RELIGION IN THE NEOLIBERAL AGE

Ashgate AHRC/ESRC Religion and Society Series

Series Editors:

Linda Woodhead, University of Lancaster, UK
Rebecca Catto, University of Lancaster, UK

This book series emanates from the largest research programme on religion in Europe today – the AHRC/ESRC Religion and Society Programme which has invested in over seventy-five research projects. Thirty-two separate disciplines are represented looking at religion across the world, many with a contemporary and some with an historical focus. This international, multi-disciplinary and interdisciplinary book series will include monographs, paperback textbooks and edited research collections drawn from this leading research programme.

Forthcoming in the series:

Understanding Muslim Chaplaincy
Sophie Gilliat-Ray, Stephen Pattison and Mansur Ali

Religion in Consumer Society
Brands, Consumers and Markets
Edited by François Gauthier and Tuomas Martikainen

Contesting Secularism
Comparative Perspectives
Edited by Anders Berg-Sørensen

Religion in the Neoliberal Age

Political Economy and Modes of Governance

Edited by

TUOMAS MARTIKAINEN
University of Helsinki, Finland

FRANÇOIS GAUTHIER
University of Fribourg, Switzerland

Routledge
Taylor & Francis Group

LONDON AND NEW YORK

First published 2013 by Ashgate Publishing

Published 2016 by Routledge
2 Park Square, Milton Park, Abingdon, Oxfordshire OX14 4RN
711 Third Avenue, New York, NY 10017, USA

First issued in paperback 2016

Routledge is an imprint of the Taylor & Francis Group, an informa business

British Library Cataloguing in Publication Data
Martikainen, Tuomas.
  Religion in the neoliberal age : political economy and modes of governance. –
  (Ashgate AHRC/ESRC religion and society series)
  1. Religion and state—History—21st century. 2. Religion and politics—
  History—21st century. 3. Religion and sociology—History—21st century.
  4. Neoliberalism—Religious aspects.
  I. Title II. Series III. Gauthier, François.
  200.9'05–dc23

Library of Congress Cataloging-in-Publication Data
Religion in the neoliberal age : political economy and modes of governance / edited by Tuomas Martikainen and François Gauthier.
    p. cm. — (Ashgate AHRC/ESRC religion and society series)
  Includes bibliographical references and index.
  ISBN 978-1-4094-4978-2 (hardcover)
  1. Religion—History—21st century. 2. Religion and politics. 3. Neoliberalism. 4. Religion and state. 5. Religion and sociology. I. Martikainen, Tuomas. II. Gauthier, François.
  BL98.R39 2013
  201'.72—dc23

2012018681

ISBN 13: 978-1-138-27492-1 (pbk)
ISBN 13: 978-1-4094-4978-2 (hbk)

Contents

Notes on Contributors   vii
Preface   xi

Introduction: Religion in Market Society   1
    François Gauthier, Tuomas Martikainen and Linda Woodhead

PART I   RELIGIONS IN THE NEW POLITICAL ECONOMY

1   Entrepreneurial Spirituality and Ecumenical Alterglobalism:
        Two Religious Responses to Global Neoliberalism   21
        Joanildo A. Burity

2   Making Religion Irrelevant: The 'Resurgent Religion' Narrative
        and the Critique of Neoliberalism   37
        James V. Spickard

3   The Decline of the Parishes and the Rise of City Churches:
        The German Evangelical Church in the Age of Neoliberalism   53
        Jens Schlamelcher

4   Catholic Church Civil Society Activism and the Neoliberal
        Governmental Project of Migrant Integration in Ireland   69
        Breda Gray

5   Faith, Welfare and the Formation of the Modern American Right   91
        Jason Hackworth

PART II   POLITICAL GOVERNANCE OF RELIGION

6   Neoliberalism and the Privatization of Welfare and Religious
        Organizations in the United States of America   109
        David Ashley and Ryan Sandefer

7   Multilevel and Pluricentric Network Governance of Religion   129
        Tuomas Martikainen

8   Regulating Religion in a Neoliberal Context:
        The Transformation of Estonia   143
        Ringo Ringvee

9   Neoliberalism and Counterterrorism Laws: Impact on Australian
        Muslim Community Organizations   161
        Agnes Chong

10   From Implicitly Christian to Neoliberal: The Moral Foundations
        of Canadian Law Exposed by the Case of Prostitution   177
        Rachel Chagnon and François Gauthier

11   Religious Freedom and Neoliberalism:
        From Harm to Cost-benefit   193
        Lori G. Beaman

Bibliography   *211*
Index   *243*

Notes on Contributors

David Ashley is Professor of Sociology at the University of Wyoming, USA. His main interests are social theory, political sociology and the sociology of knowledge. His work has been translated into several languages and he has published in numerous journals in the USA, Canada, Mexico, the UK, Germany and China. He is co-author of one of the leading social theory texts in the USA and Canada.

Lori G. Beaman, Ph.D. is Canada Research Chair in the Contextualization of Religion in a Diverse Canada and Professor in the Department of Classics and Religious Studies at the University of Ottawa. Her publications include *Reasonable Accommodation: Managing Religious Diversity* (UBC Press, 2012), *Defining Harm: Religious Freedom and the Limits of the Law* (UBC Press, 2008), 'Is Religious Freedom Impossible in Canada?' (*Law, Culture, and the Humanities*, 7/2, 2011), '"It was all slightly unreal": What's Wrong with Tolerance and Accommodation in the Adjudication of Religious Freedom' (*Canadian Journal of Women and Law*, 23/2, 2011) and 'Just Work it Out Amongst Your Selves: The Implications of the Private Mediation of Religious Freedom' (*Citizenship Studies*, 16/2, 2012, 2012). She is co-editor, with Peter Beyer, of *Religion and Diversity in Canada* (Brill, 2008). She is principal investigator of a 37-member international research team whose focus is religion and diversity (religionanddiversity.ca).

Joanildo A. Burity is Senior Lecturer and Director of the Faith and Globalisation Programme at Durham University, UK. His current research is on the expansion and socio-political activism of Latin American Pentecostals and ecumenical alterglobalists. His areas of interest include religion and globalization, religious identity and politics, religion and collective action and post-structuralist discourse theory. His publications include *Redes, Parcerias e Participação Religiosa nas Políticas Sociais no Brasil* (2006), several edited volumes and numerous articles in books and journals.

Rachel Chagnon is Professor of Law at the Université du Québec à Montréal and is the Feminist Centre coordinator. She is currently working on questions related to public policies on equality and non-discrimination. Her present project analyses the interaction between stereotypes, non-discrimination and self-regulation of the Canadian media. She has published many articles and chapters in various journals and books on issues concerning women and law.

Agnes Chong is a Doctor of Science of Law (JSD) candidate at Stanford Law School. Her dissertation examines the impact of counterterrorism laws and policies on Muslim community organizations in the United States and the United Kingdom. She is co-founder of the Stanford Program in Law & Society, a student-run organization aimed at promoting and advancing socio-legal interdisciplinary scholarship at Stanford Law School. She completed her Master's degree as a Stanford Program in International Legal Studies fellow in 2009–10. Previously, Agnes worked in the community law sector in New South Wales, Australia, in various roles including solicitor, policy officer and educator. She received her LLB/BA (Communications) with First Class Honours at the University of Technology, Sydney.

François Gauthier is Professor in Sociology of Religion at Fribourg University (Switzerland), formerly at the Département de sciences des religions of the Université du Québec à Montréal (UQAM). He is also researcher at the Chaire de recherche du Canada en Mondialisation, citoyenneté et démocratie (UQAM) and at the Groupe Société, Religions, Laïcités (GSRL EPHE-CNRS, Paris). His areas of interest include the impact of consumerism and neoliberalism on contemporary societies, as well as issues linked to religion and politics, religion and public space, as well as the application of the Maussian theory of gift on religion and culture. His publications include edited volumes on Religion in Consumer Society (*Social Compass*, 58/3, 2011), Sacred and Economic Growth (*Entropia*, 11), Youth and Religion (*Jeunes et religion au Québec*, Presses de l'Université Laval, 2008) and Techno Culture and Religion (*Religiologiques*, 24), as well as numerous articles in books and journals.

Breda Gray is Director of postgraduate programmes in Gender, Culture & Society and Senior Lecturer in the Department of Sociology at the University of Limerick, Ireland. She is author of *Women and the Irish Diaspora* (Routledge, 2004), editor of the *Irish Journal of Sociology* (18/3, 2010) special issue on the transnational turn in sociology and joint-editor of the journal *Mobilities* (6/2, 2011) on methodological innovations in mobilities research. She has also published numerous journal articles and chapters in edited collections. She is principal investigator for the IRCHSS-funded research project 'The Irish Catholic Church and the Politics of Migration' (www.ul.ie/icctmp) and joint principal investigator on the Irish Social Science Platform project 'Nomadic Work/Life in the Knowledge Economy' (http://nwl.ul.ie).

Jason Hackworth is an Associate Professor of Geography and Urban Planning at the University of Toronto. Much of his work focuses on the various ways that economic metanarratives, such as neoliberalism, shape local policy and development outcomes in North American cities. Recently, he has written about the various ways that faith-based social welfare is positioned as a justification for neoliberalism in the North American context. He is the author of two books,

Faith-Based: Religious Neoliberalism and the Politics of Welfare in the United States (University of Georgia, 2012) and *The Neoliberal City: Governance, Ideology, and Development in American Urbanism* (Cornell University Press, 2007). His articles have appeared in number of different journals including *Environment and Planning A*, *The International Journal of Urban and Regional Research*, *Urban Affairs Review* and *Urban Geography*.

Tuomas Martikainen is a Professor in Ethnic Relations in the Swedish School of Social Science at the University of Helsinki, Finland. His areas of interest include contemporary religious and ethnic diversity, governance of religion, religion in consumer society and the incorporation of immigrant Muslims in Europe. His publications include *Religion, Migration, Settlement: Reflections on post-1990 Immigration to Finland* (Brill, forthcoming), *Immigrant Religions in Local Society: Historical and Contemporary Perspectives in the City of Turku* (Åbo Akademi University Press, 2004), several edited volumes and numerous articles in books and journals.

Ringo Ringvee is a historian of religion with a special interest in contemporary religious diversity, minority religions and the interaction between politics and religion. His publications include articles in books and journals on minority religions and their legal situation in Estonia and in other Baltic countries. He is the head of the Estonian Institute for the Study of Religions, member of the research group of the Centre of Excellence in Cultural Theory at the University of Tartu and he holds the post of Adviser at the Religious Affairs Department at the Estonian Ministry of the Interior.

Ryan Sandefer is Chair and Assistant Professor in the Department of Health Informatics and Information Management at the College of St Scholastica (Duluth, MN, USA). He is currently working on the Regional Extension and Assistance Center for Health Information Technology (REACH) project funded by the Office of the National Coordinator for Health Information Technology. His areas of interest include the politics of healthcare, health policy and health information technology.

Jens Schlamelcher is Scientific Assistant at the Centre for Religious Studies, Ruhr University, Bochum, Germany. He is currently working on processes of marketization of the Protestant Church in Germany, which is also the topic of his Ph.D. thesis. Being trained in sociology and anthropology, Jens Schlamelcher has a strong foundation in the systematic branch of religious studies, where he tries to integrate different approaches such as systems theory, governmentality studies, post-structuralism and post-colonialism. Historically, his specialist field of interest is religion in late modernity, with a particular focus on Christianity.

James V. Spickard is Professor of Sociology at the University of Redlands, where he teaches social theory, the sociology/anthropology of religion, research methods and courses on the ethical implications of social policy. He is the author of over 60 journal articles and book chapters on such topics as non-Western social theory, the sociology of religious experience, human rights, globalization and religious social activism. He was the senior editor of *Personal Knowledge and Beyond* (NYU, 2002), which furthered the reflexive movement in the ethnographic study of religions. He recently co-edited *Religion Crossing Boundaries* (Brill, 2010) on transnational dynamics in contemporary African-based religions. His current projects include a co-authored book on religious experience, a book on current sociological theories of religion and a co-authored book on basic research design.

Linda Woodhead is Director of the £12m UK Religion and Society research programme, which has run from 2007–12. She is based at Lancaster University, where she is Professor of the Sociology of Religion. Her research involves theoretical and empirical explorations of religion, with a particular focus on religious change in contemporary Western societies. Her publications include *A Sociology of Religious Emotion* (2010, with Ole Riis) and *The Spiritual Revolution* (2005, with Paul Heelas).

Preface

Sometime in February 2008, Tuomas sent out a query on the Diaspora mailing list he manages to probe for scholars interested in topics related to religion and economy and neoliberalism in particular. We met in Montreal a couple of months later, as Tuomas was at the University of Ottawa as part of a postdoctoral project. After a long walk through the colourful, multi-ethnic streets of Montreal, a few drinks and good chat, we felt that, although we were both coming from quite different places, we were somehow onto something. A couple of minutes before the closing of the call for proposal, we submitted a hurriedly drafted outline for a panel on 'Religion in Consumer Society: Towards a Global Comprehensive Analytic' which materialized at the ISSR Conference in Santiago de Compostella in 2009. This was the beginning of a common journey that we believe is just beginning.

The Compostella panel was a success, namely because we had the pleasure and honour to host a paper by Linda Woodhead, whom we both respected and admired. This energy was contagious, a feeling that something like a small revolution, a recasting of paradigms, a reopening of possibilities might be nascent. The panel led to the three of us co-editing an issue of *Social Compass* (*58/3*) on the theme 'Religion in Consumer Society'. We followed with another ISSR panel in Aix-en-Provence in the summer of 2011, for which we received close to 50 proposals. The panel was the longest standing of the conference, and there simply wasn't enough time in the conference to align them all. By then the feeling we were onto something only grew. The time was ripe for new approaches, and new questions. The panel attracted a mix of established scholars seeking alternatives, and young scholars following their intuitions and meeting with our appreciations that something was missing in secularization approaches, that the cultural, social and political pull of economics today was being overlooked. This book is a product of the Aix meetings and of our attempts to seek out promising avenues. It would have been impossible without the firm encouragements from many of our colleagues, some of whom are also dear friends. We would like to thank all of them, including Jim Spickard, Peter Beyer, Philippe Portier, Andrew Dawson, Deirdre Meintel, Grace Davie and so on. We would also like to extend very special thanks to Linda Woodhead, who has inspired us, supported us and critiqued us in the most honest and valuable of ways. She was kind enough to suggest that Ashgate publish this series of two books in the Religion and Society collection, which is undoubtedly the preferred platform for the dissemination of these ideas.

Finally, we would like to thank Professor Peter Nynäs and the Post-Secular Culture and Changing Religious Landscape in Finland (PCCR) Centre of Excellence at Åbo Akademi University for hosting a meeting of the authors in December 2011 in Turku. MA Linda Annunen gave a helping hand in the organization of the event as well as with the bibliography of this book. PCCR also provided resources to us for linguistic review, conducted with great professionalism by Sarah Bannock. The event was supported by the Donner Institute and the Transnational Governance of Islam: The Cases of Canada, Finland and Ireland Project (Academy of Finland, University of Helsinki).

In Turku and Paris, 8 March 2012
Tuomas Martikainen,
University of Helsinki, Finland
François Gauthier
Fribourg University, Switzerland

Introduction:
Religion in Market Society

François Gauthier, Tuomas Martikainen and Linda Woodhead

Introduction

'We live in the age of neoliberalism.'[1] Such a strong statement from influential political scientists says much about the importance that economics has attained in all aspects of social life in the last three decades. What, indeed, is globalization without the planetary expansion of 'the market', of consumerism, of management techniques, and the infectious dissemination of neoliberal thinking as the 'only alternative'? Yet, if scholars have hinted at the profound impact of these developments on such diverse areas as economics, politics, international relations, ideology, culture, law and so on, their impact on religion has been a more neglected subject of enquiry. The starting point of this volume is the observation that the new form of political economy which has become dominant since the 1980s has had, and continues to have, profound consequences on religious organizations and on religious belief, practice and expression worldwide – and deserves more scholarly attention.

In the West, the advent of neoliberalism combined with consumerism coincided not only with a deepening crisis in the welfare state and the collapse of many state-subsidized, union-dominated, manual industries, but with growing affluence, the expansion of cultural, service and 'knowledge' industries, the growth of property ownership and the entry of a majority of women into the workforce. New media began to proliferate, and existing media were increasingly deregulated, that is to say removed from state control. During the same period traditional religion continued to suffer a steep decline. Churches with historic links to nation-states were particularly affected. The presence of non-Christian world religions, magnified by post-war migration, was increasingly felt.

These changes coincide with intensifying globalization. Globalization is a cultural phenomenon, with interlinked social, political, economic and religious dimensions. As Roland Robertson puts it: 'globalization as a concept refers to both the compression of the world and the intensification of consciousness of the world as a whole'.[2] It is both 'the concrete structuration of the world as a whole' and the

---

[1] Alfredo Saad-Filho and Deborah Johnston, 'Introduction', in Saad-Filho and Johnston (eds), *Neoliberalism: A Critical Reader* (London, 2005), p. 1.

[2] Roland Robertson, *Globalization: Social Theory and Global Culture* (London, 1992), p. 8.

'production and reproduction of the world as the most salient plausibility structure of our time'.[3] As a consequence, the religious field in a growing number of non-Western countries has witnessed significant and ongoing transformations which have links with changes in the West. While agreeing with Eisenstadt[4] that the paths of modernity (or modernization) are variegated, we also think that there is sufficient evidence to support the hypothesis that current transformations affecting religion (both religious institutions and religious phenomena in general) are best understood if cast as integral to the recent shaping of culture by economics (both consumerism and neoliberalism) considered from a global, not only Western, perspective.

For decades, work on religion has been cast within the paradigm of secularization, with most debates centring on the question of the demise or revival of religion. While works such as those of José Casanova[5] and David Martin[6] have clarified the concept of secularization by making sense of its multifarious meanings and scouring away its sometimes highly ideological groundings, still the framework of secularization falls short in providing an adequate interpretation of the complex and novel landscape of religion today. One reason is its embeddedness in a national paradigm. But as globalization shifts emphasis to the dialectic between the local and the global, and as the nation (the nation-state as a polity, a social and cultural community and a territory) and its borders are made porous, its unquestioned legitimacy as the sole basis for thinking about religion and society is challenged. The same can be said to some extent about the North/South, Western/non-Western divides that structured scholarship for most of the twentieth century, and which underlies the assumption of secularization theory that the (secular) West represents the cutting edge of social progress which the rest of the world will follow.

While those who study religion had been living in some isolation for decades, often shunned by their social scientist and humanities colleagues (what was the use of studying religion if it was going to be dissolved by modernization?), the situation is changing. In his latest book, Bryan S. Turner argues that religion stands at the heart of many contemporary political and social developments, 'and therefore the study of religion and religions has achieved an intellectual and political urgency and importance it has not had for decades.'[7] Post-9/11 developments in securitization and law, the new importance of issues related to religion and the public sphere, the shifting of post-Cold War and post-colonial geopolitics and so on have attracted new voices to the discussion, stemming from such disciplines as political science, law, philosophy, urban studies and economics. It is noteworthy

---

[3]   Ibid., p. 53.

[4]   Shmuel N. Eisenstadt, *Fundamentalism, Sectarianism, and Revolution* (Cambridge, 1999).

[5]   José Casanova, *Public Religions in the Modern World* (Chicago, 1994).

[6]   David Martin, *On Secularization: Towards a Revised General Theory* (Farnham, 2005).

[7]   Bryan S. Turner, *Religion and Modern Society. Citizenship, Secularisation and the State* (New York, 2011), p. x.

that few had prior background in the study of religion. The result has been an unprecedented intellectual effervescence which some less enthusiastic scholars consider a babble of confusion. While inter-, cross- and trans-disciplinarity are important to the revived study of religion, it has not yet led to renewed conceptual and theoretical discussion, and there is still a tendency for new discussions of securitization, law, identity and politics to remain cloistered in their own theoretical or popular frameworks, such as multiculturalism and integration, the justifiability of using religious reasons in political debate or the idea of a clash of civilizations.[8]

Refreshed outlooks are needed to address pressing issues in the study of religion today, including changed relations between religion and state in a more globalized environment; the increasing devolution of regulative power to the judiciary; the rise of new forms of religion (be it fundamentalist currents, Pentecostals or new spiritualities); the increase in the public visibility of religion; the growing importance of issues of identity and recognition; the impact of electronic media on religion and so on.

Since recent talk of 'postsecularism' does not open a sufficiently renewed perspective, because of its remaining ties to a grand narrative of secularization, where can we turn? There can no longer be a single answer or a single metanarrative. But a fruitful approach is to probe for structural shifts and towing undercurrents. One of the most fundamental in terms of its widespread impacts is surely that to do with a changed economic order, and associated ideologies. Hence, by looking at the changing relations between religion and economy we may find a new way to think about some of the issues of today. Although religion and economy is by no means a new topic, it has attracted less attention than religion and politics in Western scholarship. But if the importance of the (national) state-politics nexus has been shaken then our thinking needs to shift as well to take more account of linkages between religion and the economic.

Religion and Economy

Classical Interpretations of Religion and Economy

Classical interpretations of relations between religion and the economy include Karl Marx's radical theory of society in which economics figure first and foremost within his infrastructure/superstructure model. Marx thus heralded a reduction of society to its materialistic and 'economical' infrastructure, cast as the arena of class struggle and domination (with cultural aspects serving a secondary function of legitimization). One recalls Marx and Engels's famous phrase in which religion (understand: Western Christianity and Catholicism in particular) is the 'people's opium': a soporific smokescreen veiling an essentially harsh economic reality.

---

[8] Samuel P. Huntington, *The Clash of Civilizations and the Remaking of the World Order* (New York, 1996).

Leaving aside the less influential and more complex case of Georg Simmel, that of Max Weber – who like Simmel considered himself to be an economist rather than a sociologist – commands our attention. Weber's seminal and ambitious sociology devoted an impressive portion of its enquiry to religion, and an important fraction of that to issues regarding religion and economics. His hermeneutical approach examined the influence of religious ethics with respect to the economic field in general and economic activity in particular, seeking to understand why and how capitalism, modernization's driving force, flourished as it did in the West and not elsewhere. His understanding of the history of the West as involving progressive rationalization leading to a complete disenchantment[9] (*Entzauberung*) of the world, as well as his thesis of an 'elective affinity' between Calvinist protestant ethics and the burgeoning ethics (the 'spirit') of capitalism are well known. Rather than reducing social reality to economics as did Marx, Weber attempted to show the two-way relations linking religion (more precisely: salvation and religious ethics) and economics. Weber's work continues to provide inspiration and theoretical groundwork for analyses today. Its interest, however, was in the birth of industrial capitalism, rather than the life of late or advanced capitalism,[10] and in production rather than consumption.[11] It exemplifies the implicit nationalism discussed above, in taking as its framework bounded economic and social units (particularly national and imperial ones), rather than the less territorialized, more global flows of capital and culture which we see today.[12]

The economic and religious situation of the present day has changed significantly from the times of either Weber or Marx. In the terms of those who have theorized the most recent shift, in the late 1970s the world moved from an era of 'Fordist' industrial capitalism dominated by large-scale factory enterprises distinguished by economies of scale and rationalized, standardized production methods, to a 'post-Fordist' era distinguished by more flexible modes of production, global dispersal of labour processes, a cultural turn and 'time-space compression'.[13] In this situation, capitalist enterprises become much harder for nation-states and politicians to control and regulate; organized labour and trade unions diminish in significance; classes and 'identities' proliferate; markets become increasingly segmented; identity becomes more closely tied to the purchase and display of

---

[9]   Jean-Claude Passeron, 'Introduction', in Max Weber, *Sociologie des religions* (Paris, 1996).

[10]   Luc Boltanski and Ève Chiapello, *Le nouvel esprit du capitalisme* (Paris, 1999).

[11]   Birgit Meyer, 'Pentecostalism and Neo-Liberal Capitalism: Faith, Prosperity and Vision in African Pentecostal-Charismatic Churches', *Journal for the Study of Religion*, 20/2 (2007): pp. 5–28.

[12]   Andreas Wimmer and Nina Glick Schiller, 'Methodological Nationalism and Beyond: Nation-State Building, Migration and the Social Sciences', *Global Networks*, 2/4 (2002): pp. 301–34.

[13]   For example, David Harvey, *The Condition of Postmodernity: An Enquiry into the Origins of Cultural Change* (Oxford, 1990).

consumer goods; the speed with which goods are manufactured and consumed increases; management arises as an autonomous field of enterprise and scholarship with respect to 'human relations' within – and without – the workplace; 'governance' replaces government in a shift towards networked organization, flexibility, mobility, 'real time' responsiveness and individual responsibility; and the significance of advertising, marketing, the circulation of symbols and a class of 'cultural creatives' increases. Most significantly, Western societies have shifted from being production-capitalist to being finance and consumer-capitalist.

A Typology of Recent Religion/Economics Articulations[14]

How has religion been articulated with economics with respect to these changes? The existing work on this topic can be surveyed in four main categories, as follows.

A first ensemble of works focuses on the growth of consumer culture and its negative impacts on religion. A strong note of *Kulturpessimismus* haunts this work as a result of either or both: 1) a Marxist or neo-Marxist perspective which equates the development of capitalism with growing contradiction, alienation and reification; 2) a nostalgic perspective according to which the break with traditional forms of religion, culture and community amounts to a loss of social and moral substance. An influential example is Daniel Bell's lament at the damage done to church Christianity and solid production values like those depicted by Weber by the acids of shallow, hedonistic consumerism.[15] In a more minor tone, a mournful hue pervades accounts by many sociologists of religion of the abandonment of traditional forms of practice and belief. An example is Danièle Hervieu-Léger, who has been at the forefront in analysing recent reconfigurations of religious phenomena, and who must be credited as having been more sensitive than most with respect to emerging forms, including youth religion. Yet her definition of religion as being essentially traditional, based on 'the chains of memory', implicitly discredits contemporary forms characterized by the reconfiguration of tradition, and in the end can only regret the increased drive to 'consume' more intense, emotional experiences.[16] A similar case is that of Françoise Champion who has written extensively on what she calls the '*nébuleuse mystique-ésotérique*'[17] and for whom contemporary 'spiritualities' are no longer religious, only degraded forms of what religion once was. A variation of this critique concerns the growth of 'consumeristic' forms of spirituality, which are said to lack the moral depth and social cohesiveness of more traditional religion – a theme expounded at length

---

[14]   The following is an extended version of François Gauthier, Tuomas Martikainen and Linda Woodhead, 'Introduction: Religion in Consumer Society', *Social Compass*, 58/3 (2011): pp. 291–5.

[15]   Daniel Bell, *The Cultural Contradictions of Capitalism* (New York, 1976).

[16]   Hervieu-Léger, Danielle, *Religion as a Chain of Memory* (Cambridge, 2000).

[17]   Françoise Champion and Danièle Hervieu-Léger (eds), *De l'émotion en religion. Renouveaux et traditions* (Paris, 1990).

in Carrette and King's *Selling Spirituality* in which it is claimed that 'spirituality has in fact become a powerful commodity in the global marketplace – a cultural addiction that reflects orthodox politics, curbs self-expression and colonises Eastern beliefs'.[18] Not only nostalgia for past forms of real or imagined community, but perhaps for more traditional gender relations, is very near the surface in such laments, since consumerism, 'shopping' and 'shallow' spirituality tend to be coded as feminine, whilst production and the 'solid' values of more rational forms of historic religion tend to be coded as masculine.[19]

A second, less pessimistic body of work considers not so much how consumer capitalism has led to religious decline and decay, but how it has stimulated change in religious institutions, and in the religious landscape as a whole. Peter Berger[20] was one of the first to deal with this theme, as he discussed how, as churches became more 'bureaucratized' and alike, they simultaneously had to differentiate their various products and niches in order to survive. Wade Clark Roof has expanded on these ideas, suggesting the morphing of the religious field into a 'spiritual marketplace', an expression gaining in popularity.[21] As with expressions such as '*à la carte*' and 'pick and choose' religion, and with the whole field of Rational Choice Theory, it is not clear whether the 'market' serves merely as a metaphor, or something more, with discussion often sliding from the first to the second. Drawing from Weber, scholars such as Jörg Stolz[22] have invested in an approach concerned with 'salvation goods', with some interesting insights. However, the import of concepts and terminology from the field of economics is often done lightly, without further theoretical discussion. What does it mean to say that religion presents itself as in a market, and what is a market? Are 'salvation goods' like any other goods, be it a carpet cleaning service or gold watches? Is consuming a religious text different from consuming a Mars Bar? Such questions have by all means not received the amount of attention they require. More profoundly, can concepts issued from one field translate to another, and specifically to that of religion so easily without a prior epistemological discussion?

---

[18]　Jeremy Carrette and Richard King, *Selling Spirituality: The Silent Takeover of Religion* (Abingdon, 2005), p. back cover.

[19]　Ann Douglas, *The Feminization of American Culture* (New York, 1977); Meredith McGuire, *Lived Religion: Faith and Practice in Everyday Life* (Oxford, 2007); Linda Woodhead, 'Real Religion, Fuzzy Spirituality', in Dick Houtman and Stef Aupers (eds), *Religions of Modernity: Relocating the Sacred to the Self and the Digital* (Leiden, 2010), pp. 30–48.

[20]　Peter L. Berger, *The Sacred Canopy: Elements of a Sociological Theory of Religion* (Garden City, 1967); Peter L. Berger, *Heretical Imperative: Contemporary Possibilities of Religious Affirmation* (New York, 1980).

[21]　Wade Clark Roof, *Spiritual Marketplace: Baby Boomers and the Remaking of American Religion* (Princeton, 1999).

[22]　Jörg Stolz (ed.), *Salvation Goods and Religious Markets: Theory and Applications* (Bern, 2008).

Rational Choice theorists in the sociology of religion fit this second category insofar as they illuminate the religious field by treating it as a market in which different suppliers compete with one another to meet demand, and in which differentiated supply fares better than monopolistic provision.[23] Such work assumes a classical economic account of a marketplace composed of utilitarian-minded 'rational actors', and therefore has less to say about contemporary consumer society, with its emphasis on the emotional dimensions of the creation, supply and satisfaction of consumer demand.[24] Celebrating 'free markets' while condemning 'monopolies' (national churches), it furthers the colonization of the social sciences by economic discourse,[25] thereby reducing social phenomena to a very particular model of the economy instead of enabling an understanding of the dialectical rapports between social phenomena and economic factors. Religious market and choice theories are founded on the contestable assumption of a naturalized 'law of supply and demand',[26] while neglecting the social and structural determinations shaping individual choices and religious offers: in essence, instead of analysing religion and economic articulations, Rational Choice and market theories force-fit the former within a contestable understanding of the latter. While the first category of work on religion and economy proceeded from a negative value judgment about their modern conjunction, this second category lies at the symmetrical opposite, breathing (neo)liberal enthusiasm with respect to the inherently beneficial nature of 'free markets', individual choice and pluralism.

Thirdly, there is a large body of literature on 'prosperity religion' deriving from both the anthropology and sociology of religion, most notably in relation to the study of global Pentecostalism. Early work on the latter tended to interpret its growth, particularly in the form of a Charismatic upsurge from the 1970s onwards, in terms of its ability to forge strong work ethics and supportive networks – in

---

[23] Rodney Stark and William Sims Bainbridge, *The Future of Religion: Secularization, Revival and Cult Formation* (Berkeley, 1985); analysis by R. Stephen Warner, 'Work in Progress Toward a New Paradigm for the Sociological Study of Religion in the United States', *The American Journal of Sociology*, 98/5 (1993): pp. 1044–93.

[24] We will come back to this issue in the introduction to the second follow-up volume.

[25] In 1974, University of Chicago economist Gary S. Becker (the same infamous department as that of the neoliberal Milton Friedman) published an article which stated that non-economic social interactions could be understood using the 'simple tools of economic theory'. Becker championed a sociological approach which considered individuals as 'resources'. Gary S. Becker, 'A Theory of Social Interaction', *Journal of Political Economy*, 82/6 (1974): pp. 1063–93. Gary S. Becker, *The Economic Approach to Human Behavior* (Chicago, 1976) followed two years later. It would take about a decade before this approach would be applied to religious facts, aforehand considered to be the most heterogeneous to those of economics.

[26] The theory of supply and demand as a naturalized mechanical and trans-historical law of nature has been subject to debate within the field of economics. See namely, Alain Caillé, *Dé-penser l'économique. Contre le fatalisme* (Paris, 2005); André Orléan, *L'empire de la valeur* (Paris, 2011).

other words, the focus was Weberian, concerned with production values, rather than religion and consumption. Since capitalism is driven by both consumption and production, this perspective, as Meyer[27] pointed out, told only half the story. Likewise, Pentecostalism does not just appeal because of its work ethic: it appeals because it promises salvation under the form of worldly as well as spiritual prosperity. Of course, Pentecostalism is not the only form of contemporary religion which promises wealth, blessings and the fulfilment of personal potential by both magical and rational means: much recent New Age and Christian spirituality, including Rick Warren's 'purpose-driven' brand of Christianity and associated mega-churches, and some forms of Islam, Hinduism and Buddhism do something similar.[28] This growing body of work on prosperity religion worldwide marks an important advance in the study of religion because it is interested not only on the impact of economic change *on* religion, but on the emergence of forms of religio-ethno-economic practice which are completely integral to consumer capitalism, such as the apparent revival of magic, witchcraft, sorcery, occultism and divination.[29] The 'disenchantment' or 'demagification' of the world as a result of production capitalism has ceded its place to a re-enchantment of the religious field in tune with the pressures of the new financial and consumption-driven, globalized capitalist economy.

Finally, there is an emerging body of work taking note of the new neoliberal political economy, but usually focusing on certain specific institutional areas. The key areas have been welfare provision, faith-based organizations, governance and securitization. Common too is a renewed interest in public authorities' work with religious organizations for the public good. Often the interpretation of a state's interest is given in a normative tone, by either heralding a re-emergence of religion or seeing it negatively as an instrumentalization of religion. The tenor is often mixed in the study of welfare provision and faith-based organizations. Whereas the wide-ranging consideration of the role of religions in welfare provision in Europe by Grace Davie et al.[30] and analysis of FBOs' contribution to development

---

[27]   Meyer, 'Pentecostalism and Neo-Liberal Capitalism'.

[28]   For a selection of readings, see Linda Woodhead and Paul Heelas, *Religion in Modern Times: An Interpretive Anthology* (Oxford, 2002), pp. 173–213.

[29]   John L. Comaroff and Jean Comaroff, 'Millenial Capitalism and the Culture of Neoliberalism', in John L. Comaroff and Jean Comaroff (eds), *Millenial Capitalism and the Culture of Neoliberalism* (Durham, 2001), pp. 19–25; John L. Comaroff and Jean Comaroff, *Ethnicity Inc.* (Chicago, 2009).

[30]   Anders Bäckström and Grace Davie with Ninna Edgardh and Per Pettersson (eds), *Welfare and Religion in 21st Century Europe: Volume 1: Configuring the Connections* (Farnham, 2010); Anders Bäckström, Grace Davie, Ninna Edgardh and Per Pettersson (eds), *Welfare and Religion in 21st Century Europe: Volume 2: Gendered, Religious and Social Change* (Farnham, 2011).

work by Gerald Clarke and Michael Jennings[31] seem to welcome the new salience of religion, Jason Hackworth's[32] and Adam Dinham's[33] studies raise significant questions about the agendas of states and their embedded interests. The study of new forms of governance points out challenges to historical church-state relations which arise in the implementation of new rationalities of regulation based in New Public Management or in international law. These developments are even more evident in the securitization of religious and, especially, Islamic organizations, whereby wholly new institutional structures emerge in complex forms, varying from network cooperation to mastering security and dialogue. However, only rarely do these studies aim to connect such developments to a broader socio-economic reality, with some interesting exceptions.

In an attempt to draw together the several, and fragmented, insights about religion and economy offered by these different bodies of literature, this volume and its sister volume suggests that the changes which they partially document are best understood in relation to one another and set against the backdrop of wider socio-economic changes catalyzed by the spread of consumerism and the neoliberal ideology. Rather than highlighting the diffuse, disorganized, fragmented and deregulated aspects of contemporary religion, our claim is that recent mutations in the religious field run across other fields such as politics and can often be analysed in similar terms. They are not unregulated, but their modes of regulation differ radically in many respects from earlier more hierarchical, centralized forms of institutional authority which became naturalized by conceptual tools including secularization, the public/private division and implicit methodological nationalism. The intent behind this hypothesis is not the enunciation of a new totalizing and uni-factorial, all-encompassing and *uber*-explanatory theory pledging the understanding of social reality with respect to economics. This would merely be participating in a reduction to the economic, which is precisely what needs to be analysed. What this approach stresses is how the present situation in societies across the world and how the development of transnational and global realities have been shaped through the growing impact of economic factors on social life, above all through the coupling of intensified consumerism as a dominant cultural ethos (hand in hand with the growth and development of electronic media) with neoliberalism as a cultural and political ideology (affecting 'governance' at all levels, and increasing the sway of 'management').

---

[31] Gerald Clarke and Michael Jennings (eds), *Development, Civil Society and Faith-Based Organizations: Bridging the Sacred and the Secular* (Basingstoke, 2008).

[32] Jason Hackworth, 'Neoliberalism for God's Sake: Sectarian Justifications for Secular Policy Transformation in the United States', in Arie Molendijk, Justin Beaumont, and Chris Jedan (eds), *Exploring the Postsecular: The Religious, the Political, the Urban* (Leiden, 2010), pp. 357–79.

[33] Adam Dinham, *Faiths, Public Policy and Civil Society: Problems, Policies, Controversies* (Basingstoke, 2009).

This approach does not entail a radical shift in how we understand religion, but it does mean that we seek to sensitize ourselves to the ways in which consumerism and neoliberalism might be articulated with the field of religion. The influence of our contemporary form of 'political cultural economy' on other fields and on the ways in which social and cultural realities have been developing must be recognized and allowed to fertilize the study of religion: this does not entail or proceed from either positive or negative value judgments, and can potentially work at all levels of social reality: individual, relational, local, national and supra-national.

As the title suggests, the present volume, *Religion in the Neoliberal Age: Modes of Governance and Political Economy*, is concerned with the institutional dimensions of this approach. It explores some of the issues involving the changing landscape of relations between religions and states with respect to the pressures exerted by market-oriented, neoliberal modes of governance and management, as well as some changes occurring within religious organizations. A second volume will follow under the title *Religion in Consumer Societies: Brands, Consumers, Markets*, and will focus on the more diffuse interplays between religion and consumerism, management and branding from a perspective concerned with the vast and complex varieties of religion as lived, be it with respect to transformations within traditional institutional religions, charismatic trends, quest culture, contemporary spiritualities or life coaching.

Religion and the New Political Economy

Modernity, Liberalism, and the Emergence of the Market

Secularization theory is a theory of modernity, or rather modernization, which focuses on the destiny of religion. If we are to analyse the rapports between religion, the political and the economic, it is worthwhile to also consider the story of modernity with respect to the political and the economic. One way of doing so is to define modernization in terms of the emergence of the nation-bound, bureaucratic state as well as a capitalist, market-based economy. The autonomization of the political with respect to religion was captured by modern thinkers who envisioned a government whose legitimacy would be founded on the sovereignty of the people rather than on onto-theological bases. Meanwhile, economic relations were kept rather tightly 'embedded'[34] within the social and its hierarchies, and did not begin to truly autonomize before the eighteenth century, as intimated in the works of thinkers such as François Quesnay and John Locke,

---

[34] Karl Polanyi, *The Great Transformation: The Political and Economic Origins of Our Time* (Boston, 2001).

who both set the stage for Adam Smith's *Inquiry into the Nature and Causes of the Wealth of Nations*, published in 1776 and foundational for political economy.[35]

The project of modernity revolves around answering the modern question *par excellence*: how is a social order composed of individuals possible outside of a theological framework?[36] Answers have tended towards either the political or the economic. In republican theories of the social contract, the state is the central actor in social regulation. This option stresses a strong government, a positive, civic definition of liberty and a substantive conception of the political body. The other major modern option, embodied in classical liberalism like that of Locke, Adam Smith and James Mill, favoured a radical conception of individualism coupled with the market as the central organizing force in political and social life. Thus the market arises as reality, concept and programme.

Far from referring strictly to a technical mechanism of regulation of economic activity through the harmonization of prices according to the variables of supply and demand, the market appears as a moral system of social regulation based on the optimal expansion of human freedom, conceived essentially in terms of economic activities and rights to property. In other words, the market appeared in modernity as an economic answer to a political question, that of social regulation within an immanent frame. The idea of the market was designed as an alternative to political models involving authority: realizing automatic adjustments, and proceeding to transfers and redistributions without requiring that individual wills need play a role.[37] Such is the meaning behind Adam Smith's famed but somewhat misleading idea of the 'invisible hand' of the market, better explained as the spontaneous harmonization of individual – often conflicting – interests. For classical liberalism, the system by which prices are produced is a value-neutral process that also produces social harmony, provided the state is confined to a role that guarantees security. At the time Smith's *Wealth of Nations* was published, England (as all of Europe) was not a capitalist, industrial, market society, but rather a commercial society with a strong central government. Hence the 'market' was born as a political utopia; it was an ideology before anything like a stock

---

[35]   In this book, Smith allied two arguments which allowed for the autonomization of economics: first that the economic domain was a coherent system with its own laws, which were laws of nature which corresponded to the very dynamics of the universe. Second, that free exchange benefited to both parties, and thus that the free pursuit of individual interests tended towards the production of a common good. See Louis Dumont, *Homo aequalis I. Genèse et épanouissement de l'idéologie économique* (Paris, 1985); Pierre Rosanvallon, *Le libéralisme économique. Histoire de l'idée de marché* (Paris, 1989); Simon Clarke, 'The Neoliberal Theory of Society', in Saad-Filho and Johnston, *Neoliberalism*, pp. 50–59.

[36]   Gerard Delanty, 'The Foundations of Social Theory', in Bryan S. Turner, *The New Blackwell Companion to Social Theory* (Oxford: Blackwell, 2009), pp. 19–37.

[37]   Rosanvallon, *Le libéralisme économique*, p. 11.

market existed in reality.[38] In Karl Polanyi's words, the idea of a 'market society' preceded the institutionalization of a 'market economy'.[39]

Liberalism has slowly become one of the most influential of modernity's political ideologies, one whose emphasis is on the individual rather than the collective, on freedom rather than equality. Jason Hackworth writes how liberalism asserts that the highest virtue of society

> is the degree to which its individuals are allowed to pursue pleasure. Individuals are the best to know what and how to want, and society should be structured in a way to let them pursue this goal, the realization of pleasure. This pursuit can be believed natural (Hume) or part of a social contract (Locke), but all agree that individual autonomy should be venerated above all else.[40]

Contrary to republicanism and socialism, which value a political conception of human liberty that finds its expression through civic participation,[41] the liberal conception of liberty is radically private, even pre-social and apolitical, its standard being economic entrepreneurship.

In Karl Polanyi's[42] interpretation, the *laissez-faire* attitude that presided well into the early 1900s was a main cause of the rise of nationalisms which led to two World Wars and the Great Depression. As a consequence, the period that followed 1945 was characterized by a reactive inclination towards state regulation of economic activities, productive and financial, and the implementations of measures and policies set to limit inequalities. It is in this context that John Maynard Keynes's argument that markets did not tend 'naturally' towards equilibrium justified a more interventionist model of the state, giving way to the creation of welfare states across the West. It is in this context of heightened social concerns that egalitarian liberalism emerged in the wake of John Stuart Mill's prior attempt at reconciling classical liberalism with the more interventionist principles of Bentham's utilitarianism and a partly Christian-inspired concern for greater equality. The political liberalism of the likes of Keynes, Dewey, Dworkin, Nagel and Rawls flourished in tune with the '*moral* liberalism' of the 1960s *zeitgeist*, yet its core remains focused around individual autonomy and the model of the market, tempered by the necessity to secure certain welfare rights alongside personal rights through 'value-neutral', objective and rational procedures. Egalitarian liberalism did not alter the foundations of

---

[38]   Rosanvallon, *Le libéralisme économique*; Dumont, *Homo aequalis*.

[39]   Polanyi, *The Great Transformation*.

[40]   Jason Hackworth, *The Neoliberal City: Governance, Ideology, and Development in American Urbanism* (Ithaca, 2007), p. 4. See also Catherine Audard, *Qu'est-ce que le libéralisme? Éthique, politique, société* (Paris, 2009).

[41]   Alain Caillé and Roger Sue (eds), *De gauche?* (Paris, 2009); Maurizio Viroli, *Républicanisme* (Paris, 2011).

[42]   Polanyi, *The Great Transformation*.

liberalism and favoured a reduction of the power of the political body, a weakening of nationalism and an essentially procedural conception of the state.

The Neoliberal 'Revolution'

At the same time in the post-war period, the Austrians Friedrich von Hayek and Ludwig von Mises and the American Milton Friedman emerged as forerunners in the attack on egalitarian liberalism and the Keynesian legitimization of the welfare state. Neoliberalism emerged as a project to renew classical liberalism's pillars of individual liberty, limitation of the role of the state and freedom of the markets. Neoliberalism quickly became an enterprise aimed against socialism and egalitarian liberalism on the grounds that state intervention naturally inclined towards totalitarianism and 'liberty-cide'. Inspired by Walter Lippmann who wrote that 'the state must limit itself to the administration of justice between men going about their business',[43] the neoliberal movement coalesced around Hayek's Mont Pelerin Society meetings which spawned over one hundred influential think tanks around the world. While it is true that neoliberalism cannot be conceived as a 'pure' theory,[44] it can be associated with the slogan 'less state, more market', with the role of the state limited to the guarantee of propriety rights, contractual liberty and military spending. In the neoliberal perspective, individual liberty is conceived in economic terms, and the 'market' – the mechanism of price – is to play a central role in all aspects of social regulation.

If classical liberalism found in the workings of the market and its 'spontaneous harmonization of interests' is the model for optimal social regulation, neoliberalism goes a step further by redefining the social sphere as a form of economic field. Thus the economic field comes to include and subsumes all forms of social life and human action. The transformation is complete: from being embedded within the social, the political and the religious, the neoliberal age is that in which market economics are henceforth that in which other social realities are said to be themselves embedded.[45]

---

[43]   Audard, *Qu'est-ce que le libéralisme?*, p. 344. In 1938, Lippmann hosted what is held to be the first 'neoliberal' conference, in Paris, in which participated many eminent scholars of the time, including Raymond Aron, Wilhelm Röpke, as well as von Mises and his young disciple, Hayek. See, Serge Audier, *Le colloque Lippmann* (Paris, 2008). The Lippmann Conference is mentioned by Michel Foucault as being an important moment in the shift from a Taylorist type of hierarchical authority to a horizontal and network type of authority in *Naissance de la biopolitique* (Paris, 2004), p. 138.

[44]   Jamie Peck, 'Geography and Public Policy: Constructions of Neoliberalism', *Progress in Human Geography*, 28/3 (2004): pp. 392–405.

[45]   Analytics such as Rational Choice Theory, salvation goods and the spiritual marketplace therefore start from a neoliberal epistemology, the ideology of which is thus naturalized, and legitimized. The value of such analytics is very poor as a consequence, as they merely mime what they set out to understand, smuggling as they do so a particularly

Neoliberal ideas began to spread from the very late 1970s onwards as they were transformed into a political-economic programme thanks to the implementation of deregulation policies in the governments of Deng Xiaoping (1978) in China, Margaret Thatcher (1979) in Great Britain and the influence of Paul Volcker at the US Federal Reserve and President Ronald Reagan (1981) in the USA.[46] The neoliberal programme was also promoted and made effective through the growing influence of non-governmental international agencies such as the World Bank, the International Monetary Fund (IMF), the World Trade Organization (WTO), private think tanks and, increasingly, bond-rating firms (Standard & Poor's, Moody's, Fitch).[47] As Michael Freeden has argued, neoliberalism did not emerge from cultural or social needs so much as in relation to the characterization of economic necessities as interpreted by some of the economic and financial elite.[48] It often presents itself as an austere programme that finds legitimacy in complying with the supposedly scientific facts of economic reality; one which insists on being the only rational governmental option, as Thatcher's famous insistence on there being 'no alternative' vividly illustrates.[49] Neoliberal policies are seen as 'necessary adjustments to ineluctable economic laws'.[50]

After the 1980s, neoliberalism turned into an increasingly dominant political and cultural ideology, especially after the fall of communist alternatives:

> It strongly influences the lives of billions of people in every continent in such
> diverse areas as economics, politics, international relations, ideology, culture
> and so on. In less than one generation, neoliberalism has become so widespread
> and influential, and so deeply intermingled with critically important aspects of
> life, that it can be difficult to assess its nature and historical importance.[51]

Both Thatcher's and Reagan's programmes were somewhat makeshift and piecemeal, and neither 'became paradigmatic, but each contributed to construct what became an evolving transnational programme of creatively destructive institutional transformations'.[52] While deregulation had already permeated

---

impervious brand of ethnocentricism in which the historic and social context of the emergence of such realities are thwarted.

[46]   There were antecedents though, as Milton Friedman was directly employed in redesigning Chile's economic policies after the 1973 military coup that overthrew Salvador Allende's government and put Augusto Pinochet in power.

[47]   Hackworth, *The Neoliberal City*.

[48]   Quoted in Audard, *Qu'est-ce que le libéralisme?*, p. 348.

[49]   Today, it is countries such as Greece and Italy for whom there is no alternative but neoliberal austerity and privatization.

[50]   Neil Brenner, Jamie Peck and Nik Theodore, 'Variegated Neoliberalization: Geographies, Modalities, Pathways', *Global Networks* 10/2 (2010): p. 214.

[51]   Saad-Filho and Johnston, 'Introduction', p. 1.

[52]   Brenner et al., 'Variegated Neoliberalization', p. 214.

political forces to the left of the political spectrum in the 1980s (as in the 'reality check' of socialist President François Mitterrand in France), the breakdown of the Soviet Empire was understood as undermining the very foundations of Marxism-inspired left politics. The classical 'alternative' to economic liberalism did indeed implode, leaving left-wing politics at a loss as to how to renew their pledge for an egalitarian society, a situation that still endures today.[53] A neoliberal inclination lay at the heart of Tony Blair's reform of the Labour Party in Great Britain, as it did in Bill Clinton's version of the Democratic programme in the USA in the 1990s. Today, neoliberalization has affected the political spectrum in virtually every country, albeit with different intensities and variable results. As Brenner et al. have noted, neoliberalization as a whole has been variegated, unstable, patterned, experimental, discontinuous, contradictory, locally specific, and yet intensely global, as well as contested, and it has affected all levels of government – transnational, national, regional and municipal.[54] The overall result has been a profound reshaping and reweaving of relations between state, market, civil society and individuals, under the pressures of a politically guided intensification of market rule and commoditization. Neoliberalism is therefore intimately tied to the processes of economic globalization and its intensification of an 'increasingly transnational field of market-oriented regulatory transfer'.[55]

It is difficult to explain the irresistible rise of the neoliberal ideology in the space of three decades, after nearly four decades of prosperous welfare-statism. Authors have written about historical causes, such as the deficiencies of welfare bureaucracies, inflation rates, oil crashes and so on, as they have written about the ways in which the neoliberal agenda managed to create a consensus among the economic and political elite (the so-called Washington Consensus). Yet this does not go far in explaining how neoliberalism, which denies being ideological and has never constituted an explicit and systematic political programme, has penetrated the *zeitgeist* enough to become a *cultural* ideology which in turn allows for neoliberal policies to impose themselves as the only alternative.

The Culture of Economics: From Consumerism to Management

It can be argued that the social acceptance of neoliberalism depends on a wider shift within Western societies, one which has to do with the rise of *consumerism* as a dominant cultural ethos. We will further examine the history, nature, dynamics, functions, varieties and stakes of consumerism in the second volume of this project. In brief, mass consumption gave way to consumerism after the 1950s and has resulted in a profoundly morphed household, social and cultural reality, one in which the abundance and the circulation of objects and the continuous appeal to

---

[53]   One reason for this, as commentators such as Louis Dumont (cf. *Homo aequalis*) have noted, is that Marx's theory shares the materialist foundations of capitalism.

[54]   Brenner et al, 'Variegated Neoliberalization'; See also Hackworth, *The Neoliberal City*.

[55]   Brenner et al, 'Variegated Neoliberalization', p. 185.

desire is central. Consumerism as an ethos and matrix of lifestyle is inextricably tied to the development and democratization of communication technologies. Together, they act as vectors for cultural globalization. While the spread of consumption goes hand in hand with marketization and commoditization within this new type of society, which we can call 'consumer' or 'market society', consumerism is not to be understood analytically as the expansion of meaninglessness, simulacra and alienation, as neo-Marxist interpretations would lead us to think. Nor is it to be understood as being primarily and essentially emancipatory, as liberalist enthusiasm would like us to believe.

One way to explain the appeal of consumerism, its drive, is to see how it provides a formidable vehicle for the extension and radicalization of the modern individualistic culture of authenticity and expressivity as defined by Charles Taylor.[56] We expand in the second volume on how this perspective differs from the 'spiritual marketplace' and Rational Choice approaches, but here simply argue that consumerism has acted as a powerful cultural vector which has naturalized commoditization while enchanting economic practice and its new value of consumption rather than production, thus disseminating and naturalizing an economic rapport to the world, society, others and human existence itself. Consumerism entails an ever-growing expanse of commoditization. By expanding the market in the spaces opened through state and welfare reform, neoliberalism is reinforced as an ideology and presented as the sole Rational Choice, while marketization in turn fortifies consumerism as a desirable ethos.

Consumerism was well installed in the late 1970s when neoliberalism expanded from the political economy to governmental policy. This period is also that of the emergence of management[57] as a new 'science' within the universities and the workplace. Management lies at the crux of the economy, politics, society and culture. Management is not part of neoliberalism as such, even if neoliberal principles form the core of today's management discourses and techniques. Some of its aspects, including rationalization, were noticed by Weber and seen to be central to the process of modernization. Yet, as with consumerism, management has infused social life to the point where it provides the language with which personal and social aspirations and realities can themselves be expressed.[58]

Neoliberalism finds alignment with both consumerism and management. Both the latter operate as new forms of social regulation realized through the dynamics of the market. This new regulation shuns commanding vertical, disciplinary, authority-based modes in favour of more fluid, context-dependent, horizontal, 'rhizomatic', technical and voluntary types of regulation. One remarkable consequence of the successful dissemination of the new political economy's ideas

---

[56]   Charles Taylor, *Sources of the Self: The Making of the Modern Identity* (Cambridge, 1989); Charles Taylor, *The Malaise of Modernity* (Toronto, 1991).

[57]   We will also come back to management in the second volume.

[58]   Vincent de Gaulejac, *La société malade de la gestion. Idéologie gestionnaire, pouvoir managérial et harcèlement social* (Paris, 2005).

has been the meteoric rise of the term 'governance' in the place and stead of the now marginalized concept of government.

Neoliberalism is continuous with the liberal tradition in its preference for juridical and technical conceptions of regulation. As Jules Duchastel has noted, the neoliberal ideology distinguishes between two spaces: that of the market, whose subterranean laws are said to ensure an optimal and just balance, and that of regulation, which should be kept to as simple an expression as possible.[59] First introduced by O.E. Williamson, the term governance was developed within the field of business administration, and valued transparency, objectivity and the democratic participation of shareholders in the process of management and decision-making.[60] It also evolved in the context of urban administration in order to differentiate between the exercise of government and the strategic action of various parties with vested interests. In its history, the concept of governance has mirrored the shift from political power proper towards a market-based regulative process. Governance does not so much replace government as it acts out a change in the very grammar of politics; one that champions technical and judicial processes over so-called value-ridden, arbitrary political regulation. This mutation entails a change in the teleology of regulation, no longer expressed in terms of the 'common good' but as achieving efficiency (defined in economic terms of cost-effectiveness) and 'objective' utility.

Governance has been defined as a production technique for norms, rules and procedures, and as a way to answer a variety of conflicting interests. It has developed in the field of economics before migrating to other social fields. It testifies to a situation in which the state no longer assumes an overruling authority. The state has seen its sovereignty eroded and its legitimacy challenged by market forces in a globalized world, where the loci of power have been multiplied and political structures shaken.[61] 'Governance' conveys an economic understanding of society and polity. It helps to naturalize the market, construct the self-evidence of an economic worldview and discourage alternative modes of representation and regulation. In some cases it even legitimizes an ultra-liberal, de-historicized conception of society as comprised of agglomerations of individual interests. Actors are not cast as having rights, nor are their actions aimed towards the common good. Actors are depicted in terms of the shareholder, defined by the interests and size of market share.[62] Society becomes contractual.

---

[59] Jules Duchastel, 'Du gouvernement à la gouvernance. Crise ou ajustement de la régulation néolibérale', in Raphaël Canet and Jules Duchastel, *La régulation néolibérale. Crise ou ajustement ?* (Montréal, 2004), pp. 17–47.

[60] Duchastel, 'Du gouvernement à la gouvernance', p. 22.

[61] Duchastel, 'Du gouvernement à la gouvernance', pp. 22–3.

[62] Duchastel, 'Du gouvernement à la gouvernance', pp. 43–4.

About this Volume

The effects of neoliberalism, consumerism, marketization, management and 'governance' have been widespread. They have received scholarly attention with respect to politics, polity, education, law, security and other fields, but very little attention has been paid to their interplays with religion. The following chapters chart various aspects of these dynamics. Part I, Religions in the New Political Economy, will focus on religious responses to neoliberalism, and present how religious organizations have responded to the emergent market society. Part II, Political Governance of Religion, looks at how the changed political economy has affected the opportunity structures for religious actors, and discusses how political governance shifts the boundaries of acceptable and desired religious agency. The chapters are briefly introduced at the beginning of the two sections.

PART I
Religions in the New Political Economy

This section considers relations between religion and the new cultural political economy. What opportunities and constraints does it provide? How have both new and old religious organizations responded and made use of these new opportunities? The chapters explore a variety of ways in which beliefs, practices, theologies, symbols and rituals function within it.

Joanildo A. Burity's chapter looks at two different cases in South America, a continent that has undergone significant neoliberal reforms. He considers how neo-Pentecostal spirituality embodies 'neoliberal ideas and values of entrepreneurialism, self-assertiveness and transactional spirituality', and how ecumenical organizations and networks act as mobilizers in the anti-globalization movement. Both operate with a local/global nexus of neoliberal ideology, including the neo-Pentecostals' promise of 'God's superabundant wealth', which stands in contrast to ecumenical efforts to undermine the current political economy.

James V. Spickard continues Burity's exploration of the religious critique of neoliberalism by looking at resurgent religion in the context of the simultaneous growth of neoliberal ideologies among both Western intellectuals and comparable elites in the global South. He points to the liberal churches' ability to disentangle neoliberal ideology, while simultaneously being marginalized in public debate.

Jens Schlamelcher looks at processes of transformation within the German Evangelical Church in the age of neoliberalism. The Church is both a moral agent critiquing the marketization of society, but is also itself in a financial crisis caused by shrinking membership. The connection between the Church and its members is becoming increasingly distanced, to such an extent that the latter are increasingly seen as 'customers'. Through 'city-churches', the Church tries to reach out to its 'clientele again' by presenting novel types of religious spaces, which, according to Schlamelcher, 'de-Christianizes' these spaces in the process. The consumerist city-churches remain 'a social form without any obligations, which makes no demands with respect to religious affiliation or on individual ethical conduct'.

Breda Gray's chapter offers a powerful and synthetic post-Foucaudian analysis of governmentality. Gray analyses the shifting role of the Catholic Church in the Republic of Ireland with specific reference to the governmental project of immigrant integration. She unveils the neoliberal mode of governing 'at a distance' whilst enrolling individuals in new forms of regulation. The 'risks' of social exclusion are outsourced to civil society, where the scandal-ridden Catholic Church is attempting to claim new legitimacy. But religious and faith-based organizations become increasingly embedded in an 'audit culture' and, in the process, become instrumentalized by the state.

Jason Hackworth analyses the links between neoliberalism and the privatization of welfare in the United States. He considers how certain evangelical Christian theologians began to re-evaluate their views on welfare to make alliance with the neoliberal right – an uneasy alliance from which the Religious Right has nevertheless benefited. Hackworth analyses faith-based organizations and their many manifestations, providing a fourfold typology: FBOs as extensions of the welfare system, FBOs as enhancements of welfare, FBOs as catalysts for change and FBOs as alternatives to the state.

Chapter 1
Entrepreneurial Spirituality and Ecumenical Alterglobalism: Two Religious Responses to Global Neoliberalism

Joanildo A. Burity

The relationship between religion and neoliberalism is far from unidirectional. As the latter spread globally, it produced impacts on, but also responses from, religious identities and organizations. In the process it has become clear that a one sided 'impact' theory is insufficient to render intelligible the relational, a(nta)gonistic settings in which new forms of spirituality and religious organization have emerged, changed and proactively faced the challenges posed by recent transformations of the social bond and the public sphere. The need for a contextual analysis is not required, in a situation such as this, just for the sake of 'richer' and more nuanced pictures of the situation. Rather, it is only through the actual entanglements and intimations of global/local dynamics that one can properly capture the complex configuration of the relationship of religion and neoliberalism in globalizing times.

Given the hegemonic nature of neoliberal ideology, which has crystallized in various ways in terms of economic, political and cultural practices/policies wherever it has spread, while not relying on any single or centralized source of dissemination or control but supported by powerful actors, the link between religion and neoliberalism goes beyond consumerism. It is clearly more than a question of how market and managerial practices have infused the logic of religious organization and personal spirituality. As the grip of neoliberal ideas, motifs and propositions morphed into a governmentality of entrepreneurship, competition, deregulation, privatization of public services and stimulus to public-private partnerships driven by efficiency and competition, networked governance, risk-taking and consumerism, *hegemony* becomes a key explanatory factor. As such, it spans across very different dimensions of the social, is sanctioned by and through state policies and various forms of media and educational discourses and reaches or relates to different *social logics*,[1] including religious ones.

[1]   Jason Glynos and David Howarth, *Logics of Critical Explanation in Social and Political Theory* (London, 2008); Ernesto Laclau, 'Identity and Hegemony: The Role of Universality in the Constitution of Political Logics', in Judith Butler, Ernesto Laclau and Slavoj Žižek, *Contingency, Hegemony, Universality: Contemporary Debates on the Left* (London, 2000), pp. 44–89; Ernesto Laclau, *The Populist Reason* (London, 2005).

Neoliberalism has also acquired a certain historical trajectory which calls for attention to time and space. The initial 'dogmatic' and 'destructive' phase bent on antagonizing statist discourses was followed by other configurations in many places, depending on the degree of opposition faced by neoliberals or on how (un)successful neoliberal-inspired policies were.[2] There is, in this context, much to be learned by attending to the deployments of such entanglements and intimations in peripheral and emergent regions of global capitalism. The criss-crossing and disseminative nature of asymmetric social, economic and political exchanges in the current juncture encounters place and context in ways that both evince (counter)claims from the underside of global processes aimed at the 'centre stages' of world politics and bring those dynamics 'home' to advanced capitalist societies. This comes about through the impact of migration on domestic attitudes to national identity and otherness; resonances of perceived (sometimes relentlessly fabricated) global threats; global financial crises; outbreaks of conflicts and acts of violence reverberating from 'outside' national boundaries or the margins of society; expressions of global solidarity and the impact of transnational networking or social activism; implementation of decisions and policies agreed at the level of existing structures of global governance under pressure from emerging societies; or changes in international law.

Those claims can take various forms and shapes and generally name distinct patterns of emergence of new global actors, such as states, civil groups/movements and religions. To name only a few: demands for global justice coming from social and religious movements; religious 'reverse missions' from the periphery; intellectual critiques of colonial complicities in knowledge production by Global North academics; or political demands for participation in the institutions of global governance.

The following analysis will examine the proactive way in which religious positions relate to neoliberalism and its economic and political expressions. I will stress the comprehensive, but decentred, multilayered and contested nature of global neoliberal hegemony, and the importance for Northern contexts of developments taking place in the South.

Two particular Christian discursive formations stand out in the spaces where religion meets neoliberalism; a) *Pentecostalism* and b) *ecumenical organizations and networks* acting as mobilizers in the *alterglobalist movement*. Both discourses operate within a local/global nexus, as their articulatory character involves a *non-territorial* focus based on their understandings of mission and religious mobilization, but is also *firmly rooted* in territorial experiences of community and individualization. Pentecostalism and religious alterglobalism also operate according to logics

---

²   Boaventura de S. Santos, 'Para Uma Reinvenção Solidária e Participativa do Estado', in Luiz Carlos Bresser Pereira et al. (eds), *Sociedade e Estado em Transformação* (São Paulo, 2001); Boaventura de S. Santos and César Rodríguez-Garavito, 'Law, Politics, and the Subaltern in Counter-Hegemonic Globalization', in Boaventura de S. Santos and César Rodríguez-Garavito (eds), *Law and Globalization from Below: Towards a Cosmopolitan Legality* (Cambridge, 2005), pp. 1–26.

which seek to extend their reach and grasp over large spatio-temporal domains through equivalential or differentialist practices, thus relating to wider clusters of social relations and hegemonic practices by activating (agonistic) aggregative or particularistic strategies and by engaging other social forces, religious or not.

Through equivalential practices Pentecostals and alterglobalists 'translate' different religious, social, economic or political demands or identities into a particular discourse of spirituality which is presented as capable of addressing personal and collective crises; and they offer material provision and subjective recomposition/reassurance in situations of uncertainty, risk and dislocation. Religious discourse thereby seeks to articulate a variety of social demands, organizing and mobilizing them under a new principle, and disputing existing hegemonic discourses. In contrast, through differentialist expansion those discourses stress the specificity of their identities or their nonconformity with an existing state of affairs. Differentialist discourses claim access to representation and recognition, thus challenging 'invisibility', 'marginalization' and 'discrimination'.[3]

Neoliberalization and Religion: Complicating the Narrative

The last few decades witnessed unforeseen and unstable relations between neoliberalism and religious movements. They were unforeseen to the extent that new (religious) actors came to the fore in several parts of the world who had long been minoritized and/or confined to their national bounds. This negative minoritization which involves the activation of asymmetric attempts to reduce some identities, groups and discourses to a marginal position, to refuse them access to the public sphere, also produces a positive counterpart as some of those agents strive to shape a pluralistic public sphere where difference and equality are simultaneously asserted. The emergence and spread of minority groups/discourses and attempts to subordinate these to a 'minor status' are important aspects of the picture, highlighting another way of grasping the scalar nature of social agency in a globalized world. According to Connolly,[4] drawing on Deleuze and Guattari, minoritization is a process whereby 'numerous constituencies of multiple types cross old borders and enter into relations with a "majority" culture that often makes up an actual minority of the populace'.[5] He links the intensification of this process to the prevalence of global capital, though he rejects claims that the latter only produces homogenization.[6]

---

[3]   On my use of equivalence and difference, cf. Laclau, 'Identity and Hegemony'; Glynos and Howarth, *Logics*.

[4]   William E. Connolly, *Capitalism and Christianity, American Style* (Durham, 2008). See also Tariq Modood, 'Their Liberalism and Our Multiculturalism?', *British Journal of Politics and International Relations*, 3/2 (2001): pp. 251–4.

[5]   Connolly, *Capitalism*, p. 323.

[6]   Ibid., p. 323.

The period was also marked by growing instability, as institutional frameworks together with the values and narratives that underpinned them became slackened, ineffective and contested. The demise of socialism, the crises of military dictatorships in Southern Europe and South America, the world recession of the 1980s and the undeniable expansion of globalization aroused myriad social movements and other contestants. In this context, neoliberal and religious discourses can be seen as seeking to provide anchorage points or new principles of social recomposition to those fractured realities.[7]

In fact, without giving due attention to the multilayered relation between neoliberalism and religion, one risks conflating them unwarrantedly or attributing a unidirectional causal link between them: this is highlighted, for instance, by Meyer, who argues against a facile, direct relationship between Pentecostalism and neoliberal capitalism.[8]

Neoliberalism emerged in Latin America in the late 1980s as both a *locus* and a *medium* of discourse. As a *locus*, the *neoliberal* idiom sought to gather (hegemonize) a number of grievances against the immodest power of the state in a continent plagued by military dictatorships and a tradition of interventionist, modernizing state policies. It thus sought to act as a democratizing force. It also capitalized on a certain critique of the ideological underpinnings of such state interventionism, calling for a 'post-developmentalist' approach[9] based on 'market freedom', competition, decentralization, deregulation, consumer-oriented economic practices, openness to foreign capital and global markets.

As a *medium*, the neoliberal *idiom* offered a grammar of discourse to express the uncertainties of the regime crisis leading to democratization in Latin American countries in the 1980s, to curb and avert expectations of radical democratization and to accept globalization and state reforms as irresistible. The idiom of neoliberalism

---

[7]   See Arturo Escobar, 'Beyond the Third World: Imperial Globality, Global Coloniality and Anti-globalization Social Movements', *Third World Quarterly*, 25/1 (2004): pp. 207–30; Santos and Rodríguez-Garavito, 'Law, Politics'; Dagnino, 'Participation, Citizenship and Democracy: Perverse Confluence and Displacement of Meanings', in Catherine Neveu (ed.), *Cultures et Pratiques Participatives: Perspectives Comparatives* (Paris, 2007), pp. 353–70; Joanildo Burity, 'Reform of the State and the New Discourse on Social Policy in Brazil', *Latin American Perspectives*, 33 (2006): pp. 67–88; and 'Inequality, Culture and Globalization in Emerging Societies: Reflections on the Brazilian Case', in Jan Nederveen Pieterse and Boike Rehbein (eds), *Globalisation and Emerging Societies: Development and Inequality* (Basingstoke, 2009), pp. 185–200.

[8]   Birgit Meyer, 'Pentecostalism and Globalization', in Allan Anderson et al. (eds), *Studying Global Pentecostalism: Theories and Methods* (Berkeley, 2010), pp. 114–30.

[9]   Luiz Carlos Bresser Pereira, *Development and Crisis in Brazil, 1930–1983* (Boulder, 1984); Joel Wolfe, 'Populism and Developmentalism', in Thomas H. Holloway (ed.), *A Companion to Latin American History* (Malden, 2010), pp. 347–64; Ramón Grosfoguel, 'Developmentalism, Dependence Theory in Latin America', in Mabel Moraña, Enrique D. Dussel and Carlos A. Jáuregui (eds), *Coloniality At Large: Latin America and the Postcolonial Debate* (Durham, 2008), pp. 307–32.

sought to dispute the power of naming the new post-dictatorship scenario against the more radical construction of a democratization from below that had become a credible alternative through liberal democratic and left-wing oppositional politics.

The ambiguous locus and medium of the neoliberal idiom, with its emphasis on liberty, choice, weakening state power and enhancing economic efficiency and affordable consumption, blurred the frontier with other (anti-statist) discourses in which 'democracy' and 'social justice' became floating signifiers,[10] sometimes indistinguishable in their provenance and precise meaning. A 'perverse confluence'[11] came about between right-wing liberal discourses and popular democratic discourses, dramatically enacted in and through the political coalitions formed after the transitions to civilian rule in the continent.[12]

The articulation of neoliberalism to public religious discourse in post-dictatorship Latin America took place against this backdrop in various ways, by allowing a new religious minority to emerge, politicizing its views of crucial points of definition for the new order that was being constructed, and viscerally opposed to atheism and communism. Given the porous boundaries separating confessional Protestant identities, the relentless circulation of preachers, churchgoers, TV and radio broadcasting and publications helped disseminate the prosperity gospel theology within Christian churches and preconceptions about radical democratic discourses. This favoured an ethic of acquisition and consumption as God-given entitlements and was reinforced by opportunities for churches to join the call to engage in partnerships in governmental compensatory policies in the 1990s.[13] However, a concerted reaction emerged throughout the 2000s from various sectors within non-Pentecostal churches which changed the picture. It led to a partial delegitimation of neoliberal policies, pointing to their destructive impact on labour relations, social policies, the environment and cultural identities. Radical Christian critiques of neoliberalism managed to attract attention and positive responses from religious constituencies, also strengthening secular anti-neoliberalisms.[14]

Considering the general background against which the neoliberal hegemony had to operate in Latin American countries, the idea of a full-blown sway and grip on religious forms and discourses is therefore an inaccurate characterization of the context. The overlaps between the transformation of the political space through democratization, the advance of neoliberalization and the delegitimating

[10] Laclau, *Populist Reason*.

[11] Dagnino, 'Participation'.

[12] Joanildo Burity, *'Reform'* and *Redes, parcerias e participação religiosa nas políticas sociais no Brasil* (Recife, 2006); Janet Newman and John Clarke, *Publics, Politics & Power: Remaking the Public in Public Services* (London, 2009), pp. 138–9.

[13] Paul Freston, *Evangelicals and Politics in Asia, Africa and Latin America* (Cambridge, 2004); Donald E. Miller and Tetsunao Yamamori, *Global Pentecostalism: The New Face of Christian Social Engagement* (Berkeley and Los Angeles, 2007).

[14] Bruce E. Benson and Peter G. Hetzel (eds), *Evangelicals and Empire: Christian Alternatives to the Political Status Quo* (Grand Rapids, 2008); Burity, *Redes*.

effect of greater inequality as well as the pluralization of cultural and social identities for the emergence of new forms of resistance and political regrouping[15] need to be acknowledged in order to make proper sense of the moving positions of religious agents.

The Religious Context: Spirituality and the Neoliberal Challenge

One of the areas in which the analysis above can be usefully illustrated is that of the rehabilitation of religious identity and organizations by secular intellectuals, politicians and civil society groups. It is clear that the spread of neoliberalism was carried forth through a relentless subjective reworking so as to foster the image of a competition-driven agent, bent on disseminating both the logic of the market and its acquisitive, consumerist values. Forging a new subjectivity is coeval with the institutional re-engineering which neoliberals set out to promote as a condition for both the achievement and the free development of market sovereignty. Combining the wide reach of such cultural technologies with the expansionist zeal of the prophets of deregulation, privatization and consumerism, it would not be long before neoliberal 'spirituality' crossed paths with religious ones.

Such reverberations and overlaps across various spiritualities conform to what Connolly calls the 'evangelical-capitalist resonance machine'.[16] In his case, the focus lies on Christian right groups in America that have hardly any correspondents amongst public religious actors in Latin America. Even by American standards this religious right does not merely coincide with the evangelicals as a whole.[17] Carrette and King also develop a cogent argument on the 'second privatization of religion' (the first one dating back to the nineteenth century, under the influence of Romanticism) as a result of the 1980s' hegemonization of culture by the economic discourse of neoliberalism.[18] Like Connolly, they do not address Pentecostalism, rather focusing on Asian spirituality and the corporate takeover of religion as a subjectivization tactic to shape 'neoliberal' selves. Both approaches, however, hint at the more general nature of two important processes: the stress on (and rehabilitation of) religious identity or, more vaguely, spirituality and the *political* nature of its colonization by the transactional and acquisitive logic of market. As

---

[15] Federico Montero, 'Reflexiones preliminares sobre discriminación, ciudadanía y políticas públicas en el MERCOSUR', in F. Montero et al. (eds), *Hacia una ciudadanía plena. Los desafíos de las políticas antidiscriminatorias en el MERCOSUR* (Buenos Aires, 2009), p. 29.

[16] William Connolly, *Capitalism and Christianity*.

[17] Harvey Cox, 'Old-time Religion', *The Boston Globe*, 10 July (2006), <http://www.boston.com/news/globe/ideas/articles/2006/07/09/old_time_religion>, accessed 10 March 2011.

[18] Jeremy Carrette and Richard King, *Selling Spirituality: The Silent Takeover of Religion* (Abingdon, 2005), pp. 44–7.

I will comment later, the Latin American case provides yet another articulation of religious identity, politics and neoliberal discourse.

It is also true that 'the left' has multiplied, fragmented and reduced its ability to enact traditional conceptions of economic egalitarianism and social libertarianism clothed in a secularist outlook. Failures to harness mass support, along with the political marginalization or defeat of its more radical groups, have curtailed the traditional left's secular hubris, making it more amenable to accept and seek partnerships with religious groups. In different countries, the growing relevance of the Pentecostal vote has acted as a further incentive to seek alliances with this religious group.

Thus, the neoliberal cultural experiment in creating a new subjectivity for its hegemonic project of recharting the whole extension of the social according to the logic and practices of global capitalism encountered religious identities on the side both of compliance and contestation. This shows a facet of how religion and governmentality can become imbricated.[19] According to Springer:

> Neoliberalism-as-ideology gave way to neoliberalism-as-governmentality via the entrenchment of what Stephen Gill (1995) refers to as 'market civilization', or the transformative practices through which capitalist expansion became tied to a legitimating neoliberal discourse of progress and development. Neoliberalism then is an assemblage of rationalities, strategies, technologies and techniques concerning the mentality of rule that facilitate 'governance at a distance' (Barry et al. 1996; Larner 2000) by delineating a discursive field in which the exercise of power is 'rationalized' (Lemke 2001), thereby encouraging both institutions and individuals to conform to the norms of the market.[20]

Secondly, it met with forms of religion with an explicit global vocation and perfectly at home in the world of mobility, networking and communications made possible by new technologies and the globalist imaginary. Pentecostalism and ecumenism are two outstanding sites of global religion and in that sense they run parallel to global neoliberalism.

It is a case of a redrawing of the private/public, religion/politics distinction, and of a dissemination of religious agency across traditional social boundaries. The current juncture has facilitated the proactive expression of traditional religious reservations being confined to the realm of private life, through the direct entanglement of religious agency in ongoing disputes for the (re)ordering of global-local configurations.

---

[19]   Kevin Lewis O'Neill, 'But Our Citizenship Is in Heaven: A Proposal for the Future Study of Christian Citizenship in the Global South', *Citizenship Studies*, 13/4 (2009): pp. 333–48. See also Simon Coleman, *The Globalisation of Charismatic Christianity: Spreading the Gospel of Prosperity* (Cambridge, 2000).

[20]   Simon Springer, 'Violence Sits in Places? Cultural Practice, Neoliberal Rationalism, and Virulent Imaginative Geographies', *Political Geography*, 30 (2011): p. 95.

Pentecostalism and Neoliberal Discourse: A Transactional Spirituality of Acquisition and Consumption?

There are two main patterns of relationship between Latin American Pentecostalism and neoliberalism. Only the more recent one, *neo-Pentecostalism*, can be seen as an organic expression of a spirituality and organizational framework which is in tune with the neoliberal ideology and mode of governance.

Neo-Pentecostalism in Latin America describes a branch of the Pentecostal movement within Protestantism reaching back to the mid-1970s and firmly associated with the prosperity gospel (health and wealth) movement. Following the known Protestant fissiparous pattern, hundreds of local churches, 'ministries' and small denominations have emerged, most of their founders coming from participation in traditional Pentecostal churches, or from having been converted in other neo-Pentecostal ones. Neo-Pentecostalism should not be confused with the Charismatic movement which spread within mainline denominations and the Roman Catholic Church in the late 1960s. Its main features are nicely summarized by Silva as:

> the abandonment (or moderation) of asceticism, the valorisation of pragmatism, the use of business management techniques in running churches, emphasis on the theology of prosperity, the use of the media for the work of mass proselytism and religious advertising (leading to the name 'electronic churches') and the centrality of the theology of the spiritual battle against other religious denominations, especially the Afro-Brazilian religions and spiritism.[21]

The second pattern, which I will call *Traditional Pentecostalism*, is clearly majoritarian and needs to be captured in context, showing its convergences more at the level of political activism than in terms of substantive theological and spiritual connections to the market culture. It represents what is more commonly understood by Pentecostalism.[22]

In both cases it is a question of active engagement, not of passive reflection or external impact, but the entrepreneurial character of Pentecostal pastoral and

----

[21]   Vágner Gonçalves da Silva, 'Neo-Pentecostalism and Afro-Brazilian Religions: Explaining the Attacks on Symbols of the African Religious Heritage in Contemporary Brazil', *Mana*, 3/se (2007): p. 2. See also David Lehmann, *Struggle for the Spirit: Religious Transformations and Popular Culture in Brazil and Latin America* (Cambridge, 1996); Ricardo Mariano, *Neopentecostais: sociologia do novo pentecostalismo no Brasil* (São Paulo, 1999); Paul Freston, 'The Transnationalisation of Brazilian Pentecostalism: The Universal Church of the Kingdom of God', in André Corten and Ruth Marshall-Fratani (eds), *Between Babel and Pentecost: Transnational Pentecostalism in Africa and Latin America* (London, 2000), pp. 196–215; Ari Pedro Oro et al., *Igreja Universal do Reino de Deus: Os Novos Conquistadores da Fé* (São Paulo, 2003); and David Martin, *Pentecostalism: The World Their Parish* (Malden, 2003), pp. 71–118.

[22]   Keith Warrington, *Pentecostal Theology: A Theology of Encounter* (London, 2008).

theological discourse presents a family resemblance with neoliberalism. The entrepreneurial component of Pentecostal identification enacts in distinctive and sometimes overlapping ways *spiritualities of self-assertion, community and prosperity.*

Traditional Pentecostalism's version of an entrepreneurialism of the poor is more attuned to the encouragement to fend for oneself, not waiting for or relying on state-sponsored social provision (but not rejecting it either). This is possible because the Spirit's baptism fills the believer with divine power, regardless of gender, ethnicity or social standing, strengthening self-esteem and autonomy, and prompting that believer to take risks in faith. According to Almeida, this is, however, more akin to an 'ethics of providence', in which 'economic upward mobility does not have a strong religious value and material needs are never fully met, but provided for case by case as a "divine succour", many times as the result of face-to-face reciprocity ties that a more communitarian religiosity favours'.[23]

This spirit-filled entrepreneurialism is thus supported and sanctioned within a *community* of reference. Traditional Pentecostalism values and cultivates *encumbered selves*, providing them with both group recognition and supporting social networks through which mutual help, access to opportunities and encouragement to keep trying, venturing, challenging conventions and prejudices (particularly in the case of the poor, ethnic minorities, women and young people). Although the autonomy to make religious decisions against family traditions is prized, and self-trust and initiative are continuously inculcated, the promise of blessings comes in tandem with a shared, orderly life within the religious community. As Venables puts it with reference to Chilean Pentecostalism, 'Pentecostals are refashioned as a collective actor within the community'.[24] And he adds, 'within the community Pentecostals find a web of religious solidarity that helps them, through various mechanisms already identified, to achieve a relative improvement in their life conditions; an improvement which is an outcome, not a cause, of their action'.[25]

In contrast to this prevailing pattern, a highly strident and performative alternative has attracted most attention lately. Latin American neo-Pentecostalism, originating among the poor and by far outnumbering the white middle-class prosperity gospel churches, has become a veritable religious expression of neoliberal discourse. It emerged in the mid-1970s, especially in Brazil, and spread quickly to other South American countries, the United States and Europe (starting

---

[23]   Ronaldo Rômulo M. de Almeida, A expansão pentecostal: circulação e flexibilidade, *Centro de Estudos da Metrópole* (2006), pp. 11–12, my translation, <http://www. centrodametropole.org.br/v1/pdf/2007/ ronaldo_pentecostalismo.pdf>, accessed 10 April 2011.

[24]   Juan Pablo Venables B., *Diferentes e Integrados: Estudio acerca de la ética del trabajo en el Movimiento Pentecostal de la Región Metropolitana* (Santiago, 2007), p. 136, my translation, <http://www.cybertesis.cl/tesis/uchile/2007/venables_j/sources/venables_j. pdf>, accessed 24 June 2011.

[25]   Ibid.

with Portugal), but today stretches in all directions (the Brazilian Universal Church of the Kingdom of God is said to operate in over 160 countries). Making intensive use of the media, neo-Pentecostals clearly embody neoliberal ideas and values of entrepreneurialism, self-assertiveness and transactional spirituality. Calculating and bent on minimising 'suffering' at all costs, so that enjoyment of material blessings can face no constraints, neo-Pentecostal spirituality resembles *speculative investment*, aiming at the highest returns with the least effort: God owns all riches and the extension of his blessings is unlimited; therefore, every believer may lay claim to this superabundant wealth *through giving* and *putting God to the test* as a faithful and hyper-competent *broker* of each offering received. Despite the massive celebrations held by charismatic preachers, communication is clearly pitted at the individual level, and the community only serves to provide evidence – through endless testimonies – of the efficacy of giving and trusting God to receive individual blessings within a kind of instrumental community of ritual.[26] It is a case of a *spirituality of acquisition and consumption* by an *unencumbered self*.

If one adds the strenuous institutional activism of church leaders to enlarge or build new mega meeting places, acquire more sophisticated media equipment and outlets, provide a plethora of items for religious consumption (from publications and DVDs to tourist packages) and, in some cases, highly publicized charity-run social projects, the full range of entrepreneurship – both individual and corporate – comes clearly to the fore. Many of these churches also run special services or meetings (sometimes on a weekly basis) where people are taught how to handle their finances and how to start their own small businesses. Self-reliance, risk-taking and diligence are key inculcated values. Political brokering has become a permanent, institutional affair, with regular participation in elections since the mid-1980s all over Latin America, some churches funding their own candidates and monitoring their performance when elected through professionalized political committees. This is thought to complement their self-understanding of their mission: exercising pressure and influence to secure unrestrained religious freedom and public visibility (particularly in competition with the majority Catholic Church), and to promote traditional religious morality against more liberal gender, sexual, bio-technological agendas.

Despite the explicit endorsement of arguments and ideas clearly compatible with or advocated by neoliberal discourse at local or global levels, neo-Pentecostals need to be assessed in a rather more cautious or qualified way. First, their unrelenting call for giving (money) is inscribed in a religious logic of God's sovereignty which introduces a different consideration into the plain logic of market investment and returns: God's will or designs for each individual is ultimately unfathomable and the believer faces an inherent risk beyond faith of failing to receive the goods. It may also be a case of unconfessed sin or overindulgent behaviour which prevents or holds off access to God's riches. Such circumstances are unavoidably part of

---

[26]   Mary Ruth Gomes Esperandio, 'Subjetividade, religiosidade contemporânea e globalização: o caso da Igreja Universal do Reino de Deus', *Protestantismo em Revista*, 9 (2006): pp. 31–47, <http://www3.est.edu.br/nepp>, accessed 10 May 2011.

religious discourse and far removed from the strict logic of investment and returns. Second, neo-Pentecostal corporate politics has alternated between different political projects in the region and it is not given in their identity that only conservative choices will be made. Within the tradition of political coalitions that forms part of Latin American politics, certain neo-Pentecostal churches have become partners in the recent wave of progressive (and leftist) governments in South America. There is strong evidence, moreover, that such political activism has involved support for broadly affirmative social welfare policies. Third, the ways in which people respond to the official discourse of giving and entrepreneurship do not always conform to religious leaders' expectations: women often present themselves on behalf of their children, husbands, relatives, even friends; some people (including dissenting leaders) challenge the authenticity of the evidence provided, refuse to give as required or become disillusioned with frustrated expectations; others have complained of the absence of pastoral care from their pastors, whose 'mass performance' lacks genuine engagement with ordinary people's specific needs. Such qualifications both raise issues about actual religious commodification and marketization and forms of interpretation uncritically cast in terms of the religious economy discourse.

Finally, as both Traditional Pentecostal and neo-Pentecostal churches ride the globalizing tide and expand well beyond their original cultural and organizational contexts, they are faced with new challenges, whether on the side of their new audiences (especially immigrant, ethnic diaspora and national majority cultures) or on the side of the political and juridical requirements or constraints which they have to meet. The ability to face up to these challenges varies dramatically, but highlights the pressures toward identity-assertion and negotiation, and the need to confront cultural difference as well as very different religious contexts and demands from their original ones.

Neoliberalism, Consumerism and the Religious Left: Alterglobalism and Resistance

The religious left in Latin America is centrally referenced in two leading models; liberation theology and ecumenism, which largely coalesced in the 1970s, despite their distinctive Catholic and Protestant variants and have been displaced and constrained at denominational or hierarchical levels, but thrived in the domain of religious social activism and public governance (whether locally, nationally and transnationally). Since the early 1980s, a new generation of evangelicals, turned politically radical, joined the ranks of social activism, seeking a middle ground between the two former theological and pastoral models. 'NGOization' has become the destiny of many who were pushed out of church structures or local congregations for their political views and practical engagements. An important network of such organizations emerged out of manifold initiatives and has increasingly become articulated nationally and transnationally.

Alterglobalism, also called the global justice movement or, rather inaccurately, the anti-globalization movement, is clearly related to the experience of the World

Social Forum, emerging out of the street protests against WTO and neoliberal governance in the late 1990s and as a response to the World Economic Forum. In this context a remarkable variety of movements and organizations rallied under the motto 'Another World is Possible', calling for an alternative globalization.[27] A strong connection to Latin America, particularly with Brazilian (religious and non-religious) NGOs, is an original feature of the movement.

The emergence of an alterglobalist religious movement in Latin America is directly connected to this web of organizations, groups and circulating individual activists. Their articulation was also instrumental to one of the most powerful experiments associated with alterglobalism: the World Social Forum. Ecumenical spirituality and organizational webs were openly set against neoliberalism and its global project. As a 2004 report from the World Council of Churches put it, in a nutshell:

> Why is the ecumenical community challenging the ideology and practice of economic globalization? Globalization, as under-girded by the neo-liberal ideology, competes directly with the ecumenical vision of a united humanity where diverse communities and peoples live in solidarity with each other.[28]

Loosely connected to the transnational web of ecumenical agencies, comprising regional church representative bodies, religious NGOs and secular organizations funded by ecumenical development agencies, Latin American ecumenical networks also laid roots in the general emergence of 'civil society' as a nodal point for radical democratic aspirations. The ecumenical umbrella and the NGO form provided the necessary strength for the difficult post-dictatorship period in which democratizing tasks and neoliberal projects crossed paths, producing demobilization and technocratic governance. Through reference to values of solidarity, sustainability, direct democracy, religious and cultural resistance, an alternative was upheld through small-scale 'social projects' and 'formation' events. A religious alterglobalism[29] drawing on decades of grassroots church

---

27   Escobar, 'Beyond the Third World'; Simon Tormey, *Anti-Capitalism: A Beginner's Guide* (Oxford, 2005); Boaventura de S. Santos, 'A crítica da governação neoliberal: O Fórum Social Mundial como política e legalidade cosmopolita subalterna', *Revista Crítica de Ciências Sociais*, 72 (2005): pp. 7–44; Jeremy Gilbert, *Anticapitalism and Culture: Radical Theory and Popular Politics* (Oxford, 2008); Chairman Lévy, 'Influência e Contribuição: a Igreja Católica Progressista Brasileira e o Fórum Social Mundial', *Religião & Sociedade*, 29/2 (2009): pp. 177–97; Dimitrios Theodossopoulos and Elisabeth Kirtsoglou (eds), *United in Discontent: Local Responses to Cosmopolitanism and Globalization* (New York, 2010).

28   World Council of Churches, The Ecumenical Presence at the 4th World Social Forum, *World Council of Churches*, 21 January (2004), <http://www.oikoumene.org/en/resources/documents/wcc-programmes/public-witness-addressing-power-affirming-peace/poverty-wealth-and-ecology/neoliberal-paradigm/the-ecumenical-presence-at-the-4th-world-social-forum.html>, accessed 25 November 2010.

29   A wealth of materials representing a broad definition of religious alterglobalism, particularly the World Social Forum, can be found in the World Council of Churches

work organically linked with place-based popular movements came to target a nonterritorial adversary with an enormous capacity to morph into national and local discourses of modernization, anti-statism, rights-claiming (as *consumers* of private *and* public goods/services) and stimulus for people to take the solution to their problems into their own hands. But rather than letting go of the notion of globalization, these groups launched a contest for its 'true' meaning: a globalization of solidarity, environmental sustainability and social justice and an acceptance of cultural pluralism based on networked forms of participation.

Adopting theories of complexity coming from the natural sciences, Escobar highlights how 'emergence' and 'adaptation' are apt concepts to account for the logic of alterglobalism:

> In this type of situation, simple beginnings lead to complex entities, without the existence of a master plan or central intelligence planning it. They are bottom-up processes, where agents working at one (local) scale produce behaviour and forms at higher scales (eg the great anti-globalisation demonstrations of the last few years). Simple rules at one level give rise to sophistication and complexity at another level through what is called emergence: the fact that the actions of multiple agents interacting dynamically and following local rules rather than top-down commands result in visible macro-behaviour or structures. Sometimes these systems are 'adaptive'; they learn over time, responding more effectively to the changing needs of their environment.[30]

A counter-discourse of global spirituality is emergent, traceable through an ecumenical participation in the World Social Forum which proposed a 'spirituality of resistance' (2003);[31] a 'spirituality of life and human dignity' (2004);[32] or 'life in dignity' (2005).[33] After a rather discreet visibility in 2001 and 2002, the religious participation within the Forum grew significantly as from 2003. That

---

website (www.wcc-coe.org/wcc/what/jpc). An attempt to recast liberation theology as a global theology of cultural pluralism, interreligious dialogue, deep ecological cosmology, embracement of networked forms of mobilization and global civil society activism, led to the World Forum on Theology and Liberation. The Forum has been held in connection with each World Social Forum, since 2005, a few days before the main event, and signals a global reconversion of the liberation theology movement, away from conventional Third Worldism (cf. www.wftl.org/default.php?lang=en-us&t=padrao&p=capa&m=padrao).

　　30　Escobar, 'Beyond the Third World', p. 222.

　　31　'Another World is Possible. The World Council of Churches and other ecumenical organizations at the third World Social Forum', *World Council of Churches*, <wcc-coe.org/wcc/what/jpc/wsf-e.html>, accessed 5 March 2011.

　　32　Ibid.

　　33　'"An authentic, alternative voice": The WCC and other ecumenical organizations at the fifth World Social Forum', *World Council of Churches*, <http://www.wcc-coe.org/wcc/what/jpc/wsf-2005-e.html>, accessed 5 March 2011.

year, for instance, three workshops were held on the theme 'A Spirituality of Resistance' led by the 'Ecumenical Caucus', set up by the WCC, the Lutheran World Federation, the Ecumenical Alliance for World Action, the Latin American Council of Churches and a group of Brazilian churches and religious NGOs. One of the WCC presidents, the Argentinian Methodist Bishop Federico Pagura, also featured in the event's 'Testimonies' section.

The progressive wing of the Catholic Church has also been involved in the World Social Forum experience from the very beginning. According to Lévy, not only a very large proportion of Brazilian activists played a crucial role at the inception of the Forum, but around half of them were, or had directly been, associated with liberation theology and church pastoral groups.[34] Lévy also raises an important qualification regarding how the liberationist background of the original conception of the Forum produced a distinctive outlook when compared with more traditional leftist traditions:

> Such features comprise diversity, respect for the other and the defence and promotion of democratic values and practices at all decision-making levels. They include, particularly, the understanding of the Forum as an open and horizontal structure and a tool for raising awareness and enhancing participation for all. Another remarkable influence is the relevance granted to spirituality, symbolism and celebration in the Forum, which define its spirit and go well beyond intellectualism.[35]

In stark contrast to the Pentecostal register of discourse, religious alterglobalism speaks with a 'secular' voice, combining academic theology and appropriations of social scientific discourse to produce a second order religious reflection on world affairs and social struggles.[36]

---

[34] Chairman Lévy, 'Influência e Contribuição', pp. 178–9.

[35] Ibid., p. 179, my translation.

[36] A case of alterglobalist ecumenical discourse can be found in the 'Faith, Economy and Society Programme' sponsored by the Latin American Council of Churches (CLAI). As an example, I mention the workshop 'External Debt, the State of the Art and Alternatives for the Construction of Another International Financial Architecture'. The workshop was organized in September 2007 by CLAI and co-sponsored by Bread For All, the Friedrich Ebert Foundation (German Social Democracy) and Jubilee 2000 Guayaquil. Its final statement is a highly technical economic analysis of Latin American countries' external debt issues, without a trace of theological language (cf. http://www.clailatino.org/fes/deudaexterna2007/documento%20final.html). It clearly expresses a leftist position and does not say a word on how religious readers should relate the analysis to their faith or spiritual values. The text is really aimed at a different interlocutor: the state and Latin American political elites. Another statement is the Guatemala Declaration (October 2008), resulting from the AGAPE Consultation on 'Linking Poverty, Wealth and Ecology: Ecumenical Perspectives in Latin America and the Caribbean', sponsored by the World Council of Churches, the Latin America Council of Churches and the Christian Ecumenical Council

But the World Social Forum is very much aware of the public salience of religious identities and mobilization. Beyond the deep involvement of religious groups during the Brazilian editions of the Forum, the meetings in Mumbai (2004) and Nairobi (2007) brought this fact into even sharper relief. On the other hand, it is always a case of local and national organizations that have tried diligently to promote a combination of radical democratization and interreligious and intercultural dialogue, walking on a tight rope between the assumption of convergence and solidarity and a call to exercise agonistic respect towards irreducible differences.

The Pentecostal voice, instead, tends to either privilege the oracular, authoritative pronouncements of pastors and political representatives, or to operate through the media and in congregational gatherings. Besides, the theological justification of ecumenical discourse also resorts to a grammar of uncovering or discerning as the underlying dynamics of the 'kingdom of God' takes place in the midst of things – in everyday life as well as in political and economic practices, locally as well as translocally. In this sense, though the register of discourse changes significantly, the encompassing Pentecostal belief that religion is about the whole of life is also present in religious alterglobalism, allowing for its articulation of discourses of economic justice, environmental protection, sustainable livelihoods, cultural and religious pluralism and global governance based on empowered civil society participation.

Alterglobalists do mind the local, including church levels, as sites where the battles of communication and mobilization take place, building up hegemonic chains of equivalence and recruitment of activists. But again the logic differs: the written word predominates; primers are prepared and workshops conducted in churches in order to study those resources. This is where theology comes in most explicitly, as opposed to emotional preaching targeted at prompting immediate individual emotional responses.

Ecumenical organizations in Latin America have shown an acute awareness of the *political* nature, not only of global neoliberalism as their main adversary, but also of the articulation of a discourse of solidarity at the very junction of local *and* global. This means betting on the emergence of small beginnings at certain tipping points, as argued by Escobar, and engaging in painstakingly woven connections and persuasive strategies to bring in new partners to the conversation. They follow existing network nodes and make extensive use of both communication technologies and the range of international meetings, where an ever-growing number of 'civil society representatives' have rendered the notion of a 'movement of movements' at least conceivable.

---

of Guatemala (cf. http://www.oikoumene.org/en/resources/documents/wcc-programmes/ public-witness-addressing-power-affirming-peace/poverty-wealth-and-ecology/neoliberal- paradigm/agape-consultation-guatemala-declaration.html).

Concluding Remarks

Religious models of response to the globalization and hegemony of neoliberalism take place in a complex context, involving local and global dimensions and strategies. Their articulatory practices involve a non-territorial focus based on more traditional views of mission as proselytizing and seeking control of state power, or on networking models of religious mobilization drawing from social movement cultures. The ways in which such responses reflect or resist the grip of consumer culture and the hypercommodification of social life vary starkly, as I have shown, but they are also brought home through similarities and contrasts which underlie the agonistic relation that unfolds between them.

Similarities involve: a common a(nta)gonistic grammar: Pentecostal spiritual warfare *versus* ecumenical ideological/theological contestation of neoliberalism; an anti-idolatric register of discourse, whether in Pentecostal demons of corruption or moral licentiousness, or in ecumenical critiques of market ideology; a call for crucial decisions about obedience to God and enjoyment of salvation as taking place in this world, here and now.

There are of course contrasts, too: Pentecostal conversion(ism) *versus* ecumenical ethical activism as the proper manifestation of obedience to God; cosmological dualism *versus* multidimensional, inner-worldly interpretation of everyday personal and social struggles; pragmatic compromises with secular economic and political ideologies *versus* principled resistance to neoliberalism in the name of a pluralistic approach to cultural identities, political views and modes of community.

The final outcomes of each side of these comparisons and contrasts are far from settled. Questions remain, particularly in light of frequent boundary-crossings and ambiguities: is Pentecostal spirituality unequivocally a case of religious neoliberalism opposed to the alterglobalist position? Is ecumenical alterglobalism a mere theological gloss on the secular discourse of the global civil society? What is the constitutive place of (secular) neoliberalism in both cases? In what ways do they also go beyond neoliberalism? Strategic moves, events taking place beyond each side's purview, misplaced expectations and contingent experiences will continue to play their part in the unfolding of these important carriers of change in our times. Riding on or against the neoliberal wave, spiritual entrepreneurialism and religious alterglobalism are relationally implicated in their common attempt to transfigure the world (to come).

Chapter 2

Making Religion Irrelevant:
The 'Resurgent Religion' Narrative
and the Critique of Neoliberalism

James V. Spickard

The past three decades have seen a spate of scholarly theorizing about the world's seemingly vibrant 'conservative' religions.[1] Variously identified as 'new fundamentalisms', 'resurgent religion', and the like, much of this scholarship types radical Islam, nationalist Hinduism and both Pentecostal and Fundamentalist Christianity as reactions to global modernity. In effect, it sees them as religious responses to social and theological dislocation: as revitalization movements that give their followers the practical and conceptual tools to reformulate their lives while allowing them to imagine that they are maintaining religious traditions.

Not all scholars take this view.[2] Enough do, however, to lend weight to the recent public discourse that identifies religion with an effort to restore an authoritarian past. Among other things, this discourse has demonized conservative Christians and Muslims[3] and has made best-sellers of the recent books by the so-called 'New

---

[1]   James Davidson Hunter, *American Evangelicalism: Conservative Religion and the Quandary of Modernity* (New Brunswick, 1983); Martin E. Marty and R. Scott Appleby (eds), *Fundamentalisms Observed* (Chicago, 1991); Martin E. Marty and R. Scott Appleby, *The Glory and the Power: The Fundamentalist Challenge to the Modern World* (Boston, 1992); Benjamin R. Barber, *Jihad Vs McWorld: Terrorism's Challenge to Democracy* (New York, 2001); Peter L. Berger (ed.), *The Desecularization of the World: Resurgent Religion and World Politics* (Grand Rapids, 1999); Philip Jenkins, *The Next Christendom: The Coming of Global Christianity* (Oxford, 2002); Gabriel A. Almond, R. Scott Appleby and Emmanuel Sivan, *Strong Religion: The Rise of Fundamentalisms Around the World* (Chicago, 2003).

[2]   For example, Christian S. Smith, *American Evangelicalism: Embattled and Thriving* (Chicago, 1998); Andrew M. Greeley and Michael Hout, *The Truth About Conservative Christians: What They Think and What They Believe* (Chicago, 2006).

[3]   George M. Marsden, *Fundamentalism and American Culture: The Shaping of Twentieth-Century Evangelicalism: 1870–1925* (New York, 1980), pp. 199ff; Karim H. Karim, *Islamic Peril: Media and Global Violence* (Montreal, 2003); Samuel P. Huntington, *The Clash of Civilizations and the Remaking of World Order* (New York, 1996).

Atheists'.[4] It has also driven moderates and progressives from American churches. As Michael Hout and Claude Fischer have shown, a growing number of Americans left organized religion in the 1990s because it had embraced a conservative political agenda.[5] In effect, they said 'If that's religion, I want no part of it.'

It is not my purpose here to say whether anti-modern religion is surging, much less whether this is (or would be) a good or a bad thing. Instead, I am studying the consequences of the common belief that religious conservatism is becoming a stronger force in the contemporary world. This chapter places the resurgent-religion discourse in the context of the simultaneous growth of neoliberal ideologies among both Western intellectuals and comprador elites in the global South. It asks what happens if religion is seen as a remnant of an ignorant and authoritarian past, resisting global progress. It argues that framing the choice as '*Jihad versus McWorld*' (to use Benjamin Barber's felicitously stark phrasing) insulates neoliberalism from religious critique. I do not claim that this is intentional; it does, however, let the world's dominant politico-economic ideology off the hook by destroying the credibility of any religiously based disapproval. This has tangible and unfortunate consequences for the conduct of public life.

The Conservative Religion Hypothesis

It is a well-known sociological trope that the founders of our discipline thought religion would vanish in the modern age. From Marx's comment about 'the opium of the people' to Durkheim's identification of religion with the 'primitive' to Weber's frets about worldly disenchantment, mainstream sociology long thought that supernaturalist religions were on the wane. Secularization theory in its various forms presented a complex analysis of religious decline, which seemed to fit the European case rather well.[6] For example, Steve Bruce presented figures to show that religious membership in Britain dropped from 30 per cent to 14 per cent of the adult population between 1900 and 1990, while by the mid-1980s just 2 per cent of Scandinavians attended weekly services.[7] Grace Davie argued that lack of religious belonging does not mean a lack of religious belief, yet it does indicate a loss of

---

[4]   Richard Dawkins, *The God Delusion* (New York, 2006); Sam Harris, *The End of Faith: Religion, Terror, and the Future of Reason* (New York, 2004); Christopher Hitchens, *God is Not Great: How Religion Poisons Everything* (Toronto, 2007).

[5]   Michael Hout and Claude S. Fischer, 'Why More Americans Have No Religious Preference: Politics and Generations', *American Sociological Review*, 67/2 (2002): pp. 165–90.

[6]   For example, Bryan R. Wilson, *Contemporary Transformations of Religion* (London, 1976); David A. Martin, *A General Theory of Secularization* (Oxford, 1978); Karel Dobbelaere, *Secularization: A Multidimensional Concept* (London, 1982); Steve Bruce, *God is Dead: Secularization in the West* (Oxford, 2002).

[7]   Steve Bruce, *Choice and Religion: A Critique of Rational Choice* (Oxford, 1999), pp. 213–17.

institutional vitality.[8] American Mainline Protestantism has been in similar decline since the 1970s.[9] True, many people now favour non-institutional forms of religion, sometimes calling themselves 'spiritual, not religious'.[10] Yet, as Bruce argued:

> The road from religion embodied in the great European cathedrals to religion as a personal preference and individual choice is a road from more to less religion. From the Middle Ages to the end of the twentieth century, religion in Europe (and its offshoot settler societies) has declined in power, prestige, and popularity.[11]

Notoriously, though, religion has not disappeared. Indeed, certain kinds of religion have now taken centre stage, and not those with which Euro-American 'thought-leaders' are particularly comfortable. Resurgent Islam is in the daily news, but conservative Christianity is also growing and not just in the US. As Philip Jenkins wrote in his best-selling *The Next Christendom*, Christianity is attracting new followers around the world, especially in the developing countries, and they are of a particular type. In his words:

> The [Christian] denominations that are triumphing all across the global South are stalwartly traditional or even reactionary by the standards of the economically advanced nations. ... [They] have either been Roman Catholic, of a traditionalist and fideistic kind, or radical Protestant sects, evangelical or Pentecostal. ... In addition, rapid growth is occurring in non-traditional denominations that adapt Christian belief to local tradition [such as] African indigenous churches.[12]

Such churches are supernaturalist, mystical, and often puritanical. 'In this thought-world, prophecy is an everyday reality, while faith-healing, exorcism, and dream-visions are all basic components of religious sensibility.'[13] This is no secularized 'death of God' Christianity, nor a bloodless liberal deism. It is a vibrant, engaged, theologically conservative movement to save souls and to improve believers' daily lives. For Jenkins, this is Christianity's future: within a few decades, he says, 75–80 per cent of Christians will be traditionalists from the global South.[14]

---

[8]   Grace Davie, *Religion in Britain since 1945: Believing Without Belonging* (Oxford, 1994).

[9]   Wade Clark Roof and William McKinney, *American Mainline Religion: Its Changing Shape and Future* (New Brunswick, 1987).

[10]   Meredith B. McGuire, *Lived Religion: Faith and Practice in Everyday Life* (New York, 2008); Robert C. Fuller, *Spiritual, but not Religious: Understanding Unchurched America* (New York, 2001).

[11]   Bruce, *Choice*, pp. 7–8.

[12]   Jenkins, *The Next Christendom*, p. 7.

[13]   Ibid., p. 6.

[14]   Philip Jenkins, 'Believing in the Global South', *First Things*, December (2006), <www.firstthings.com/article/2007/01/believing-in-the-global-south-17>, accessed 23 July 2011.

The leading edge of Islam is similarly traditionalist and militant – though mostly not *jihadist*, as is commonly imagined in the West. Variously described as 'fundamentalist', 'Islamist', or 'Islamicist',[15] recent socio-intellectual movements in the *Dar al Islam* have emphasized strict adherence to the Qur'an and the Hadith, which they see as records of the pure Islam practiced by Mohammed and his companions. *Salafis*, to use a common (if broad) Arabic term for one branch of the movement, oppose religious innovations in either theology or practice. *Wahhabis* (followers of Muhammad ibn Abd-al-Wahhab) are even more puritanical. Neither is necessarily political, though both typically advocate the superiority of *Shari'ah* (Islamic law) for regulating human conduct. The vast majority of these Islamists reject violence, though the perpetrators of the various anti-Western massacres of the last two decades have identified themselves with Islamist views.[16] Like traditionalist Christianity, traditionalist Islam is growing. The Pew Forum on Religion and Public Life estimates that the world's Muslim population will increase by 35 per cent by 2030, to about 26 per cent of the world's people. Their survey of 25,000 African Christians and Muslims shows both groups to be (on average) equally religiously conservative, devoted to traditional beliefs and practices, and upholding traditional moral standards.[17]

Just reading the newspapers, one could similarly point to resurgent Hindu nationalism as embodied in the Indian *Bharatiya Janata Party* and the cultural movement for *Hindutva*, or to the role of militant Sinhalese Buddhism the Sri Lankan civil war.[18] Here, also, politicized religion is not the whole story. The root story is that militantly conservative, traditionalist religion seems to be a growing force in the contemporary world. Secularization theory did not expect this outcome.

Famously, advocates of the so-called 'market model' of religion did expect it.[19] In their view, religion's strength depends on the structure of the religious 'market', in which churches compete for adherents. Two market factors weakened European

---

[15]   Martin Kramer, 'Coming to Terms: Fundamentalists or Islamists?', *Middle Eastern Quarterly*, Spring (2003): pp. 65–77.

[16]   Mark Juergensmeyer, *Terror in the Mind of God: The Global Rise of Religious Violence*, 3rd edn (Berkeley, 2003); Olivier Roy, *Globalized Islam: The Search for a New Ummah* (New York, 2004).

[17]   Pew Forum on Religion and Public Life, 'The Future of the Global Muslim Population: Projections for 2010–2030', 27 January (2011), <pewforum.org/Global-Muslim-Population. aspx>, accessed 16 July 2011; Pew Forum on Religion and Public Life, 'Tolerance and Tension: Islam and Christianity in Sub-Saharan Africa', 15 April (2010), <pewforum.org/executive-summary-islam-and-christianity-in-sub-saharan-africa.aspx>, accessed 16 July 2011.

[18]   Stanley J. Tambiah, *Buddhism Betrayed? Religion, Politics, and Violence in Sri Lanka* (Chicago, 1992).

[19]   See Rodney Stark and William Sims Bainbridge, *A Theory of Religion* (New York, 1987); Laurence R. Iannaccone, 'Why Strict Churches Are Strong', *American Journal of Sociology*, 99/5 (1994): pp. 1180–211; Rodney Stark and Roger Finke, *Acts of Faith: Explaining the Human Side of Religion* (Berkeley, 2000).

religion as a whole: state support for a particular church – the legacy of the *cuius regio, eius religio* policy that ended the religious wars of the seventeenth century – and the recent abdication by those state churches of the supernaturalism that (claim the market advocates) constitutes religion's chief appeal. In this analysis, American religion is more vital than Europe's both because America lacks a state church and also because its most vital churches emphasize a salvation-oriented 'old-time religion'. Market theorists say that American Mainline Protestantism has lost ground precisely to the degree that it has gone 'up-market', appealing to intellectuals rather than to the masses while emphasizing social ethics over saving souls. Yes, there is room for liberal religion in the marketplace, but such religions are not big sellers. Most people seek religions that put them on the right side of life's cosmic powers – however those powers are conceived of in a particular cultural milieu.[20] So-called 'conservative' religions do this; market theorists expect them to grow wherever religions are free to meet people's needs.

There is, however, a third approach. At least since the mid-twentieth century, some sociologists have explained the rise of militantly traditionalist religions as a direct response to modernity itself. Rather than modernity leading to irreligion, as secularization theorists claimed, modernity's trials produce a conservative religious reaction. Some examples illustrate this line of thinking.

Examples

The claim that modernity provokes a conservative reaction goes back at least to the early twentieth century, when it was used as an explanation for American fundamentalism. As historian George Marsden described the matter:

> A fundamentalist is an evangelical who is angry about something ... [or, more precisely,] who is militant in opposition to liberal theology in the churches or to changes in cultural values or mores, such as those associated with 'secular humanism'. ... Fundamentalists are not just religious conservatives, they are conservatives who are willing to take a stand and to fight.[21]

Scholars from Stewart Cole to Richard Hofstadter argued that in America this anger is particularly strong across the rural/urban cultural divide.[22] The shift in power to cities and away from small towns – everywhere part of the modernization process – led to increased religious strife. At root, Hofstadter attributed the fundamentalists' rancor to status anxiety:

---

[20] Stark and Bainbridge, *A Theory of Religion*; Stark and Finke, *Acts of Faith*.

[21] George M. Marsden, *Understanding Fundamentalism and Evangelicalism* (Grand Rapids, 1991), p. 1.

[22] Stewart Cole, *History of Fundamentalism* (Hamden, 1931; reissued 1963); Richard Hofstadter, *Anti-Intellectualism in American Life* (New York, 1962).

> By the end of the [nineteenth] century, it was painfully clear to fundamentalists that they were losing much of their influence and respectability. ... [Their response] was shaped by a desire to strike back at everything modern.[23]

Historian William McLoughlin similarly wrote that 'fundamentalism represented the "Old Lights" who always appear in a time of religious change'.[24] The withdrawal of some fundamentalists from the northern denominations into their own sects only encouraged the sense that their time was passing. The dominant view was that 'conservative religion would die out as modernity advanced'.[25]

That did not happen, but the effort to explain conservative religion as an attempt to turn back the clock continued. To take one famous example: in response to the 1980s rise of the Christian Right in American politics, the membership growth of conservative churches and the decline of the Protestant Mainline, and perhaps above all the Iranian revolution, the American Academy of Arts and Sciences and the University of Chicago undertook 'The Fundamentalism Project' to study those trends. Recognizing that non-Protestant groups were labelled 'fundamentalist' only by analogy, Martin Marty, the Project's co-leader, described a 'family resemblance' among militantly conservative religions that, included the following elements among others:

- Fundamentalism is always reactive, reactionary.
- Fundamentalisms engage in ... selective retrieval, picking and choosing certain 'fundamentals', ... [which] always come from some earlier, ... normative stages in one's own sacred history.
- Fundamentals are used for setting boundaries. ... The result is always an exclusive or separatist movement.
- With absolutism comes authoritativeness and authoritarianism.
- They take shape as reactions to moral relativism or the relaxation of standards of conduct.[26]

In short, the 'fundamentalisms' the Project would study were reactive, backward looking and aggressively anti-modern, pushing back at what they saw as a world gone wrong.

Eight years, several conferences and numerous volumes later, Marty affirmed these descriptors.[27] He found a growth in the number and strength of 'primarily

---

[23]   Hofstadter, *Anti-Intellectualism in American Life*, p. 121.

[24]   William McLoughlin, 'Is There a Third Force in Christendom?', *Daedalus*, XCVI/ Winter (1967): pp. 43–68, cited in Marsden, *Fundamentalism and American Culture*, p. 200.

[25]   Marsden, *Understanding Fundamentalism and Evangelicalism*, p. 63.

[26]   Martin E. Marty, 'Fundamentalism as a Social Phenomenon', *Bulletin of the American Academy of Arts and Sciences*, 42/2 (1988): pp. 20–22.

[27]   Martin E. Marty, 'Too Bad We're So Relevant: The Fundamentalism Project Projected', *Bulletin of the American Academy of Arts and Sciences*, 49/6 (1996): pp. 22–38.

religious or religiously connected movements that were intense, impassioned, separatist, absolutist, authoritarian, and militant'.[28] From the resurgent Protestantisms of Northern Ireland and the Americas through the Jewish and Muslim sectarian movements in Israel and the West Bank, and from the Sikh and Hindu eruptions in India to the various forms of radical Islam in the Arab world and elsewhere, militantly conservative religion sought to retake the world from secular modernity. Though the Fundamentalism Project's many detailed case studies overwhelmed any simplified summation, its overall results left the impression that resurgent religions wished to turn back the clock to a world that was both simpler and morally more certain than the one in which we all live. In Marty's words:

> Anyone who is not a member of a fundamentalist movement ... will see that much of what goes on within such fundamentalisms is threatening – even devastating – to other kinds of fundamentalists, to more moderate coreligionists ..., to their neighbors and rivals, to governments, and to the idea of civil society.[29]

There seemed to be no hope that such movements could peacefully coexist in a religiously plural world.

If Marty tempered his eloquence with an historian's sense that reality is always more complex than our explanations of it, Benjamin Barber's best-selling *Jihad vs. McWorld* drew a starker distinction.[30] He described a world rent by two opposing forces: global commerce, which dissolves all traditional forms of life, and a renewed tribalism that seeks to re-establish a local purity purged of all modern complexities and accretions. The former, symbolized by transnational consumer capitalism (McDonald's, Hollywood, MTV, News Corp, and theme parks) erodes national boundaries. It undercuts democracy by removing people's control over their economic and cultural lives. The latter, actualized by ethnic warfare and religious sectarianism, lives 'for anti-Western antiuniversalist struggle'.[31] It undercuts democracy by refusing to recognize the legitimacy of any force but its own. Both forces attack the contemporary nation-state, one dissolving it from without and the other fracturing it from within. Barber was not sanguine about democracy's ability to withstand this dual onslaught:

> The collision between the forces of disintegral tribalism and reactionary fundamentalism I have called Jihad (Islam is not the issue) and the forces of integrative modernization and aggressive economic and cultural globalization I have called McWorld (for which America is not solely responsible) has been brutally exacerbated by the dialectical interdependence of these two seemingly

---

[28] Ibid., p. 24.

[29] Ibid., pp. 27–28.

[30] Barber, *Jihad vs McWorld*.

[31] Ibid., p. 207.

oppositional sets of forces. ... Democracy is caught between a clash of movements, each of which for its own reasons seems indifferent to freedom's fate.[32]

The image was clear: the 'parochialism, antimodernism, exclusiveness, and hostility to "others" ... that constitute ... Jihad' – which can be found in most world religions – arises from two forms of resentment.[33] On the one hand, McWorld trivializes and homogenizes all human values; on the other, it does nothing for 'those mired in poverty and despair as a consequence of unregulated global markets and of a capitalism run wild because it has been uprooted from the humanizing constraints of the democratic nation-state'.[34] '*Jihad*' is a religio-tribal reaction to these events. It is a moral and political crusade to revitalize a threatened way of life. It is, to use Anthony Wallace's label, a 'revitalization movement' – a concept I shall examine in a moment.[35] First, however, let me cite one more scholarly example, this one a bit more complex.

In 2000, Mark Juergensmeyer published a prescient book about religious violence, entitled *Terror in the Mind of God*.[36] In it, he examined recent cases of violence in five religious traditions, from Christian bombers of abortion clinics in the US to Jewish and Muslim suicide attacks in Israel and the West Bank, to the Aum Shinrikyo attack in Tokyo's subways. He also interviewed some of the perpetrators: the Reverend Michael Bray, who fire-bombed seven American clinics; Mahmud Abouhalima, the 'mastermind' of the 1993 World Trade Center bombing; the Sikh militant Simranjit Singh Mann; and others. He found, unsurprisingly, that these men saw themselves at the centre of a cosmic war. They saw themselves involved in a spiritual battle against the forces of darkness, one fraught with moral significance. Above all, their struggle was embedded in the social tensions of the present era. Radical religious ideas, in Juergensmeyer's view,

> have given a profound and ideological clarity to what in many cases have been real experiences of economic destitution, social oppression, political corruption, and a desperate need for the hope of rising above the limitations of modern life. The image of cosmic struggle has given these bitter experiences meaning, and the involvement in a grand conflict has been for some participants exhilarating. ... [It helps assuage] the sense of personal humiliation experienced by men who long to restore an integrity they perceive as lost in the wake of virtually global social and political shifts.[37]

---

[32] Ibid., p. xii.

[33] Ibid., p. 205.

[34] Ibid., p. xii.

[35] Anthony F.C. Wallace, 'Revitalization Movements: Some Theoretical Considerations for Their Comparative Study', *American Anthropologist*, 58/2 (1956): pp. 264–81.

[36] Juergensmeyer, *Terror in the Mind of God*.

[37] Ibid., p. 248.

Here, militant religion provides a path forward to those seeking to escape social chaos and moral decay by turning back the clock to a purer era. It is not the only path available, but it is by no means rare in the contemporary age.

Revitalization Movements

Juergensmeyer, Barber, and the Fundamentalism Project describe militantly traditionalist religion as a means of defending a threatened moral universe. In their narrative, religious activists seek to renew that universe, to give it strength and clout against a world they think has gone bad. Activists oppose the evils of modern life, so they act to restore what they regard as the purity and goodness of former times – and they do so aggressively. Religion for them needs to reorder the world.

The anthropologist A.F.C. Wallace described several classes of such revitalization movements, which he defined as 'deliberate, organized, conscious effort[s] by members of a society to construct a more satisfying culture'.[38] In his view, these movements occur at times of individual and social stress. People find themselves unable to continue their accustomed lives, perhaps as the result of war or economic dislocation, perhaps from encounters with new peoples and new ways of being, perhaps because technological changes have thrown their lives into confusion. In any case, their ways of making sense of the universe no longer work. In response, individuals may react regressively, seeking solace in 'alcoholism, passivity and indolence, ... disregard of kinship and sexual mores, irresponsibility ..., states of depression and self-reproach'.[39] These are, said Wallace, symptoms of a cultural disorder: the inability of established conceptual 'mazeways'[40] to produce satisfying answers for how to live in the world in which people now find themselves.

If this behavioural and conceptual dislocation becomes widespread, Wallace wrote, entire groups can find their accustomed mazeways inadequate. Such groups have several different options. Some may choose wholesale change, much as the adherents of the 'Vailala Madness' (c.1919–c.1930), the John Frum Movement (c.1930–c.1960), and other Melanesian 'cargo cults' threw out ancient practices and imitated Western ways.[41] More often, groups reorganize old ways of thinking, folding in new elements and a new sense of purpose while retaining a felt connection with the past. The Handsome Lake religion of the Seneca (1719–1815) and the Peyote Religion among the Navajo are examples from Native American history.[42] Sometimes, as was the case with the Ghost Dance religion of the American

---

[38]   Wallace, 'Revitalization Movements', p. 265.

[39]   Ibid., p. 269.

[40]   Ibid., p. 266.

[41]   Peter Worsley, *The Trumpet Shall Sound: A Study of 'Cargo' Cults in Melanesia* (London, 1957).

[42]   Anthony F.C. Wallace, *The Death and Rebirth of the Seneca* (New York, 1972); David F. Aberle, *The Peyote Religion Among the Navajo* (New York, 1966).

Great Plains,[43] groups re-embrace tradition, hiding the newness of their religious teachings beneath an ideology of returning to the old. The Ghost Dance taught adherents to turn their backs on White trade goods, reject cultural innovations, and refocus their lives on the traditional world. That, and dancing, would cause the Whites to leave. This was about as realistic as the accompanying belief that wearing 'ghost dance shirts' would supernaturally stop army bullets, but it did not keep Plains Indians from trying. The result was death and martyrdom – not unlike that of today's suicide bombers, who seek a similar unearthly reward.

Applied to our current topic, the various fundamentalist groups examined by Marsden, and, by Marty, Appleby, and their associates, along with Barber's tribally oriented '*Jihad*' and Juergensmeyer's religious terrorists as all think they are reviving a traditional, supernaturally valued way of life. In actual fact they are changing tradition, emphasizing certain parts and discarding others, then using the result to give themselves a meaningful way of engaging the world. American fundamentalist groups, for example, have become more political than had previously been the case, have aggressively sought to transform everything from public school systems to national laws, and have notoriously embraced cutting-edge technology to spread their message. Contemporary *Salafis* and *Wahhabis* have redefined ten centuries of tolerant Islam as 'un-Islamic', have removed the traditional subtlety from Islamic law, and have created a global *jihad* to defend the borders of *Dar al Islam*.[44] Hindu nationalists have tried to impose a belligerently purified Hinduism on the messy reality of traditional Indian religious life. In these cases, as in others, the combination of new and old gives adherents a revitalized cosmic vision.

At least, so goes the narrative. Seeing militantly traditionalist religions as revitalization movements highlights some key elements of those groups' worldviews and behaviours. It further explains why such religions have arisen in the contemporary world. Put simply, it attributes resurgent traditionalism to the massive social dislocations of the last many decades. Like secularization theory, it says that such changes have religious consequences, but unlike secularization theory it says that modernity can produce more religion as well as less. Modern stresses lead some people move from religious to secular mazeways; it leads others to reinvigorate their religious views, militantly. Resurgent religious conservatism is thus a way of coping with a changed world.

As noted above, my point, here, is not to evaluate this way of understanding contemporary religious trends. I do, however, wish to highlight some of the consequences of affirming this view. To do so, I must first review the socio-intellectual context that currently dominates world political and economic thinking.

---

[43]   James Mooney, *The Ghost Dance Religion and the Sioux Outbreak of 1890* (Washington, 1896).

[44]   Roy, *Globalized Islam*.

Neoliberalism in the World System

As other contributors to this volume have noted, neoliberalism has been the leading economic discourse of the last 30 years. Neoliberal economists champion free markets, free trade, welfare reform, economic deregulation, and privatization.[45] These policies, advocates say, spur economic growth. They are also supposed to allow countries to prosper by producing those goods and services for which they have some comparative advantage. Low-wage, low-education countries are supposed to contribute cheap manual labour; high-wage, high-education countries get to contribute scientific and technological innovation.

While well intentioned, these policies have done tremendous damage to poor people around the world. To mention a few examples: Swan and Vaitla showed how the International Monetary Fund's neoliberal-inspired 'structural adjustment' policies created severe hunger in Niger where little had previously existed;[46] Greenberg showed how these policies undercut agriculture in the Dominican Republic;[47] my own fieldwork in Nicaragua revealed the connection between the loss of state subsidies and the growth in squatter settlements in the Managua city dump. By ignoring social structures and thinking only about markets, neoliberalism amounts to what former World Bank economist Joseph Stiglitz called 'market fundamentalism'.[48] This is the belief – against evidence – that all economic problems are the result of government regulation and that deregulation and free trade will always and everywhere generate wealth. Many observers thought that the market failures of 2008–10 would have disproved this view,[49] but the political rhetoric surrounding the 2011 and 2012 US and European debt crises showed that it is still alive and well. More than that: neoliberal economic philosophy has set the terms of the current economic debate without leading to a solution.

In neoliberal theory, free markets are supposed to maximize the growth of the total economic system, though not necessarily of every part of it.[50] The theory assumes, however, that all players have equal access to the resources, knowledge, and other tools necessary to play the economic game. Unfortunately, they do not. Stiglitz won his 2001 Nobel Prize in part for tracking the consequences of unequal information access; he concluded that 'unfettered markets often not only do not

---

[45]   See Manfred A. Steger and Ravi K. Roy, *Neoliberalism: A Very Short Introduction* (New York, 2010).

[46]   Samuel Hauenstein Swan and Bapu Vaitla, *Hunger Watch Report 2007–2008: The Justice of Eating* (London, 2007), Chapter 2.

[47]   James B. Greenberg, 'A Political Ecology of Structural-Adjustment Policies: The Case of the Dominican Republic', *Culture and Agriculture*, 19/3 (1997): pp. 85–93.

[48]   Joseph E. Stiglitz, *Globalization and Its Discontents* (New York, 2003).

[49]   For example Wonhyuk Lim, 'Demise of the Anglo-American Model of Capitalism', *Global Asia*, (Winter 2008): pp. 58–60.

[50]   Milton Friedman, *Capitalism and Freedom* (Chicago, 1962).

lead to social justice, but do not even produce efficient outcomes'.[51] Government regulation is thus needed to rescue markets from themselves.

Neoliberalism also fails to consider the impact that power differences have on economic life. Rather than being a 'flat' economic world,[52] our international economy is dominated by a developed 'core' of advanced capitalist nations, surrounded by a less developed 'semi-periphery' and 'periphery'.[53] Most trade flows between the core while peripheral regions possess fewer resources, have less complex trade relations and thus have less opportunity to better themselves. The core dominates economically, militarily and politically. To cite just one example, core countries can craft exceptions to their own calls for free trade, so they can continue subsidizing their own farmers while insisting that peripheral and semi-peripheral countries stop doing so.[54] Thus subsidized American rice exports drove Haitian rice farmers from their own domestic market, exacerbating poverty, hunger and social tensions in that already poor country.[55]

Moreover, each nation has internal inequalities, which recent research has shown reduce social welfare in all types of political system.[56] Economic inequality has increased over the last 30 years in most of the countries listed in the OECD's 2011 annual report – precisely the years in which neoliberalism dominated public policy.[57] The same pattern is present between countries: net capital flows from rich countries to poor countries dropped dramatically as international investment in poorer countries dried up.[58] Simultaneously, the richest 1 per cent of the world's population has garnered an increasing share of both national and international wealth.[59]

Neoliberalism predicts none of this, yet this is perhaps the biggest economic story of the last few decades. Why, then, has the neoliberal approach not been

---

[51]   Beppe Grillo, 'The Pact with the Devil by Joseph E. Stiglitz', January (2007), <www.beppegrillo.it/eng/2007/01/stiglitz.html>, accessed 23 July 2011.

[52]   Thomas L. Friedman, *The World Is Flat: A Brief History of the Twenty-First Century*, expanded and updated edn (New York, 2006).

[53]   Immanuel Wallerstein, *World-Systems Analysis: An Introduction* (Durham, 2004).

[54]   Indian Ministry of Agriculture. 'Agricultural Subsidies (PSE) in Selected OECD Countries and India', 2003, <agricoop.nic.in/statistics/stock2.htm>, accessed 18 August 2011.

[55]   Josiane Georges, 'Trade and the Disappearance of Haitian Rice', TED Case Studies Number 725, June (2004), <www1.american.edu/TED/haitirice.htm>, accessed 9 February 2012.

[56]   Timothy Powell-Jackson et al., 'Democracy and Growth in Divided Societies: A Health-Inequality Trap?', *Social Science and Medicine*, 73/1 (2011): pp. 33–41.

[57]   OECD, 'Society at a Glance 2011 – OECD Social Indicators', *OECD*, <www.oecd.org/els/social/indicators/SAG>, accessed 23 July 2011.

[58]   Maurice Obstfeld and Alan M. Taylor, 'Globalization and Capital Markets', *NBER Working Papers Number 8846*, March (2002).

[59]   Boston Consulting Group, 'Shaping a New Tomorrow: How to Capitalize on the Momentum of Change', (31 May 2011), <www.bcg.com/media/PressReleaseDetails.aspx?id=tcm:12-77753>, accessed 23 July 2011.

swept from the intellectual stage? Perhaps the answer lies in whom it serves. Neoliberalism has favoured the world's richer countries and has favoured the richest segments of those countries far more than others. If we had space and data, we could ask whether these groups have enough control over politics and intellectual life to keep neoliberalism on the intellectual agenda, despite its flaws.[60] That is not, however, the point of this chapter. It is time to return to the discourse of resurgent religious conservatism, to see what role it plays on this stage.

Religion as Ethical Critique

Religions are not just organizations specializing in the transcendent;[61] they are also sources of ethical critique. They tell individuals what is right and wrong; they also tell societies, governments, corporations and religious organizations – their own and others – how they should act in the world. Their moral authority stems from their role as arbiters of the divine, of life's purposes or of whatever a given religion sees as its core concern.

Examples are not hard to find. The flight against human slavery was championed by religious people, from the sixteenth century's Dominican Bartolomé de las Casas through the eighteenth and nineteenth century Quaker anti-slavery activists to the Protestant Abolitionists of the American pre-Civil War years. Lest we imagine this to be a purely Christian phenomenon, Yu Hyongwon (1622–73) criticized Korean slavery on the basis of Confucian ethical teachings. Similarly, most of the major American activists for women's suffrage were religious;[62] the African American Civil Rights movement was begun and largely run by clergy, whose position as church leaders gave their movement great moral power. Catholic social encyclicals, from Leo XIII's 1891 *Rerum Novarum* (on the conditions of the working class) through Benedict XVI's 2009 *Caritas in Veritate* (on the problems of global development), have outlined a distinctive social agenda on matters of poverty and wealth, economics, society and the state. Though grounded in both the Bible and in Christian tradition, those teachings are not simply rooted in the past. Their ethical insights evolve alongside the world to which they are applied – without, however, losing their capacity to criticize injustice.

---

[60]   See G. William Domhoff, *Who Rules America? Challenges to Corporate and Class Dominance*, 6th edn (New York, 2009).

[61]   Stark and Bainbridge, *A Theory of Religion*; Richard K. Fenn, *Key Thinkers in the Sociology of Religion* (New York, 2009).

[62]   Lucretia Mott, Susan B. Anthony, Martha Wright, Mary Ann McClintock and Jane Hunt were all Quakers; Lucy Stone was a Congregationalist-turned-Unitarian; only Elizabeth Cady Stanton opposed religion and that because of its history of suppressing women. See Margaret Hope Bacon, *Mothers of Feminism: The Story of Quaker Women in America* (San Francisco, 1986).

None of this is news. Religion's ability to have its critiques taken seriously has been affected, however, by the growth of the discourse that I analysed at the beginning of this chapter: the view that religion is increasingly conservative in the modern world, that religion seeks to turn back the clock to an earlier and more authoritarian age and that it seeks to impose its moral and theological agenda on others.

To see how, let us start with a trivial example, Austin Cline's online review of Juergensmeyer's book on religious terrorists.[63] Posted at Cline's 'Agnosticism/ Atheism' website, the review is generally positive until it reaches Juergensmeyer's conclusion that the best antidote to religious terrorism is more appreciation of religion's role in 'giv[ing] spirit to public life and provid[ing] a beacon for moral order'.[64] Cline dismisses this conclusion as misguided. 'Better' religion will not drive out 'worse' religion, he says, because all religions are 'false at the very least and likely harmful or even dangerous'. Other pages at the site make the same argument: all portray religion as belief-centred, supernaturalist and authoritarian. This site's image of religion is similar to what Hout and Fischer report motivates the increasing number of American 'Religious Nones': resurgent conservative religion is seen as advocating a socially destructive, authoritarian agenda, and all religion is tarred with this brush.[65]

This discourse hinders religions' ability to generate ethical critique in two ways. First, it identifies religion with the past, usually typified as 'unenlightened'; religion is thus presented as lacking the scientific knowledge needed to evaluate the contemporary world. For example, American fundamentalism's long fight against biological evolution, its claims for the scientific inerrancy of the Bible and the like have led many observers to distrust all religions' intellectual grasp of the world. Even religious scientists are reluctant to make public their own religious commitments, for fear that their colleagues will think less of their work.[66]

Second, the discourse presents religion as at best authoritarian, typically intolerant, and at worst violent, none of which helps it solve current problems. Europe's conflict between religion and reason was always overdrawn, but this opposition remains a cultural trope, feeding distrust of religious authorities who demand obedience instead of making reasoned arguments. To many, the Inquisition remains a vivid image of what happens when religion controls state power. Post-revolution purges in clerical Iran, reports of Saudi religious police assaulting women, and the like reinforce this history. And Juergensmeyer's interviews bring

---

[63]   Cline, Austin, 'Review', *Agnosticism/Atheism Website*, (not dated), <atheism. about.com/library/books/full/aafprTerrorMindGod.htm>, accessed 18 August, 2011.

[64]   Juergensmeyer, *Terror in the Mind of God*, p. 248.

[65]   Hout and Fischer, 'No Preference'; Gerardo Marti, *Hollywood Faith: Holiness, Prosperity, and Ambition in a Los Angeles Church* (New Brunswick, 2009).

[66]   Elaine Howard Ecklund, *Science Vs. Religion: What Scientists Really Think* (New York, 2010).

us face to face with men (and some women) who will kill on behalf of their gods. Is it even safe to consider religious critique, if this is what religion entails?

It is relatively easy to see how these factors undercut religions' ethical voice. If religion is based in the past, and if its comments about science are ideological and scientifically uninformed, why should anyone suppose that its ethical pronouncements are any different? They become all too easy to dismiss – particularly for socio-political elites wishing to deal with their challenge. *Argumentum ad hominem* becomes *argumentum ad religiones*. All religions are tarred.

The Result

The net result of all this is to undercut religious criticisms of contemporary political and economic practices. It is not just conservative religious criticism that suffers; all religious criticism finds itself isolated and dismissed. In the United States (to take the country I know best), the 1980s were the last decade that paid significant attention to mainstream religious critiques of governmental policy. The Nuclear Freeze Movement had church origins and support.[67] The Sanctuary Movement was a church-based network opposed to US wars in Central America.[68] The Catholic Bishops' pastoral letters on peace and on economic justice engendered reasoned and thoughtful debate from opponents as well as supporters.[69] Since then, the growth of the Religious Right, the Catholic Church's turn toward anti-abortion politics and the clergy sex scandals – both Catholic and televangelist – have been the main religious news stories. The Freeze failed, the Central American wars ended, and the Bishops' letters have been forgotten. There has been much religious commentary on public affairs, but it has gotten no significant traction. Neoliberalism reigns.

This is not to say that neoliberalism is free from critique. Stiglitz (2003) has criticized neoliberal policies, as have other prominent economists.[70] Their analysis has been quite scathing, but it has been based on utility, not ethics. They point out that neoliberalism does not produce wealth (except for the few), it does not

---

[67] David S. Meyer, *A Winter of Discontent: The Nuclear Freeze and American Politics* (Westport, 1990).

[68] Ann Crittenden, *Sanctuary: A Story of American Conscience and the Law in Collision* (New York, 1988).

[69] National Conference of Catholic Bishops, 'The Challenge of Peace: God's Promise and Our Response', (1983), <www.usccb.org/sdwp/international/TheChallengeofPeace. pdf>, accessed 26 July 2011; National Conference of Catholic Bishops, 'Economic Justice for All: Pastoral Letter on Catholic Social Teaching and the U.S. Economy,' (1986), <www. usccb.org/jphd/economiclife/pdf/economic_justice_for_all.pdf>, accessed 26 July 2011.

[70] Stiglitz, *Globalization and Its Discontents*; Paul Krugman, *The Return of Depression Economics and the Crisis of 2008* (New York, 2008); Ha-Joon Chang, *Bad Samaritans: The Myth of Free Trade and the Secret History of Capitalism* (New York, 2007).

create stable economies, nor does it foster sustainable economic growth. Instead, it creates poverty, destabilizes poor countries, and produces misery among the less fortunate. They basically say that neoliberalism does not work. A religious critique – even a conservative one such as Nasr's[71] – would challenge the neoliberal notion of 'success' itself, by questioning whether untrammelled economic growth improves the human condition.

A few economists do question the established measures. Amartya Sen, among others, has called for better, more moral measures of economic success than mere growth.[72] His Nobel Prize came, in part, because he combined ethical reflection with his economic reasoning. His approach is rare, however, and it has not placed ethics at the centre of his profession.

The point is: neoliberalism's continued intellectual hegemony stems not from its success at describing how economies work in the real world, but – at least in part – from the weakness of its natural opponents. Religious social criticism used to be taken seriously. The fact that it is not today says something about contemporary religion's loss of credibility. That loss, in turn, results in part from the popular image of religions as being rooted in the past, as being authoritarian, intolerant, and even violent. *Prima facie*, the discourse that I have described here, in which religion is seen as becoming increasingly conservative, traditionalist, and right-wing, has contributed to this trend.

---

[71]   Seyyed Hossein Nasr, *Islam in the Modern World: Challenged by the West, Threatened by Fundamentalism, Keeping Faith with Tradition* (New York, 2011).

[72]   Amartya Sen, *Inequality Reexamined* (Cambridge, 1992); Amartya Sen, *Development as Freedom* (Oxford, 1999).

Chapter 3

The Decline of the Parishes and the Rise of City Churches: The German Evangelical Church in the Age of Neoliberalism

Jens Schlamelcher

This chapter examines the ways in which the Evangelical Church of Germany, one of the country's oldest institutions, is affected by social and cultural changes associated with the rise of consumerism and neoliberal governance. On the one hand, the Church as a moral agent expresses concerns about global marketization,[1] claiming, with the authority of theological arguments, that social solidarity and mutual care are being undermined by the impersonal and asocial nature of the market, which promotes the survival of the fittest. Furthermore, the Church defines itself as something like an island of community in this sea of the neoliberal free market. In this way the Church sees itself as having something to 'offer' in view of this situation – namely the recognition of individuals as people and not merely as customers.

However, the Evangelical Church is also an institution with certain organizational aspects. As such, it is one of the biggest employers in Germany,[2] providing services in health, education and religion. As an organization, the Church is dependent on funding and thus is greatly affected by neoliberal reforms. This holds true for its subsidiary organizations in the welfare and education sectors. Current empirical investigations show that within schools, hospitals and other facilities run by the Church, the process of internal and external marketization has been well under way since the middle of the 1990s.[3] Total quality management, management by objectives and temporary contracts of employment as the main instruments of internal marketization have been widely deployed. Furthermore, the shift of their finance structure from preservation of the *status quo* (*'Bestandssicherung'*) to flat

---

[1] Evangelische Kirche in Deutschland, *'Evangelische Kirche gegen Ökonomisierung des Sozialen'* (1998), www.ekd.de/presse/1831.html, accessed 28 December 2011.

[2] About 550,000 individuals are employed in Church institutions; 4,220,000 of them are members of the *Diakonische Werk*, the umbrella organization of the welfare institution of the Evangelical Church in Germany.

[3] Heinrich Bedford-Strohm (ed.), *Von der "Barmherzigkeit" zum "Sozial-Markt": Zur Ökonomisierung der sozialdiakonischen Dienste. Jahrbuch Sozialer Protestantismus* (2 vols, Gütersloh, 2008), vol. 2.

rate per case (*'Fallpauschale'*)[4] has also resulted in strong competition for clients in their segments, making 'customer orientation' a key imperative.

This chapter aims to address processes of change in those areas where the Church performs if not exclusively, at least primarily, religious functions. These are located in the parishes, as well as in newly established extra-parochial sites, such as the so-called 'city churches'. While other church organizations – mainly schools, hospitals or homes for the elderly – are deeply integrated into the state welfare system (they receive their funding either directly from the state or from national insurance funds), the parishes are characterized by a greater autonomy from the state, and hence in principle are less directly affected by the neoliberal-inspired reforms which have affected the welfare system. Their funding is based on the Church tax (*Kirchensteuer*); every member of the Church pays an amount that is equivalent to nine per cent of his income tax to the Church. This church tax system, established shortly after the Second World War, has ensured the comparable wealth of the Evangelical (as well as Catholic) Church in Germany, compared to the churches in other countries. However, this financial structure is also the reason for the present crisis in the Evangelical Church. While its income had been rising steadily until 1992, it is now in a state of steady decline. This is due to a number of reasons. The main ones are changes in the demographics of the population – the German population is growing older and retired persons do not pay church taxes – and the tendency on the part of taxpayers to quit Church membership.[5]

Thus a reduction of income – which is to say, the same factor that has caused the welfare state to downsize on the road to neoliberalism – now affects the Church. In order to simply ensure its continued existence as an organization, the Church is thus forced to proceed in two ways: first, it has to downsize and economize. Second, it has to attract new, or former, members in order to 'grow against the trend'.[6]

---

[4]   This means that where formerly the financier, mainly the state, would cover the financial needs of an institution such as a hospital or a school (preservation of *status quo*), it now 'pays' the institution for any single 'case' – the hospital will now get a certain amount of money for any case treated, the school a certain amount of money for any pupil *per annum*.

[5]   Every year, between 0.5 and 1 per cent of members quit the Church. Most often than not, the decision to quit is based on financial reasons. Whenever the state increases taxes, it is more likely for Church members to compensate for their loss of income by saving on the church tax and quitting. Since most of the official members of the Evangelical Church do not believe in the foundations of Protestant theology and evaluate their membership status more on financial than on religious reasoning, the German Evangelical Church is a good example of 'belonging without believing', in contrast with the observation of Grace Davie from the institution's point of view. Grace Davie, 'Believing Without Belonging: Is this the Future of Religion in Britain?', *Social Compass*, 37/4 (1990): pp. 455–69.

[6]   See Evangelische Kirche in Deutschland, *Kirche der Freiheit: Perspektiven für die Evangelische Kirche im 21. Jahrhundert*, (2006), <www.ekd.de/download/kirche-der-freiheit.pdf>, accessed 28 December 2011.

These organizational (as opposed to theological) imperatives have sparked an explosion of neoliberal discourses within the Church.[7] Often drawing on theological reasoning, it is argued that the Church, especially in the period of the flourishing Early Church, has always functioned like an enterprise. As such, it is advisable and appropriate to adopt instruments such as marketing strategies and processes of enhancing customer orientation. Thus 'growing against the trend' shall be achieved by turning the Church into a species of trading company. These discourses, often in the form of official documents from churches at the national level, however, encounter a twofold problem. On the one hand, they are faced with a barrage of criticism. Based mainly on opposing theological arguments as well as on sociological ones,[8] calls in favour of a neoliberal restructuring are more often than not refuted. This may also be a problem for the neoliberal project of restructuring the state. But the difference for the Church is its second problem, namely, the lack of legislative power of the Church boards. The Evangelical Church in Germany is, unlike the Catholic Church, based on a democratic structure, which ensures that the parishes and church districts have a high degree of autonomy. Thus, whatever happens in the Church is less a consequence of decrees from 'above', but of decisions made from 'below'.

This chapter addresses these bottom-up processes. First, it looks into social transformations within the parishes which have occurred due to the loss of financial income. How do these parishes manage to downsize and economize; and what are the social consequences of this? Second, it asks what steps the Evangelical Church is taking to attract new members. For reasons which will become clear, extra-parochial sites such as the city churches have become an important area of scrutiny in this study.

This analysis of the transformations of the German Evangelical Church at the level of the parishes and its establishment of extra-parochial sites is based on a qualitative method. Fieldwork was conducted in a number of parishes and at one of the city churches and included several interviews which were interpreted on the basis of the methods of objective hermeneutics. As most of the changes affect the social *Gestalt* of the Church, this chapter will first outline a conceptual understanding of social forms in general. It will then proceed with a reference to the German Evangelical Church parish system and its programme as it was established from the late nineteenth century onwards, before presenting the empirical findings of current changes. As will be shown, the German Evangelical Church experiences the age of neoliberalism not only as a period of accelerated decline, but also as one of social and religious transformation.

---

[7]   Jens Schlamelcher, 'Unternehmen Kirche? Neoliberale Diskurse in den deutschen Großkirchen', in Walter O. Ötsch and Claus Thomasberger (eds), *Der neoliberale Markt-Diskurs: Ursprünge, Geschichte, Wirkungen* (Marburg, 2009), pp. 213–56.

[8]   Many of the critiques are inspired by sociological theorists such as Niklas Luhmann, or even Michel Foucault.

Theoretical Background: Communities, Organizations and Markets as Social Forms

The discussion of the analysis presented below is based on an analytical distinction between what are called in German sociology *Sozialform* ('social forms').[9] Based on systems theory,[10] society in general may be described as having three levels. At the macro level, the so-called functional systems of society, such as the economy, law, education, politics, the arts and religion, facilitate social operations in a very general sense. The micro level consists of such interactions as acts of communication (or '*parole*' as it is referred to in structuralism). Various social forms exist between these levels of functional systems and interactions. They give structure to these interactions; thus it makes a difference if interactions are embedded in a market-like customer-client relationship, or in an organization based on hierarchy and impersonal social relations, or within communities in which individuals are personally included. Let me briefly outline some general traits of these three social forms, which are relevant to my argument:

* The community is the oldest social form; it is based on the integration of individuals as embodied persons. Every aspect of the individual may be of relevance for the community. The basic principle of exchange is general reciprocity, or the 'gift economy', as outlined by Marcel Mauss. A third aspect of relevance here is that virtually every item of communication is legitimate. Communities may endure for a very long period of time. Because they are based upon personal ties, communities are only able to include a limited number of individuals. They tend to construct a strict boundary between individuals who are 'in' and those who are 'out' of the community. Often, communities demand high degrees of commitment from individuals and they tend to place constraints on individual decision-making.
* In contrast with that of the community, market interaction is based on a pure rationality of use. Individuals establish short-term social relations in order to exchange desired goods. Within markets, the personality of individuals has no relevance. The only point of interest in the other is that they possess desired goods and are willing to exchange.

---

[9]   The theorizing of social forms has a long tradition in German sociology, with significant contributions by Ferdinant Tönnies and Georg Simmel. In recent German sociology, the conceptual, ideal-typical distinction of social forms into communities, organizations and markets is now widely accepted. See Helmut Wiesenthal, 'Markt, Organisation und Gemeinschaft als "zweitbeste" Verfahren sozialer Koordination', in Wieland Jäger and Uwe Schimank (eds), *Organisationsgesellschaft – Facetten und Perspektiven* (Wiesbaden, 2005), pp. 223–64.

[10]   See Niklas Luhmann, 'Interaktion, Organisation, Gesellschaft: Anwendungen der Systemtheorie', in Niklas Luhmann, *Soziologische Aufklärung, Vl. 2: Aufsätze zur Theorie der Gesellschaft* (Opladen 1975), pp. 9–20.

- Like markets,[11] organizations are a very recent development in the history of social forms. In the late eighteenth century, they replaced the premodern social form of personal hierarchies (between liege lord and vassal, master craftsman and journeyman and so on). Organizations are social units which integrate individuals – as do markets – in an impersonal way. They do this by abstracting and extracting one aspect of the individual – his manpower – which presupposes an analytical distinction between both, a phenomenon which is very peculiar to modernity. Furthermore, organizations are constructed upon the principle of instrumental reason. They virtually buy labour power in order to pursue certain rational goals (such as the maximization of profit). This results in the heavy dependency of organizations on financial resources. It is money that keeps the operations of the organizations, based on the purchase of labour power, going. As has been argued above, the main shifts in the 'age of neoliberalism' are in relation to organizations.

The Social Form of the Church

Using this analytical distinction, the social form of the Church is best understood as being driven by the tension that arises between being organizational and communal.[12] In modern times and under the heavy impact of secularization as well as the structural individualization of religion and the weakening influence of the Church, this tension between communal and hierarchical organization has undergone an important twist. The Church *organizations*, now modernized bureaucracies, have declared *community* to be the goal of their organizational programme. The *Gemeindereformbewegung* (parish reform movement), originating in the late 1890s, claimed that the parishes,[13] which were situated at the intersection of the Church and the people and which were responsible for the transmission of religious orthodoxy, should be transformed into 'animated communities'. Emil Schulze, who gave rise to this movement, articulated it thus: '[i]t is our goal to transform the parishes into associations, whose members will know and love each other and who will prove their love by reciprocal pastoral care'.[14] A lot of effort was undertaken

---

[11]   Cf. the introduction to this volume. See also Karl Polanyi, *The Great Transformation: The Political and Economic Origins of Our Times* (Boston, 1944).

[12]   For a more detailed analytical description see Jens Schlamelcher, 'Kirchliche Vergemeinschaftungsformen im Prozess der Vergesellschaftung', *Evangelische Theologie*, 70/6 (2010): pp. 439–50.

[13]   On the history and role of the parishes and the evolution of its mission in France-Germany with a comparative approach, see Olivier Bobineau, *Dieu change en paroisse. Une comparaison franco-allemande* (Rennes, 2005).

[14]   Emil Schulze, *Die Reform der evangelischen Landeskirchen nach den Grundsätzen des neueren Protestantismus* (Berlin, 1906), p. 121, my translation.

to put this community programme into practice. First, the average size of the parishes was reduced by means of the establishment of new parish foundations; this was in order to ensure that the priest and every one else in the parish would know each member personally. Second, parish councils were established based on a democratic procedure which gave every member of the parish the opportunity to take part in decision-making. Third, community halls were built in which the various functional assemblies of the church members could take place.

However, the success of this organizational programme was partial, at best. Clusters of local communities have indeed been formed, but only a few people from each locality have become involved in these communities. Instead of reaching all official members, the overall effect was to widen the gap between those who were part of the communalized nucleus and those who where not: the difference between core members and distanced members was exacerbated. The programme inevitably resulted in a logical paradox: communities, as outlined above, have tended to become closed social systems which include only a limited number of members; furthermore, it constructs a boundary between those who are in and those who are out. Thus, the success of the parish reform movement was also the reason for its failure, when measured against its claim to re-establish a people's church. After all, the parish reform movement did not halt the growing distance between the majority of individuals and the Church.

Especially since the late 1960s, this process of distanciation has seemed to accelerate, as statistical data revealing increasing rates of members leaving the Church, declining rates of attendance at sermons and the tendential shrinkage of the core communities has shown. This process has remained the trend up until now: every year sees less attendance at sermons, every year more individuals are leaving the Church than entering. However, this does not hold true for the financial income of the Church. Due to rising salaries and the linking of Church funding to income tax, the financial revenues of the Church were flourishing until the early 1990s. This enabled the Church to compensate for its institutional decline with an organizational upgrade. After the process of founding new parishes came to a halt in the late 1960s, the Church continued to invest in its community programmes by employing more people, mainly priests (most parishes would allow more than one priest), secretaries, church musicians and social workers. While the nucleus communities became ever smaller, the numbers of salaried personnel in the parishes increased.

This unequal development of institutional decline, allied with organizational upgrading lasted until the early 1990s. From then on the financial income of the Church has tended slowly to dry up. In the last 15 years, many parishes have encountered a loss of financial power by a factor of more than 30 per cent. Statistical data show that this combination of institutional and organizational decline will continue and even accelerate in the coming decades. The very 'future of the Church' – a tellingly secular self-conception – is under threat, by reason of a continuing loss of members, but most of all, by reason of a loss of income. From now on, the Church will have to economize, firstly by deploying its income more efficiently. Secondly, in order to counter its institutional and organizational decline, it will have to increase its membership and therefore it must become more attractive, or, as the neoliberal vocabulary would have it, more 'customer-oriented'. The following sections will now investigate the structural consequences of this double necessity.

Parishes' Response to Financial Austerity

As our empirical findings show, austerity is the single most important agent of change in the parishes. They are now forced into a process of organizational downsizing involving reductions in personnel, abandonment of buildings such as churches or community halls and cutbacks in activities. Furthermore, a wave of parish fusions has occurred since about the year 2000, leading to a decrease in the number of parishes, and an increase, statistically, in the average number of parish members.

Financial austerity is by and large an organizational issue, since, as argued above, it is money which fuels organizational activity, ensuring the continuation of its operations, which in turn consist of the consumption of labour power. Parishes themselves are, as argued above, best understood as a hybrid of community and organization. How does financial austerity affect the social form of the parish? How do economizing and downsizing – the necessary adaptations of the parish-as-organization to financial austerity – affect the parish-as-community? The results show that economizing and downsizing have enabled the parish-as-organization to sustain its organizational functionality, while the parish-as-community is heavily affected by the eroding impact of these organizational adaptations. This is due to the fact that the organization tends to withdraw many of the resources it formerly provided to establish and sustain the parish community. Thus, the organizational crisis brought about by financial austerity causes a shift in the balance between the parish-as-community and the parish-as-organization and the shift moves the centre of balance towards the latter. This shift can be illustrated in various ways.

An initial measure of economic downsizing can be made by charting the extent of the outsourcing of certain functions of the parish-as-organization, a good example of this being administrative work which had formerly been conducted by the parish secretary in the parish office. Whilst these offices had performed what appears to be a simple, easy to outsource organizational function, however, they had also served as platforms for personal interaction. In the Church slang they were often referred to as the 'coffee hangout'. In this way, the parish office had functioned as a hinge between the parish-as-organization and the parish-as-community. Now, most parishes have closed their offices; administrative work (such as does not affect the decision-making of the parish) is now handed over to an autonomous organization that will also cover the basic administrative needs of other parishes. Individual parishes will pay for this service and since in recent years a number of organizations designed to provide administrative services have evolved, the parishes can now choose between suppliers to get the cheapest price. Thus, a process of internal marketization has taken place; this will ensure the sustaining of organizational functionality (administration), but with the effect that the function of the parish office as a resource for interaction and community is removed.

A similar process of marketization has taken place in the healthcare services of the parish. Healthcare had formerly been conducted by the district nurse together with volunteers. The nurse, being salaried by the parish, had had a great deal of autonomy in her work and could also afford to use her working time for interaction with people in need who would otherwise be suffering from loneliness. In recent years, the position of the district nurse has been discontinued and healthcare services have been outsourced to the local arm of the *Diakonisches Werk*. This organization is financed by the German health insurance system. Hence the *Diakonische Werk* receives a fixed amount of money for every patient with certain needs (each 'case'). Additional time for interaction is thus not rewarded; in order to keep the finances balanced, as many 'cases' as possible have to be treated in the smallest possible number of hours worked. However, strong competition among different suppliers should ensure the high quality of the work. This has the effect that the formerly religious aspect of healthcare has now also completely vanished, since according to the secular, neoliberal market ethos, the 'customers' should not be imposed upon by religious communication.

Another aspect of the changes which have occurred due to financial austerity is the process of a de-professionalization of the priest. The general responsibilities of a priest consist of official ceremonies (including sermons, baptisms and so on), pastoral care (mainly as a result of personal interactions) and parish management. Our research results show an important shift in the balance of these responsibilities. Over the last ten years, parishes have been reducing their numbers of priests. The reduced numbers of priests are now faced with a situation in which they have to care for ever more people, since the percentage of reduction of priest positions is much faster than that of parish members. At the same time, these smaller numbers of priests still have to carry the load of management duties. The priests we interviewed showed a clear tendency towards reducing the professional aspects of their work, mainly, the pastoral care in which they would be personally communicating with their parishioners, to a bare minimum. Home visits which were routine in the past have now become a rare pastoral activity. This feeds the trend of a de-professionalization and managerialization of the role of the priest: less pastoral interaction, more management.

Finally, parishes, often in the context of a fusion or collaboration with other parishes, tend to abandon some of their buildings, such as churches or community halls. These buildings, however, were formerly the focal point of personal interactions, meetings and joint activities of the community. Many of the mostly elderly members of the core communities displayed high levels of identification with these buildings and with 'their' parish. Most often, the abandonment of these buildings leads to splits in the core communities. The unintentional effect of the fusions on the parishes is the production of winners and losers. The winners are the parish communities whose buildings will be maintained and often renovated. The losers are ripped away from 'their' church and community hall; often, they do not feel 'at home' in the buildings they attribute to the 'other' parish. The integration of communities in the context of fusions is likely to fail, which leads to diminishing degrees of participation among the losers.

These developments show that the parishes can hardly keep up with their promise to offer a space for community and mutual interaction in the age of neoliberalism. Not only have they offered a form of community that is not very attractive for the majority of the population, but the financial crisis has caused a process of erosion, in which the parish-as-organization has, by and large, withdrawn all the resources needed to sustain these communities. These core communities can sometimes, due to a high level of voluntary commitment, compensate for the removed organizational support. However, the capacity of the parishes for any 'outreach' has been shrinking. Instead of 'growing against the trend', these developments rather tend to accelerate the decline of the Church. This is the reason why many church officials have lost faith in the missionary power of the parishes. Aspirations for growth have thus shifted away from the parishes to extra-parochial sites, such as the newly established city churches, whose main function is to attract people without any affiliation to the parishes, the Church, or even religion, in general. The following sections deal with the Church's aspirations for renewed growth.

Attracting New Members: Low Threshold Offers

Even without the problems brought about by financial austerity, it may be argued that the parishes are failing to attract a majority of individuals in the contemporary context of Germany. In the 1970s and 1980s, when money was available, the process of falling away from the Church – what might be called 'de-churching' and in German is spoken of as *Entkirchlichung* – was still continuing. Nevertheless, attracting people has always been a religious imperative of the Church, and in the context of financial austerity, this has also become an organizational necessity. The wealth, even the existence of the church-as-organization depends on its income, which is based on the Church tax. But how to attract new members in the specific social environment of contemporary Europe, in which most individuals are religiously 'unmusical', at best? From the point of view of secularization theory, it may be argued that the parishes did a very good job of sustaining levels of commitment to the Church. But from the corporate consultant's point of view, the parishes, along with their programmes of community building, seem to be a failed strategy so that the current organizational urgent need to attract new members has stimulated a neoliberal discourse within the Church which centres on the notion of 'customer orientation'. From the corporate consultant's point of view, there is no such thing as secularization;[15] the single reason why the Church is in crisis

---

[15] This argument has also been made in the rational choice approach in the study of religion. See, among others, Rodney Stark, 'Secularization R.I.P.', *Sociology of Religion*, 60/3 (1999): 249–73.

is because it has not been sufficiently 'customer-oriented'. To a certain degree, these discourses can be seen to make theological sense. After all, isn't customer orientation not just another, contemporary word for mission?

On the other hand, the contestation and widespread refutation of the application of the idea of 'customer orientation' is also founded on theological arguments. Does the Church not have to address individuals as persons and not as objects of financial interest? More importantly, can a Church founded on the Word of God be open to the wishes and interests of 'customers'? Indeed, as rather less sophisticated neoliberal voices might argue, bringing the Gospel to the people *is* the ultimate in customer orientation. What company has anything better to offer than salvation from eternal misery? However, a problem arises if those potential 'customers' do not have any interest in this 'ultimate good'. At this point, the term customer orientation is highly problematic and often rejected, but the need to attract new people is not.

Instead of customer orientation, another term promises to unite those in the Church who propose a neoliberal agenda with those who resist it. It is referred to as the 'low threshold offer' (*niederschwelliges Angebot*). Low threshold offers are made much of as the basis for future Church projects, superseding the failed project of organized communalization. By making 'low threshold offers' the Church hopes to 'reach' the large majority of individuals without an affiliation to their parish, the Church or even religion in general. Thus, low threshold offers are the latest strategy for 'growing against the trend'.

The term 'low threshold offer' first came up in the 1960s and already had the connotation of bringing in people who would otherwise not feel attracted to the Evangelical Church. This strategy formed part of the communities' reform movement. Parish halls, for example, which would also be a site for non-religious cultural events, were conceived of as places of 'low threshold offers'. For the reasons outlined above, however, many church officials have lost faith in the missionary power of the parishes. Parishes do suffer from '*milieu* restriction': for one thing, their members are perceived as being 'overaged'. These communities are now perceived as something that repels rather than attracts new people. Instead, hopes for growing against the trend are placed onto new, extra-parochial sites, such as especially the new pastoral form of the city church. While the parishes are sometimes perceived to be an archaic model, extra-parochial sites such as the city churches have received widespread interest. Thus, while the term 'low threshold offer' is not new, the exemplary site for the making of this kind of offer has changed – from the parishes to the city churches.

City churches are a very recent phenomenon, but their emergence into the European religious landscape seems to be as important as the emergence of the 'mega churches' in the Christian world outside of Europe. A city church is somewhat like a parish-as-organization: that is to say it is run by salaried personnel such as priests, secretaries and sextons – but it does not have a parish community. It does conduct religious events that are directed towards these outsiders, however. Indeed, the emergence of the 'city church' is a consequence of secularization.

Parishes in the centres of big cities faced a situation in which their parish communities were dying out. This was due to a shift in the population; the typical *milieu* of the Church, elderly and conservative families, have left the centre of the cities, while at the same time other groups such as single people and migrants without Christian backgrounds have moved in. Thus, the parishes in the centre were stripped of their parish communities, while at the same time they continued to inhabit the oldest and most representative church buildings. In the late 1980s, the idea came up of using these buildings as centres for religious events which were open to everyone – thus attracting those people who would not be attracted by the usual offers of the parishes.

The city church investigated in this chapter is situated in the centre of a West German city within the metropolitan Ruhr area. It offers a whole range of organized events of a religious character to anyone who is interested; the target group being the people in the city. The following list gives an incomplete overview of the activities on offer: feminist acts of worship (a monthly event which is led by a musician), chants of healing and power (a monthly event), dance meditations, tango dance classes and tango acts of worship (less than monthly), contemplation sessions, healing touch sessions, religious lectures and so on. The personnel consists of two priests, a secretary and a sexton. It is housed in a one of the most famous church buildings of the city, which dates back to the twelfth century. Recently, the interior space has been renovated. Seat benches were substituted with portable chairs, and parquet flooring was laid on top of the stone floor. Thus, the interior space has been turned into a multi-functional hall which is suitable for dance sessions, while its sacred character has been conserved – the shrine, the windows and the religious artefacts are still in place.

Despite the fact that city churches have gained a wide reputation, they have not been studied so far. There are no quantitative data available on how many people attend the events of city churches on a regular or occasional basis. The city church I observed had a clientele of about 200 people. Its sermons and the feminist acts of worship were better attended than would be the average for participation in church services in a typical parish. However, the proportional attendance as measured against the sphere of influence is much smaller than that of the average parish.[16] Given that the sphere of influence of this city church is a whole city of more than 600,000 people, the number of participants looks very small. Thus, the idea of 'growing against the trend' by means of the establishment of city churches seems not to be very realistic. Most of the attendees in the city church I observed belong to an educated, middle-aged middle class with rather liberal orientations. Some people I interviewed have had a close relationship to the Church ever since. Sometimes, they enjoy the activities in the city church in addition to those of their parishes. Thus, it is also not clear if and how many people with a distanced relationship to the Church are attracted by this city church at all.

---

16   About 4 per cent of the parish members attend the church service on a regular basis.

The Social and Religious Profile of the City Churches

Before addressing the empirical findings on the nature of these 'low threshold offers', the term itself merits attention. One reason for its current success may be that it does not bear any of the theologically unacceptable characteristics which the term 'customer orientation' entails. The Church does not have to prostitute itself in order to meet the interests of its potential 'customers'. Firstly, the idea of the 'threshold' constructs a boundary between the two spaces it separates. Secondly, the term indicates that it is the threshold, and not the space behind it, (the church) which is the obstacle: the lower the threshold, the more people are likely to enter in. This further suggests that the space behind the threshold is no different from before, merely that the borderline (threshold) separating the 'inner' from the 'outer' space is easier to cross. The 'inner' space, the church itself, is conceived of as being untouched, unchanged. This, of course, is theologically acceptable. The texts of official documents as well as those of practical theologians promoting low threshold offers are very clear about the identity of the Church. Its remit is – incontestably – to spread the Gospel, and low threshold offers are only one (under the current cultural conditions, the most important) means to achieve this goal.

However, the empirical findings cast doubt on the veracity of this description. One remarkable finding of our research is that the low threshold offers conducted by the city church may have considerably low thresholds, both in a social and in a religious sense. But the important point is that neither these events, nor the city churches as a whole actually do function as, or constitute, a threshold. This is due to the fact that people attracted by the events of the city church will not then move on into any of the 'inner spaces' of the church, for example, by becoming a member of the parish; people who are attracted will simply return to these regular events and become regular guests. Thus, instead of functioning as a threshold, the city church actually creates a new space within the Church. This space is characterized by a genuine social form and genuine religious content.

The Social Form of the City Church

Compared to the parish communities, the events offered by this city church indeed have a low social threshold. They are open to everyone and do not entail any moral commitment to become part of the church community in any long-term sense. Some of these events request fees.[17] Thus, these events may have an economic threshold, but a very low social threshold, as is typical for the market situation.

---

[17]   Entry into the feminist acts of worship is free. Other activities such as the chanting for healing and empowerment or the tango dancing acts of worship ask entry fees of between 4 and 12 euros per participation. The fee is equal for everyone and independent of church membership status.

One can come, consume and go, without being subjected to any further demands. There is no request for any personal commitment.

But this type of advertised, well-organized event which is directed towards newcomers with no obligation for any personal interaction is only part of the story. After having crossed the threshold of the church door, part of what is offered within the closed social system of the organized event is the experience of an ephemeral and ever-evolving community. This is achieved mostly by transforming the attendees of these events from being merely 'consumers' into collective 'producers'. For example, in the chanting of healing and empowerment songs, people come and pay the entry in order not to listen to songs as in a concert, but in order to collectively sing them, often in canon. This experience of being part of a religious performance stimulates an atmosphere of community, even among foreign participants.

Thus, the social *Gestalt* of these events may be referred to as a form of instant community building (situative *Vergemeinschaftung*), characterized by the following features: first, it depends on a parent organization which can engage in a supplier-customer relationship. Second, it instantly develops a community within the organized event which is limited in time. Third, it is based on bringing together individuals into temporarily held constellations: there is no enduring form of membership. Finally, it is repeatable and can be experienced again, by simply attending the next organized event a month later.

Drawing on the analytical differentiation of social formations into markets, organizations and communities, the social *Gestalt* of the city churches consists of a complex entanglement of these social formations without any of them losing their distinctive qualities. In particular, what the city churches *offer* is a certain kind of instant and situative *Vergemeinschaftung* within their *organized* events. This ephemeral community building among foreign visitors – along with its distinctive religious profile – determines the social attractiveness of these city churches.

The Religious Profile of the City Church

The highest religious thresholds are religious creeds, dogmas, doctrines or, to put it concisely, the formulation of religious truths. They can either be believed and accepted, or refuted. Within a secular society, such religious truths may attract some, but will also repel many individuals.

The city church we looked at for this study seems to attract the aforementioned religiously 'unmusical' individuals by abandoning anything that comes close to creed, belief and dogma. The religious contents we observed may be conceived of as an oscillation between a religious semantics that comes close to conforming to contemporary Protestant theology and a religious semantics that comes close to the so-called 'new religiosity' and a spirituality that does not conform to contemporary Protestant theology. Christian elements are selected and adapted for a new religiosity, consisting of the following features:

- a clear emphasis that the core of religion is religious *experience*, hence the forefronting of the mystic tradition. Mystics, as emphasized, can be found in the Christian tradition, but also in many other religious traditions;
- an absence of doctrine and dogma. The notion of religious truth is neither communicated nor demanded. The Bible serves, at best, as an illustration. Jesus, if mentioned at all, is referred to as *exemplum*, but never as *mysterium*;
- a strong tendency towards inner-worldly transcendence; religion as a means of coping with everyday life, not a way in which to relocate the individual into a better world to come. A religious semantic which lacks any character of revelation or salvation, as defined historically in Christianity.

This abandonment of religious truths also includes an act of abstraction, where everything that comes close to concreteness, such as creed, dogma and so on, such as are found in 'traditional' Christianity, but also in other religions, are levelled into one core message of universal spirituality. This is often reached by a certain coupling of difference and elision: cultural and religious differences are looked for in order to find everywhere the same. Behind the differences, it is proclaimed, there is unity. It is claimed that all religions adore a deity. This deity may be called (randomly) God, Mother Earth, Allah or by the name of some Sanskrit or American Indian deity. The naming and appellation of a single transcendent authority has thus become arbitrary.

Besides the institution of low thresholds with regards to beliefs and dogmas, there is another religious aspect in this city church that advertises its easy accessibility. It has often been observed that one aspect of the new religiosity or contemporary spirituality is a democratization of religious virtuosity. Everyone is capable of achieving religious virtue. The question is how much effort, measured in time, work and also money (in order to pay for the course fees) is put in. New religiosity may be conceived of as a continuum – in some instances, the new religious 'sects' (in the Weber-Troeltschian sense of the word) demand a high level of personal commitment, while at the other end of the spectrum the obligation for personal commitment is very low-level. The religiosity of the city church here observed is situated at the latter pole of this continuum. Indeed, the notion of religious virtue is completely abandoned. People are invited to come, take part in religious communication, feel better and go. There is no demand for any consideration of ethical conduct, or for religious practices such as regular prayer. Religious activity is thus reduced to a participation in the events on offer.

These social and religious features of the city church reveal that this is a space within the Evangelical Church with a maximum adaptation towards the consumer society and religious individualism. Religious communication is barred from making any constraints on belief, commitment or any requirements for personal effort such as religious learning, moral behaviour and so on. Religion has thus become an item of *consumption*: one may come, participate in religious communication, and then leave it behind and go back to an ordinary, everyday, secular life.

Further, it may help individuals to cope ethically with their daily lives in the age of neoliberalism, which is dominated by the demands of production and consumption. The city church has something to offer more highly educated people with a critical perspective on the economy. These people are faced with the dilemma of a moral refutation of the double function of production/consumption and the evident impossibility of escaping from these economic constraints. Impressed and relieved by the spiritual experience in the city church, which implies the feeling of connectivity and being part of a greater whole against the backdrop of individual atomism which is typical of capitalist society, people leave the service and return – bad consciences unburdened – to producing and consuming.

Conclusion

This chapter has addressed processes of transformation within the German Evangelical Church in the age of neoliberalism. On the one hand, this is the story of an accelerated decline. The parish communities especially suffer from the withdrawal of resources which the church organization could provide. Thus, the balance within the social form of these parishes between community and organization shifts towards the latter. As a moral agent, the Church does mount a critique of the marketization of society; but faced with its own financial crisis, processes of marketization are also taking place within its domain. Bereft of its communities, the Church takes on the character of a typically consumer-oriented organization: making no demands of commitment on its 'customers'. Thus, a process of isomorphism is taking place in which the Church becomes a reflection of its social environment. The Church is not, as it may conceive of itself, an island of community resisting the sea of neoliberalism. Rather, it has become part of the sea itself.

However, the need of the Church to attract the religiously 'unmusical' majority has further inspired processes of transformation – ones in which it has also developed religious forms which are characteristically customer-oriented: a social form without any obligations, which makes no demands with respect to religious affiliation, or on individual ethical conduct. However, in a sense, it proves to bear those elements of customer orientation which lead to a wide refutation of the term into the vocabulary of the Church: if the Church, from a theological point of view, is bound to promulgate the Gospel (and this is nowhere contested in the present theological debates), the space of the city churches may be conceived of as de-Christianized.

Chapter 4
Catholic Church Civil Society Activism and the Neoliberal Governmental Project of Migrant Integration in Ireland

Breda Gray

Introduction

This chapter examines the shifting role of Catholic Church civil society activism in the Republic of Ireland (henceforth Ireland) with specific reference to the governmental project of immigrant integration. As Mooney argues, immigration 'has become a strategic issue on which the Catholic Church asserts its prophetic voice in the modern public sphere', but in different ways across national contexts.[1] The theoretical approach underpinning the chapter is informed by Foucault's work on governmentality[2] and 'governmentality studies' scholarship.[3] Governmentality is

---

[1]   Margarita Mooney, 'The Catholic Bishops Conferences of the United States and France. Engaging Immigration as a Public Issue', *American Behavioral Scientist*, 49/11 (2006): pp. 1455–56.

[2]   Michel Foucault, *The History of Sexuality, vol. 1. An Introduction* (London, 1979); Michel Foucault, 'The Subject and the Power', in Hubert Dreyfus and Paul Rabinow, *Michel Foucault: Beyond Structuralism and Hermeneutics* (Brighton, 1982), pp. 208–26; Michel Foucault, 'Governmentality', in Graham Burchell, Colin Gordon and Peter Miller (eds), *The Foucault Effect: Studies in Governmentality* (Hemel Hempstead, 1991), pp. 87–104; Michel Foucault, 'Security, Territory, and Population', in *Michel Foucault, Ethics: Subjectivity and Truth*, Paul Rabinow (ed.) (New York, 1997), pp. 67–71; Michel Foucault, *Security, Territory, Population. Lectures at the College de France 1977–78*, translated by Graham Burchell (Basingstoke, 2007); Michel Foucault, *The Birth of Biopolitics: Lectures at the College De France 1978–79*, translated by Graham Burchell (Basingstoke, 2008).

[3]   Peter Miller and Nikolas Rose, 'Governing Economic Life', *Economy and Society*, 19/1 (1990): pp. 1–31; Peter Miller and Nikolas Rose, *Governing the Present: Administering Economic, Social and Personal Life* (Cambridge, 2008); Graham Burchell, Colin Gordon and Peter Miller (eds), *The Foucault Effect: Studies in Governmentality with Two Lectures by and an Interview with Michel Foucault* (Chicago, 1991); Mitchell Dean, *Governmentality: Power and Rule in Modern Society* (London, 1999); Mitchell Dean, *Governing Societies* (Maidenhead, 2007); Nikolas Rose, *Powers of Freedom. Reframing Political Thought* (Cambridge, 1999); Thomas Lemke, '"The Birth of Bio-politics" – Michel Foucault's Lecture at the Collège de France on Neo-liberal Governmentality', *Economy*

concerned with the processes by which technologies of domination and technologies of the self intersect. And, insofar as Foucault saw religion as part of the political technology of governing the self[4] and as 'an immanent process of governmentality',[5] the focus here is on how these processes are manifest in twenty-first century Catholic Church governmental projects on immigrant integration in Ireland.

There is a deep disenchantment with the Catholic Church in Ireland largely due to child sexual abuse scandals and the Church's cover up of these. However, even as public debate becomes more hostile towards the Church, the turn to religious organizations as agents in the governance of migrant integration can be seen as opening up new spaces of authority for the Catholic Church. In this chapter I argue that neoliberal modes of governing 'at a distance',[6] while appearing to promote the autonomy of churches and individuals, actually enrol them in new forms of regulation. This is achieved through policy agendas that blur the boundaries of state, market and civil society. Examples include the policy focus on migrant 'risk' management and a turn to religious organizations as sites of 'citizenization',[7] as well as the contracting out of services and associated intensification of 'audit culture'.[8]

Nation-states across Europe increasingly rely on immigrants in the insistent drive towards competitiveness in the globalized economy. For example, immigration is factored into economic policies as states compete to attract the best talent available globally and fill gaps in service provision created by welfare state restructuring. However, the economic interests that promote migration as a necessary condition of national competitiveness also cause a fragmentation or 'rending of the social fabric'.[9] Immigration also gives rise to religious and cultural diversification which is in turn problematized in terms of 'risks' to social cohesion, often through the threat of religious extremism. These 'risks' are increasingly seen as most effectively managed by individuals themselves as members of civil society and religious groups rather than as citizens of the state. Thus, the solution takes the form of acting upon the dynamics of religion and civil society.

---

and Society, 30/2 (2001): pp. 190–207; Thomas Lemke, 'Foucault, Governmentality, and Critique, Rethinking Marxism', 14/3 (2002): pp. 49–64; Thomas Lemke, 'An Indigestible Meal? Foucault, Governmentality and State Theory' (2007), <www.thomaslemkeweb.de/publikationen/IndigestibleMealfinal5.pdf>, accessed 10 November 2011.

4 Jeremy R. Carrette (ed.), Religion and Culture, By Michel Foucault (Manchester, 1999).

5 Jeremy R. Carrette, Foucault and Religion: Spiritual Corporality and Political Spirituality (London, 2000), p. 139.

6 Miller and Rose, Governing the Present.

7 James Tully, 'Political Philosophy as a Critical Activity', Political Theory, 30/4 (2002): pp. 533–55.

8 Marilyn Strathern, 'Introduction: New Accountabilities', in Marilyn Strathern (ed.), Audit Cultures: Anthropological Studies in Accountability, Ethics and the Academy (London, 2000), p. 1.

9 Foucault, The Birth of Biopolitics, pp. 305–6.

Perceived as the site of moral forces that bind individuals in durable relations, religious and faith-based organizations (FBOs) are called on to act on conduct to ensure social cohesion. But to govern through religious authority and affiliation requires that these are rendered technical. So, for example, the varying forms of partnership between Catholic church actors, civil society organizations and philanthropic foundations in Ireland combine pastoral power based on 'care' for 'vulnerable' immigrants with the calculative technologies of 'targets', 'performance indicators' and 'benchmarking'. The combination of these technologies, albeit with an emphasis on the calculative, is a key feature of an emergent 'audit culture' in Ireland promoted by philanthropic funding foundations and legitimated by claims of enhanced transparency and accountability that are already a feature of public sector reform.

This chapter begins by differentiating between the Foucauldian approach to neoliberalism adopted here and the model of neoliberalism advanced in mainstream political theory and sociology. This is followed by an overview of neoliberal political rationality as articulated by Foucault and scholars of governmentality and a discussion of the ways in which this rationality might shape migrant integration governance through religious or faith-based organizations. A further section brings these theoretical debates to bear on how the Catholic Church has come to play a central role in the governance of migrant integration in Ireland, primarily by means of the pastoral power of identifying and responding to individual and collective 'need' and creating a reciprocal relationship between the 'shepherd' (Catholic Church actors) and 'flock' (immigrant service users and church members). I then examine the ways in which these pastoral technologies combine with calculative technologies in the implementation of neoliberal rationalities of governance. Following the preferred method in governmentality studies, discourses of governance in policy texts are analysed, but equally, this chapter assumes that 'mentalities of rule' are embodied in the institutional landscape which interacts in complex ways with policy texts and events.

Framing Neoliberalism Theoretically

Liberalism as a political ideology is 'organized around a commitment to individual liberty' but is perhaps of more practical import as a 'project of government'.[10] Although aimed at rule through the free activities of autonomous citizens, liberalism constitutes some as lacking the minimal capacities for autonomous action, thus establishing a hierarchical order of 'cultivated inhabitants of civilized states' with capacities for individual autonomy and others 'at a greater or lesser distance from that condition'.[11] Social or egalitarian liberalist understandings of the state tend to see it as intervening to promote autonomy and 'to mitigate social

---

[10] Barry Hindness, 'Neo-liberal Citizenship', *Citizenship Studies*, 6/2 (2002): p. 133.
[11] Ibid.

inequalities and injustices thrown up by the operation of the market economy'.[12] In contrast, neoliberal state restructuring is seen as involving a move away from such state intervention, focusing instead on the active promotion of economic growth through the free market as the most effective and socially productive mode of resource allocation in a globalized world.[13]

While also acknowledging the shifting role of the state, mainstream sociological analyses of neoliberalism tend to frame it more broadly. Lemke[14] identifies three main streams of sociological analysis: first, neoliberalism is seen as an ideology or 'faulty theory ... that must be replaced by a right or emancipatory – which means scientific or "impartial" – knowledge'.[15] Second, neoliberalism is understood in terms of the 'triumph of capitalism over the state' and the 'extension of economy into the domain of politics', leading to calls for the regulation and taming of capitalism.[16] The third approach emphasizes individualization and the celebration of flexibility and mobility, all of which are seen as threatening humanist values and traditional collective bonds.[17] The problem with these approaches for Lemke is that they ignore the work that dualisms such as ideology/emancipatory knowledge, economy/state, public/private individual/collective do 'in constituting and stabilizing liberal-capitalist societies'.[18] With Lemke and others, I see Foucault's account of neoliberalism as offering a more productive approach to the study of contemporary neoliberal transformations.

For Foucault, neoliberalism is to be seen as 'neither ... a theory nor as an ideology, but rather ... a practice, or ... political technology'.[19] In this context, a political technology or rationality is understood as 'a specific form of normative political reason organizing the political sphere, governance practices, and citizenship ... [that] articulates the nature and meaning of the political, the social, and the subject'.[20] So from this perspective, the focus shifts to specific variants of neoliberal 'practices of governance rather than either epochs or generalized modes of power-knowledge'.[21] Moreover, social power relations are not seen as emanating directly 'from structural economic relations, but are instead made and

---

[12]   Lois McNay, 'Self as Enterprise: Dilemmas of Control and Resistance in Foucault's *The Birth of Biopolitics*', *Theory, Culture & Society*, 26/6 (2009): p. 56.

[13]   David Harvey, *A Brief History of Neoliberalism* (Oxford, 2005).

[14]   Lemke, 'Foucault, Governmentality, and Critique, Rethinking Marxism'.

[15]   Ibid., p. 54.

[16]   Ibid.

[17]   Ibid.

[18]   Ibid.

[19]   Ben Golder, 'Foucault and the Genealogy of Pastoral Power', *Radical Philosophy Review*, 10/2 (2007): pp. 160.

[20]   Wendy Brown, 'American Nightmare: Neoliberalism, Neoconservatism, and De-Democratization', *Political Theory*, 34/6 (2006): p. 693.

[21]   Mariana Valverde, 'Genealogies of European States: Foucauldian Reflections', *Economy and Society*, 36/1 (2007): p. 160.

re-made every day in the encounters among individuals and groups that make up institutions'.[22] This approach sees neoliberalism not simply as an 'ideological rhetoric ... a political-economic reality, or ... a practical antihumanism, but above all ... [as] a political project that endeavors to create a social reality that it suggests already exists'.[23]

From this perspective, the separation of church, state and the economy can never be assumed. Instead, the focus is on how the lines of separation and connection between these are themselves elements of governance.[24] The emphasis is on how neoliberal rationalities produce forms of knowledge that become the 'truth' of the situation and contribute to particular forms of regulation and configurations of institutions.[25] So, rather than simply a retreat of the state,[26] as heralded by some analyses of neoliberalism, what is perhaps more evident is a reformulation of state/ civil society and public/private relations such that religious non-governmental organizations (RNGOs) and faith-based organizations (FBOs) are becoming more significant governmental actors, or governmental in new ways. As civil society becomes more intertwined with both the state and market, religious and faith-based organizations (alongside other civil society agencies) become structurally linked to market-oriented state agendas and associated projects of social cohesion and integration. I am not concerned, therefore, with debates regarding typologies of RNGOs or FBOs, because the discussion here is focused on such organizations as effects, or artefacts, of neoliberal political projects.[27]

The shift away from welfare state governance through the social, which is increasingly identified with a culture of dependency and a failure of self-care, does not necessarily mean a retreat of the state. Instead, it is possible to trace a reconfiguration of the role of the state as intervening now to promote autonomy and self-care in the form of entrepreneurship of the self.[28] However, the shepherd-

---

[22]   Ibid., p. 161.

[23]   Lemke, 'Foucault, Governmentality, and Critique, Rethinking Marxism', p. 60.

[24]   Lemke, 'Foucault, Governmentality, and Critique, Rethinking Marxism'.

[25]   Lemke, 'Foucault, Governmentality, and Critique, Rethinking Marxism', p. 55.

[26]   The term 'state' is used here, not in the sense of a unitary actor, but to mean an ensemble of institutions, rationalities and practices of power (that can be contradictory and conflicting) that acts both on the individual and the population as a whole.

[27]   My main focus is on Catholic Church-initiated or run organizations, or what Berger calls religious NGOs. She defines these as being 'a unique hybrid of religious beliefs and sociopolitical activism at all levels of society ... [and] seek[ing] to fulfill explicitly public missions', see: Julia Berger, 'Religious Nongovernmental Organizations: An Exploratory Analysis', *Voluntas: International Journal of Voluntary and Nonprofit Organizations*, 14/1 (2003): p. 16. However, she notes that 'the extent to which religious identity defines the organization's structural, strategic, and service dimensions' varies and suggests 'that degrees of "religiosity"' can be present across organizations from the self identity of workers and organizational goals to decision-making processes and organizational fields (Ibid., p. 25).

[28]   McNay, 'Self as Enterprise'.

flock game of pastoral power that was incorporated into the secular administrative apparatus of welfare state provision for the vulnerable and marginalized has not disappeared. To some degree, this form of pastoral power is relocated in civil society (including religious) organizations – all actors in a marketized social domain competing to attract funding based primarily on a demonstrated ability to respond to 'need' most efficiently. As the market becomes the model for regulating and coordinating the activities of actors across all domains of social life, the focus of governance turns to the promotion of competition, efficiency, individual choice and responsibility. As such, economic and social policy agendas converge and civil society organizations are tasked with rendering individual subjects 'responsible' for their own integration through 'self-care' and making the 'right' choices.[29] This often involves immigrants being made responsible for acquiring the appropriate 'norms and values' as markers of integration.[30]

Power works here mainly as a form of 'guidance ... that is, governing the forms of self-government, structuring and shaping the field of possible action of subjects'.[31] As such, neoliberalism differs from liberal welfarism[32] or social liberalism[33] 'in imagining responsibility for governance shifting towards agents operating beyond the state' such as RNGOs or FBOs, and 'a corresponding move towards these agents governing through their freedom'.[34] Thus, enactments of responsibility are often encouraged by way of participation in civil society, religious or faith-based groups which are seen as having particularly effective influencing capacities. Having introduced the approach to neoliberalism adopted in this chapter, I proceed in the following section to consider the key tenets of neoliberal governmentality in more detail.

Towards Neoliberal Governmentality

Noting the multiplicity of governmentalities, Miller and Rose identify three broad 'families' of governmentalities: classical liberalism, social government and neoliberalism. In classical liberal governmentalities the state limits itself 'by designating zones exterior to it – private life, the market, civil society ... that [have] ... their own density and autonomy'.[35] Social government, or governing

---

[29] McNay, 'Self as Enterprise'; Lemke, 'Foucault, Governmentality, and Critique, Rethinking Marxism'; Rose, *Powers of Freedom*.

[30] Willem Sckinkel and Friso van Houdt, 'The Double Helix of Cultural Assimilation and Neo-liberalism: Citizenship in Contemporary Governmentality', *British Journal of Sociology*, 61/4 (2010): p. 704.

[31] Lemke, 'Foucault, Governmentality, and Critique, Rethinking Marxism', p. 52.

[32] Randy K. Lippert, *Sanctuary, Sovereignty, Sacrifice: Canadian Sanctuary Incidents, Power, and Law* (Vancouver, 2005).

[33] Rose, *Powers of Freedom*.

[34] Lippert, *Sanctuary, Sovereignty, Sacrifice*, p. 6.

[35] Miller and Rose, *Governing the Present*, p. 17.

'from the social point of view', is deemed necessary to 'combat the twin threats of unbridled market individualism and communist revolution', such that subjects are transformed 'into social citizens with social rights'.[36] Here the state is 'the ultimate guarantor of the welfare of the individual' through social insurance and social welfare.[37] I dwell a little on this second mode of governmentality to consider the pastoral power that is central to its operation. Foucault argues that pastoral power as 'a model and matrix for procedures for the government of men, really only begins with Christianity'.[38] This modality of power works through relations of 'care' which require 'a complete obedience of [one] individual to another individual'.[39] This relationship of obedience is never at an end because 'one obeys in order to be obedient' and this 'state of obedience' is new insofar as it involves 'the complete renunciation of one's own will'.[40] The pastor here experiences 'his responsibility as a service, and one that makes him the servant of his sheep'.[41] The pastor must 'take charge of and observe daily life in order to form a never-ending knowledge of the behaviour and conduct of the members of the flock he supervises'.[42]

With this form of power Foucault identifies the emergence of 'absolutely specific modes of individualization' based on procedures of '[a]nalytical identification, subjection, and subjectivation'.[43] Knowledge of the conscience and its direction are central to the workings of pastoral power. Moreover, the pastoral power relationship is based on the personal example of the pastor.[44] For Foucault, the pastorate 'involves the history of the subject' and, as such, 'is a prelude to governmentality'. This is because it establishes particular kinds of relationships; constitutes 'a specific subject' whose merits are analytically identified, who is subjected to continuous networks of obedience, and is subjectified by means of the compulsory extraction of truth.[45] With the secularization of these relationships and processes, they spread into the whole social body and are perhaps most obviously evident in the welfare state, or what Miller and Rose[46] call governing through the social. Here, the pastoral power relationship is based on the impersonal expertise of the 'psy' and 'social professions'. In this chapter, I argue that pastoral power has not disappeared with the reformulation of state, market, civil society relations, but is dispersed across civil society and works in a complex relationship to neoliberal rationalities of rule.

---

36   Ibid., pp. 17–18.

37   Ibid., *Governing the Present*, p. 18.

38   Foucault, *Security, Territory, Population*, pp. 147–48.

39   Ibid, p. 175.

40   Ibid., pp. 177–8.

41   Ibid., p. 179.

42   Ibid., p. 181.

43   Ibid., p. 184.

44   Thomas Biebricher, 'Faith-based Initiatives and Pastoral Power', *Economy and Society*, 40/3 (2011): pp. 399–420.

45   Ibid., pp. 184–5.

46   Miller and Rose, *Governing the Present*.

Miller and Rose's[47] third family of governmentality is neoliberalism, or 'advanced liberalism', which expanded in the latter decades of the twentieth century, but was prefigured by the German ordo-liberals of the Freiburg School in the 1930s and 1940s and the Chicago School in the 1960s. For the German ordo-liberals, classical liberal thought was wrong in seeing the market as a natural phenomenon and promoting *laissez-faire* policies. Instead, they conceived of the market in anti-naturalistic terms and as requiring political intervention in order to keep it alive and functioning. As such, 'the state and the market are not juxtaposed but ... one mutually presumes the existence of the other'.[48] Rather than the state correcting market dysfunction, they argued that economic rationality or the market should be used to correct social dysfunctions.[49] This was not about the carving out of a space of freedom from the state as in classical liberalism, but about initiatives to promote those entrepreneurial and self-responsible dispositions necessary to market functioning.

From this perspective, state roll-back is not seen as 'a decline of state sovereignty' but as promoting new 'forms of government that foster and enforce individual responsibility, privatized risk-management, empowerment techniques, and the play of market forces and entrepreneurial models in a variety of social domains'.[50] The state should keep out of correcting market dysfunction and direct its interventions towards creating the right environment for economic growth. So, instead of intervening to mediate the effects of the market or to facilitate the redistribution of income, the focus of social policy would be to enable individuals achieve adequate income to insure against risks on the basis of private resources.[51]

As the task of neoliberal social policy is 'economic growth' through the market, 'competitive mechanisms' are seen as playing 'a regulatory role at every moment and every point in society'.[52] The optimum conditions for market functioning can be promoted by lessening the anti-social consequences of competition, or anti-competitive blockages, in two key ways: first, through the universalization of the entrepreneurial form within the social body through the promotion of competition underpinned by the principle of 'equal inequality for all'; and second, through a redefinition of law so that economic liberty both founds and legitimates the state and state sovereignty is 'limited to guaranteeing economic activity'.[53] As such, law is not conceived as the effect of a collective will, but 'brings into play a conception of individual freedom which is not so much judicial in essence as a de facto recognition and consideration of the independence of the governed'.[54] In this

---

47 Ibid.
48 Lemke, 'The Birth of Bio-politics', p. 193.
49 Foucault, *The Birth of Biopolitics*, p. 191; McNay, 'Self as Enterprise', p. 58.
50 Lemke, 'Foucault, Governmentality, and Critique, Rethinking Marxism', p. 3.
51 Foucault, *The Birth of Biopolitics*, p. 144.
52 Foucault, *The Birth of Biopolitics*, pp. 144–5.
53 Lemke, 'The Birth of Bio-politics', pp. 195–6.
54 Jacques Donzelot, 'Michel Foucault and Liberal Intelligence', *Economy and Society*, 37/1 (2008): p. 125.

approach, utility becomes 'the main criterion for working out the limits of powers of public authority'.[55] Law operates more as a norm and functions in a regulatory way rather than as a technique of sovereignty.

Instead of the promotion of *equality*, the focus is on *inclusion* such that all individuals are kept 'in the framework of "equal inequality" which ensures competition precisely because there is no exclusion'.[56] In short, social policy 'is no longer a means for countering the economic, but a means for sustaining the logic of competition'.[57] So for the ordo-liberals, market mechanisms and competition require neoliberal practices of government including political regulations and social interventions that code 'social existence as an enterprise' mediating the economic and social domains.[58]

This view was developed by the Chicago School which redefined 'the social sphere as a form of the economic domain'.[59] Here 'the economic is not a firmly outlined and delineated area of human existence, but essentially includes all forms of human action and behavior'.[60] As such, social relations and individual behaviour are 'deciphered using economic criteria and within economic terms of its intelligibility' and 'the economic matrix … enables a critical evaluation of governmental practices by means of market concepts'.[61] The promotion of economic efficiency and competitiveness becomes the permanent goal in the neoliberal problematic of security.[62] Unlike the welfare-state model which relied on social scientific expertise, this mode of rule involves the 'mastery of formal rationality as embodied in the intellectually lowlier "grey sciences", above all accounting, auditing and law'.[63] Technologies of benchmarking, audit and performance produce 'calculating individuals' within 'calculable spaces', all of which are incorporated within 'calculative regimes'.[64]

In contrast with the liberal economic subject, which is one of exchange, the neoliberal subject is one of competition but requires the constant intervention of the state to ensure social conditions conducive to constituting such economic subjects of competition. By adopting market values in all areas of her life, this subject

---

[55]   Michel Foucault, 'Sécurité, territoire, population: Cours au Collège de France (1977–78), ed. M. Senellart (Paris, 2004), p. 45, in Donzelot, 'Michel Foucault and Liberal Intelligence', p. 126.

[56]   Donzelot, 'Michel Foucault and Liberal Intelligence', p. 124.

[57]   Ibid.

[58]   Lemke, 'The Birth of Bio-politics', p. 197.

[59]   Ibid.

[60]   Ibid., pp. 197–8.

[61]   Ibid., p. 198.

[62]   Dean, *Governing Societies*, p. 126.

[63]   Nikolas Rose, 'Governing 'Advanced' Liberal Democracies', in Andrew Barry, Thomas Osborne and Nikolas Rose (eds), *Foucault and Political Reason: Liberalism, Neo-liberalism and Rationalities of Government* (London, 1996), pp. 55–6.

[64]   Peter Miller, 'Accounting and Objectivity: The Invention of Calculating Selves and Calculable Spaces', *Annals of Scholarship*, 9/1–2 (1992): p. 61.

becomes an entrepreneur of herself, interpellated as an acquisitive entrepreneurial and self-responsible consumer.[65] As such, all government and civil society actors are subject to rationalities of choice and cost-benefit analyses that reproduce them as consumer citizens. The goal is 'to devise a state capable of creating, through its own programs and initiatives, the voluntaristic, entrepreneurial and self-responsible dispositions upon which market rationality draws'.[66] Moral responsibility is equated with rational deliberation by the individual, who makes choices among different options and bears responsibility for her actions.[67] Here neoliberalism works both as a strategy of rule and to reframe individual agency whereby all subjects, whether political, consumer or service user, are 'autonomous choosers'.[68] Decisions are made as choices, but choices are shaped through the stimulation of entrepreneurial market behaviour across civil society. This is a marketized civil society of competing organizations all involved in the act of 'governing', either as a replacement of the state, or in partnership with state agencies, with philanthropic foundations and/or businesses.

Many see religious and faith-based organizations gaining significance as agents of neoliberal governance due to their perceived unique capacities in the shaping of the conduct of conduct. For example, McClain argues that '[f]aith-based groups appeal to general religious values to encourage clients to become self-sufficient and change self-defeating attitudes and behaviour'.[69] Others suggest that religious or faith-based organizations are seen as more holistic agents of service provision than the state, and best able to mobilize volunteers in projects such as migrant integration.[70] As such, religious and faith-based actors are framed as 'best able' to 'compete effectively in the emerging neoliberal social policy arena'.[71]

Over the past decade or so, North American and European states have turned to FBOS in response to issues of immigration, integration, the politics of recognition

---

[65]   Brown, 'American Nightmare'.

[66]   Sam Binkley, 'The Work of Neoliberal Governmentality: Temporality and Ethical Substance in the Tale of Two Dads', *Foucault Studies*, 6 (2009): p. 68.

[67]   Brown, 'American Nightmare'.

[68]   Nick Lewis, Wendy Larner and Richard Le Heron, 'The New Zealand Designer Fashion Industry; Making Industries and Co-constituting Political Projects', *Transactions of the Institute of British Geographers*, 33/1 (2007): p. 43.

[69]   Linda McClain, *Unleashing or Harnessing "Armies of Compassion"?: Reflections on the Faith-Based Initiative* (Boston, 2009), p. 396, <www.bu.edu/law/faculty/scholarship/.../Faith-based-McClain.html>, accessed 10 May 2011.

[70]   Rebecca Sagar, *Faith, Politics, & Power: The Politics of Faith-Based Initiatives* (New York, 2010); Sara Silvestri, 'Islam and Religion in the EU Political System', *West European Politics*, 32/6 (2009): pp. 1210–39; David Ley, 'The Immigrant Church as an Urban Service Hub', *Urban Studies*, 45/10 (2009): pp. 2057–74.

[71]   Anne Marie Smith, 'Neoliberalism, Welfare Policy, and Feminist Theories of Social Justice', *Feminist Theory*, 9/2 (2008): p. 132.

and the perceived 'risks' of religious extremism.[72] In the US, for example, the debate about church-state separation has been reframed 'to suggest that such separation creates discrimination against religious groups ... [and] to remedy this, government must actively reach out to religion in a spirit of cooperation and integration, rather than separation'.[73] However, Sager argues that this governance through religious organizations is not really about social solutions, but acts symbolically to bring about a shift in the relationship between state and religion legitimating governance through religion. A strengthening of the role of religious organizations in the governance of integration and social cohesion is also noted across European countries through techniques of faith, but also through an emphasis on their capacity to achieve results and meet targets.[74]

Tadros suggests that because of their 'unique concern with the spiritual and moral capacities of those they seek to serve', religious organizations are best placed to shape the 'capacities at the root of people's ability to transform their own condition and that of those around them' and, therefore, are ideal vehicles of neoliberal governance.[75] However, this interpretation tends to assume a coherent neoliberalism that is successful in creating isomorphic subjects and overlooks the ways in which neoliberalism coexists with, appropriates and subverts other rationalities and techniques of governance. A more nuanced account may be possible by attending to specific governmental practices that establish neoliberalism in a particular socio-historical context. In the following section I examine the case of the Catholic Church in Ireland and its potential revitalization as an agent of migrant integration at a time when the 'risks' of migration are problematized in relation to religious identities and modes of affiliation.

Migrant Integration, the Catholic Church and the Marketization of Irish Civil Society

Although the religious structure of Irish society has been predominantly Catholic since the inception of the state in the 1920s, the numbers claiming a religion other

---

[72]   Mariz Tadros, *Faith-Based Organizations and Service Delivery Some Gender Conundrums, Gender and Development Programme* (Geneva, 2010), <www.unrisd. org/80256B3C005BCCF9/(httpAuxPages)/.../Tadros.pdf>, accessed 10 May 2011.

[73]   Sager (2010): p. 8; see also Chapter 5 (Hackworth) in this collection.

[74]   Justin Beaumont, 'Faith Action on Urban Social Issues', *Urban Studies*, 45/10 (2008): pp. 2019–34; Paul Cloke, Andrew Williams and Samuel Thomas, 'FBOs and Social Exclusion in the United Kingdom', in Danielle Dierckx, Jan Vranken and Wendy Kerstens (eds), *Faith-based Organisations and Social Exclusion in European Cities. National Context Reports* (Leuven, 2009); Julia Mourão Permoser, Sieglinde Rosenberger and Kristina Stoeckl, 'Religious Organizations as Political Actors in the Context of Migration: Islam and Orthodoxy in Austria', *Journal of Ethnic and Migration Studies*, 36/9 (2010), pp. 1463–81.

[75]   Tadros, *Faith-Based Organizations and Service Delivery Some Gender Conundrums, Gender and Development Programme*, p. 6.

than Roman Catholic or Church of Ireland trebled in the 15 years to 2006, largely due to immigration.[76] The evangelical sector grew considerably, but the two fastest growing religions and those with the highest proportions of immigrants were 'Orthodox [Greek, Russian and Coptic] and Islam'.[77] There was an increase of 6.3 per cent in those identifying as Roman Catholic between 2002 and 2006 with 92 per cent of Irish nationals and 50.8 per cent of non-Irish nationals falling into this category.[78] Amongst immigrants, over 80 per cent of the Polish, Filipino and Lithuanian and over 50 per cent American and French residents in Ireland in 2006 were Catholic, with Roman Catholicism being the religion of 26 per cent of Nigerian immigrants.[79, 80] However, my concern in this chapter is less with the small increase and diversification of Catholic Church membership than with the emergence of Catholic Church-initiated and run initiatives directed towards migrant integration.

Honohan and Rougier argue that although 'the dominant position of Catholicism has been seen as a driver of intolerance of diverse religious perspectives in Ireland ... another view ... holds that because Ireland has traditionally been a religious society it may be more hospitable to religious minorities'.[81] While these propositions require further empirical investigation, the evidence to date with regard to Muslims suggests that the perception of Ireland as a religious society has enabled the relatively smooth carving out of a space for Islam in Ireland.[82] It is also true to say that Catholic Church actors, through their lobbying for immigrant rights, and the establishment of pro-migrant organizations open to those of all religions and none, have significantly shaped the governance of migrant integration in Ireland.[83] These Catholic actors find themselves simultaneously engaged in pastoral care, advocacy, protest, management and government roles.

---

[76]   Malcolm Macourt, 'Mapping the "New Religious Landscape" and the "New Irish": Uses and Limitations of the Census', in Olivia Cosgrove, Laurence Cox, Carmen Kuhling and Peter Mulholland (eds), *Ireland's New Religious Movements* (Cambridge, 2011), p. 39.

[77]   Desmond A. Gillmor, 'Changing Religions in the Republic of Ireland, 1991–2002', *Irish Geography*, 39/2 (2006): p. 113; Macourt, 'Mapping the "New Religious Landscape" and the "New Irish"'.

[78]   Iseult Honohan and Nathalie Rougier, 'Tolerance and Cultural Diversity Discourses in Ireland', European University Institute, Florence Robert Schuman Centre for Advanced Studies (2010).

[79]   Central Statistics Office, Census 2006: Non-Irish Nationals Living in Ireland (Dublin, 2008).

[80]   Muslims, although a very small section of the population, represented the third largest religious category in 2006 – up 13,400 from 2002 to just over 32,500, see: Honohan and Rougier, 'Tolerance and Cultural Diversity Discourses in Ireland', p. 13.

[81]   Honohan and Rougier, 'Tolerance and Cultural Diversity Discourses in Ireland', p. 25.

[82]   Oliver Scharbrodt and Tuula Sakaranaho, 'Islam and Muslims in the Republic of Ireland', *Journal of Muslim Minority Affairs*, 31/4 (2011), p. 479.

[83]   Breda Gray, 'Making Migration a Public Issue: The "Network-making Power" of the Irish Catholic Church', in Mary Gilmartin and Alan White (eds), *Ireland and Migration* (Manchester, 2013).

Since the 1990s, the central role of the Irish Catholic Church in education and to a lesser extent in the domains of health and welfare has come under pressure due to the diversification of Irish society, clerical sexual abuse scandals and secularizing trends. These challenges to the traditional position of the Church are mirrored by 'a general decline in [the Church's] influence over the state and other social institutions' as it becomes increasingly subject to media investigation, interrogation and contestation.[84] But despite this public contestation, the project of migrant integration has been led by Catholic Church actors since the mid-1990s. Variously motivated by social justice, charity and social entrepreneurship, these actors responded to the social effects of state immigration and integration policies shaped by labour market requirements and minimal legal obligations towards asylum seekers and refugees under the 1951 UN Convention.[85]

This church response is in line with a history of Irish Catholic Church civil society activism informed by the principle of subsidiarity. This principle holds that the transfer to the larger or higher authority of that which can be performed and provided by the lesser and subordinate bodies is wrong. The presumption underpinning this tenet of Catholic teaching is that state intervention 'should never "destroy or absorb" the lesser intermediate bodies'.[86] Irish social Catholicism in the first half of the twentieth century set itself against class politics and the state as an expression of the national community.[87] The emergence of the modern secular state across Europe was seen as a threat to the role of the Church as the rightful agent of welfare. Moreover, the Church principle of subsidiarity asserted in the papal encyclical *Quadragesimo Anno* (1931) discouraged the assumption by the state of major social or economic responsibilities and emphasized instead the transfer of existing responsibilities and powers to corporatist institutions. This legitimated Irish Catholic Church 'attempts to establish an alternative institutionalisation of social and economic power'.[88] During the 1930s and 1940s church social teaching continued to oppose class-based social organization and the labour movement, employers' federations and organizations of farmers, all of which were seen as potentially socially disruptive forces.[89] In response to the emergence of European welfare states in the 1940s and 1950s, L'Estrange notes

---

[84]   Susie Donnelly and Tom Inglis, 'The Media and the Catholic Church in Ireland: Reporting Clerical Child Sex Abuse', *Journal of Contemporary Religion*, 25/1 (2010): p. 1.

[85]   Gerry Boucher, 'Ireland's Lack of a Coherent Integration Policy', *Translocations*, 3/1 (2008): pp. 5–28.

[86]   *Mater et Magistra* (1961) and *Quadragesimo Anno* (1931), in John A. Coleman, 'Catholic Social Thought and Civil Society', (2006), pp. 9–10, <www.cuhk.edu.hk/crs/ catholic/CCS/download/Civil%20Society_Coleman.doc>.

[87]   Sean L'Estrange, *Catholicism and Capitalist Social Order in Ireland, 1907–1973: An Historical Institutionalist Analysis* (Belfast, 2004), p. 134.

[88]   L'Estrange, *Catholicism*, p. 139.

[89]   Ibid.

that Irish social Catholicism gave rise to 'innumerable polemics against State welfare provision, particularly in the field of health'.[90] Moreover,

> the overwhelming majority of such writing remained staunchly opposed to direct State intervention in the economy, and generally supportive of private enterprise and market forces as the default option for economic development [and] though market failure could justify the State in stepping in to make good the deficiencies in private enterprise, the burden of proof for defining a legitimate case of market failure remained exceptionally heavy.[91]

However, Coleman notes that 'Catholicism has never held that government is best which governs least'.[92] Instead, the specific role identified for the state is 'to "encourage, stimulate, regulate, supplement and complement" the action of intermediate groups'.[93] In this way at least, the principle of subsidiarity can be seen as lining up with the neoliberal rationality of shaping practice and subjectivity at a distance through the community and the family.[94]

During the twentieth century, Catholic social activism in Ireland defined problems of social order 'as problems of community' with such problems being resolved by forms of community building that 'relied on the sanctity of the patriarchal family'.[95] Society was conceived as a 'community of communities' and was to be protected as such.[96] This conception of Irish society was 'set against both independent class-based organizations and the State as the organized expression of the national community'.[97] L'Estrange suggests that this view that community building could resolve social problems prefigures the introduction of the governmental practice of 'social partnership' in 1987.[98] This formalized partnership mechanism involved agreeing 'programmes for government' between the government, representatives from the business world, civil society organizations and, from the mid-1990s, the voluntary and community sector, including Catholic Church organizations. Immigrant integration was identified as a target of

---

[90]   Ibid., p. 153.

[91]   Ibid.

[92]   Coleman, 'Catholic Social Thought and Civil Society', p. 2.

[93]   Ibid.

[94]   Linda McClain, *Unleashing or Harnessing 'Armies of Compassion'?: Reflections on the Faith-Based Initiative*, p. 369.

[95]   Sean L'Estrange, 'A Community of Communities – Catholic Communitarianism and Societal Crises in Ireland, 1890s–1950s', *Journal of Historical Sociology*, 20/4 (2007): pp. 560, 557.

[96]   Ibid.

[97]   L'Estrange, 'A Community of Communities', p. 566; Eoin Devereux, 'Saving Rural Ireland – Muintir na Tire and Its Anti-Urbanism 1931–1958', *The Canadian Journal of Irish Studies*, 17/2 (1991): pp. 23–30.

[98]   Ibid.

governance in the Social Partnership Agreement, *Sustaining Progress* (2003–05), which set the policy agenda for this period and stated that 'Government and the social partners agree on the desirability for the development of a comprehensive policy framework on migration' (2003: section 2.5).

Although social partnership is currently under pressure due to the fiscal crisis and austerity measures, the conception of Ireland as a community of communities and the pervasive assumption that the state is 'unfit to accomplish the "conduct of conduct" on its own' both hold sway.[99] To date, social partnership has provided a framework in which actors with diverse agendas and interests engage in consensual governance in the 'best interests' of Irish society. Indeed, over time, the term 'to partner' has become 'the proper, civilized way to relate'.[100] For example, Gaynor argues in relation to social partnership that

> there is no longer any room for groups not committed to a problem-solving discourse employing what have become the normative communicative methods of 'reasonable' evidence-based argumentation.[101]

However, insofar as social partnership operates as 'a community of communities', it continues to provide a context in which Catholic Church actors can participate in the sectoral politics that are active despite the appearance of consensus.[102]

Formal social partnership arrangements can be understood as a key element in an assemblage of techniques of governance that are reconstituting state-civil society relationships in Ireland. These include public sector reform, recognition of the 'community and voluntary sector' as partners with the state and the promotion of active citizenship. The ongoing project of public sector reform is partly addressed through the mechanisms of social partnership and involves the promotion of managerial accountability and an imperative to justify all public sector practices 'on the grounds of economic efficiency'.[103] Another aspect of this reform is the shift to a contract culture in which 'the legitimacy of actions is defined in terms of the agreed exchange between the respective parties'.[104]

In keeping with the promotion of partnership and contract culture, the government White Paper on the Community and Voluntary sector identifies civil

---

[99]   Randy Lippert, 'Rationalities and Refugee Resettlement', *Economy and Society*, 27/4 (1998): p. 393.

[100]   Lippert, 'Rationalities and Refugee Resettlement', p. 392.

[101]   Niamh Gaynor, 'Associations, Deliberation, and Democracy: The Case of Ireland's Social Partnership', *Politics and Society*, 39/4 (2011): pp. 497–519.

[102]   Ibid.

[103]   George Taylor, *Negotiated Governance and Public Policy in Ireland* (Manchester, 2005), p. 121.

[104]   Ibid.

society organizations as 'essential partners in economic and social development'.[105] This call to partnership is justified on the basis that the state is 'not the answer to every problem, but just one player among others'.[106] The paper acknowledges that although '[m]any services [had] been initiated and run by religious organizations', these organizations are now being replaced by 'statutory sector and other voluntary organizations'.[107] While the White Paper acknowledged the decline of religious – mainly Catholic Church-based – organizations in the community and voluntary sector, the Taskforce on Active Citizenship Report asserted that 'organizations involved in ... religious dimensions of Irish life', amongst others, have the 'ability to achieve trust, cohesion and confidence in ways that governments cannot'.[108] In the period when these documents were published, church-initiated or church-run organizations were centrally engaged in shaping the governance of immigrant integration. As such, the secularization of the community and voluntary sector does not mean an eventual disappearance of Catholic Church actors, but their presence may take new forms and become more concentrated in specific areas. It is also possible that at a time of disaffection amongst Irish citizens, the civil society activism of church actors is more welcome amongst immigrant groups.

Church-initiated and church-run organizations for migrants in Ireland take many forms. For example, the Refugee Project (later to become the Refugee and Migrant Project) was set up by the Irish Bishops' Conference in 1999 and provided pastoral care to refugees and asylum seekers as well as awareness and information within the Church and beyond until its wind down in 2011. Meanwhile, many religious orders including the Vincentians, Dominicans, Holy Ghost, Columban, Mercy and Little Sisters of the Assumption were key actors in initiating a national network of advocacy and welfare services especially for asylum seekers and refugees. Although in many cases staffed by lay people, some of these are identifiably religious NGOs, often with social justice rather than, or combined with, apostolic or evangelical aims.

Another church response to immigration has been at the level of individual clergy or religious actors who were instrumental in initiating pro-migrant NGOs.[109] While most of the episcopal and religious order-run organizations are identifiable as Catholic Church organizations, those NGOs initiated by individual clergy or religious actors have developed into secular agencies and accommodate religiosity and secularity in a variety of ways at an organizational level. These include the

---

[105] Department of Social, Community and Family Affairs, White Paper on a Framework for Supporting Voluntary Activity and for Developing the Relationship between the State and the Community and Voluntary sector (Dublin, 2000), p. 16, section 2.32.

[106] Ibid., p. 9, section 1.2.

[107] Ibid., p. 17, section 2.38.

[108] Report of the Task Force on Active Citizenship (Dublin, 2007), p. 43.

[109] A further, although more difficult to trace, response is that of individual clergy and religious actors who act in an individual capacity, providing advocacy and support for particular groups of migrants, often from countries where they worked as missionaries.

Immigrant Council of Ireland, the *Migrant Rights Centre Ireland, NASC. The Irish Immigrant Support Centre; Doras Luimni* and the *Irish Refugee Council*. The work of these organizations is directed primarily by technical expertise in social policy, community work, human rights, legal skills, efficient systems and financial management. However, continuing church connections are visible insofar as religious founders remain important spokespersons for some organizations; many have ongoing funding from founders' congregations; and most have clerical or religious members on their management boards. Many of these organizations have been central in the recent development of Irish city and county Integration Plans.

Alongside these Catholic Church-initiated organizations, FBOs have multiplied 'among "new" minority communities'.[110] However, the lack of 'a longstanding infrastructure of policy and practice in relation to ethnic diversity' in Ireland has hindered their ability to develop 'the social and economic capital necessary both to achieve sustainability and to function strategically'.[111] For example, although the institutionalization of Islam has progressed considerably in recent years, Scharbrodt and Sakaranaho argue that 'the "respect for religion" in Ireland works well in order to keep the status quo [and] ... does not sufficiently address the issues of cultural and religious difference'.[112] As such, those organizations initiated by and/or run by Catholic Church actors have an advantage over minority religion-led initiatives. Indeed, the national infrastructure of migrant integration services established by Catholic clergy and members of religious orders is testimony to the advantageous position of the Church.

The pivotal position occupied by these organizations has also been enabled by the unique position of the Catholic Church amongst civil society actors in having access to buildings and the capacity to organize and mobilize volunteers.[113] Church actors were able to seek seed-funding through religious orders and other sources to initiate projects which, in the absence of any substantive state funding, were subsequently able to ensure medium-term sustainability by attracting funding from the two philanthropic funding sources: Atlantic Philanthropies and the One Foundation. Atlantic Philanthropies funded pro-migrant organizations under its reconciliation and human rights programme. A central aspect of its funding work involves 'supporting organizational development, such as strategic planning, board development, fundraising and succession planning'[114]. The One Foundation is '[f]ounded on strong business principles' and pursues 'active philanthropy' in order

---

[110]   Alice Feldman, Deo L. Ndakengerwa, Ann Nolan and Carmen Frese, *Diversity, Civil Society and Social Change in Ireland: A North-South Comparison of the Role of Immigrant/'New' Minority Ethnic-led Community and Voluntary Sector Organisations* (Dublin, 2005), p. 6.

[111]   Ibid.

[112]   Scharbrodt and Sakaranaho, 'Islam and Muslims in the Republic of Ireland', p. 480.

[113]   Gray, 'Making Migration a Public Issue'.

[114]   The Atlantic Philanthropies website.

to generate long-term solutions to issues such as 'the integration of minorities'.[115] It aims to 'provide high level entrepreneurial knowledge, skills and resources, and work closely with non profits to maximize the value of [One Foundation] investment'.[116]

Both philanthropic foundation funders have set particular social justice agendas and take a 'calculative' approach to the achievement of service targets and outcomes, thus promoting an 'audit culture' associated with neoliberal forms of governance. As the Catholic Church-initiated NGOs gained capacity, they became secularized and were made more accountable through the targets and performance indicators set by philanthropic foundation funders. Those Catholic Church actors involved were able to maintain legitimacy as religious actors through their unique pastoral commitment and their social entrepreneurship, such that these organizations have come to be seen as both socially innovative and holistic in their approach to the achievement of integration.[117] The legitimacy of church actors was partly achieved by way of a kind of disaffiliation 'from the mother organization', namely, the Catholic Church in Ireland.[118] As such, the wider discrediting of the institutional Church is overcome through an uneasy compromise that brings pastoral power as a holistic response to migrant 'need' together with neoliberal rationalities of rule. This pragmatic compromise enables such organizations to act on society to bring those migrants on the border into the game, for it is only through inclusion in the game that individuals are governable, as they come to govern themselves according to economic laws.[119]

The particular role of the Catholic Church was inflected in new ways with the development of a state-based infrastructure for migrant integration in 2007. A Minister of State for Integration was appointed and the Office of the Minister for Integration (OMSI) was established to develop and coordinate integration policy across government departments, agencies and services. This was followed by the publication of an integration policy document '*Migration Nation: Statement on Integration Strategy and Diversity Management*' (MN) in 2008, which set out the key principles of state policy on integration.[120] *Migration Nation* acknowledges a

---

[115]   The One Foundation website.

[116]   Ibid.

[117]   For example, Sr. Stanislaus Kennedy (Religious Sisters of Charity) established Social Innovations Ireland (SII) out of which grew the Immigrant Council of Ireland (srstan.ie).

[118]   Xabier Itçaina, 'The Roman Catholic Church and the Immigration Issue: The Relative Secularisation of Political Life in Spain', *American Behavioral Scientist Journal*, 49/1 (2006): p. 1482.

[119]   Donzelot, 'Michel Foucault and Liberal Intelligence', p. 130.

[120]   *Migration Nation: Statement on Integration Strategy and Diversity Management* (Dublin, 2008). The Irish Naturalisation and Immigration Service (INIS) had been established in 2005 to provide a 'one stop shop' in relation to asylum, immigration, citizenship and visas. However, in the same year as the *Migration Nation* document was

Europe-wide concern regarding the 'radicalization of Muslims' that has 'not so far come to the fore in Ireland'.[121]

Honohan and Rougier suggest that unlike other EU countries, neither the 'security' issue, nor 'Muslim radicalization' have been emphasized in Ireland.[122] They account for this partly on the basis that

> [t]he Muslim community in Ireland is quite different [from other EU countries] in terms of its varied geographic origins and socio-demographic composition ... and the fact that the Irish Government and institutions have sought to establish a dialogue with the Muslim community and have allowed for some accommodation of religious practices.[123]

Nonetheless, *Migration Nation* states that 'integration policy will have to address the security and social cohesion issues which arise from such immigration'.[124] It also identifies Muslim radicalism as 'one of the greatest challenges in European integration thinking' and calls for effective Muslim representation in ongoing dialogue focusing on the clarification of 'civic responsibilities' of migrants which 'has been a major component in international intercultural dialogue events'.[125] However, given the socio-historical positioning of different faiths and religious groups in Ireland, the grounds of such dialogue cannot be equal.[126] Therefore, this key policy strategy of inter-faith dialogue includes immigrants in the 'framework of equal inequality' which promotes competition by ensuring there is no exclusion.[127]

Noting the central role of faith groups and organizations in promoting inclusion and social cohesion, *Migrant Nation* states:

> Migration has affected all faith-based groups by increasing the demand for their religious services and pastoral care ... Many congregations have been re-vitalised by the arrival of migrants. All of the faith-based groups have expanded the range and scope of their activities in response to the needs of newly-arrived migrants. ... Because of their attachment to their religious beliefs and practices

---

published, the National Consultative Committee on Racism and Interculturalism (NCCRI) and the National Action Plan against Racism (NAPR), both state-funded bodies seen as central to the project of integration, were abolished and funding was cut for language support classes in schools.

121 *Migration Nation*, p. 36.
122 Honohan and Rougier, 'Tolerance and Cultural Diversity Discourses in Ireland', p. 4.
123 Ibid.
124 *Migration Nation*, p. 34.
125 Migration Nation, pp. 36–7.
126 Scharbrodt and Sakaranaho, 'Islam and Muslims in the Republic of Ireland'.
127 Donzelot, 'Michel Foucault and Liberal Intelligence', p. 124.

many migrants look to religious authorities for information and assistance on settling in Ireland.[128]

The document goes on to note a need to 'assist the faith-based groups in carrying out work related to integration' by holding discussions with these groups 'with a view to putting in place arrangements to financially support that aspect of the groups' activities'.[129] Through state funding for such organizations, the pastoral power formerly embedded in the welfare state is made to work through diverse civil society organizations which must be entrepreneurial in carving out their presence and sustaining it. As key actors in this field, Catholic Church-initiated or run organizations have much to gain if and when this policy is fully implemented. Although the Ministry for Integration was abolished with the formation of a new government in 2011, *Migration Nation* remains the basis of state policy on migrant integration.

We are left with the question of how to account for this notable evidence of Catholic social activism at a time when the institutional church is discredited and when neoliberal governing rationalities emphasize freedom and personal responsibility? In response, I argue that the religious authority of the Catholic Church actors, although much contested, is enlisted into governmental programmes as an intervention motivated by an apparently holistic approach to human well-being (addressing all needs, from spiritual to economic) that works *with* the apparent freedom of civil society, RNGOs and FBOs as well as migrants themselves in the governance of integration. Such an 'unfolding of the formally political sphere upon non-political agencies'[130] involves the creation of conditions for competition and choice in the project of migrant integration. This 'appeal to the values of civil society' legitimizes 'approaches to the reform of public services and public provision that breach earlier modes of separation of Church and State'.[131, 132]

Church, FBO, state and market relations are re-envisioned through manageable, measurable and collaborative technologies of performance measurement and their effectiveness in integrating the 'wrong kinds' of immigrants by building their capacities for participation. This is not a 'natural' process but requires the inculcation of skills in order to develop 'self governing entities that exercise choice'.[133] Through an assemblage of rationalities and techniques of neoliberal governance (social partnership, public sector reform, community and voluntary sector recognition and mobilization, active citizenship, migrant integration through religious affiliation) we can identify the emergence of favourable conditions for

---

[128]   *Migration Nation*, p. 44.

[129]   Ibid., p. 45.

[130]   Dean, *Governing Societies*, p. 116, emphasis in original.

[131]   Ibid., 117.

[132]   Of course, while most liberal democracies adopted some mode of separation of church and state, this has never been the case in the socio-political context of Ireland.

[133]   Lippert, 'Rationalities and Refugee Resettlement', p. 382.

church actors to compete in a marketized civil society. Here the project of migrant integration through Catholic Church-based social justice initiatives involves preventing limit cases of exclusion which impede individuals from participating in a society of 'structured inequalities'.[134]

Conclusion

Although the public role of the Catholic Church is more visibly contested than at any time since the formation of the state, the growth of the Muslim population and public focus on religious diversity in Ireland over the past decade have put religion on the public agenda in new ways. Moreover, the problematization of immigration as an issue of integration and, to some extent, in terms of the (potential) threat of religious extremism, has created the conditions for Catholic Church actors to take up this governmental project. However, given the depletion in church personnel and resources and the absence of state funding, it has been necessary for church actors to partner with philanthropic foundations. So, in similar ways to Spain,[135] but in contrast with France and Quebec where principles of *laïcité* and 'open secularism' apply respectively, the decline of the Catholic Church as a dominant social institution in Ireland does not necessarily mean the demise of church influence as a civil society actor.

This chapter examines the transformations wrought by neoliberal political rationalities in relation to the public role of Irish Catholic Church actors in the governance of migrant integration. By drawing on Foucauldian and neo-Foucauldian work on governmentality, the Catholic Church, RNGOs, FBOs, civil society and the state are discussed as assemblages of practices rather than as unified institutions and emerge as artefacts of neoliberal governmentality. The neoliberal state is distinguished from the welfare state which protected against the vagaries of the market insofar as it intervenes primarily to create favourable market conditions for economic growth, competition and entrepreneurship of the self.

The displacement of pastoral power from state welfare apparatuses to a marketized civil society has facilitated the reappearance of the Catholic Church, despite a depletion in its personnel and capital in recent decades. Now sited in civil society organizations including religious and faith-based organizations, pastoral power can be seen as a necessary condition for neoliberal governance insofar as it renders capable those constituted as incapable.[136] Unlike its workings through the welfare state, it now relies on the entrepreneurial conduct of service providers, service users and, in some cases, church members, to engage wisely in the marketized domains of civil society and religious practice. Furthermore, this shift of pastoral power involves the creation of hybridized religious spaces that

---

[134]   McNay, 'Self as Enterprise', p. 64.

[135]   Itçaina, 'The Roman Catholic Church and the Immigration Issue'.

[136]   Lippert, *Sanctuary, Sovereignty, Sacrifice*.

combine with secular authorities of professional expertise and audit culture such that church spaces and practices are secularizing in new ways. These shifts involve a reconfiguration of state and church relations which are reworked as the effect of neoliberal governmental technologies.[137] By carving out a civil society role in the project of migrant integration, Catholic Church actors in Ireland have reasserted a role for the Church as 'an expert in humanity'[138] and in migrant integration.[139] These church initiatives also demonstrate the ways in which neoliberalism can be enacted through religious processes and partnerships and its potential to function as a 'mobile technology' moving across domains.[140]

However, as the resources of the Catholic Church in Ireland both in terms of personnel and capital diminish, as the two time-limited philanthropic funding foundations close by 2015, and as the state remains entrenched in austerity-based budgeting for the foreseeable future, the sustainability of the current governmental model of migrant integration services is in question. Although new spaces of legitimacy have been carved out by and for the Catholic Church through neoliberal rationalities and technologies of rule, its key civil society role in the governance of migrant integration as discussed in this chapter will, no doubt, be subject to ongoing reinvention and hybridization in the years to come.

Acknowledgements

Thank you to Orla McDonnell for comments on earlier versions of this chapter. This chapter draws on research undertaken as part of the Irish Research Council for the Humanities and Social Sciences project 'The Irish Catholic Church and the Politics of Migration' (www.ul.ie/icctmp).

---

[137] Lemke, 'Foucault, Governmentality, and Critique, Rethinking Marxism'; Lemke, 'An Indigestible Meal?', p. 18.

[138] Danielle Hervieu-Léger, *Vers un nouveau Christianisme?* (Paris, 1996), p. 296, in Mooney, 'The Catholic Bishops Conferences of the United States and France', p. 1467.

[139] Breda Gray and Ria O'Sullivan Lago, 'Migrant Chaplains: Mediators of Catholic Church Transnationalism', *Irish Journal of Sociology*, 19/2 (2011): pp. 93–109.

[140] Aihwa Ong, 'Neoliberalism as a Mobile Technology', *Transactions of the Institute of British Geographers*, 32/1 (2007): pp. 3–8.

Chapter 5
Faith, Welfare and the Formation of the Modern American Right

Jason Hackworth

Does God Want You to Be a Neoliberal?

In 2006, *Time Magazine* published an issue on the prosperity gospel – an Americanized offshoot of the larger Pentecostal movement.[1] On the front cover, the magazine's editors suggestively asked 'Does God want you to be rich?' to foreground their interviews with clergy who earnestly believe that the Bible does in fact outline such a hope on the part of God. Prosperity theologians cite a number of biblical verses, but none more than *Deuteronomy 8:18* which reads:

> But thou shalt remember the Lord thy God: for it is he that giveth thee power to
> get wealth, that he may establish his covenant which he swear unto thy fathers,
> as it is this day.

Prosperity ministers, who currently occupy three of the four largest congregations in America, see verses like this one as a clear message that God does in fact want you to be rich. If you are faithful and generous (to the church) you will be rewarded. Digging a bit deeper, it is possible to find other elements of the Christian religious community within the US who invoke the Bible to justify what many view as the secular realm of welfare and economics.[2] Fellows at the Acton Institute in Grand Rapids Michigan, for example, generate dozens of policy papers detailing the synergies between entrepreneurial capitalism and Christianity. They reserve particularly sharp ire for the welfare state which they view as a betrayal of biblical and economic principles.[3] Moreover, high-profile American Religious Right leaders like Jerry Falwell and Marvin Olasky have long devoted significant attention in their

---

[1]   David Van Biema and Jeff Chu, 'Does God Want You to Be Rich?', *Time Magazine*, Sept. 18 (2006), <www.time.com/time/magazine/article/0,9171,1533448,00.html>, Accessed October 2008.

[2]   Jason Hackworth, 'Compassionate Neoliberalism?: Evangelical Christianity, the Welfare State, and the Politics of the Right', *Studies in Political Economy*, 86 (2010): pp. 83–108.

[3]   Jay Richards, *Money, Greed, and God: Why Capitalism is the Solution and Not the Problem* (New York, 2009).

theologically inspired political interventions to the economy and welfare.[4] Their position amounts to a biblically inspired neoliberalism. They cite both God and the patriarchs of neoliberalism to justify low taxes, the abolition of secular welfare and free trade. There is, in short, a small but committed and influential group of neoliberals who have very specific biblical verses to justify their beliefs. According to this line of thought, God does not only want you to be rich. He evidently wants low taxes for the wealthy, little to no state-run welfare and economic policies that emphasize free trade. God is evidently a very committed neoliberal.

Within established narratives of neoliberalism, the Religious Right and arguments of this sort play a very small role and for good reason.[5] Many of the leading proponents of neoliberalism were either very private with their religion and did not insert it in obvious ways into their economic theories, or were avowed atheists as in the case of Ayn Rand.[6] The response of the religious studies community to these movements, by contrast, has been to notice them yet marginalize them with respect to theological orthodoxy, by suggesting that they are built on an incorrect or incomplete understanding of the Bible. In the same *Time Magazine* article mentioned earlier, Rick Warren – who is not exactly what most would think of as a left-wing ideologue – scoffs at the credibility of the prosperity gospel, citing other biblical verses, mostly from the New Testament, that counter the claims made by the movement. Others have emphasized the extant or emergent power of left-leaning theologies within the political sphere.[7] Still others have side-stepped the God-as-neoliberal group altogether by focusing almost entirely on what they see as progressive incarnations of religiously inspired social welfare.[8]

---

[4]   Jerry Falwell, *Listen America* (Garden City, 1980); Marvin Olasky, *The Tragedy of American Compassion* (Washington, 1992).

[5]   David Harvey, *A Brief History of Neoliberalism* (Oxford, 2005); Jason Hackworth, *The Neoliberal City: Governance, Ideology, and Development in American Urbanism* (Ithaca, 2007); Naomi Klein, *Shock Doctrine: The Rise of Disaster Capitalism* (Toronto, 2007).

[6]   Jennifer Burns, *Goddess of the Market: Ayn Rand and the American Right* (Oxford, 2009).

[7]   Frederick Clarkson (ed.), *Dispatches from the Religious Left* (New York, 2009); E.J. Dionne, *Souled Out: Reclaiming Faith and Politics after the Religious Right* (Princeton, 2008); Jim Wallis, *The Great Awakening: Reviving Faith and Politics in a Post-religious Right America* (New York, 2008).

[8]   R. Alan Hays, 'Habitat for Humanity: Building Social Capital through Faith Based Service', *Journal of Urban Affairs*, 24/3 (2002): pp. 247–69; David Conradson, 'Expressions of Charity and Action towards Justice: Faith-based Welfare Provision in Urban New Zealand', *Urban Studies*, 45/10 (2008): pp. 2117–41; Paul Cloke, 'Deliver Us from Evil? Prospects for Living Ethically and Acting Politically in Human Geography', *Progress in Human Geography*, 26/5 (2002): pp. 587–604. For earlier versions of this thesis see: Michael Pacione, 'The Ecclesiastical Community of Interest as a Response to Urban Poverty and Deprivation', *Transactions of the Institute of British Geographers*, 15/2 (1990): pp. 193–204; David Ley, 'The City and Good and Evil: Reflections on Christian and Marxist Interpretations', *Antipode*, 6 (1974): pp. 66–74.

Some have publicly pondered how the Religious Right can avoid the Gospel of Luke and the narratives of cooperation in constructing such a narrative.[9]

I do not wish to wade into a theological argument here except to make two very simple, superficial observations: 1) whatever influence progressive theologies have in the political sphere, they are categorically overshadowed by that of the political organizations, congregations and denominations representing a Rightist view of the Bible on matters of welfare and economy within the North American context; and 2) the Bible, like any other religious text, is an exceptionally varied and internally contradictory piece of work; I am deeply sceptical of the notion that either the Right or the Left can find a singular position from this text. What I do wish to do here is to suggest that the religion-neoliberal alliance is a political one – it has fissures like any other coalition and there are important precedents from which we can learn a great deal. The US case offers a great example from which to build an analysis of this sort. On the one hand, it offers a high-profile case of an apparently smooth alliance between neoliberals and religious fundamentalists. From this alliance it is useful to consider using the term 'religious neoliberalism', both in the sense that there is a widespread devotion, almost a religious one, to neoliberalism but also, less obviously (but more importantly), the Religious Right has been crucial for providing political support for neoliberal policies even though its stated aims and mission are different.[10] Yet on the other hand, the case has much to teach us about the tensions and political difficulties of fusing these worldviews in practice. The philosophical and political fissures between religious and market fundamentalism make the puritanical notion of religious neoliberalism a politically uneasy alliance. As scholars of religion and neoliberalism begin to explore these connections in non-North American locales, a great deal can be learned from the experience where this alliance is arguably most historically rooted and politically embedded. These realms interact in a variety of ways. The point here is not to summarize all of them, but to focus on the arena where they collide in the most overt and telling way: social welfare.[11]

Religious Neoliberalism?

The prevailing narrative of neoliberalism has foregrounded the importance of secular economic scholars, concepts and justifications for its rise. The work of economists such as Friedrich Hayek, Milton Friedman and Ludwig von Mises

---

[9]   William Connolly, *Capitalism and Christianity, American Style* (Durham, 2008).

[10]   Jason Hackworth, *Faith Based: Religious Neoliberalism and the Politics of Welfare in the United States* (Athens, 2012); Jason Hackworth, 'Neoliberalism for God's Sake: Sectarian Justifications for Secular Policy Transformation in the United States', in Arie Molendijk, Justin Beaumont, and Chris Jedan (eds), *Exploring the Postsecular: The Religious, the Political, the Urban* (Leiden, 2010), pp. 357–79.

[11]   For a more complete version of this argument, see Hackworth, *Faith Based*, or Hackworth, 'Compassionate Neoliberalism?'.

are particularly central to this narrative.[12] Though once dismissed as the 'lunatic fringe' by a leading historian of liberalism as recently as the 1960s, the ideas of these scholars have become canonical in modern day neoliberalism.[13] All were engaged in the project of selectively highlighting the ideas of classical liberals – Smith, Hume, Acton, Locke and (James) Mill in particular. Hayek, Friedman and von Mises venerated various economic rationalities in the construction of society, in particular the market, property, individual freedom and state deregulation. Along with dozens of other like-minded economists, the three formed the Mont Pelerin Society to develop such ideas and advocate their diffusion.[14] The ideational influence of scholarly economic thought of this sort on the narrative of neoliberalism is difficult to overstate.

The simple fact that many of its proponents happen to be economists is not the only way in which economic thought dominates the narrative of neoliberalism's rise. A variety of other scholars have highlighted the importance of economic rationalities for this. Dumenil and Levy have, for example, foregrounded the role of tax policy. They argue that neoliberalism may have complicated ideational roots, but that its political salience is rooted in a widespread desire amongst elites to reduce their tax burden.[15] Other scholars have highlighted the importance of economic logics that are used by various institutions to promulgate neoliberalism. The logic of neoliberalism is shielded by an ostensibly non-political economics, and used to justify 'necessary' interventions by global bond-rating agencies like Moody's, large global institutions like the International Monetary Fund and think tanks like the Cato Institute.[16] The interventions of these institutions are shrouded in economistic fatalisms – 'choose the neoliberal path or else (… your economy will fail; … your state will fail; … your freedoms will be curtailed)'.

In general, the role of secular economics – as a set of ideas, as a discipline, as a justification – is central to the growing scholarly narrative that is tracing the rise of neoliberalism. To be sure, there are good reasons for such a focus. First and foremost, the revival of classical liberalism in the twentieth century was largely spearheaded by secular-minded economists. Hayek, Friedman, von Mises and their infamous Mont Pelerin Society of like-minded economists became incredibly effective activists for their cause. Second, powerful organizations like the IMF and

---

[12]   Jamie Peck, 'Remaking Laissez-faire', *Progress in Human Geography*, 32/1 (2008): pp. 3–43; Hackworth, *Neoliberal City*; Harvey, *Brief History*.

[13]   Harry Girvetz, *The Evolution of Liberalism* (New York, 1963).

[14]   Peck, 'Remaking Laissez-faire'.

[15]   Gerard Dumenil and Dominique Levy, *Capital Resurgent: Roots of the Neoliberal Revolution* (Cambridge, 2004).

[16]   Jason Hackworth, 'Local Autonomy, Bond-rating Agencies and Neoliberal Urbanism in the US', *International Journal of Urban and Regional Research*, 26/4 (2002): pp. 707–25; Jamie Peck, 'Liberating the City: Between New York and New Orleans', *Urban Geography*, 27/8 (2006): pp. 681–713; Richard Peet, *Unholy Trinity: The IMF, World Bank, and WTO* (Boston, 2003).

WTO are organized around a secular economic logic. And third, regardless of whether economic thinking can explain the rise of neoliberalism, material changes to the economy in a variety of locations around the world have been successfully used by proponents of neoliberalism. Whether it be the 'shock therapy' of mid-1990s Russian economic reconstruction or more immediate 'crises' like Hurricane Katrina or the war in Iraq, secular economic ideas have been used to sell, depoliticize and promote the growth of neoliberalism.[17]

But while there are certainly valid reasons for using a secular economic lens to understand neoliberalism's rise as an intellectual project, such an approach falls considerably short of explaining why the idea has political salience. While we can usefully trace the ideational rise of neoliberalism through economic texts, concepts and institutions, such an approach does not tell us much about why the idea has gained political traction – why it is adopted in many different countries, and why it is so appealing during times of crisis when it has such a clear track record of long- and medium-term failure. The goal of this chapter is to consider the ways in which various radical right Christian philosophical movements support neoliberalism (particularly the destruction of the welfare state) in an ideational way, and then to speculate on the actualized influence that these movements have on welfare policy. My argument is as follows. First, if neoliberalism were abstracted as an isolated secular project as laid out by its proponents including Hayek and Friedman, it would not enjoy nearly as much popular political success as it has had in the past 30 years. Its record on 'solving' economic problems is a dismal one, and there are no popular movements with neoliberalism as the central objective. Neoliberalism's ability to morph and adapt to various movements has allowed it to be coupled with ideas that have their own forms of legitimacy, from which neoliberalism can benefit.

While this angle has not yet been developed in the literature, fortunately there are a number of precedents and parallel literatures that can be used to guide and justify such a focus. First, in a general sense, the work of Max Weber is perhaps the most important and influential precedent for this approach. Weber famously argued that it is the Calvinist work ethic – particularly as exercised by Puritan sects – which conditioned societies in Europe and the US to accept the premises of liberal capitalism.[18] In particular, he highlighted the importance of the theological concept of a divine calling for a particular profession, as well as the inclination to save, work hard and avoid immediate gratification. These features, he argued, were central to the development of the form of capitalism that began in nineteenth century Europe (Germany in particular) and has diffused to much of Western Europe and North America today. Hudson and Coukos apply this logic to the 1996 Welfare Reform Act in the United States, suggesting that the deep-seated

---

17   Harvey, *Brief History*; Peck, 'Liberating the City'; Klein, *Shock Doctrine*.

18   Max Weber, *The Protestant Ethic and the Spirit of Capitalism* (New York, 2003 [1905]); Max Weber, 'Introduction to the Economic Ethics of the World Religions', in Sam Whimster (ed.), *The Essential Weber* (London, 2004), pp. 55–80.

assumptions identified by Weber had been reborn in the efforts to reform welfare – in particular, the notions of a 'deserving' and 'undeserving' poor, and the sanctity of work.[19] In a similar vein, Kahl uses a neo-Weberian approach to suggest that the socio-religious underpinnings of various societies throughout the world can be used to explain a great deal about their welfare systems.[20] The Anglo-American system, he argues, is dominated by an intense individualism, rooted to the Calvinist ethic, that opens a political space for policies like religiously based welfare. Weberian work (and the work of neo-Weberians) not only forms a justification for considering the role of divinely inspired logics on economic tendencies, but also provides some initial clues about the particular influence of Calvinist thought as it inflects modern day debates about welfare, religion and economy.

Other scholars, namely historians who are not necessarily working from a Weberian point of view, have also provided work that can serve an important role of precedence here. In particular, the work of the historian Boyd Hilton stands out. Hilton reminds us that evangelicals were among the most fervent supporters of the original classical liberals in late eighteenth-century England and Scotland.[21] To Hilton though, it was not that evangelicals were actually liberal in a classical sense, but rather that they saw the brutality of economic conditions faced by the poor as God's punishment for the Original Sin. So while the details of why the status quo existed were different – for classical liberal economists, widespread poverty was simply a 'natural' feature of the market; for evangelicals it was divine punishment – the policy implications were the same: *laissez-faire* governance.[22] These works are important not only because they draw direct connections between religious fundamentalism and classical liberalism, but because they underscore the point that this union, while politically powerful, is rooted in different logics.

A third, more contemporary group of political economists, whose work is unified more by topic than a particular school of thought, has attempted more directly to understand the interaction between evangelical Christianity and neoliberalism in the US, or what Connolly deems the 'evangelical-capitalist resonance machine'.[23] Connolly argues that a political 'machine' has created a

---

19   Kenneth Hudson and Andrea Coukos, 'The Dark Side of the Protestant Ethic: A Comparative Analysis of Welfare Reform', *Sociological Theory*, 23/1 (2005): pp. 1–24.

20   Sigrun Kahl, 'The Religious Roots of Modern Poverty Policy: Catholic, Lutheran, and Reformed Protestant Traditions Compared', *Archives Europeennes de Sociologie*, 46/1 (2005): pp. 91–126, 171.

21   Boyd Hilton, *The Age of Atonement: The Influence of Evangelicalism on Social and Economic Thought, 1785–1865* (Oxford, 1986).

22   Gordon Bigelow, in a more popular piece for *Harper's Magazine*, found a similar relationship between nineteenth century evangelicals and economists: Gordon Bigelow, 'Let There Be Markets: The Evangelical Roots of Economics', *Harper's Magazine*, 310/1860 (2005): pp. 33–8.

23   William Connolly, 'The Evangelical-capitalist Resonance Machine', *Political Theory*, 33/6 (2005): pp. 869–86.

political space in which revenge against non-believers (of neoliberalism and of Christianity) have been woven together into a powerful machine. He argues that both elements (neoliberals and evangelicals) work together in a way that magnifies the intensity of their political critique and sometimes begins to merge. He points, in particular, to the importance of the 'end times' prophesies that have been very influential amongst evangelicals. This worldview has merged with a critique of secular governmental institutions. In this view such organizations that 'persecuted' the true believers before Armageddon will be punished. In a similar work, Kintz argues that Christian fundamentalist literalism has infused economic discourses in the US to quell dissent about economic alternatives.[24] The discourse shifts to 'surrendering' to reality rather than conceiving alternatives.[25]

Faith-based 'Fusion' and the Idea of Religious Welfare

Popular conceptions of 'the Right' in the American context often lump 'conservatives' into one undifferentiated block. But there has long been a fissure between two of its main constituencies: religious fundamentalists and neoliberals (also known as economic conservatives and libertarians). Formal efforts to fuse the neoliberal and religiously conservative wings of the American Right have existed at least since the 1960s and have been covered elsewhere in great detail.[26] But it is worth revisiting a few points in this history to set the framework for understanding the contemporary importance of the idea of welfare at fusing and fraying the Right. Perhaps the most important point is that the alliance between neoliberalism and conservative religiosity in the US is neither natural nor politically tranquil. As Sager, a member of the neoliberal wing, evocatively describes it, 'Whatever alliances have been formed, libertarians have always tended to see social conservatives as rubes ready to thump nonbelievers on the head with the Bible the first chance they get, and social conservatives have always tended to see libertarians as dope-smoking devil worshippers'.[27] But the success of the Republican Party, and the Right in general, is in no small measure due to the durability of their unlikely union, particularly since the 1980s.

Prior to the 1960s, the Religious Right as the well-organized political entity that we know today did not exist. Many evangelical Christians in the US were

---

[24]   Linda Kintz, *Between Jesus and the Market: The Emotions that Matter in Right-wing America* (Durham, 1997); Linda Kintz, 'Finding the Strength to Surrender: Marriage, Market Theocracy, and the Spirit of America', *Theory, Culture and Society*, 24/4 (2007): pp. 111–30.

[25]   Wendy Brown, 'American Nightmare: Neoliberalism, Neoconservatism, and De-democratization', *Political Theory*, 34/6 (2006): pp. 690–714.

[26]   Ryan Sager, *The Elephant in the Room: Evangelicals, Libertarians, and the Battle to Control the Republican Party* (Hoboken, NJ, 2006); Hackworth, *Faith-Based*.

[27]   Sager, *Elephant in the Room*, p. 8.

either averse to politics, or remained loyal to the Democratic Party for its pro-welfare stances.[28] Recognizing the political possibilities of moving beyond the issues that divided them, high-profile conservatives began a conscious attempt to build bridges between neoliberals[29] and religious conservatives. The most famous instance took place within the pages of William F. Buckley's *National Review*, which published a series of essays in the mid-1960s designed to bridge or 'fuse' the two wings together into a political force.[30] These efforts had some success among elite conservative intellectuals, but did not have an immediate impact on rank-and-file evangelicals in the United States, in part because there was still a residual aversion to engaging in politics, and the institutions necessary for doing so effectively were not yet established.[31] Ironically, it was the presidential campaign of a Democrat, Jimmy Carter, that would serve as a political awakening for the evangelical community and the Religious Right as a political force. Carter was the first modern president to campaign openly as an evangelical Christian – albeit a centre-left one. This community, of course, quickly and decisively turned against Carter and the Democratic Party within a few years. By the 1980s, Religious Right organizations such as Focus on the Family, and new educational institutions like Jerry Falwell's Liberty University, served to organize and consolidate the political power of religious conservatives. With very few exceptions this power was used to promote candidates within the Republican Party, and when issues of economics or welfare did come up, it was used to promote an economically conservative agenda.[32]

By the 1990s, figures in the Religious Right were not simply supporting neoliberals as a matter of political pragmatism; they were beginning to build elaborate arguments around the assertion that the Bible actually lays out a template for a government without welfare and an economy without regulation.[33] Perhaps the most tangible outcome of these efforts was the movement that led to the

---

[28]   John Green, 'Seeking a Place: Evangelical Protestants and Public Engagement in the Twentieth Century', in Ronald Sider and David Knippers (eds), *Toward and Evangelical Public Policy: Political Strategies for the Health of a Nation* (Grand Rapids, 2005), pp. 35–63; Ronald Sider and Donald Knippers, 'Introduction', in Ronald Sider and David Knippers (eds), *Toward and Evangelical Public Policy: Political Strategies for the Health of a Nation* (Grand Rapids, 2005); Clyde Wilcox and Carin Larson, *Onward Christian Soldiers: The Religious Right in American Politics, Westview Press* (Boulder, 2006).

[29]   I use the terms 'neoliberal', 'market fundamentalist', 'libertarian', and 'economic conservative' more or less interchangeably in this chapter. 'Neoliberal' and 'market fundamentalist' are labels used by scholars critical of the movement, while 'libertarian' and 'economic conservative' are more frequently used as self-identifiers. In my view, the labels encapsulate a broadly similar worldview: a state that is involved in as little social welfare, taxation and economic regulation as possible (see Hackworth, 2007 for more on my arguments about this).

[30]   Sager, *Elephant in the Room*.

[31]   Green, 'Seeking a Place'; Wilcox and Larson, *Onward Christian Soldiers*.

[32]   José Casanova, *Public Religions in the Modern World* (Chicago, 1994).

[33]   Hackworth, 'Neoliberalism for God's Sake'.

establishment of Charitable Choice in 1996. Charitable Choice was a provision in the larger Welfare Reform Act which prohibited discrimination against religious providers who wanted government money to fund their efforts. It was the brainchild of Religious Right hero John Ashcroft – then a US Senator from Missouri – and was built on the assumption that churches could deliver welfare much more effectively than government. The Charitable Choice provision actually changed very little in the short term, as the Clinton Administration insisted, as had historically been the case, that places of worship build a wall of separation between their efforts to proselytize and their efforts to provide welfare. The myth that faith-based social service providers were being discriminated against served as a powerful platform for the then candidate George W. Bush's run for the presidency.[34] He promised to 'end the discrimination' by redirecting more money to religious providers. The idea was exciting to religious conservatives who felt that a dose of biblical 'tough love' was exactly what welfare recipients needed, and provided hope to neoliberals who had long felt that the government should not be in the business of social welfare.[35] It was even seen as a way to dislodge certain constituencies from the Democratic Party, such as Black evangelicals.[36]

Though the Bush administration attracted a great deal of scrutiny for uttering the phrase 'Faith-based Initiative', the actual impact on the welfare landscape was mixed at best. There was not a discernable increase in the use of faith-based organizations *vis-à-vis* secular ones, and several of the key mandates of the initiatives never came to fruition. Much less debatable, however, was the expansion and deepening of the *conversation* about the idea of faith-based welfare. Though the Bush administration had certain goals and certain faith-based institutions in mind, the public conversation around the issue revealed a great deal of variation in both the literal meaning of the concept, but also in its political utility. This variation, in my view, served to fray rather than fuse the religious-neoliberal coalition. That is, while it was an effort by the Bush administration to replace secular welfare with sectarian welfare – an idea that appealed to both religious conservatives and neoliberals in the abstract – the messy details of implementation and the varied meanings of 'faith-based welfare' eventually served to alienate *both* neoliberals and religious conservatives. What follows is an attempt to summarize some of the prominent meanings of faith-based welfare that emerged from this

---

[34] I deem it a myth in part because religious providers such as Lutheran Social Services and Catholic Charities had long received government funding. The only providers that were excluded were those who had sectarian limitations on who they hired or for whom they provided care. The only discriminatees in this case were the discriminators.

[35] Lawrence Mead, *The New Paternalism: Supervisory Approaches to Poverty* (Washington, 1997); Lawrence Mead, 'A Biblical Response to Poverty', in Mary Bane and Lawrence Mead (eds), *Lifting Up The Poor: A Dialogue on Religion, Poverty and Welfare Reform* (Washington, 2003), pp. 53–106; Olasky, *The Tragedy of American Compassion*.

[36] Sager, *Elephant in the Room*; Amy Black, Douglas Koopman, and David Ryden, *Of Little Faith: The Politics of George W. Bush's Faith-based Initiatives* (Washington, 2004).

context. As will become clear, the policy pursuit of some might have furthered religious neoliberalism, but the pursuit of others categorically would not. Pursuing an undifferentiated 'Faith-based Initiative' thus complicated efforts to consolidate religious neoliberalism.

The Varied Meanings of Religious Welfare: a Simple Typology

There has been a great deal of effort in the past decade to provide a better typological understanding of faith-based organizations,[37] particularly in understanding how and when religion is a part of the social services that they provide.[38] From this literature FBOs are positioned and understood in at least four ways: as extensions, enhancements, catalysts and alternatives (both regressive and progressive) for government-based welfare.[39] These themes are both idealized archetypes that reveal themselves in discourses, and actualized practices in which FBOs are engaged. Each entails a different set of policy implications and normative assumptions, and as such challenges a different set of political ideals.

---

[37]   This literature uses the label 'faith-based organizations' to include a variety of institutional forms that range from places of worship to religiously identified social service organizations.

[38]   Richard Hula, Cynthia Jackson-Elmoore, and Laura Reese, 'Mixing God's Work and the Public Business: A Framework for the Analysis of Faith-based Service Delivery', *Review of Policy Research*, 24/1 (2007): pp. 67–89; David Reingold, Maureen Pirog and David Brady, 'Empirical Evidence on Faith-based Organizations in an Era of Welfare Reform', *Social Service Review*, 81/2 (2007): pp. 245–83; Kevin Kearns, Chisung Park and Linda Yankoski, 'Comparing Faith-Based and Secular Community Service Corporations in Pittsburgh and Allegheny County, Pennsylvania', *Nonprofit and Voluntary Sector Quarterly*, 34/2 (2005): pp. 206–31; Thomas Jeavons, 'The Vitality and Independence of Religious Organizations', *Society*, Jan./Feb. (2003): pp. 27–36; John Hiemstra, 'Government Relations with Faith-based Non-profit Social Agencies in Alberta', *Journal of Church and State*, 44/1 (2002): pp.19–44; Eric Twombly, 'Religious Versus Secular Human Service Organizations: Implications for Public Policy', *Social Science Quarterly*, 83/4 (2002): pp. 947–61; Steven Rathgeb Smith and Michael Sosin, 'Varieties of Faith-related Agencies', *Public Administration Review*, 61/6 (2001): pp. 651–70.

[39]   Much of this literature invokes the experience of faith-based organizations before the establishment of Charitable Choice, and later the Faith-based Initiative. It is my position that these policy events (Charitable Choice and the Faith-based Initiative) were mere moments in a longer conversation that had been occurring for decades about the role of faith in welfare.

Faith-based Organizations (FBOs) as Extensions

A common theme in the aforementioned FBO literature is the revelation that many FBOs engage in social assistance that is financed by some level of government.[40] Usually, though not always, such contractual work is performed by large denominational groups (rather than congregations) such as Catholic Charities and Lutheran Social Services. Almost all federal and most state level contractual agreements in the US (and most secular, developed countries for that matter) come with some guidelines on how that money can be used. Often these include stipulations requiring the FBO to guarantee that they will not discriminate against those of other faiths in hiring or in their clientele. In order to comply, intricate efforts have been made either to secularize the operation, or to compartmentalize and separate a branch of the organization that will be dealing with government contracts (from the 'sectarian' branches of the organization that might not comply with government regulations). This tends to diminish the openly religious elements of FBOs, much to the consternation of conservatives who believe that these elements are integral to the success of the organization. In a sense then some FBOs – or at least departments in some FBOs – function as extensions of state-based welfare, committed in general to the same principles of universal access as secular government, and largely dependent on the state for funding. They are, in this view, part of the 'shadow state' that has become increasingly relevant as central governments spin off welfare work in the form of contracts to NGOs. These relationships existed for decades before Charitable Choice or the Faith-based Initiative, but the Religious Right felt that they were being excluded because they wanted to retain sectarianism in their service delivery.

FBOs as Enhancements

Not all literature emphasizes the contractual 'shadow state' functions of some FBOs. Some authors tend to emphasize the notion that FBOs may depend on government funding because of their fundraising limitations, but are better than the state at providing social services, so they should be given the latitude to use this funding however they wish, sectarian or not. This theme reveals itself in a number of forms. First, there is a variety of literature that emphasizes the role that FBOs have played historically as social service providers before and during the rise of formalized government-funded welfare and that they should be compensated for their efforts. Such work argues, based on historical work, that FBOs have displayed a compassion, possess social capital and enhance community in ways that government or secular NGO welfare could not hope to provide. Authors in this school conclude that this historical experience is a justification for contemporary funding of FBOs, but with no (or few) regulatory strings attached. This theme was a popular one within the Bush administration, which tried, with mixed success, to increase funding to, and reduce oversight on,

---

[40]   Smith and Sosin, 'Varieties'; Hiemstra, 'Government Relations'.

small congregational FBOs.[41] A second manifestation of the FBO as enhancement theme has been in the form of geographical accounts of how such a relationship (between FBO and the state) functions in countries other than the US. The work of Daly is particularly important in this regard, as he argued that Western European countries – particularly the Netherlands and Germany – offer a model in which FBOs are funded without regulation by the state.[42] A third argument has been made by conservatives who suggest that faith-based organizations are superior to government-run welfare, because they (the FBOs) are able to sort the 'deserving' from the 'undeserving' – thus the FBO as enhancement would be not only more just, but also less expensive in practice as the 'undeserving' would be removed from the care apparatus and the public would have better accountability with their tax dollars.[43] This idea is appealing to religious conservatives but not neoliberals, who feel that the state should not be involved at all in welfare.

FBOs as Catalysts for Change

Not all authors have understood FBOs to be either alternatives, extensions or enhancements of the state. Some authors have focused on the progressive possibilities of FBOs – how in particular they can be used as a vehicle to motivate the state to become more redistributive. Pacione, for example, has documented the importance of the Church of England's *Faith in the City* report in the late 1980s.[44] *Faith in the City* argued for the government to devote more resources to poverty reduction. In a sense, its position was more progressive than the official opposition at the time (though probably no more successful). More recently Beaumont and Dias have argued that the equation of FBOs as vehicles of neoliberalism is hasty and, in many cases, inaccurate.[45] They show how two Dutch FBOs (one in Rotterdam, one in Amsterdam) not only provided conventional social assistance, but also provided a vehicle for activism *against* neoliberal policies by the state. Much of this sentiment implicitly (and sometimes explicitly) harkens back to the ideas of Liberation Theology and the Social Gospel – some fragments of which have been revived in the form of a 'religious Left' that sees it as imperative to use biblical teachings as a justification for challenging the neoliberal state. Still others have pointed out how FBOs have been important components – usually

---

[41]   David Kuo, *Tempting Faith: An Inside Story of Political Seduction* (New York, 2006); Black, Koopman, and Ryden, *Of Little Faith*; John Dilulio, 'Getting Faith-based Programs Right', *Public Interest*, 155/Spring (2004): pp. 75–88.

[42]   Lew Daly, *God and the Welfare State* (Boston, 2006).

[43]   Mead, 'A Biblical Response'; Mead, *The New Paternalism*.

[44]   Pacione, 'The Ecclesiastical Community'.

[45]   Justin Beaumont, 'Faith Action on Urban Social Issues', *Urban Studies*, 45/10 (2008): pp. 2019–34; Justin Beaumont and Candice Dias, 'Faith-based Organizations and Urban Social Justice in the Netherlands', *Tijdschrift voor Economische en Sociale Geografie*, 99/4 (2008): pp. 382–92.

though not exclusively in conjunction with labour unions – in advocating for better working conditions and pay for workers.[46] Though this is obviously a 'faith-based' approach, it appeals to neither neoliberals nor religious conservatives, for fairly obvious reasons.

FBOs as Alternatives to the State

FBOs are sometimes framed as alternatives to the state within the literature. There are two forms that are useful to differentiate as they imply (and in some cases directly state) a completely different normative policy agenda. In one case, the experience of FBOs is interpreted as a justification for more state-based or state-sponsored social assistance. In the other, the experience of FBOs is framed as a justification for diminishing or completely eradicating state involvement in welfare.

Type A – as an alternative to the regressive state   some literature focuses on FBOs as alternatives to government, but not part of a normative desire to destroy state-based welfare. Rather, a number of authors have emphasized the role that FBOs – congregations in particular – have played historically (and in a contemporary sense) in providing assistance that the state either could not or would not provide. First, a variety of authors have emphasized the role that FBOs have played historically, before, during and after the rise of Keynesian welfare in the mid-twentieth century.[47] Through individual case studies and meta-analyses these authors show how FBOs are not positioned necessarily as a reason to provide less government welfare, but rather as a *de facto* safety net within contexts where regressive politics mobilized state-craft in order to deny social assistance to the poor. They were an 'alternative' because the state would not mobilize its resources to help. A second, less direct, strand emphasizes the idea that some FBOs possess qualities that the state simply cannot replicate and thus provide services that are incomparable to those provided by the state. Ley and Hays for example have shown how FBOs possess a cultural legitimacy amongst adherents of their religion that can be mobilized to motivate volunteers to help new immigrants assimilate to a new country, or build houses

---

[46]   Kristen Sziarto, 'Placing Legitimacy: Organizing Religious Support in a Hospital Workers' Contract Campaign', *Tijdschrift Voor Economische En Sociale Geografie*, 99/4 (2008): pp. 406–25.

[47]   Ram Cnaan, Stephanie Boddie and Robert Wineburg, *The Newer Deal: Social Work and Religion in Partnership* (New York, 1999); Ram Cnaan, Stephanie Boddie, Femida Handy, Gaynor Yancey and Richard Schneider, *The Invisible Caring Hand: American Congregations and the Provision of Welfare* (New York, 2002); Ram Cnaan, Stephanie Boddie, Charlene McGrew and Jennifer Kang, *The Other Philadelphia Story: How Local Congregations Support Quality of Life in Urban America* (Philadelphia, 2006); Robert Wuthnow, *Saving America?: Faith-based Services and the Future of Civil Society* (Princeton, NJ, 2004).

for the poor.[48] Though this theme is expressed in varied fragments, the important continuity is that this literature is not directed toward a normative view that would see the reduction or demolition of welfare. These authors either express the position that FBOs have picked up where the state has been negligent or, more directly, that FBOs need *more*, not less, help from the state in their social assistance programmes.

Type B – as an idealized replacement for the 'failed' state   the notion of FBOs as replacements – defined here as descriptions and practices which frame such organizations as not only better than the state but also able (or conceivably able with the right policy) of functioning as independent entities – is less common in the literature, but voiced by a variety of influential pundits. This theme has taken at least two forms in the literature. First, the idea is rooted to the notion that charities of all sorts, religious or not, were 'crowded out' by the expansion of government welfare in the 1930s, and remain so today.[49] Within this logic, the government should radically downsize, if not completely eliminate, welfare so that the charitable sector can be 'revived'.[50] In the words of Jay Richards, an Acton Institute Fellow who came out with a book in 2009 entitled *Money, Greed and God*:

> Some private charities are more effective than others, but almost all of them are more effective than larger government programs ... all of these organizations have one thing in common: they define their mission in part by what the government does or doesn't provide. If the government weren't occupying most of the charitable ecosystem, charities would be profoundly different. The ecosystem would be filled with thousands of well-funded responsive charities accountable to their donors and communities. As it is, government has invaded the ecosystem, and mostly made a mess of it.[51]

As a large component of the charitable sector, FBOs are often framed, by default, as a suitable replacement for welfare in these narratives. Second, this view has

---

[48]   David Ley, 'The Immigrant Church as an Urban Service Hub', *Urban Studies*, 45/10 (2008): pp. 2057–74.

[49]   Richards, *Money, Greed and God*; Jonathan Gruber and Daniel Hungerman, 'Faith-based Charity and Crowd-out during the Great Depression', *Journal of Public Economics*, 91/5&6 (2007): pp. 1043–69; Daniel Hungerman, 'Are Church and State Substitutes? Evidence from the 1996 Welfare Reform', *Journal of Public Economics*, 89/11&12 (2005): pp. 2245–67; Richard Steinberg, 'Does Government Spending Crowd-out Donations? Interpreting the Evidence', *Annals of Public and Cooperative Economics*, 62/4 (1991): pp. 591–617.

[50]   Jennifer Ziegler, 'Testimony to Subcommittee on Human Resources of the House Committee on Ways and Means on February 10, 2005', U.S. House of Representatives Website, <http://waysandmeans.house.gov/hearings.asp?formmode=view&id=2969>, accessed October 2006.

[51]   Richards, *Money, Greed and God*.

been promoted by those who not only have antipathy for government-based welfare, but also believe that the replacement should be religious (not a secular NGO model). Marvin Olasky is arguably the most prominent promoter of this position.[52] He has argued that government-based welfare is an abject failure primarily because it is wasteful and does not emphasize personal responsibility enough. To Olasky, such programmes should be dismantled and replaced with a locally-based, religious system that is funded by biblical tithes. Such programmes would not burden the federal government and would be able to sort the 'deserving' from the 'undeserving' poor.[53] Olasky's views have had wide influence in the US Republican Party – he was a close advisor to George W. Bush in the 1990s and is credited with coining the phrase and selling the concept of 'compassionate conservatism'.[54] This idealized model is alienating to religious progressives, but theoretically held the potential to serve as a glue for the neoliberal-religious fundamentalist coalition. But the details of implementation never led to this model, in particular because the Bush administration was keen on funding new FBOs in the process, thus enacting a model that alienated neoliberals.[55]

Conclusion

Religious neoliberalism is a political construction with a theological flavour. It is no more 'natural' than the social gospel or liberation theology, but it is supported by vastly more organized supporters and institutions. This construction – or coalition – is much more internally varied than many scholars and theologians often recognize. Many do not even acknowledge its presence; those who do routinely dismiss it as bad theology or irrelevant political economy. But for this construction to maintain itself – given its internal contradictions – issues arise around which corners of the coalition can coalesce. Social welfare, via the Faith-based Initiative, promised to be one of these issues.

---

[52]   Olasky, *The Tragedy of American Compassion*; Marvin Olasky, *Compassionate Conservatism: What It Is, What It Does, and How It Can Transform America* (New York, 2000).

[53]   Hudson and Coukos, 'The Dark Side'; Kahl, 'Religious Roots'.

[54]   Omri Elisha, 'Moral Ambitions of Grace: The Paradox of Compassion and Accountability in Evangelical Faith-based Activism', *Cultural Anthropology*, 23/1 (2008): pp. 154–89; Margaret Harris, Peter Halfpenny, and Colin Rochester, 'A Social Policy Role for Faith-based Organisations? Lessons from the UK Jewish Voluntary Sector', *Journal of Social Policy*, 32/1 (2003): pp. 93–112; Patrick Boleyn-Fitzgerald, 'Misfortune, Welfare Reform, and Right-wing Egalitarianism', *Critical Review*, 13/1&2 (1999): pp. 141–63; Ralph Dolgoff, 'What Does Social Welfare Produce?', *International Social Work*, 42/3 (1999): pp. 295–307.

[55]   Sager, *Elephant in the Room*.

Within the American political theatre, there is a synergy, if not a lock-step political alliance between religious fundamentalism and economic fundamentalism, even though the two stem from wildly different logics, appeal to different demographics and defer to very different forms of authority. The Bush administration's Faith-based Initiative was, in many ways, the political embodiment of this alliance. It was designed in part to institutionally fuse together the two wings around the concept of faith-based welfare. In the abstract, this appealed to religious conservatives because is harkened (or at least implied a harkening) to a return to a time when churches were the main source of social welfare in the US, and it appealed to secular neoliberals because it stoked hopes of a downsized welfare state. But while the Faith-based Initiative was positioned politically to bond together the two wings of this alliance, the details of implementation caused some conservatives to quickly rail against it as a divisive (for the Right) set of policies that *neither* returned welfare to the churches nor away from the state. I argue that part of this revolves around the fact that welfare, even religiously delivered welfare, is far too multifaceted and poly-motivated to serve as a bonding agent for this group alone. As a 'replacement for the state', the idea of faith-based organizations has a great deal of potential as a glue for this varied group. But the resultant conversation and existing landscape of welfare (which was already connected to the religious organizations in multiple ways) never had the effect of foregrounding this particular conception and thus complicated the idea of its role as a bonding agent. The Faith-based Initiative thus served to fray more than fuse the very coalition that it was designed to placate. It serves, if nothing else, as an actualized lesson of the political difficulties that inhibit the more complete union of market and religious fundamentalism in other societies.

PART II
Political Governance of Religion

Neoliberalism has involved not only the 'liberalisation' of rules and regulations, but – counter-intuitively – the emergence of new forms of governance and control. Our inability to identify and locate new forms of control is bound up by a reluctance to discard old theoretical tools and concepts. This section of the book tries to reverse this by looking at the political governance of religion. Some chapters explore how the state has not retreated, but created different, sometimes innovative, forms of regulation using models from the market. Others consider the expanding, regulatory power of law in relation to religion, emphasizing the influence of the contractual, legalistic aspects of neoliberalism.

David Ashley and Ryan Sandefer suggest that contemporary faith-based programmes in the United States are to some extent designed to compensate for a declining public sphere. Basing their argument in the political philosophy of Jürgen Habermas, they argue that faith-based initiatives weaken, rather than foster, ability of citizens to provide value-oriented inputs. They critique the neoliberal agenda that depoliticizes political choices, and claim that 'faith-based initiatives enable government to adjust to what neoliberalism had helped institutionalize'.

Tuomas Martikainen's chapter studies new forms of multilevel and pluricentric network governance of religion, using examples from Finland. Network governance has emerged as an increasingly popular form of state coordination, even eclipsing previous modalities of government. Embedded in New Public Management, the networks have become important means of regulation through negotiation and bargaining. Martikainen concludes that this seemingly amorphous field is in fact structured, and can be understood as an expression of a new political economy of religion.

Ringo Ringvee studies, from the perspective of religion, the political rupture of post-Soviet legal reforms which took place when Estonia made a decisive turn to neoliberalism after decades of communist rule in the early 1990s. He argues that the neoliberalization of the religious market was more profound in relation to the new enthusiasm for political liberty than it might have been in other circumstances. However, Estonia had become one of most secularized countries in the world, and the historical churches were not able to reclaim their former strength. According to Ringvee, this had to do with their historical association with repressive power – either the *German* Lutheran Church or the *Russian* Orthodox Church – and their meagre role in forming a national identity.

Agnes Chong studies the consequences of the securitization of Islam in Australia by combining a legal and an ethnographic approach. She argues that while counter-terrorism laws are not explicitly part of neoliberal restructuring, they support a neoliberalization of religious charity which leads to restrictive forms of self-governance. Older forms of giving relied on social bonds and trust; out of the fear of giving support to global terrorism organisations new forms of charity behaviour are born, as donors shop around and evaluate charities. Mutual trust is weakened and a contractual society is institutionalized in the process.

The following two chapters compose a complementary case study of the influence of neoliberalism on state-church relations from the perspective of the law in multiculturally-oriented Canada. Analysing the evolution of Canadian criminal law with respect to sexual offences, Rachel Chagnon and François Gauthier show how implicitly Christian moral foundations shaped the rules and exercise of law until the year 2000, when the effects of Rawls-inspired procedural justice completed the erosion of these religious moorings. The result has been a striking alignment of Canadian law with neoliberal principles and their individualistic and economic understanding of social reality.

Focusing on a recent judgment of the Supreme Court of Canada on an issue of religion and public space, Lori Beaman argues that such an economically sensitive approach as that proposed by this volume goes farther in providing a comprehensive analysis of the neoliberal turn in the exercise of Canadian law than secularization theory. She shows how an entrepreneurial framework and a cost-benefit argumentation threaten to erode egalitarianism, marginalize community based religious claims, and sacralise state security.

Chapter 6

Neoliberalism and the Privatization of Welfare and Religious Organizations in the United States of America

David Ashley and Ryan Sandefer

From 'Charitable Choice' to Faith-based Programmes

In 1996, President Bill Clinton signed into law the *Personal Responsibility and Work Opportunity Reconciliation Act* (*PRWOA*), which, among other things, abolished Aid to Families with Dependent Children and replaced it with Temporary Aid to Needy Families (TANF). The *PRWOA* capped lifetime relief. It also implemented a 'charitable choice' option for private and religious organizations.

Before 1996, churches or religious organizations that received federal money had to spin off separate secular, non-profit-making subsidiaries. Charitable choice changed this by giving religious organizations block grants from the Department of Health and Human Services (HHS) to fund TANF programmes with religious content. (Religious groups and organizations were still expected to offer a secular alternative to 'faith-based' assistance if one were requested.)

Expanding Clinton's programmes, in 2001 President George W. Bush established the White House Office of Community and Faith-based Organizations (WHOCFBO) and centres for faith-based and community initiatives at the Departments of HHS and Housing and Urban Development (HUD), as well as the Departments of Justice (DOJ), Labor and Education. Other centres were later added at the US Agency for International Development (USAID) and at the Departments of Agriculture, Commerce and Veterans Affairs, as well as at the office of Small Business Administration. In 2006, Bush also ordered the Department of Homeland Security to organize FBIs – according to one spokesperson because of 'the extraordinary support ... the faith-based community' had shown in the aftermath of Hurricane Katrina.[1] By 2005, 'more than $2.1 billion in grants [had been] awarded to religious organizations',[2] mostly Christian.

In 2005, state support for faith-based organizations was ratcheted up another level when the *Job Training Improvement Act* authorized *publicly funded* faith-based organizations to hire and fire staff on the basis of their religious affiliation,

---

[1] Spencer S. Hsu, 'Bush Orders DHS to Create Center for Faith-based Aid', *The Washington Post* (8 March 2006): p. A20.

[2] The White House (2007), 'HOFBCI Accomplishments in 2006'.

or lack of it. Adhering to the 1964 *Civil Rights Act*, charitable choice had allowed religious organizations to take religious orientation into consideration but was silent on whether this privilege could be extended to those receiving taxpayers' money.

As it was also with Ronald Reagan, the key, or swing, constituency for George W. Bush was (non-Church-affiliated) Christian evangelicals.[3] In the USA, church attendance is now more important in determining voting patterns than gender, income, region or age and is equally as important as race. 'Americans who regularly attend worship services and hold traditional religious views increasingly vote Republican (indeed, in 2004 they were three times more likely to vote Republican), while those who are more secular in their outlook tend to vote Democratic'.[4] It is not surprising, then, that, according to David Kuo, who was second-in-command of Bush's 'faith-based' programmes at the White House, the Bush administration promoted FBIs for partisan advantage.[5] As Karl Rove, chief White House strategist, put it at the time, evangelicals and Christians were 'nuts' but they were also politically 'invaluable'.[6] FBIs also were used to send money to organizations that were 'politically friendly' such as Pat Robertson's 'Operation Blessing.' Other programmes funded high-profile backers of Bush.

In a procedure he calls a 'farce', Kuo reports how Bush operatives handpicked 'peer-review panels' for faith-based applications such as that submitted by 'We Care America' (a new organization 'with a staff of three, all from the world of Washington politics, and all very Republican'), which ultimately received $2.5 million.[7] According to Kuo, the Bush administration actually spent 'about $20 million a year *less* "doing compassion"' than did the Clinton administration.[8] Bush made 'grand announcements' about his Christian-based programmes but was not interested in how they were implemented.[9] Nonetheless, the drive to deliver 'faith' was relentless. For instance, WHOFBCO trained 25,000 'faith-based and community leaders', HUD organized 'FREE two-day, intensive Grant Writing

[3]   Alan Cooperman and Thomas. B. Edsell, 'Evangelicals Say they Led the Charge for the GOP,' *The Washington Post* (8 November 2004): p. A01.

[4]   Pew Forum on Religion and Public Life, 'Religion and Public Life. A Faith-based Partisan Divide' (26 January 2005), <http://pewforum.org/Politics-and-Elections/Religion-amp-Public-Life-A-Faith-based-Partisan-Divide.aspx>; 'How the Faithful Voted. Political Alignments and the Religious Divide in Election 2004' (17 November 2004), available online at <http://pewforum.org/Politics-and-Elections/How-the-Faithful-Voted-Political-Alignments-amp-the-Religious-Divide-in-Election-2004.aspx>. See, also, Laura R. Olson and John C. Green, 'The Religion Gap', *Political Science and Politics*, 39 (2006): pp. 455–59.

[5]   David Kuo, *Tempting Faith. An Inside Story of Political Seduction* (New York, 2006), pp. 217–32.

[6]   Ibid., p. 229.

[7]   Ibid., p. 214ff.

[8]   Ibid., p. 220.

[9]   Ibid., p. 208.

Training Workshops for Faith-based & Community-Based Organizations' and the DOJ offered 'technical assistance' to other faith-based groups and organizations who wanted access to taxpayers' money.[10]

Faith-based programmes also refocused foreign aid. USAID, for example, gave hundreds of millions of dollars to Catholic charities and to the evangelical organization 'Food for the Hungry', which teaches hygiene and family planning but also, according to its website, works on 'developing a biblical worldview to help churches overcome false beliefs that mire them and their communities in physical and spiritual poverty'.[11]

Advocacy for FBIs and the relaxation of employment laws for religious organizations were described by the Bush administration as 'conservative' and as 'compassionate'. Yet, Bush support for FBIs was less obviously 'conservative' or 'moral' than it was – initially at least – radical and contentious.[12] By greatly expanding the number of religious organizations and groups that received public funding, Bush's FBIs went far beyond Clinton's. Many of the groups and organizations the WHOCFBO organized did not even exist before funding opportunities were institutionalized.[13] The 'Healthy Marriage Initiative,' for instance, funded by TANF and administered by HHS, offered up to $100 million annually for new faith-based and community organizations that could teach 'healthy' (typically, Christian-based) family practices.

In defence of the Healthy Marriage Initiative, HHS cites 'Twenty-Six Conclusions from the Social Sciences' to prove that children from 'healthy marriages' are 'physically healthier', 'emotionally healthier' and 'less likely to commit suicide'.[14] According to HHS, communities with a higher percentage of couples in 'healthy families' have 'higher rates of home ownership', 'lower rates of migration' and 'higher property values'.[15] Spurious correlation is packaged

---

[10]   See 'Technical Assistance Events and Resources,' The White House Faith-based and Community Initiatives, available online at <http://georgewbush-whitehouse.archives.gov/government/fbci/technical-assistance.html>.

[11]   http://www.fh.org/do/church. See, also, Farah Stockman, 'Bush Brings Faith to Foreign Aid,' *The Boston Globe* (8 October 2006).

[12]   See, for instance, the American Civil Liberties Union (21 June 2005) 'ACLU Calls on Congress to Reject Funding of Religious Activities, Says Faith Based Initiative Goes Too Far and Threatens Civil Rights', available online at <http://www.aclu.org/religion-belief/aclu-calls-congress-reject-funding-religious-activities-says-faith-based-initiative->.

[13]   One example – 'Fountain of Life' – suddenly came into existence in September 2001 when the Rev Sherron Parrish was 'blessed with a vision' (see their website available online at http://www.folim.org/go/about.) Shortly thereafter, the State of Florida approved Fountain of Life International Ministries as a 'Worship Center' and the organization received a faith-based grant of $483,383 from the taxpayers.

[14]   US Department of Health and Human Services, 'The Healthy Marriage Initiative' (2007), <http://www.acf.hhs.gov/healthymarriage/benefits/index.html>.

[15]   Ibid.

and promoted as causal explanation. It is not, though, acknowledged that an endorsement of heterosexual arrangements and federally funded programmes for Christian or religiously based practices amounts to a tacit rejection of other conceivable versions of 'family'.

According to Robert Wuthnow, 'the recent discussion about [government-sponsored, government-funded] faith-based services' is 'part of a larger debate about the future of civil society' because FBIs test 'whether the American public is willing to do its part to help one another'.[16] This suggests, however, that in promoting FBIs, the state facilitates (for example, encourages and funds), but does not create, authorize or substantively attempt to shape 'caring activity'. Other sociologists have suggested that FBIs can help develop social capital and build multi-racial progressive coalitions in deprived social neighbourhoods.[17] Yet, such capital and such coalitions tend not to emerge from the private and voluntary activities of groups and organizations. Rather, like 'Healthy Marriage', they are, indirectly, constructed by the state (usually through block grants).

In pushing their new agenda for FBIs, members of the Bush administration claimed that, in the past, government had *discriminated* against private, charitable and religious organizations, and that this needed to change. Hence, it was time to introduce a 'level playing field' on which private, voluntary groups could compete equitably with secular organizations and public bureaucracies for government funds. In addition, Bush officials argued that private charities are *more cost-effective* than government bureaucracies.

As noted earlier, however, before 2001 there were no major impediments to religious groups or churches receiving public funding. In a study conducted for the Urban Institute, Eric Twombly found that the major 'faith-based providers on average have provided services for 37 years and receive roughly 6 per cent of their resources from direct government funding.'[18] And, as Mark Chaves and William Tsitsos have shown, it is a 'myth' that religious organizations 'face substantial discrimination when competing for government grants and contracts'.[19] Kuo points out that before 2001, faith-based programmes received 'government grants ... for

---

[16]   Robert Wuthnow, *Saving America? Faith-based Services and the Future of Civil Society* (Princeton, 2006), pp. 1–2.

[17]   See, for instance, William H. Lockhart, 'Building Bridges and Bonds: Generating Social Capital in Secular and Faith-based Poverty-to-Work Programs', *Sociology of Religion*, 66/1 (2005): pp. 45–60, and Mark R. Warren, *Dry Bones Rattling: Community Building to Revitalize American Democracy* (Princeton, 2001).

[18]   Eric C. Twombly, 'Religious versus Secular Human Service Organizations: Implications for Public Policy', *Social Science Quarterly*, 88/4 (2002): p. 958.

[19]   Mark Chaves and William Tsitsos, 'Six Myths about Faith-based Initiatives,' *The Christian Century* (12–19 September 2001), p. 20. See, also, Mark Chaves and William Tsitsos, 'Congregations and Social Services: What They Do, How They Do It, and With Whom', *Non-profit and Voluntary Sector Quarterly*, 30/4 (2001): pp. 660–83.

many years'.[20] In some programmes, there was a long-standing *bias* in favour of faith-based organizations. In the 1990s, for instance, Habitat for Humanity, a Christian organization, received more than half the funds HUD disbursed to NGOs.[21]

The argument that FBIs deliver social services more efficiently than secular and bureaucratic alternatives is as little supported by the evidence as is the claim that these organizations are crippled by discrimination.[22] According to Twombly, 'faith-based providers on average spend considerably more on management and administration than do secular groups'.[23] Yet these are not more effective than those that are secular.[24] Although he is generally supportive of FBIs, even Wuthnow concedes there is 'no evidence on the whole of recipients viewing faith-based organizations more favorably than secular nonprofits'.[25] Indeed, a study released by the Pew-funded Roundtable on Religion and Social Welfare Policy found that 'the White House has relied on largely anecdotal evidence to support the view that faith-based approaches produce better long-term results'.[26]

Charged by Congress with evaluating their effectiveness, the United States Government Accountability Office (GAO) also concluded in 2006 that FBIs were not more effective than secular organizations.[27] In addition, the GAO documented a total lack of accountability. There is no standardized definition of a 'faith-based' organization, and reliable methods for evaluating faith-based organizations have never been developed. The GAO additionally noted that many government-funded FBIs failed to separate 'religious activities from federally funded program services',[28] and they seldom offered an alternative to Christian-based services.

[20]   Kuo, p. 180.

[21]   Ibid.

[22]   Chaves and Tsitsos, 'Six Myths about Faith-based Initiatives'. See, also, Alan Cooperman, 'Faith-based Charities May Not Be Better, Study Indicates', *The Washington Post* (25 May 2003): p. A07.

[23]   Twombly, p. 954.

[24]   Mark. J. DeHaven, Irby B. Hunter, Laura Wilder, James W. Walton and Janet Berry, 'Health Programs in Faith-based Organizations: Are they Effective?', *American Journal of Public Health*, 94/6 (2004): pp. 1030–1036.

[25]   Wuthnow, *Saving America*, p. 215. See, also, Robert Wuthnow, Conrad Hackett and Becky Yang Hsu, 'The Effectiveness and Trustworthiness of Faith-based and Other Service Organizations: A Study of Recipients' Perceptions', *Journal for the Scientific Study of Religion*, 43/1 (2004): pp. 1–17.

[26]   Cited in Amy Sullivan, 'Faith Without Works,' *Washington Monthly*, October 2004, available online at <http://www.washingtonmonthly.com/features/2004/0410.2sullivan.html>.

[27]   Government Accounting Office, 'Faith-based and Community Initiative. Improvements in Monitoring Grantees and Measuring Performance Could Enhance Accountability,' (Washington: United States Accountability Office, June 2006), pp. 49–50, [GAO-06-616], available online at <http://www.gao.gov/new.items/d06616.pdf>.

[28]   Ibid. See 'Highlights' of the report.

What *did* set the Bush-sponsored FBIs apart was that they tended to flaunt the values of evangelical Christians and to claim that people could not be helped or healed unless they were 'born again' in Christ.[29] Although this observation is contentious and socially divisive, it was popular with many Christian fundamentalists who recognized in Bush's 'compassion agenda' and numerous speeches about 'faith' a vision that strategically linked US policy at home and abroad with Divine Will. As Henry Giroux put it: 'Religious fundamentalism' was mated with 'market fundamentalism to form an ideology of American supremacy'.[30] Faith-based programmes were thus part of a larger agenda that portrayed the world in simplistic, black-and-white terms, demanded mass, unthinking loyalty and encouraged voters to substitute religious dogma and authority for analysis, reflective understanding or practical concern about public welfare. In brief, rather than focus on how social problems might reliably be addressed, Bush's policies were highly divisive: they fostered what Simone Chambers calls 'bad civil society', in other words, 'one that promotes or is hospitable to particularistic civility – that is, a civility that does not cross group boundaries'.[31]

In order to understand how civil society and political liberalism are supposed to work together, we need to turn to a brief examination of how sociology classically has parsed modernity.

Faith-based Programmes and the Erosion of Civil Society

Beginning with Auguste Comte and Herbert Spencer, and ending with Jürgen Habermas and Talcott Parsons, the development of liberal democratic society was characterized as typically an 'evolutionary' process of social differentiation. We call this the 'standard sociological model' (SSM). As classically defined by Parsons nearly 50 years ago,[32] the SSM emphasized differentiation among: (1) the economy; (2) the state; (3) the societal community; and (4) a fiduciary

---

29   Helen Rose Ebaugh, Paula F. Pipes, Janet Saltzman Chafetz and Martha Daniels, 'Where's the Religion? Distinguishing Faith-based from Secular Social Service Agencies', *Journal for the Scientific Study of Religion*, 42/3 (2003): p. 422.

30   Henry Giroux, 'Neoliberalism and the Demise of Democracy. Resurrecting Hope in Dark Times,' *Dissident Voice* (7 August 2004).

31   Simone Chambers, 'A Critical Theory of Civil Society', in Simone Chambers and Will Kymlicka (eds), *Alternative Conceptions of Civil Society*, (Princeton, 2001), pp. 90–112. See, also Simone Chambers and Jeffrey S. Kopstein, 'Bad Civil Society,' *Political Theory*, 29/6 (2001): pp. 838–66.

32   Talcott Parsons, *Societies: Evolutionary and Comparative Perspectives* (Englewood Cliffs, 1966).

subsystem.[33] Such differentiation facilitates social distance, self-reflection and the relative autonomy of life spheres.[34]

Highly differentiated, complex societies have to articulate the objectivist, instrumentalist domination of capital and administration with the messy, and often unruly, sphere of communicative action. As formulated by Parsons and Habermas, the solution is to have the economic and political subsystems specialize in managing (not producing) the societal community. In traditional societies, cultural energy, purpose and motivation emerge within a largely pre-reflective lifeworld. In modern liberal societies, the major nexus between the state and the lifeworld is the political party, which attempts to capture the administrative capacity of the polity in pursuit of policies that can garner support from below.

Modern societies, then, are complex systems that incorporate both instrumental and communicative forms of rationality. Following Habermas, we can define these two types of rationality: (1) as a 'system' of technical control and planning; and (2) as a lifeworld of communicative action (see Figure 6.1)[35] With the assistance of institutional arrangements, communicative action enables subjects to define and to implement solidarities, values and commitments. (This process can be unreflective, or relatively self-reflective. According to Habermas, when it is self-reflective it becomes more rational.) Political liberalism requires that the steering capacities of the state do not overwhelm or entirely colonize communicative action. Accordingly, different spheres of social action (for example, 'strategic' versus 'moral') need to be appropriately differentiated and institutionalized.

One problem with the SSM is that it largely assumes that political liberalism inexorably (and, presumably, irreversibly) emerged as part of an 'evolutionary process'. Parsons, for instance, believed that structural differentiation in leading nations such as the United States was an evolutionary breakthrough.[36] More recently, the neo-conservative Francis Fukuyama went a step further by announcing that, in a sense, history now had come to an end because liberal democracy had proven itself to be the 'final' and irreversible solution to the problem of political rule.[37] Citing the USA as the epitome of social progress, Parsons had pointed out earlier that the Nazi state had not just been a military

---

[33]   Talcott Parsons, *Politics and Social Structure* (New York, 1969) and *The System of Modern Societies* (Englewood Cliffs, 1971). See, also, Jürgen Habermas, *The Theory of Communicative Action, Vol. 1: Reason and the Rationalization of Society*, Thomas McCarthy (trans), (Boston, 1984); *The Theory of Communicative Action, Vol. 2: Lifeworld and System: A Critique of Functionalist Reason*, Thomas McCarthy (trans), (Boston, 1987), pp. 199–299; *The Philosophical Discourse of Modernity. Twelve Lectures*, Frederick Lawrence (trans), (Cambridge, 1987), pp. 336–67.

[34]   Anthony Giddens, *The Consequences of Modernity* (Stanford, 1990).

[35]   Habermas, *The Theory of Communicative Action, Vol. 2*, pp. 113–97.

[36]   Parsons, *Societies: Evolutionary and Comparative Perspectives*.

[37]   Francis Fukuyama, 'The End of History,' *National Interest*, 16 (Summer, 1989): pp. 3–18.

	Economy	*The State*
SYSTEM ▶ (of administration and goal-orientation). Based on (means-end) strategic action constituting instrumental power	e.g., market forces, class relations Principle of Organization is the Exchange of Equivalents. (Rationalized by capitalism) Output: Consumable values	e.g., government, the judiciary, administrative agencies Principle of Organization is Rational Planning. (Rationalized by bureaucracy and formal law) Output: Administrative/ judicial decisions

THE PUBLIC SPHERE is rooted in the lifeworld and mediates between the state and the societal community. To varying degrees it is shaped both by groups controlling the state and by events in the lifeworld

	Societal Community	*Fiduciary Subsystem*
LIFEWORLD ▶ (Socio-cultural system) Based on (ends-oriented) communicative action and creating communicative power	e.g., roles, statuses, primary and secondary groups Principle of Organization is Social (Moral) Solidarity Output: Norms, meanings, beliefs that promote social integration or a sense of belonging	e.g., values, beliefs, commitments, faith Principle of Organization is Holistic Meaning Output: The stability and predictability of communal and social arrangements (trust)

**Figure 6.1 Differentiation of system and lifeworld under modernity
(adapted from Talcott Parsons and Jürgen Habermas)**

threat to Western democracy, but was also intrinsically *anti-modern* in that it demanded blind acceptance of 'natural' culture displayed by regressive, irrational, totalitarian expressions of power.

Unlike fascist Germany though, liberal states always have had to depend 'on cultural boundary conditions they could not themselves reproduce ...'.[38] Once they were able no longer to 'feed parasitically on the remains of tradition',[39] liberal societies became increasingly dependent on inputs of legitimacy or 'generalized motivations' from the lifeworld.[40] However, 'communicatively produced power' (which is based on trust, commitments, values and ideology) is 'a scarce resource, which organizations compete for and officials manage, but which none of them can

---

[38]   Jürgen Habermas, *Legitimation Crisis* (Boston, 1975), p. 76.
[39]   Ibid.
[40]   Habermas, *Legitimation Crisis*, p. 49.

produce'.[41] Consequently, the liberal state is hostage to something it cannot entirely master: 'nourished by normative preconditions that it cannot itself guarantee'.[42]

Civil Society

The Bush administration declared that FBIs would help revitalize and 'energize' civil society.[43] But, on the face of it, this is a puzzling claim, for, as a tertiary sphere, grounded in the lifeworld, and supposedly situated outside markets and the state, 'civil society' is 'a realm of life *institutionally separated* from territorial state institutions'.[44] In modern, liberal societies the socio-cultural system provides cultural outputs that shape civil society, and the state processes these as raw inputs. Civil society is not a part of government because it is private and voluntary. It is not market-driven because it focuses on general welfare and the public good. Rather, it comprises 'legally protected *non-governmental* institutions' that are 'non-violent, self-organizing, self-reflexive, and permanently in tension with each other and with the state institutions that "frame", constrict and enable their activities'.[45]

Following Habermas, we believe 'civil society' is best conceptualized as a 'public sphere' (*Öffentlichkeit*) of communicatively formed political discourse that mediates between the societal community and administrative decisions monopolized by political specialists (see Figure 6.1). Of course, this sphere will be strengthened and enhanced by voluntary associations, strong family ties, social capital and civic organizations that promote social inclusion.[46]

According to Habermas, the public sphere emerged in the eighteenth century when wealthy, powerful and influential individuals began to use salons, reading-

---

[41]   Jürgen Habermas, *Between Facts and Norms: Contributions to a Discourse Theory of Law and Democracy*, William Rehg (trans), (Cambridge, 1996), p. 149. See, also, Habermas, *Legitimation Crisis*, p. 70.

[42]   Habermas, *Between Facts and Norms*, p. 251.

[43]   Organizing Statement of The White House Office on Faith-based Initiatives and Community Organizations (2001). 'Rallying the Armies of Compassion', (2001), <http://archives.hud.gov/reports/rally.pdf>.

[44]   John Keane, *Civil Society: Old Images, New Visions* (Stanford, 1998). See, also, Jeffrey Alexander, *The Civil Sphere* (New York, 2006).

[45]   Ibid., p. 6; emphasis supplied.

[46]   Civil society has also been defined as voluntary, 'associational life' that creates 'social capital', for example, Michael Edwards, *Civil Society* (Cambridge, 2004), pp. 18–71. See, also, Alexis de Tocqueville, *Democracy in America* (New York, 1945); Robert Putnam, 'The Strange Disappearance of Civic America,' *American Prospect*, 7 (Winter 1996): p. 24; Theda Skocpol, *Diminished Democracy. From Membership to Management in American Civic Life* (Norman, 2004). Other theorists have equated it with the 'good society', the 'setting of settings', where 'all are included, none are preferred'. See, for instance, Michael Walzer, 'The Civil Society Argument', in Chantal Mouffe (ed.), *Dimensions of Radical Democracy: Pluralism, Citizenship, Community* (London, 1992), pp. 89–107.

houses, coffee-houses, periodicals and parliament to constitute a 'public'.[47] The self-cultivation of the bourgeoisie – its interest in literature, architecture, music, philosophy and more self-reflective forms of religion – provided the basis for a new, more reflexive lifeworld as well as the emergence of politically engaged individuals and groups capable of self-cultivation (and capable, too, of acknowledging that they could constitute communities of self-education).

In recent years, the public sphere has weakened considerably. Yet, it was under threat from its very inception. For example, as political specialists began to play an increasingly important role in government, 'much of the argument and activity constitutive of the public sphere' began to take place not among individuals or between groups and organizations, but 'within the confines of the state between professional politicians'.[48] As organized political parties increasingly replaced associations of individuals, debate was 'increasingly subordinated' to tactical and strategic considerations concerning 'the competition for power'.[49] Consequently, political parties were less focused on representing than in helping to define a constituency (and its concerns).[50] By the late twentieth century, parties relied on polls and on focus groups, not so much to discover what supporters wanted, but to learn how to 'sell' to them. Ultimately, public communication was hijacked by the business of mass media, and communicative action was displaced by the system imperative of money. 'Where the early public sphere tended to "level up", the modern media, in its pursuit of the widest audience, is inclined to "level [or dumb] down"'.[51]

In this chapter, we suggest that contemporary faith-based programmes are to some extent designed to compensate for a declining public sphere. FBIs allow administrative power to produce, manage and then invoke what subsequently can be tapped as a basis of communicative support. Yet, because of such dedifferentiation, FBIs *weaken*, rather than foster, citizens' abilities to provide value-oriented inputs. When political discourse is penetrated and reorganized by instrumental power, actors lose access to resources that might shape or change public policy. Instead, they are defined – and (as we have seen), even brought into existence – by their willingness to be colonized and manipulated. Some of the more reflective religious groups and organizations seem to understand this and, as a result, understandably oppose the kind of faith-based programmes federal bureaucracies seek to implement and then to own.[52]

---

[47]   Jürgen Habermas, *The Structural Transformation of the Public Sphere: An Inquiry into a Category of Bourgeois Society*, Thomas Burger (trans), (Cambridge, 1989).

[48]   Nick Crossley and John Michael Roberts (eds), *After Habermas: New Perspectives on the Public Sphere* (Oxford, 2004), p. 5.

[49]   Ibid.

[50]   Ibid.

[51]   Ibid., p. 6.

[52]   See, for instance, Brian C. Anderson, 'How Catholic Charities Lost its Soul,' *City Journal*, (Winter, 2000), <http://www.city-journal.org/html/10_1_how_catholic_charities.html>.

Political Liberalism as a Type of Social Formation

Political liberalism was based initially on a religiously defined conception of the 'natural liberty' of the pre-social individual.[53] Yet, as modernity became more reflexive, intellectuals acknowledged that political liberalism was founded less on pre-social fixities or theological certainties than on a theory (or, for Marx, on an ideology) of '"limited" government, civil liberties, toleration and the protection of a sphere of privacy *against the state*'.[54] Because of this arrangement, modern, liberal society could never rely on a 'natural' political culture or an 'administrative production of (fiduciary) meaning'[55] Rather, 'capitalist democracy' not only had to defend, but also had to *define* boundary relations between, on the one hand, a voluntary, self-constituting sphere of value and meaning and, on the other, procedures and decisions organized by the state.

The classic early-modern formulation and defence of such a sphere of privacy was developed by James Madison in his 'Memorial and Remonstrance Against Religious Assessments' of 1785.[56] Madison, an American statesman and political theorist, was the fourth President of the United States and played a major role in helping to draft the US Constitution and author the Bill of Rights. As he cogently suggested in his 'Memorial and Remonstrance', a failure to separate religion from government would be harmful to *both*. Religion, Madison points out, is a duty we owe our Creator 'precedent both in order and time and in degree of obligation' to the claims of public authorities. Religious duty cannot be compelled, but must be directed by reason. To confuse what we owe the Deity with what we owe our fellow citizens is injurious to both: it is 'an arrogant pretension falsified by the contradictory opinions of Rulers in all ages ... and an unhallowed perversion of the means of salvation'.[57]

Madison, then, lucidly and compellingly defined the appropriate boundary conditions between, on the one hand, the socio-cultural domain of fiduciary meaning and, on the other, the administratively rational state. He thereby *solved* the problem of how to differentiate administrative procedures and decisions from private commitment – a solution, which, as we argue below, the New Right has perversely discarded, as it insistently reintroduces the original problem Madison helped fix.

By the middle of the nineteenth century, bourgeois society was progressively and extensively imposing market relations on everyday life as it increasingly

---

[53]   See John Locke's 'Second Treatise of Government', 1689.

[54]   Ellen Meiksins Wood, *Democracy Against Capitalism: Renewing Historical Materialism* (Cambridge, 1995), pp. 227–8, note 21, emphasis supplied. See also, Habermas, *The Philosophical Discourse of Modernity*, p. 83ff.

[55]   Habermas, *Legitimation Crisis*, p. 70; emphasis removed.

[56]   Available online at http://atheism.about.com/library/FAQs/cs/blcs_txt_MadisonMR. htm.

[57]   Ibid.

colonized (neutralized resistance from) the societal community. Although this did not pose any direct threat to religion, *per se*, this 'colonization of the lifeworld', as Habermas expresses it,[58] did lessen the need for an autonomous production of political legitimacy because, as Marx pointed out,

> [t]he institution of the market can be founded on the justice inherent in the exchange of equivalents; and, for this reason, the bourgeois constitutional state finds its justification in the legitimate relations of production. This is the message of rational natural law since Locke. The relations of production can do without a traditional authority legitimated from above.[59]

Of course, markets and formal law in early-modern society did not *entirely* subjugate the socio-cultural system. In the USA, at least, the separation of state and religion held firm. Moreover, semi-autonomous families and vocational occupational groups institutionalized comparatively high levels of privatism. Hence, the civil sphere continued to be shaped by socio-cultural inputs that neither the state nor capital could dominate. Sometimes (and, often, from a religious perspective) these even expressed a rejection of, or an aversion towards, market rationality and the authority of the state.[60]

By the beginning of the last century, however, capitalism was based less on the family firm or on small businesses than on exceedingly well-organized and concentrated forms of production. And, as John Dewey pointed out in the 1930s, 'when it came to the problem of organizing the new forces and the individuals whose mode of life they radically altered into a coherent social organization, possessed of intellectual and moral directive power, liberalism was well-nigh impotent'.[61]

It was necessary, then, for 'liberalism' to reinvent itself – this time more self-consciously as mass 'liberal democracy'. A social-democratic version of political liberalism which, subsequently, was developed most extensively in Western Europe, centred on various forms of corporatism and statism. These largely were a response to market failure and to working-class forms of organization.

In early liberal bourgeois society, the public sphere was relatively unproblematic because all politically qualified actors brought to the table *some* commonality of interest that could be taken for granted. But, by the end of the nineteenth century, this arrangement was in jeopardy. As soon as the identification of liberty with the unfettered free market was challenged, the state both had to acknowledge, and to deal with, a wider conception of substantive justice. The solution to such

---

58   Habermas, *The Theory of Communicative Action*.

59   Habermas, *Legitimation Crisis*, p. 22.

60   Some churches in the United States, for instance, were at the forefront of the anti-slavery movement.

61   John Dewey, *Liberalism and Social Action* (Amherst, 1991), pp. 58–59.

'demand overload' or 'rationality crisis'[62] turned out to be, first, a new, more organized, version of '*civil* privatism' (that is, 'political abstinence combined with an orientation to career, leisure and consumption'[63]), second, market populism (which began to emerge in the USA in the 1920s) and, third, an expansion of formal, Weberian administrative rationality.

Corporatism and social democracy, then, did not block, but increasingly channelled and organized political demands. During this period, in order to ensure that social protest and potentially ruinous fiscal demands from below could be contained,[64] the advanced capitalist state had to ensure that the 'administrative system' be kept 'as far as possible' from the 'legitimating system'.[65] Yet, a *political* programme that promotes depoliticization (including political abstinence, civil privatism, proceduralism, increasing indifference – fragmentation, even) is inherently problematic. As the political theorists, Gabriel Almond and Sidney Verba archly noted, the 'democratic citizen' was now expected to be 'active, yet passive; involved, yet not too involved; influential, yet deferential'.[66]

At some point, the processes of depoliticization just outlined begin to undermine liberal hegemony. This is because administrative power is starved of communicative inputs that allow it to represent itself as a legitimate entity. Another way of putting this is to say that the state suffers from a decline in its ability to produce and then to use political goods such as 'equality', 'peace', 'justice', 'freedom', 'tolerance' and 'democracy'. Associated with such a 'rationality crisis' are precipitously falling levels of trust.

By the end of the last century, while 'effectiveness' (for example bureaucracy, knowledge, technology, manipulation and so on) continued apace, civic involvement began to decline.[67] An increasing emphasis on market populism, which, by the 1960s far exceeded anything seen in the 1920s, and – more recently – the development of innovatory and highly profitable instruments of debt creation became a substitute for this shrinking civil sphere. As a result, political rule became increasingly administrative or technical. Partisan or ideological differences between the two major political parties diminished in importance.

---

[62]   Habermas, *Legitimation Crisis*, pp. 61–7. 'Rationality crisis' refers to the inability of the state to steer the societal community effectively. In the late twentieth century it tended to be associated with fiscal crisis.

[63]   Ibid., p. 37; p. 74.

[64]   Jürgen Habermas, 'Equal Treatment of Cultures and the Limits of Postmodern Liberalism', *The Journal of Political Philosophy*, 13/1 (2005): p. 4.

[65]   Habermas, *Legitimation Crisis*, pp. 69–70.

[66]   Gabriel A. Almond and Sidney Verba, *The Civic Culture: Political Attitudes and Democracy in Five Nations* (London, 1989), pp. 343–4.

[67]   Robert D. Putnam, 'The Strange Disappearance of Civic America', p. 24.

Faith-based Initiatives and Neoliberalism

Neoliberalism jettisons the social-democratic compromise between capital and organized labour, which was based on the principle that 'the state should focus on full employment, economic growth, and the welfare of its citizens and that state power should be freely deployed, alongside of or, if necessary, intervening in or even substituting for market processes to achieve these ends'.[68] The earlier endorsement of 'embedded liberalism' – a 'regulatory environment that sometimes is restrained but in other instances led the way in economic and industrial strategy'[69] – was replaced by 'disembedded' 'market (consumer-driven) democracy'. Those unable to adjust to these new circumstances are abandoned to their unhappy fate and the conception of 'liberty' is redefined

> to encompass the mere purchase of consumer needs, which take the place of natural needs; indeed they *become* natural needs. The mass market caters to individual 'needs' and the satisfaction of these needs becomes the political expression of liberty. [As a result] citizens routinely convey a lack of social responsibility, which is implicated in the weakening of liberty since it can find no way to be expressed in the social order.[70]

In short, 'neoliberalism' asserts that the general welfare 'is best advanced by liberating individual entrepreneurial freedoms and skills within an institutional framework characterized by strong private property rights, free markets and free trade'.[71] It is associated with the increased mobility of capital, an emphasis on financial markets, privatization, debt creation, a redistribution of wealth and income (upward) and an increased reliance on the state to justify these transformations ideologically.[72] Hence, neoliberalism weakens the nation-state but also defines a new role for it.

Associated with neoliberalism are the New Right policies promoted by neoconservatives. Essentially, these seek to weaken the hold of embedded liberalism. They favour dogmatic ('natural') authority, based on automatic patriotism and on reactionary, anti-modern versions of religious fundamentalism. Allegedly, contemporary Christian evangelicals vote for New Right candidates because they believe they 'share their values'. But it is far more likely that, in a larger context, New Right interest in religion is but the deference it shows to expediency. If what is least examined becomes most valuable to political leaders we should not be surprised when 'natural' culture (for example, 'normal' sex,

---

[68]   David Harvey, *A Brief History of Neoliberalism* (Oxford, 2005), p. 10.

[69]   Ibid., p. 11.

[70]   Tim Duvall, 'The New Feudalism: Globalization, the Market and the Great Chain of Consumption', *New Political Science*, 25/1 (2003): p. 93.

[71]   Harvey, *A Brief History of Neoliberalism*, p. 2.

[72]   Ibid., pp. 160–164.

'traditional' marriage, an insistence on Christian dogma) becomes the political coin of the day.

In 2008, presidential candidate Barack Obama opposed many New Right policies. However, like Bill Clinton before him (and like Tony Blair, Gordon Brown or David Cameron in the UK), President Obama was unable or unwilling to challenge, let alone reverse, many of the neoliberal, structural and global changes that have dispersed social-democratic and corporatist forms of rule since the 1980s. Although Obama (like Cameron) was uncomfortable with some facets of neoliberalism, neither he nor Cameron, were able, or inclined, to challenge or reject it directly.

The Obama administration responded to FBIs in the same way as it responded to the Bush administration's foreign policy: it seamlessly continued them. On 5 February 2009, Obama signed a new executive order that effectively replaced Bush's Office of Faith-based and Community Organizations with 'The Office of Faith-based and Neighborhood Partnerships'. He also *expanded* FBIs by appointing a new Advisory Council on 'faith-based' issues. In short, the Obama administration effectively helped solidify and legitimate what the previous administration had championed. As a result, contentious 'reforms' initiated by Bush were normalized. Yet, because Obama was viewed differently by the media, his 'faith-based initiative ... generated little of the critical press coverage associated with President Bush's earlier effort'.[73] Indeed, as *The New York Times* (somewhat sardonically) opined shortly after the new President's inauguration:

> Nearly everyone now takes for granted the wisdom, constitutionality and inevitability of some form of federal financing for community social services run by religious groups. Who anymore can imagine that the United States managed to exist for over 200 years without the government providing any direct aid to faith and its works?[74]

Faith-based initiatives enable government to adjust to what neoliberalism has helped bring about. But, as mentioned previously, the administrative promotion of FBIs as a substitute for what is freely willed from below additionally masks, and even worsens, legitimation deficits. As communicative power declines, political rule increasingly is starved of the semi-autonomous inputs political liberalism once depended on in order to legitimate its particular form of hegemony. In addition, the sphere of privacy that liberalism allegedly emerged to protect in the first place shrivels.

---

[73] Pew Forum on Religion and Public Life, 'Media Coverage of the Faith-based Initiative in the First Six Months of 2001 and 2009' (12 August 2009), <http://pewforum. org/Social-Welfare/The-Starting-Line.aspx#accounting>.

[74] Susan Jacoby, 'Keeping the Faith. Ignoring the History', *The New York Times* (28 February 2009): p. 11.

Legitimation and Motivation Crisis

According to Habermas, the stress points of advanced capitalism were, as we have seen: (1) a 'rationality' (political) crisis and (2) a 'legitimation' (socio-cultural) crisis where sufficient inputs of loyalty and commitment (not merely attention) are lacking. We believe this latter crisis is endemic and has been growing over the last 20–30 years. As Robert Putnam has discovered, since the 1970s civic and political engagement, tolerance and trust, together with 'social capital' (the development of networks, norms and trust), has declined precipitously.[75] As a result, Americans are less likely to vote, less likely to trust government, less likely to volunteer and less likely to get involved in civic organizations. Americans today are less happy with their lives than were their parents and they have fewer close friends.

Examining 'America's Civic Condition', the Brookings Institution recently summarized that involvement in voluntary associations is still relatively high in the USA, compared with Western Europe, but it has not grown for a generation. Fraternal organizations and female auxiliaries have suffered deep losses since the mid-1970s. On the other hand, church-affiliated groups are strong, and evangelical denominations have added members in the last 30–40 years. However, 'as fundamentalist denominations encourage the faithful to rely on one another, there is evidence that they promote distrust of outsiders'.[76] Ironically, this 'helps voter turnout, because a fervent dislike for others motivates people to vote'.[77]

The voluntary sector in the USA is more in flux than in collapse. But, as the Brookings Institution summarizes:

> No one doubts that many forms of participation in official political institutions and activities have declined in recent decades or that Americans are less inclined to express trust in political leaders – and in one another. [Moreover] trust in government has fallen more precipitously than interpersonal trust. Much of the decline took place in 1963–75, an era defined largely by Vietnam and Watergate. And perhaps, to a significant extent, the decline was justified. But there now exists, at least at the extremes, evidence of paranoia rather than healthy distrust. According to a recent study by the University of Virginia's Post-Modernity Project, a fifth of Americans believe that the governing elite is 'involved in a conspiracy'.[78]

---

[75]   Robert D. Putnam, *Bowling Alone: The Collapse and Revival of American Community* (New York, 2000). See, also, Putnam, 'The Strange Disappearance of Civic America'.

[76]   Peter Levine and William M. Galstone, 'America's Civic Condition: A Glance at the Evidence', *Brookings Institute*, (4 January 2012), <http://www.brookings.edu/articles/1997/fall_civilsociety_galston.aspx>.

[77]   Ibid.

[78]   Ibid.

Considerable data exist, then, to support the overall thesis that problems of political legitimacy have grown since the 1960s. Given widespread distrust in, and apathy about, government, it is, perhaps, not surprising that many US 'citizens – particularly the youngest – seem to be shifting their preferred civic involvement from official politics to the voluntary (not necessarily civic) sector. If so, de Tocqueville's thesis would have to be modified: far from acting as a school for wider political involvement, postmodern civil life increasingly might serve as a refuge from (and alternative to) it'.[79]

Summary and Concluding Remarks

The fundamental contradiction of any *capitalist* social formation is that the state must always frame political deliberation so that 'the asymmetrical distribution of chances for the legitimate satisfaction of needs' is unacknowledged.[80] Addressing this issue in *Legitimation Crisis*, and in the earlier *Structural Transformation of the Public Sphere*, Habermas grappled with an issue that had also troubled earlier members of the Frankfurt School: the threat to liberal democracy resulting from a shrinking and deformation of the public sphere.

Faith-based initiatives are a response to the 'legitimation' and 'motivation' crises described and predicted earlier by Habermas.[81] Siding with critical theory against the SSM (but – like Habermas – incorporating many insights of the SSM), our argument and conclusions are as follows.

The advanced capitalist state dealt with market failure by assuming enhanced responsibility for economic growth and social welfare. As a result, accumulation increasingly depended on the state's ability to promote market-replacing and market-substituting policies, thereby creating the threat of dangerous, uncontainable forms of politicization.

Over the last three or four decades, a more managed and circumscribed public sphere was degraded further by mass-mediated forms of communication, the rising significance of 'focus groups', the spectacularization of politics,[82] the declining significance of the nation-state, the increasing mobility of capital, global labour arbitrage and the commercialization of 'public debate'.

These processes worsened both the 'legitimation' and 'motivation' crises. The latter suggests that the requisite quantity of motivations for the state is not forthcoming; the former occurs when the socio-cultural system changes 'in such a way that its output becomes dysfunctional for the state and for the system of

---

[79] Ibid.

[80] Habermas, *Legitimation Crisis*, p. 27.

[81] Habermas, *Legitimation Crisis*, pp. 47–8, 68–75, 75–92.

[82] Guy Debord, *The Society of the Spectacle* (New York, 1994). In the 1970s, Debord suggested presciently that the politics of the future would increasingly be based on the state's response to 'terrorism'.

social labor'.[83] Organized capitalism distanced administrative mechanisms from the system of legitimacy. This meant that there continued to be no expectation of any 'administrative production of meaning'. As a result, the state was required to govern on the basis of its own procedures. But this led to legitimation deficits that threatened the authority, power and scope of government. A weakened state is less able to resist neoliberalism, which favours globalized markets at the expense of national solidarities.[84]

A major difficulty confronting governing elites in the USA over the last two or three decades is the crisis in motivation. In early America, religious orientations emerging from a relatively autonomous lifeworld often shaped vital and highly consequential motivational inputs.[85] However, it is increasingly difficult for religion today to supply 'communicative needs'. Lacking discursively redeemable norms based in relatively autonomous religious communities, religion (like other postmodern identity movements) has increasingly 'retreated into the regions of subjective belief'.[86] Today, the postmodern state may have little alternative but: (1) to help engineer, and respond to, the non-rational fears and fantasies of increasingly mass-mediated constituents; and (2) to mediate among splintered and segmented – largely identity-based – new social movements (many of which are enthusiastically promoted and celebrated by postmodern sociologists).

Both the George W. Bush and Obama administrations have attached state policies to the religious/moral justifications that emerge from an increasingly *sponsored* and constructed lifeworld. This solves the problem of a 'lack of input' from below by co-opting and reinforcing it from above. Still, broaching boundary conditions between: (1) administrative procedures; and (2) the system of legitimacy is risky. First of all, unless the authoritarian option of *requiring* meaning is successfully and totally institutionalized, opposition, and, hence, enhanced segmentation, will ensue. Second, any steering failure makes the state vulnerable to attack from below in the form of endless, vacuous claims that government should be promoting not these particular values but some others. In no way is this likely to be a recipe for political order.

In 2008, Barack Obama received far higher levels of support from Christian evangelicals than did Bill Clinton either in 1992 or 1996. In what was described by *The New York Times* as 'the most intensive effort yet by a Democratic candidate to reach out to self-identified evangelical or born-again Christians', the Obama campaign launched a major initiative to pry Christian fundamentalists 'away from

---

[83] Habermas, *Legitimation Crisis*, p. 75.

[84] Economic globalization weakens the nation-state. But weak nation-states are less able to resist global economic rationalization.

[85] The classic study is Max Weber, *The Protestant Ethic and the Spirit of Capitalism*, trans. Talcott Parsons (New York, 2003 [1905]).

[86] Habermas, *Legitimation Crisis*, p. 77.

their ... attachment to the Republican Party'.[87] Obama operatives also recognized that, since the 1980s, rigid partisan affiliation was on the decline: voters today are increasingly likely to describe themselves as 'independent'. Still, although Obama managed to close the electoral 'God gap', he did not end it. 'Fifty-five per cent of the one-quarter of the electorate who go to church weekly or more still preferred Republican John McCain, as against an opposing 43 per cent, according to exit polls cited by the Pew Forum'.[88]

The fact that (in differing degrees and with divergent levels of enthusiasm) New Right policies were to some extent adopted by both major parties in the USA (as well as by 'New Labour' in the UK) suggests that they are not partisan, but a tactically useful – perhaps necessary – response to structural change. Within their own frame of reference ('natural' economic relations; the remains of traditional society), bourgeois politics were relatively unorganized. By contrast, those of advanced or organized capitalism focused more on the capture of 'natural' administration and were increasingly restrictive or negative in scope. This served to strengthen the nation-state – albeit at the expense of communicative rationality. By contrast, the postmodern agenda of the New Right defends the freedom of global money flows, reduces the domain of public accountability (not, necessarily, authority) and encourages 'a return of the repressed' in the form of unreflective culture.

In modern, liberal, society the public sphere sought to reconcile the particular needs and aspirations of relatively self-reflective (private) individuals with the powerful capabilities of strong, centralized states. For Habermas, such an arrangement necessitated 'a truth dependent mode of socialization', which is to say a mode of identity formation (citizenship) based on generalizable, well-grounded principles.[89] Later, Habermas hoped that liberal democracy could be vested in a 'well-secured private autonomy' founded in 'valid law' 'nourished by the communications of an unsubverted public sphere rooted in the core private spheres of an undisturbed lifeworld via the networks of civil society'.[90]

In *Legitimation Crisis*, however, Habermas suggested that the dissolution of the public sphere (by means of a dedifferentiation of system and lifeworld) would – as he rather alarmingly phrased it, at the time – lead to 'the end of the individual'.[91] What he meant by this was that individuals would no longer be able to locate transcendent or quasi-transcendent bases for reflectively grounded modes of political will-formation. Hence, the state would be free to implement 'decision

---

[87] John M. Broder, 'Obama Courting Evangelicals Once Loyal to Bush', *The New York Times* (1 July 2008), <http://www.nytimes.com/2008/07/01/us/politics/01evangelicals.html?pagewanted=1&_r=1>.

[88] Bruce Nolan, 'Obama Narrows, But Doesn't End, Electoral "God gap"', *The Pew Forum on Religion and Public Life* (13 November 2008), http://pewforum.org/Religion-News/Obama-narrows-but-doesnt-end-electoral-God-gap.aspx.

[89] Habermas, *Legitimation Crisis*, p. 142.

[90] Habermas, *Between Facts and Norms*, p. 408.

[91] Habermas, *Legitimation Crisis*, p. 136; pp. 141–2.

processes' without recourse to 'generalized motivations, values and interests'.[92] Under these circumstances, the state would have to rule 'positivistically' (try to generate legitimacy out of the appearance of legality),[93] or, in addition (as we are now suggesting), it could consolidate 'natural' culture by invoking and facilitating the 'faith-based' 'communities' it had helped to construct in the first place.

What is anathema to the New Right is the idea of 'positive liberty',[94] which advocates the extension and discovery of communicatively based ideas of freedom. According to the New Right, markets always and inevitably deliver social goods far more effectively than does government, and, by the first part of this century, this ideology helped drive the development of risky financial instruments that were predatory and unsupervised. But when government was compelled to bail out the financial organizations that had developed such instruments it became apparent that risk had been socialized from the very beginning. In a parallel manner, contemporary political elites sought administratively to socialize commitment as they 'privatized' (relinquished democratically mandated responsibility for) the public sphere. Faith-based initiatives, in other words, function chiefly to simulate a type of legitimacy for political elites that, thanks to capital and the state, the lifeworld no longer can deliver by itself.

---

92   Ibid, p. 132.

93   Habermas, *Between Facts and Norms*, p. 253.

94   See Isaiah Berlin, 'Two Concepts of Liberty', in Isaiah Berlin, *Four Essays on Liberty* (London, 1969), pp. 1–54.

Chapter 7
Multilevel and Pluricentric Network Governance of Religion

Tuomas Martikainen

Introduction

Interest in the governance or management of religion has become an increasingly fruitful perspective in the study of contemporary religion over the last decade.[1] It is based on the empirical observation that states have shown a growing interest in regulating religions in order to suppress or promote certain forms of religious behaviour.[2] Much of the scholarly debate has revolved around radical and potentially violent religion and, especially, Islam.[3] However, other religions have also been taken into account in these studies, including new religious movements and 'cults'.[4] Even though the state's concern has often been related to terrorism, we have also witnessed the emergence of state activity in the promotion of good relations between different religions, including the 'dialogue of religions',[5] as well as support for many kinds of 'faith-based organizations' in the interests of general welfare.[6]

---

[1] For example, Timothy A. Byrnes and Peter J. Katzenstein (eds), *Religion in an Expanding Europe* (Cambridge, 2006); Veit Bader, *Secularism or Democracy? Associational Governance of Religious Diversity* (Amsterdam, 2007); Paul Bramadat and Matthias Koenig (eds), *International Migration and the Governance of Religion* (Montreal, 2009); Bryan S. Turner, *Religion and Modern Society: Citizenship, Secularisation and the State* (Cambridge, 2011).

[2] For example, Turner, *Religion*, pp. 172–93; Jonathan Laurence, *The Emancipation of Europe's Muslims: The State's Role in Minority Integration* (Princeton: Princeton University Press, 2012).

[3] For an overview, Marcel Maussen, *The Governance of Islam in Western Europe: A State of the Art* (Amsterdam, 2007); Matthias Koenig, 'How Nation-States Respond to Religious Diversity', in Bramadat and Koenig, *International*, pp. 293–322.

[4] For example, Phillip Charles Lucas and Thomas Robbins (eds), *New Religious Movements in the Twenty-First Century: Legal, Political, and Social Challenges in Global Perspective* (London, 2004).

[5] For example, Levent Tezcan, 'Interreligiöser Dialog und politische Religionen' *Aus Politik und Zeitgeschichte*, 28–29 (2006): pp. 26–32.

[6] For example, Adam Dinham, *Faiths, Public Policy and Civil Society: Problems, Policies, Controversies* (Basingstoke, 2009); see also Chapter 5 (Hackworth) and Chapter 6 (Ashley & Sandefer) in this volume.

This chapter stems from two concerns related to the study of the governance of religion today. First, historical church-state relations are an increasingly outdated model with which to describe and analyse the myriad of ways in which states interact with religions. There are growing numbers of state and other actors which are active in these relations, and the classical church-state relations are merely one among many relevant ones.[7] Second, due to the emergence of novel forms of state guidance through public administration reforms (the so-called 'New Public Management'[8]), the role of state-led, hierarchical steering mechanisms is now of less importance than earlier.[9] This chapter accepts the proposition that network governance as a specific form of relationship is of increasing salience and that it functions through a different logic from that of hierarchical modes of governance.[10] The perspective that will be applied in this chapter also takes it as self-evident that neoliberalism and globalization are the driving forces behind the emergence of network governance, but as they have already been elaborated in the introductory chapter, they shall not to a large extent be discussed in the following.

The aim of this chapter is to develop a heuristic tool through which we are better able to identify important actors in the governance of religion, to clarify how network governance processes are conducted and to illustrate what this new perspective implies for a classical analysis of church-state relations. The chapter is laid out as follows. First, it discusses, briefly, existing studies on the governance of religion. Second, it makes clear the differences between state, market and network-centric forms of governance, and presents multilevel and pluricentric governance networks as a specific modality of regulation. Third, the chapter illustrates by examples from Finland how multilevel, pluricentric and networked governance helps to clarify the nature of contemporary governance of religion, and it also briefly reflects on the inherent tensions and problems that this system brings along with it. The chapter concludes by stating that this complex and seemingly amorphous field is best understood as an expression of a new political economy of religion in which network governance has emerged as a new modality of regulation alongside historical church-state relations.

---

[7] For example, Koenig, 'How Nation-States Respond to Religious Diversity', in Bramadat and Koenig, *International*, pp. 293–322; Marcel Maussen and Veit Bader, 'Introduction', in Marcel Maussen, Veit Bader and Annelies Moors (eds), *Colonial and Post-Colonial Governance of Religion: Continuities and Ruptures* (Amsterdam, 2011), pp. 15–17.

[8] For example, Christopher Pollitt, Sandra van Thiel and Vincent Homburg (eds), *New Public Management in Europe: Adaptations and Alternatives* (Basingstone, 2007).

[9] For example, Kees van Kersbergen and Frans van Waarden, '"Governance" as Bridge between Disciplines: Cross-disciplinary Inspiration Regarding Shifts in Governance and Problems of Governability, Accountability and Legitimacy', *European Journal of Political Research*, 43 (2004): p. 143.

[10] Eva Sørensen and Jacob Torfing, 'The Democratic Anchorage of Governance Networks', *Scandinavian Political Studies*, 28/3 (2005): pp. 197–8.

Studies on the Governance of Religion

'Governance' is a concept that has replaced the notion of 'government' in many analyses in recent decades. Whereas 'government' customarily referred to hierarchical modes of regulations, 'governance' implies a more complex logic that includes various forms regulation, persuasion and so on to gain a desired policy outcome.[11] For example, Veit Bader defines governance as states' 'regulation, including mechanisms of action co-ordination and enabling non-market (self-) regulation'.[12] As governance has only recently become a concept used in the study of religion, the following brief discussion of existing scholarship also notes fields of study that have been interested in the state regulation of religion, even though they might not have used the concept of 'governance'. The aim here is not to provide a full presentation of the field, but rather to highlight some areas that are of relevance to the current chapter.

First, in the study of secularization the main focus has been on general social developments, including institutional differentiation, rationalization, industrialization, urbanization and privatization, and the theories have then discussed their societal and cultural implications for religious organizations and religiosity. The state is implicitly presented as a specific, historically formed container of these more general processes that has through law and other norms provided a 'place' of religion. The nation-state is also a common frame in these studies.[13] In historical terms, the role of the Westphalian system has been highlighted to clarify the special position of (majority and minority) churches in Europe.[14] However, secularization theory's main contender, the rational choice theory of religion, focuses much more on the state's regulative role and how that provides space for religious competition. In brief, they argue that the more the state regulates religion, and, especially favours certain majority religions, the less there will be religious competition and, ultimately, religions will be of less importance. In these studies, however, the role of the state is associated mostly with regulating the openness and fairness of the 'religious economy'.[15] The role of other than state-led regulation is not central in these approaches.

Second, the study of church-state relations, or more broadly of religion and law, focuses on the legal dimension in terms of how religions are regulated and how

---

[11] Anne Mette Kjær, *Governance* (Cambridge, 2004), pp. 1–7.

[12] Bader, *Secularism*, p. 50.

[13] For an overview, see James Spickard, 'Narrative versus Theory in the Sociology of Religion: Five Stories of Religion's Place in the Late Modern World', in James Beckford and John Walliss (eds), *Religion and Social Theory: Classical and Contemporary Debates* (Farnham, 2006), pp. 163–75.

[14] For example, Peter J. Katzenstein, 'Multiple Modernities as Limits to Secular Europeanization?', Byrnes and Katzenstein, *Religion*, pp. 30–31.

[15] For example, Rodney Stark and Roger Finke, *Acts of Faith: Explaining the Human Side of Religion* (Berkeley, 2000), pp. 198–203.

they cooperate with the state. These studies carefully present, analyse and often compare different legislative contexts in different societal spheres and countries, and how these rules steer religious organizations and affect religious freedom. Such studies include discussions of the role of national constitutions, different areas of legislation and church financing, among others.[16] Lately, studies of religion and law have increasingly noted the role of international law and human rights norms on religion.[17] Matters that fall outside of the legal framework are of less interest. While the law is obviously important, such a perspective misses, according to Marcel Maussen and Veit Bader, for example, issues of self-regulation, non-state actors' agency and actual policy implementation.[18]

Third, the study of governing Islam in Europe has emerged as a central area in debating the state's role in relation to religion. According to Marcel Maussen's overview of the field, central topics of interest have included mosque establishment, Islamic schools, transformations of religious authority, representation, political mobilization and headscarf debates. In terms of analysis, studies have looked at opportunity structures, state-church relations, colonial legacy and transnationalism, among others.[19] As part of the study of Islam in the West, much interest has been directed at the role of security and terrorism. It has been argued that Muslims have been securitized and that an exclusive focus on national security is also producing new mergings with immigrant integration, security and minority policy, whereby Muslims are drawn into closer relationships with the state.[20] The studies on the governance of Islam in Europe have been in the forefront of bringing more nuanced forms of governance into focus.

Fourth, growing out of the interest in Muslim immigrants in Western countries, but joined with a broader perspective of international migration and immigrant cultural and religious diversity, a field on 'religion and immigration' has emerged. The studies often look at particular communities within a local, regional or national setting. The most well known of these are the US-based 'new immigrant religion' studies in several gateway cities,[21] but similar studies have also been conducted

---

[16]   For example, Gerhard Robbers (ed.), *State and Church in the European Union* (Second Edition, Baden-Baden, 2005); Lisbet Christoffersen, Kjell Å Modéer and Svend Andersen (eds), *Law & Religion in the 21st Century – Nordic Perspectives* (Copenhagen, 2010).

[17]   For example, James T. Richardson, 'Religion, Law, and Human Rights', in Peter Beyer and Lori Beaman (eds), *Religion, Globalization and Culture* (Leiden, 2007), pp. 391–405.

[18]   Maussen and Bader, 'Introduction', p. 17.

[19]   Maussen, *The Governance of Islam in Western Europe*.

[20]   For example, Jonathan Laurence, 'Muslims and the State in Western Europe', in Arianne Chebel d'Appolonia and Simon Reich (eds), *Immigration, Integration, and Security: America and Europe in Comparative Perspective* (Pittsburgh, 2008), pp. 229–53; Ayhan Kaya, *Islam, Migration and Integration: The Age of Securitization* (New York, 2009).

[21]   For an overview of US research, see: Wendy Cadge and Elaine Howard Ecklund, 'Immigration and Religion', *Annual Review of Sociology*, 33 (2007): pp. 359–79.

in many other countries.[22] In this scholarship, there seems to be less focus on regulatory power as such, but the communities are rather seen as emancipatory vehicles for the groups in question as well as negotiation partners with other local institutions. However, several insightful commentaries have emerged from the scholarship on the differences in the inclusion processes of new immigrants, also related to state power.[23] Many of these insights do, however, rest on methodological nationalism,[24] even though the role of transnational networks is often noted.

Fifth, the study of welfare provision by religious organizations, including both historic churches and more recent faith-based organizations, has been of growing interest during the last decade. While not focusing on governance as such, the studies highlight changes in states' relation to religions in welfare provision that are based on New Public Management policies outsourcing previous state-run services to civil society organizations, also in developmental work.[25] These new relationships are influenced by historical models of church-state relations,[26] but in themselves they promote a new rationality for them. However, there is a tendency in some of the literature to applaud the growing role of religious organizations in welfare provision and as active agents in civil society, and provide a less critical focus on the new political economy of which they are part. As contributions in this volume and elsewhere[27] show, the role of neoliberal restructuring in advanced industrial societies is often one of instrumentalizing religion-based welfare provision and charity in efforts to reduce state costs. Nevertheless, the study of FBOs' and others' welfare provision is significant, as it illustrates novel forms of networks and state coordination.

---

[22]   For an overview of European research, see: Michael Stausberg, 'Exploring the Meso-levels of Religious Mappings: European Religion in Regional, Urban, and Local Contexts', *Religion: An International Journal*, 39/2 (2007): pp. 103–8.

[23]   For example, José Casanova, 'Immigrants and the New Religious Pluralism: A European Union/United States Comparison', in Thomas Banchoff (ed.), *Democracy and the New Religious Pluralism* (Oxford, 2007), pp. 59–83; Nancy Foner and Richard Alba, 'Immigrant Religion in the U.S. and Western Europe: Bridge or Barrier to Inclusion?', *International Migration Review*, 42/2 (2008): pp. 360–392.

[24]   Andreas Wimmer and Nina Glick-Schiller, 'Methodological Nationalism and Beyond: Nation-state Building, Migration and the Social Sciences', *Global Networks*, 2/4 (2002): pp. 301–34.

[25]   For example, Gerard Clarke and Michael Jennings (eds), *Development, Civil Society and Faith-Based Organizations* (Basingstoke, 2008).

[26]   Eva Jeppson Grassman, 'Welfare in Western Europe: Existing Regimes and Patterns of Change', in Anders Bäckström and Grace Davie with Ninna Edgardh and Per Pettersson (eds), *Welfare and Religion in 21st Century Europe: Volume 1. Configuring the Connections* (Farnham, 2010).

[27]   For example, Dinham, *Faiths*; Anders Bäckström and Grace Davie with Ninna Edgardh and Per Pettersson (eds), *Welfare and Religion in 21st Century Europe: Volume 1. Configuring the Connections* (Farnham, 2010).

In conclusion, this brief overview of some of the key debates shows clearly that the state and different forms of regulation are again firmly on the agenda of the sociology of religion and related fields that reflect upon contemporary religion. On the one hand, there seems to be a consensus emerging that national differences in the regulation of religion are a key explanatory factor in understanding the varied outcomes in different countries.[28] On the other hand, seemingly contrary to this notion is also a broad consensus that there are many similarities in the responses of states to increased religious diversity.[29] My own position is to argue for a continuing, but weakened path dependency of national regimes that is supplemented by both new forms of governance networks and an increasing international layer of policy formation that can provide varied outcomes in different contexts.[30] At times, the two regimes converge and overlap, but ultimately they function through different logics and target somewhat different issues. Thereby the following discussion should be seen as an attempt to map out an emerging new regime of governing religion that may or may not challenge the historical models.

Governance Networks

A starting point in the study of governance networks is to distinguish between three modalities of cooperation between public and private organizations. The first one of these is the classical state bureaucratic model of a *unicentric* or hierarchical modality, where 'state rule is based on the undisputed centrality of the sovereign state that turns everybody else into subjects of the law'.[31] Rules are conducted via laws and regulations, which are implemented and enforced by public administration. Not following the rules leads to legal sanctions. The second modality is that of the market, the *multicentric* form, where competition is 'based on an infinite number of self-interested actors who are not bound by any common agendas, purposes or commitments'.[32] The procedural rationality of market competition relies on the 'invisible hand' leading to optimal allocation of goods and services, and is based on the fear of loss. The third form is the *pluricentric* modality of governance networks that 'involve a large number of interdependent

---

[28]   For example, Joel Fetzer and Christopher Soper, *Muslims and the State in Britain, France, and Germany* (Cambridge: Cambridge University Press, 2005).

[29]   For example, Matthias Koenig, 'How Nation-States Respond to Religious Diversity', in Bramadat and Koenig, *International*.

[30]   I discuss the same issue from a welfare state perspective in: Tuomas Martikainen, 'The Global Political Economy, Welfare State Reforms, and the Governance of Religion', in Peter Nynäs, Mika Lassander and Terhi Utriainen (eds), *The Post-Secular Society* (London, 2012), pp. 71–93.

[31]   Sørensen and Torfing, 'The Democratic Anchorage of Governance Networks', p. 197.

[32]   Sørensen and Torfing, 'The Democratic Anchorage of Governance Networks', p. 197.

actors who interact in order to produce a public purpose'.[33] Decision-making takes place through negotiations, and compliance is achieved via trust and political obligation that lead over time to self-regulation.

Governance networks are thereby a specific and distinct modality of state regulation that differs from the classical unicentric and market-based multicentric modality through the interdependency of involved actors and the centrality of negotiation and mutual trust in the network. Eva Sørensen and Jacob Torfing define governance networks as follows: they are

> (1) a relatively stable horizontal articulation of *interdependent*, but operationally *autonomous* actors, (2) who interact through *negotiations* that involve bargaining, deliberation and intense power struggles, (3) which take place within a *relatively institutionalized framework* of contingently articulated rules, norms, knowledge and social imaginaries, (4) that is *self-regulating* within limits set by external agencies and (5) which contribute to the production of *public purpose* in the broad sense of visions, ideas, plans and regulations.[34]

Governance networks are flexible and more sensitive to complex social problems, and they can be important for gathering information and considering competing solutions, because the network participants often have detailed knowledge that is not otherwise available to policymakers. Governance networks may be especially suited for creating consensus and reducing the risk of failure in policy implantation.[35] What exactly forms a governance network remains to be looked at case by case, but to illustrate a few we could look for networks including both religious and public authority representatives. These would include, for example, temporary groups formed around specific social problems, or permanent or *ad hoc* associations that focus on specific questions or projects. The bonds between different actors can be loose or institutionally more strictly defined. These may also altogether create 'shadow networks' where key individuals are able to monitor and guide development, leading to a form of 'meta-governance'.[36]

Multilevel governance takes as its point of departure the interdependency of actors on different political and territorial tiers, including the global, transnational, national, regional and local. Hence, relevant actors in any particular case can be positioned in different political and territorial tiers or levels of organization, but in one way or another are dependent on each other.[37] An example of multilevel

[33] Sørensen and Torfing, 'The Democratic Anchorage of Governance Networks', p. 197.

[34] Sørensen and Torfing, 'The Democratic Anchorage of Governance Networks', p. 197. Numbering is added by the author.

[35] Sørensen and Torfing, 'The Democratic Anchorage of Governance Networks', pp. 198–9.

[36] Sørensen and Torfing, 'The Democratic Anchorage of Governance Networks', p. 202.

[37] Ian Bache and Matthew Flinders, 'Themes and Issues in Multi-level Governance', in Ian Bache and Matthew Flinders (eds), *Multi-level Governance* (Oxford, 2004), p. 3.

governance has been the role of the European Union in creating local change through framework funding. As the EU promotes the subsidiarity principle, it has meant a new, more extensive relationship between the EU and local or regional bodies that in some instances surpasses state-led policies.[38] While the study of multilevel governance has its origins in the study of European integration, it is useful also in explicating well the increasingly complex relationships of global interconnectivity.

Multilevel and pluricentric network governance as a perspective is well suited to a study of the complex and interwoven, seemingly amorphous constellations where state regulation is somehow part of the whole. Pedersen, Sehested and Sørensen have modelled the perspective through three key areas and their interconnections. These are: (1) network-based relations and connectivity, (2) meanings and storytelling and (3) institutions and meta-governance. Networks communicate with institutions and create meaning and narratives that eventually start to frame the issues that the network is about.[39] Pedersen et al. stress the role of narrative framings in the process of coordination that 'provide *dynamic, decentered, interactive, situated,* and *overlapping linkages that promote communication between otherwise disconnected stories and practices'*.[40] The authors' emphasis on the centrality of common narratives is understandable through the reliance of governance networks on a shared agenda and, often, on funding from external sources, as these ultimately legitimate and make possible the networks' existence.

The Case of Finland – an Illustration and Discussion of Governance Networks

Network governance in a broad sense of the term is not new. States have previously also regulated and cooperated through many kinds of constellations and modalities with religions, even if these have not been in the focus of scholarship. For example, Central European corporatism often includes churches as key actors in the provision of social welfare.[41] What is new, though, is the extent to which governance networks deal with issues of contemporary religious diversity, and how (potentially) transformative these are.[42] In the following shall be illustrated how Christian, Islamic and Jewish religious organizations in Finland have entered

---

[38]   Patrick Ireland, *Becoming Europe: Immigration, Integration, and the Welfare State* (Pittsburgh, 2004), p. 172.

[39]   Anne Reff Pedersen, Karina Sehested and Eva Sørensen, 'Emerging Theoretical Understanding of Pluricentric Coordination in Public Governance', *The American Review of Public Administration,* 41/4 (2011): pp. 388–90.

[40]   Anne Reff Pedersen, Karina Sehested and Eva Sørensen, 'Emerging Theoretical Understanding of Pluricentric Coordination in Public Governance', p. 389. Italics in original.

[41]   Bader, *Secularism,* pp. 60–61.

[42]   For example on the role of Islamic councils, see: Laurence, *Emancipation.*

new relationships both with each other and with the Finnish state during the 1990s and 2000s.

Finland gained its independence from tsarist Russia in 1917. Prior to that it was an eastern province of Sweden until 1809, whereby it had become a Catholic and, since the Reformation, Lutheran outpost of Northern Europe. The Lutheran Church was the dominant, majority church, that together with a small Finnish Orthodox Church, had a favoured position in public law in relation to other religions, but its role as the state church no longer continued in the independent nation-state. While some connections between the state and the Lutheran Church remained, these were mainly severed during the 1990s. The two churches have had a large degree of autonomy, but also some obligations, including having to care for most of the graveyards in Finland. Minority religions, especially minor Protestant churches, but also Jewish and Muslim communities, have enjoyed complete religious freedom since 1922, but their societal position has been marginal.[43] While historically a poor, peripheral European region and, later, state, Finland rose to high levels of prosperity and built a well-developed, social democratic welfare state in the post-World War II period. In postwar Finnish society, there was little room for religion, which seemed to be waning in importance anyway due to increasing secularization. The regulation of religion tended to give it further autonomy.

Towards the end of the 1980s, Finland started to implement changes in public administration which were inspired by New Public Management (NPM), leading to the outsourcing and privatization of formerly state-run activities. The turn of the 1990s brought along important changes in the geopolitical space, where Finland had so far manoeuvred in the shadow of the Soviet Union, while not officially being part of the Eastern Bloc. The collapse of Soviet rule in 1991 contributed to a deep economic recession in Finland, but also opened a window of opportunity for more pro-Western policies. In 1995, Finland joined the EU in a move that was to have long-lasting effects in many areas of society, including further reforms in public administration and the strengthening role of NPM and associated policies. One of the consequences of these reforms was an increasing use of projects and networks, in addition to market-based solutions, in public administration.[44]

Whereas public administration reforms at the time seemed unrelated to questions of religion, they were to have an impact after some time. As a follow up to the fall of the Soviet Union, Finland over the next few years became the target

---

[43] Markku Heikkilä, Jyrki Knuutila and Martin Scheinin, 'State and Church in Finland', in Gerhard Robbers (ed.), *State and Church in the European Union* (Baden-Baden, 2005), pp. 520–523.

[44] For example, Risto Heiskala, 'Kansainvälisen toimintaympäristö muutos ja Suomen yhteiskunnallinen murros', in Risto Heiskala and Eeva Luhtakallio (eds), *Uusi jako: Miten Suomesta tuli kilpailukyky-yhteiskunta?* (Helsinki, 2006), pp. 22–3, 31–4; Aimo Ryynänen and Asko Uoti, 'Kunnallinen itsehallinto ja uusi hallintotapa', in Ilari Karppi and Lotta-Mari Sinervo (eds), *Governance: Uuden hallintotavan jäsentyminen* (Tampere, 2009), pp. 220–221.

of new waves of immigration somewhat unexpectedly, and, hence, the numbers of immigrants started to rapidly grow. Among the new immigrants were many ethnic Finns returning from the former Soviet Union, as well as asylum seekers, including many Muslims.[45] After joining the EU, Finland also became eligible to use the EU's framework funding, among other issues, which was to play a major role in immigrant integration. In the governance of immigration issues, both projects and networks (these two are often interlinked) have become prominent tools for advancing immigrant integration. Embedded in the approach are NMR tools, including 'best practices', 'networking', 'knowledge sharing', 'mainstreaming' and so on. This meant that over time, at least in immigration services, networking became a fundamental element of everyday working practice.[46]

While religious organizations are not often included in immigrant projects, at times they have participated. In the existing literature, at least Lutheran[47] and Muslim[48] organizations have become part of both immigrant projects and governance networks, although for different reasons. While the Lutheran Church had been engaged in minor social work even earlier, it gained a role and, especially, visibility, in poor relief and welfare provision in the aftermath of the economic recession of 1990–93, when it distributed food aid to the unemployed. The images of 'bread queues' where people waited for their weekly portion became major news and a key event in the collective memory of the recession. Especially the Salvation Army, but also the Lutheran Church, became known for distributing this food aid. In time, immigrants (of many religions) also became recipients of such services. Projects and networking with other organizations and the public sector became a key element in these new services, not to mention EU framework funding. The Church has also been vocal in public about the downsides of neoliberal policies, including their impact on the national welfare model.[49] Hence, the Lutheran Church has entered into the realm of new forms of poor relief and welfare provision as a service provider that has both taken advantage of novel types of public funding, as well as being critical of neoliberalism. Through these activities it has also been positioning itself against the dominant political ideology of its time, distancing its

---

[45] Tuomas Martikainen, Kathleen Valtonen and Östen Wahlbeck, 'The Social Integration of Immigrants in Finland', in James S. Frideres and John Biles (eds), *International Perspectives: Integration and Inclusion* (Montreal, 2012), pp. 127–46.

[46] Salla Tuori, *The Politics of Multicultural Encounters: Feminist Postcolonial Perspectives* (Åbo, 2009), pp. 35–8.

[47] For example, Anne Birgitta Pessi, Olav Helge Angell and Per Pettersson, 'Nordic Majority Churches as Agents in the Welfare State: Critical Voices and/or Complementary Providers?', *Temenos*, 45/2 (2009): pp. 207–34.

[48] For example, Tuomas Martikainen, 'The Governance of Islam in Finland', *Temenos*, 43/2 (2007): pp. 243–65.

[49] Mikko Malkavaara, 'Nälkä ja köyhyys kirkon asiaksi – Näkökulmia laman ja markkinakilpailun aikana', in Virpi Mäkinen (ed.), *Lasaruksesta leipäjonoihin: Köyhyys kirkon kysymyksenä* (Jyväskylä, 2002), pp. 296–303.

identification with the state that, despite the official separation of church and state, has remained strong.

The trajectory for the Muslim organizations' cooperation with public authorities in Finland is somewhat different. Unlike many Western states, Finland has had a small Muslim community ever since the 1870s. The Tatars settled in a few urban areas starting from the 1870s until the 1920s. They have a well-developed community structure with mosques and associations, but have always some kept some distance from the state. While there was a slow influx of Muslims to post-war Finland, it was not until the 1990s that the numbers began to quickly rise, from an estimated 4,000 in 1990 to 50,000–60,000 individuals in 2010. As about two-thirds of the Muslims were refugees, it meant that in the context of the Finnish welfare state, they ended up in close contact with public authorities. Many ended up unemployed or in education, implying that social workers, employment offices and public schools soon had, as clients or pupils, people of ethnic and religious backgrounds other than what had previously been customary.[50] All through the 1990s public authorities in various sectors of the state apparatus were coming to terms with immigrants of different religious backgrounds, of whom some also demanded – or were thought to be asking for – special treatment, because of their ethnic and religious backgrounds. Besides basic human interaction, a common way to solve these (real or imagined) problems involved creating social projects which allowed access to extra resources and were increasingly seen as an effective solution in public administration. Also the immigrants organized themselves. Literally hundreds of new immigrant associations were founded in the 1990s and continued to promote various causes into the 2000s, among them significant numbers of religious organizations. Also worthy of note is the fact that those national groups with the most contact with public authorities were over-represented among the immigrant associations.[51] Many of the religious associations were quick to establish contact with, or were contacted by, public authorities in order to solve pressing issues.[52] In other words, during the 1990s there grew a multitude of local projects, associations, networks and *ad hoc* cooperative organizations to promote and disentangle new issues related to growing ethnic and religious diversity.

As we arrive at the 2000s, public administration reforms have been implemented for over a decade already and NPM policies have shaped the available policy options and preferences in problem solving. Now we also start to see an increase in efforts to create permanent structures for the representation of new, immigrant origin diversity in the population on the national and international levels. To name some of the more central ones: (1) *the Advisory Board for Ethnic Relations*

---

[50] Tuomas Martikainen, 'Finland', in Göran Larsson (ed.), *Islam in the Nordic and Baltic Countries* (London: Routledge, 2009), pp. 76–89.

[51] Miikka Pyykkönen, 'Integrating Governmentality: Administrative Expectations for Immigrant Associations in Finland', *Alternatives*, 32 (2007): pp. 197–224.

[52] Tuomas Martikainen, *Immigrant Religions in Local Society: Historical and Contemporary Perspectives in the City of Turku* (Åbo, 2004), pp. 244–6.

(ETNO), run by the Finnish Government, was founded in 1998 and has later evolved into an expert body with national and regional boards which involves the representation of civil society organizations; (2) *the Ombudsman for Minorities* was created in 2002 to protect the rights of new ethnic minorities, among others; (3) *the Islamic Council of Finland* (SINE) was founded in 2006 to represent the various Muslim organizations in Finland – this institution was based on an initiative of the Ombudsman of Minorities; (4) *the Dialogue among Civilizations Group* was founded as part of the Ministry of Foreign Affairs in 2006; (5) *the Cooperation Forum of Religions in Finland* (USKOT-RESA) was founded in 2011, based on a religious dialogue forum started by the President of Finland in 2001, and it has representatives from Christian, Jewish and Muslim organizations. What had happened?

In the aftermath of 9/11 and, especially, the Muhammad cartoons controversy of 2005–06, the Finnish authorities started to pay more attention to religious radicalism in general and Islam in particular. This was in part due to external pressure from the EU, the USA and the United Nations, whereby the threat of Islamic terrorism was noted, relevant legislation was implemented and resources for counterterrorism surveillance were increased.[53] In addition to these 'hard' measures, more emancipatory lines of reasoning started to take shape, namely those calling for social inclusion and cultural/religious dialogue. The first one of these expressed more or less the rationale of the Finnish welfare state, whereby an individual's background should not be a disadvantage in her life. This notion is, however, somewhat transformed in the public policy reforms, and instead of society's responsibility, one's own responsibility is elevated to a higher role. This is primarily what the many immigrant projects aim at doing. The second main stream concerns cultural and religious dialogue, and we have seen a rapid growth of many associations, projects, networks and so on promoting a fruitful dialogue of religions.[54]

Common features for all these new constellations are that they essentially interact with their social and institutional environment through networks. Only rarely are there formal, hierarchical structures that define this interaction, or if there is, it applies only to a limited extent to all participants. There is also significant overlap in both individual and institutional membership of the governing bodies or councils of these organizations. They also combine local, national and, at times, international interests from various sectors of society that do not necessarily have much in common elsewhere. The organizations draw their legitimacy from proposing to function as a negotiation mechanism for the common good,

---

[53] Toby Archer and Leena Malkki, 'Terrorismin- ja radikalisaation vastaisuuden nousu Suomessa', in Tuomas Martikainen and Marja Tiilikainen (eds), *Islam, hallinta ja turvallisuus* (manuscript in review).

[54] For example, Tuomo Melasuo, Matti Pesu and Outi Tomperi (eds), *Impivaarasta pyramideille: Kulttuurienvälinen vuoropuhelu ja suomalainen kansalaisyhteiskunta* (Tampere, 2011).

including societal harmony and good ethnic relations. There are no models for such constellations in church-state relations in Finland. The closest that exist are governmental boards concerned with issues related to Roma and Sami populations, which are both historical minorities in Finland, and even there the focus is more on legal rights and the responsibilities of the state *vis-à-vis* the minority in question. In sum, they are paradigmatic examples of multilevel and pluricentric governance networks and meta-governance of new ethnic and religious diversity in Finland.

So, if we are indeed witnessing the formation of a new modality of church-state relations, as I have argued here, what does this imply? First of all, it signals that the legal, formal relations might today be of less importance than they were earlier. This brings in a question of democracy, as significant negotiations and consensus formations take place outside of democratically elected bodies, such as parliament, even if the processes themselves have democratic approval. Second, it elevates interreligious relations to key status in contemporary religious dynamics. Questions of the inclusion or exclusion of these networks may become significant for individual groups and communities, and may affect their ability to function. Third, it requires the sensitivity to identify the significant actors at different levels and an ability to evaluate the nature of these relationships. Fourth, it requires more focus on governance networks in research, with respective theoretical and methodological tools to identify key developments and actors. Finally, it challenges the academic specialization of the study of religion, to learn about areas with which it has had little to do historically, such as international relations, public administration and social policy.

Conclusion

This chapter has presented multilevel and pluricentric governance networks as a new and increasingly important modality in the state's efforts to regulate religion. It is seen to be part of a wider change in the global political economy that on its behalf is a result of globalization in the broadest sense and the associated ideology of neoliberalism, as well as the changes on the regulation of religion which may well for the most part be a mere side-effect of these changes. The results of changing patterns of governance, however, are not as random and unsystematic as it might be thought. Rather, we have seen multiple efforts to coordinate religion for many different ends, including good ethnic relations, social cohesion, better (or less costly) provision of welfare and so on. Whereas the actual (national) contexts of these shifts in emphasis matter and respond in their own ways, still the general direction of movement is towards a closer relationship between many (if not all) religious organizations and the state.

Network governance does not replace previous forms of government, but has grown along with and beside them. In the long term they may be incorporated into law and other existing institutions, but even as such, they will change the existing modality of government on religion. As a network governance of religion has risen alongside the pluralization of the religious field, we may expect it to have its most significant role precisely in governing ethnically and religiously diverse societies. At least individuals and organizations attached to these networks will be transformed in the process, which, of course, is the intention of governance in the first place. How far interreligious networking will reach remains an open question, but it has the ability to create new power blocks and to exclude those not wished welcome.

Acknowledgements

The article has been written in association with Transnational and Local: The Social Integration of Immigrant Communities Project, funded by the Academy of Finland (project number 131720).

Chapter 8

Regulating Religion in a Neoliberal Context: The Transformation of Estonia

Ringo Ringvee

I am not an economist. I am a practical man. I had read only one book on economics. This was Milton Friedman's *Free to Choose*. I must say that to my mind all the ideas which were presented there looked to be very practical. I was not too well informed. I did not know that not many countries, or rather no country at all had ever used the same policies. It looked very logical to me. Hence I introduced these things. They have worked very well in Estonia and are now being followed in lots of other countries.

Mart Laar, the Prime Minister of the first Cabinet of Ministers of the Republic of Estonia (1992–94).[1]

Introduction

The disintegration of the Soviet Union and the fall of its satellite regimes in Central and Eastern Europe in the late 1980s and the early 1990s were followed by social and political reforms that changed the economic as well as the ideological/ political landscape in Europe considerably. The reforms and transition processes from totalitarian-political and state-regulated economic regimes to democratic free market systems were influenced by local, historical traditions as well as by global influences and the general attitudes of the times. In the transition processes from totalitarian to democratic systems, individual choice, the rule of law, personal freedom and free markets were the key issues for social transformation. One of the ideologies that were introduced in the transition states of Central and Eastern Europe was neoliberalism (see the introductory chapter of this volume).

Estonia was one of the post-Soviet countries where, shortly after the collapse of the Soviet regime, neoliberal reforms were implemented quickly and decisively. Rapid privatization, a flat tax system and an attractive economic and political climate for foreign investors, combined with decisive orientation to the West, soon made Estonia one of the success stories among the post-Soviet transition countries entering the consumer society. A neoliberal approach was also applied to religion

---

[1] Paul Belien, 'Walking on Water: How to Do It', *The Brussels Journal* (27 August 2005), <http://www.brusselsjournal.com/node/202, accessed 4 October 2011>.

in Estonia. This involved an implementation of the principles of religious freedom, minimizing state intervention in religion, and creating a free market of religions. Estonia is a secular society, and while it has often been considered to be one of the least (institutionally) religious countries in the world, or at least in Europe, it is at the same time also considered to be one of the countries where governmental regulations on religion are minimal, and where freedom of religion is guaranteed both in the legislation as well as in practice. The main aim in what follows here is to give an analysis of the outcome of the neoliberal religious policy which was implemented in Estonia from the early 1990s, and to look at how religious institutions have adapted to the free market of religions. However, to understand the current situation of Estonian society, some historical background should be taken into account.

Religion in Estonia

Estonia is a small country in the northeast of Europe. Estonia's population was, according to official statistics gathered in January 2011, approximately 1.34 million, with native Estonian speakers numbering approximately 924,000.[2] From the thirteenth century onwards, Estonia had been ruled, respectively, by Danish and Swedish kings, the Teutonic Order, the Baltic German gentry and Russian czars; and in the seventeenth century the southern area of Estonia was, for a short time, part of the Polish-Lithuanian Commonwealth.

Estonia's religious history is a history of discontinuities. By 1224 Estonia had been Christianized as a result of the Northern Crusade. The era of the Roman Catholic Church in Estonia lasted from the thirteenth to the sixteenth century; the Lutheran Reformation reaching Estonia in 1524. Since then the Lutheran Church has been the dominant religious institution in Estonia. Even when Estonia became part of the Russian Empire in 1721, the Lutheran Church retained its dominant position due to close relations with the Baltic German gentry. Although the Russian Orthodox Church enjoyed the status of state church in the Russian Empire, it only started missionary activities in Estonia as late as the 1840s. There were two waves of religious conversion from the Lutheran Church to the Orthodox Church among native Estonian peasants; one took place in the 1840s and the other in the 1880s when the Orthodox Church took a more active role.[3] A considerable number of Estonians became members of the Orthodox Church, and the reasons for conversion have been considered to be mostly economically or politically motivated. Although there were Estonian Lutheran clergy in the nationalist movement from the 1860s onward, the majority of the Lutheran clergy were non-Estonians – mostly Baltic Germans – until the early twentieth century.[4]

---

[2]   Statistical Office of Estonia, <www.stat.ee>, accessed 20 February 2012.

[3]   Toivo U. Raun, *Estonia and the Estonians*, updated second edn (Stanford, 2001), p. 50.

[4]   See also, Steve Bruce, 'The Supply Side Model of Religion: The Nordic and Baltic States', *Journal for the Scientific Study of Religion*, 39/1 (2000): p. 42.

In 1918 Estonia established its independence as a democratic republic. In 1920 Estonia and Soviet Russia signed a peace treaty after two years of war, and the army of the Baltic German gentry was defeated on the southern border of Estonia. The first Estonian Constitution was adopted in 1920. This Constitution stipulated freedom of religion, and stated that there is no state religion in Estonia. Religious associations were considered to be self-administering and self-financing associations. In 1925 the *Religious Societies and their Associations Act* was adopted and it established the principle of equal treatment of religious associations by the state. According to the 1934 population census, Lutherans formed 78.2 per cent of the population, followed by the Orthodox population with 19 per cent.[5]

Relations between the state and religious associations started to change in the 1930s when political trends in Europe became generally more authoritarian. In 1934 a new constitution was adopted in Estonia and the parliamentarian form of governance was replaced by a presidential one. It was followed by a *coup d'état* as the acting head of state enforced the *Emergency Act* and continued to rule until 1940. In December 1934 he enforced a new *Churches and Religious Societies Act* by means of a presidential decree. This legal act introduced a differentiated approach on the part of the state towards religious associations. Churches with a membership of more than 100,000 members, namely the Estonian Evangelical Lutheran Church (EELC) and the autonomous Estonian Apostolic Orthodox Church, had a special relationship with the government. However, the state church system was not implemented. The development of closer relations between the state and the majority churches ended in 1940 due to the change in the political system.

According to the secret protocols of the Molotov-Ribbentrop Pact of 1939, Estonia belonged to the sphere of interest of the Soviet Union. In 1940 Estonia was incorporated to the Soviet Union as a Soviet Socialist Republic. The period of the Soviet regime in Estonia (1940–41, 1944–91) and the Soviet-Marxist policy of atheism succeeded in breaking the customary transmission of religious traditions, as well as to a large extent marginalizing Estonian religious institutions. The EELC, a traditional, majority church, was politically neutralized by the Soviet authorities by 1949, and was socially marginalized during the Soviet atheistic campaigns of the late 1950s and the early 1960s, which stigmatized religiosity and replaced religious rites of passage with Soviet ones.[6]

During the late 1980s the Soviet regime started to collapse and a national re-awakening was taking place in Estonia, as it was in other Baltic States. There was also a change in attitudes concerning religion and 'the Church' in general. According to the World Values Survey of 1990 'the Church' was the third most

---

[5] *Rahvastiku koostis ja korteriolud: 1. III 1934 rahvaloenduse andmed. Vihk II,* [The Composition of the Population and Housing Conditions. Data from the 1934 Population Census] (Tallinn, 1935), pp. 118–27.

[6] Raun, *Estonia and the Estonians*, p. 218.

trusted institution in Estonian society.[7] In 1990 the post of Commissioner of Religious Affairs was dissolved, and the responsibilities for the relations between the state and religion were placed in the Ministry of Culture.[8]

With the end of the Soviet regime restrictions on religious activities were abolished. Religion, and especially the EELC, was taken to be the link that connected the present with the period of independence that had ended in 1940. At the same time, new religious movements started their activities in Estonia. Although the traditional churches were critical of these new competitors in the unregulated religious sphere, there was neither an anti-cult movement nor an organized move to compete with the new arrivals. The general attitude in society towards any kind of church/religion/spirituality was positively tolerant. Religion enjoyed a positive image in the press.

As has been argued elsewhere, the deregulation of a religious economy is followed by increasing religious pluralism.[9] This also took place in Estonia during the early 1990s. Religious pluralism itself, however, does not mean that religious activity accordingly increases. In spite of claims by the rational choice/supply side theory of religion that the deregulation of religious 'markets' increases religious vitality, this did not happen in Estonia. Steve Bruce argued more than a decade ago on the religious situation in Eastern Europe, that religion flourishes in European societies with strong religio-ethnic identities, and not in religiously diverse, but secular societies where religion in general does not have much importance.[10] The example of Estonia is a good illustration of Bruce's point. Estonia is a religiously diverse country with many different old and new religious traditions. At the same time, a connection between Estonian national and religious identity is largely missing due to historical factors. Religion was not considered to be an important factor in nation building in the nineteenth century, as the Lutheran Church had close connections with the Baltic German nobility, and the majority of the Lutheran clergy were not native Estonians. The development of a closer connection between the state and the EELC from 1934 onward ended in 1940 due to the Soviet occupation. In contrast with many other European societies, the Estonian national identity is not related to any particular religious identity. The Estonian identity is much more related to language and territory. Religion and religious participation are a matter for the private sphere.

---

[7]   2009 Estonian Human Development Report 2009 (Tallinn, 2011), p. 113, <www.kogu.ee/public/eia2009/EIA2009_engredis.pdf>.

[8]   ENSV Teataja 1990, 10, 163 *Eesti NSV Valitsuse määrus nr 67 Eesti NSV Riikliku Usuameti moodustamise kohta* [Governmental Regulation No 67 of the Estonian SSR on establishing the Board of Religion], (Tallinn, 1990). Riho Altnurme, 'Relations with the State', in Riho Altnurme (ed.), *History of Estonian Ecumenism* (Tallinn, 2009), pp. 311–13.

[9]   For example, Roger Finke, 'The Consequences of Religious Competition. Supply-side Explanations for Religious Change', in Lawrence A. Young (ed.), *Rational Choice Theory and Religion: Summary and Assessment* (New York, 1997), p. 52.

[10]   Steve Bruce, 'Modernisation, Religious Diversity and Rational Choice in Eastern Europe', *Religion, State and Society*, 27/3–4 (1999): pp. 273–4.

According to the population census of the year 2000, 29 per cent of the population older than 15 years of age considered themselves to be adherents of some religious tradition. 13.57 per cent of the population considered themselves to be Lutherans, while 12.8 per cent defined themselves as Orthodox.[11] A sociological survey on religiosity in Estonia which was carried out in 2010[12] presented the country as one of the most unchurched countries in Europe. According to a survey, 16.4 per cent of the respondents considered themselves to be members of some congregation or religious movement.[13] It has been argued that in the 1990s it was most convenient for Estonians with broken religious traditions and with no religious framework not to define themselves religiously.[14] Thus Grace Davie's notion about British religiosity – believing without belonging – seems to hold true also in Estonia.[15] But what do Estonians believe in? According to the results from the 2010 survey on the religious life of the Estonian population, even the beliefs of the population who belong to Christian congregations are very heterodox.[16] The Estonian researcher Lea Altnurme has noted that in contemporary Estonia there has been 'a notable tendency toward church-free spirituality'.[17]

Deregulating the Religious 'Market'

Socio-political activism in Estonia during the late 1980s was reflected also in the field of religion. The religious institutions in Estonia were not at the forefront of the independence movement as the Roman Catholic Church was in Lithuania or in Poland. Governmental restrictions on religion and religious activities were

[11] 2000 Population and Housing Census (Tallinn, 2002), pp. 292–3.

[12] *Elust, usust, usuelust 2010* [On Life, Faith, Religious Life 2010] (2010), a sociological survey conducted by social and market research company Saar Poll from 25 March to 11 April 2010.

[13] The percentage of Estonians who considered themselves to be believers was 6.2 per cent of the respondents while that of believers among non-Estonians was 26.2 per cent. (*Elust, usust, usuelust* 2010).

[14] Raigo Liiman, *Usklikkus muutuvas Eesti ühiskonnas* [Religiosity in a Changing Estonian Society], (Tartu 2001), p. 54.

[15] Grace Davie, *Religion in Modern Europe* (Oxford, 2000), p. 3; Pille Valk, *Religiooniõpetus Eestis* [Religious Education in Estonia], in Pille Valk (ed.), *Töid religioonipedagoogikast I* (Tartu, 2008), pp. 93–4; Ringo Ringvee, *Riik ja religioon nõukogudejärgses Eestis 1991–2008* [State and Religion in Post-Soviet Estonia 1991–2008] (Tartu, 2011), p. 45.

[16] Ringo Ringvee, 'Ristiusu kohtumine teiste vaimsete praktikatega – Eestimaa kogemus' [Christianity Encountering other Spiritual Practices – the Estonian Experience], in Eerik Jõks (ed.), *Astu alla rahva hulka* (Tallinn, 2012).

[17] Lea Altnurme, 'Changes in Mythic Patterns in Estonian Religious Life Stories', *Social Compass* 58/1 (2011): p. 80.

removed gradually from 1988 onwards. Many of the Lutheran clergy were involved in the heritage protection movement, which was one of the first civic associations.

A drafting process for new legislation on religious organizations had started in the Soviet Union by 1989. In 1990 the last Commissioner for Religious Affairs in Soviet Estonia had prepared a proposal for new legislation on religious organizations. Although the draft version of the new law was published in the newspaper of the EELC, it was later withdrawn for unknown reasons. The office of Commissioner for Religious Affairs was liquidated in 1990. The staff of the Commissioner's office initiated a new governmental institution, the Board of Religion (*Usuamet*). However, the Board did not become operational as there emerged another new agency from the Ministry of Culture to take responsibility for the relations between state and religious associations. Already in May 1990 the Estonian Ministry of Culture had organized a roundtable for religious associations and governmental agencies, and for six months there were two institutions taking care of matters related to religion. In November 1990 the Religious Affairs Bureau was established at the Ministry of Culture. The staff of the Religious Affairs Bureau had no relation to the previous Commissioner for Religious Affairs office. At the same time the new staff did not represent directly any religious group in Estonia either. There was also no ready-made model for the relationship between the state and religious organizations. The new agency also ignored to some extent the ecumenical Estonian Council of Churches, which was founded in 1989 with the involvement of the Religious Affairs Commissioner.[18]

The years from the late 1980s until 1992 have been called the era of the church boom in Estonian religious history as the numbers of religious services were at a peak, as were the numbers of donating members. This period has been described as being full of confusion and enthusiasm concerning religion, both at the individual as well as the institutional level.[19] During the early 1990s there were several new religious traditions, both Christian and non-Christian, and different alternative spiritualities present in the Estonian 'religious market'.

This religious vitality soon started to decline as society stabilized and since 1993 the donating membership for the largest religious institution in Estonia, the Estonian Evangelical Lutheran Church, for example, has been steadily declining.[20] At the same time smaller Protestant denominations which had not experienced such a decline in membership during the Soviet era have maintained their membership

---

[18]   Riho Saard, 'Establishment of the Council of Churches', in Riho Altnurme (ed.), *History of Estonian Ecumenism* (Tartu, 2011), pp. 240–5.

[19]   Lea Altnurme, *Kristlusest oma usuni: Uurimus muutustest eestlaste religioossuses 20. sajandi II poolel* [From Christianity to Personal Belief: A Study of Changes in the Religiosity of the Estonians in the Second Half of the 20th Century] (Tartu, 2005), pp. 80–83, Ringvee, *Riik*, p. 40.

[20]   The loss of donating membership of the EELC has been striking – from 76,132 donating members in 1992 to 45,172 in 2001 and to 35,326 in 2010 (EELC Intranet www.eelk.ee; last accessed 20 January 2012).

at the same level for years. The Jehovah's Witnesses, who started their public activities in Estonia in 1991, became one of the fastest growing groups in Estonia in the 1990s, in spite of the negative image they were given in the media. With 4,200 active members, the Witnesses are the fifth or sixth largest denomination in Estonia.

In 1990 the Supreme Council of the Estonian Soviet Socialist Republic restored the pre-Soviet name of the Republic. In 1991 the Supreme Council of the soon-to-become independent Estonian Republic made a decision that in the future Estonian legislation should be based on the principles of the pre-Soviet Estonian legal acts active until June 1940, that is to say, before Estonia was incorporated into the Soviet Union. In August 1991 the Supreme Council of the Estonian Republic re-established Estonia's independence on the principle of restitution.

Although the idea of restitution was central in the process of rebuilding independent Estonian statehood, it was not interpreted as a return to the legislative situation that existed in 1940, but rather as a starting point for the drafting process of new legislative acts.[21] The Constitutional Assembly was formed from different pro-independence political factions in September 1991 in order to draft a new constitution. Religion-related questions were not among the important or debated ones. There was consensus that religious freedom must be guaranteed and that there was not going to be a state church. The idea of including the right to religious education in the Constitution was refused by the majority. The new Constitution was adopted by a referendum and was enforced in 1992.

The cornerstone of the governmental policy concerning religious freedom, both on an individual as well as on a collective level is stated in the Article 40 of the Constitution. It reads:

> Everyone has freedom of conscience, religion and thought. Everyone may freely belong to churches and religious societies. There is no state church. Everyone has the freedom to exercise his or her religion, both alone and in community with others, in public or in private, unless this is detrimental to public order, health or morals.[22]

The principles of religious freedom outlined in the Constitution of Estonia follow closely the Universal Declaration of Human Rights Article 18, and Article 9 of the European Convention for the Protection of Human Rights and Fundamental Freedoms. Religious freedom has been guaranteed in the legislation and also in practice, as different reports on religious freedom and/or government restrictions show.[23]

---

[21]   Raul Narits, *Seadusloome õigusliku ja regulatiivse mõju hindamine* [An Assessment of the Legal and Regulatory Impact of Legislation], (Tallinn, 2011), <http://www.riigikogu. ee/rito/index.php?id=11863>.

[22]   Constitution of the Republic of Estonia (1992).

[23]   Pew Forum on Religion and Public Life, 'Global Restrictions on Religion' (Washington, 2009). For the US State Department's annual International Religious Freedom Reports, see: <www.state.gov/g/drl/rls/irf/>.

The principle that there is no state church in Estonia defines the institutional separation of state and religion. The separation has not been interpreted as excluding cooperation between governmental institutions and religious associations however. Such cooperation may take different forms, including financial support for social rehabilitation programmes, for social care, but also the allocation of funds from the state budget for the restoration of religious buildings or objects with historical and/or cultural value, or for delegating some of the duties considered to be duties of the modern state to the religious associations (third sector), or at least making such delegation possible.

While the religious associations are considered to be self-financing associations, the Estonian Council of Churches (ECC) as a regular non-profit-making association has been an exception. In 1991 the Ministry of Finance responded to the proposal of the ECC to have tax exemptions for religious organizations with the initiative to subsidize the ECC from the state budget. This initiative from the Ministry reflected wider attitudes in society that the injustice experienced by religious organizations during the Soviet period should be somehow compensated. In 1991 the first allocation to the ECC from the state budget was made. The allocation mechanism was criticized by the Ministry of Culture. The head of the religious affairs office noted that if the state wants to subsidize churches and congregations then the state should have the right to say how the funding allocation is going to be distributed. They also mentioned that it would be more reasonable if the religious associations were self-financing associations, and donations to them were tax exempted for donors.[24] Despite occasional criticisms, the system that was established in 1991 has been considered to be the most efficient way to subsidize the majority churches that represent approximately 90 per cent of the adherents of different denominations in Estonia. While the annual allocation of funds is a response to the Soviet past, it also reflects a certain continuing authority (even if symbolic) of the churches. At the same time it might be argued that it has also affected the activities of the Council's member churches to some extent. It should be added that in the early 1990s there was also a substantial quantity of financial support coming to the EELC, for example, from other Lutheran Churches in Europe, and similarly with other religious associations. As Tamas Kodacsy has noted in the case of Hungary, where similar processes were taking place, such financial subsidies have caused 'historical churches' to become passive.[25] This has eventually impacted also on their membership. One of the deans of the EELC noted in the annual overview in 2007 that the public perception of the Church as being funded by the state or municipality has resulted in a decline of donating members in congregations.[26]

---

[24]   Archive of the Religious Affairs Department at the Estonian Ministry of the Interior, correspondence 1991.

[25]   Tamas Kodacsy, 'The Church and Democracy in Central Europe', *Religion in Eastern Europe* 1 (2004): p. 36.

[26]   Vallo Ehasalu, *EELK Valga praostkonna sõnaline aruanne 2006* [Report on 2006 of the Valga Deanery of the EELC] 31 March (2007), <www.valgapraostkond.ee/index.php ?op=3&path=Aruanne%2FS%F5naline+aruanne, accessed 19 December 2007>.

While the religious associations remain at the margins of society, the expectations of religious associations as they are expressed in public discussion, although rather rare, are often higher than the institutions are able, or willing, to carry out. It could be well said that in Estonia the churches and other religious organizations have been rather passive in public discussions of social problems, ethics or politics. The only exception to the latter took place in 2002 when the EELC expressed its full support for joining the EU before the national referendum.

The Impact of Neoliberalism

The early 1990s was the time when the neoliberal free market religious economy was introduced, as well as a time when religious freedom was extended across all the post-Soviet states. Religious life and religious associations were liberated from governmental repressions and restrictions, and state interference was minimized. The classical liberal belief that it would be best for religious associations if state intervention were minimized was strong.

The drafting process for a new legislation on religion in Estonia started in 1991. The initiative came from the Ministry of Culture, and the drafting commission also included representatives from other ministries, one legal expert and representative of the EELC, which was considered to be the most traditional of the religious associations in Estonia, as well as the most active one in society in general at that time. The approach to religious associations was liberal and egalitarian. In 1991 the representatives of the state had already assured that the new legislation would treat all religious associations equally.[27] According to the materials of the drafting commission, the religious associations were considered to be tax-exempt, non-profit-making associations, like the religious associations in the United States and Canada. The idea that the unregulated religious 'market' would thus regulate itself and that there would be no special treatment for some churches was criticized by some members of the Lutheran clergy.[28] This tension between the neoliberal state and representatives of the traditional religious institution became evident in an article by the head of the Board of Religious Affairs in the newspaper of the EELC, where they pointed out that the attempts by the Lutheran Church to get a special position or treatment in relations with the state were not acceptable.[29]

The period from 1991 to 1994 has been described as a time of 'extraordinary politics' in Estonia, characterized by radical reforms (such as, for example, rapid property reform based on a restitution principle or monetary reform) and the

[27] Andra Veidemann, '*Kirik ja riik on Eesti Vabariigis lahutatud*' [The Separation of Church and State in the Estonian Republic], *Päevaleht*, 21 February (1991).

[28] Silvester Jürjo, 'Chaplaincy', in Riho Altnurme (ed.), *History of Estonian Ecumenism* (Tartu, 2009), pp. 404–23.

[29] Andra Veidemann, '*Toimetusse helistas...*' [A Call to the Editors...], *Eesti Kirik*, 18 June (1992).

creation of a new political, economic and social order.[30] The first free parliamentary elections after re-establishing the independence in Estonia took place in September 1992. The winner of the elections was the right wing political bloc, composed of the Fatherland/Pro Patria (*Isamaa*), who won 29 parliamentary seats out of 101. Their electoral slogan 'Clean the place!' (*Plats puhtaks!*) reflected their eagerness to make a decisive break with the Soviet past. The coalition government was eventually formed by the Fatherland/Pro Patria, the Estonian National Independence Party (*Eesti Rahvusliku Sõltumatuse Partei*) and the centrist alliance Moderates (*Mõõdukad*). The government was led by the young, 32-year-old Prime Minister, Mart Laar of the Fatherland/Pro Patria Union. The first government came to be characterized by rapid and radical reforms which were implemented on a number of different societal levels. Neoliberal policy was implemented not only in economics: the freedom and responsibility of an individual was also emphasized in other areas of governmental policy. It was accompanied by changes in the Civil Service, where the former officials with a Soviet background were replaced by new civil servants, who were often young and/or inexperienced in public policy, but eager to make a difference in society and ready to take advice from abroad – specifically, from the West.[31]

The first government had a strong belief in the neoliberal presumption that the free markets will regulate themselves. The inspiration and ideological support for this came from Milton Friedman's ideas on the free market, Ronald Reagan's deregulation policy in the United States and Margaret Thatcher's practice of minimizing state involvement in the public sector in the UK, as Estonia's first Prime Minister has admitted.[32] The reforms in the economy led to rapid privatization, setting up the markets and implementation of the idea of a minimal state. Professor of Political Science at the University of California, Berkeley, Wendy Brown has defined neoliberal governance in practice as 'extending and disseminating market values to all institutions and social action'.[33] This approach became the norm in Estonia.

Although there were close personal relations between cabinet members and the EELC, there was no pressure from the political forces for special treatment of any church or religious group. The introduction into the internal directives of morning

---

[30]   Marju Lauristin and Peeter Vihalemm, 'The Political Agenda During Different Periods of Estonian Transformation: External and Internal Factors', *Journal of Baltic Studies*, 40/1 (2009): p. 5.

[31]   Lars Johannsen and Karin Hilmer Pedersen, 'Path Making: Democracy in the Baltic States Twenty Years After', *Politics in Central Europe*, 7/1 (2011): p. 66; Taavi Annus, *Governance and Law in Transition States* (Tartu, 2004), pp. 11–15. Taavi Annus (Ibid.) has noted that academic research often neglects the role of civil servants in the transition states, such as Estonia and other post-communist states.

[32]   Belien, 'Walking on Water: How to Do It'.

[33]   Wendy Brown, *Edgework: Critical Essays on Knowledge and Politics* (Princeton, 2005), p. 40.

prayers in the Parliament was mocked to such an extent that they were terminated. The neoliberal idea of a free market with minimal regulations was implemented in the field of religion in a situation where religious activity was booming, and 'the Church' was among the most trusted institutions in society. Freedom of religion was interpreted generally as a negative liberty. The idea that state and governmental institutions should not interfere in the life of religious associations was accepted both by governmental as well as religious representatives.

The liberal framework and neoliberal governance of religion was established in 1993 with the adoption of the *Churches and Congregations Act* (1993 CCA). The 1993 CCA reflected the general liberal attitudes of the period as shown above. According to the Act, all registered religious associations were equal before the law and the requirements for the registration for legal entity status as well as privileges were same for all. In contrast with many other post-Soviet countries, there was no distinction between traditional or non-traditional religious associations.

In Estonia the registration of a religious association as a legal entity has not been a mandatory criterion for a religious community to operate. There are religious communities without any legal entity status, and some communities have decided to operate as registered, regular, non-profit-making associations. The governmental agencies have not intervened on the activities of such groups. However, registration as a religious association under the *Churches and Congregations Act* grants certain privileges. These privileges have been rather insignificant and relate mostly to tax-exemptions. In December 2001 all registered religious associations became eligible to apply for the right for their clergy to conduct marriages with civil validity. Those who are considered to be members of the clergy have been defined by every religious association in their statutes. In December 2011 there were 125 clergymen and women from 12 different religious associations who had the authorization from the Ministry of the Interior to conduct marriages with civil validity.[34]

The drafting of a new legal act for regulating the founding, status, and termination of religious associations had already started in 1996, due to general changes in Estonian legislation at that time when new regulations replaced the old ones from the Soviet era. The drafting process of the new *Churches and Congregations Act* took over five years. As the existing legal framework satisfied all parties, there was no rush for a new legal act. During the drafting process the EELC proposed an idea that religious associations could regulate their relations with the state through special contracts, but it did not gain popularity either among politicians or among governmental officials. Members of the Estonian Council of Churches, besides the EELC, also expressed their concerns that this might introduce unequal treatment of religious associations by the state. Thus the idea was eventually dropped.

---

[34] For the list of the clergy see the Ministry of the Interior's website, <http://www.siseministeerium.ee/abielu-solmimise-oigust-omavad-vaimulikud/.>

The first version of the new *Churches and Congregations Act* was adopted by Parliament in 2001. It included restrictions on the registration of religious associations whose administration is located outside of Estonia. The President of the Republic refused to sign the Act, referring to the violations of the principles of autonomy of religious associations, as well as to violations of collective freedom of religion stipulated in the Constitution. Parliament abolished the restrictions, but extended the range of subjects of the property reform, reflecting the interests of the EELC. This extension, however, was considered unconstitutional by the President, who refused to sign the new version of the Act. As these changes were removed by Parliament, the *Churches and Congregations Act* was passed by Parliament on its third reading in 2002 and the President signed it.

During the drafting processes of the 2002 *Churches and Congregations Act* (2002 CCA), the discussions on the limitations on religious freedom resonated with ongoing discussions on the issue in continental Europe. The specific reference for the discussions was a group of local Satanists who had attempted to become registered as a religious association. As there was no agreement as to what could be considered a destructive sect, and there was an implicit concern that the label could be applied to any religious association, the limitations were not included in the final version of the 2002 CCA.

The main differences between the 1993 CCA and the 2002 CCA concerned mostly the registration process as the Church Register was shifted from the Ministry of the Interior to the Courts. Requirements for the religious associations applying for registration as a legal entity remained the same – it must have a statute, an association contract and at least 12 adult founding members. The only religious association that does not need a statute for registration is the Roman Catholic Church, which operates in Estonia on the basis of an agreement made in 1999 between the Estonian Government and the Holy See. Although the basic idea of minimal regulation of religion remained unchanged in the 2002 CCA, it should be noted that the regulations on religion have increased during the twenty-first century. Many of the new regulations on religion are the result of the consolidation processes of Estonian legislation into European Union law, and not from the actual need for more regulations. Estonia has been a member state of the European Union since 2004 and religion-related questions and regulations on equal treatment and on other issues have been enforced. Although this has created opposition to the EU regulations in some Christian circles, the secular (but not secularist) policy has been until now rather indifferent to these critical voices.

The Estonian State and Religions in a Neoliberal Context

Governmental attitudes toward religion and religious associations in a secular state where neoliberal policy and governance have been put into practice have been pragmatic. For a neoliberal state that is oriented to a market-rationale and individualism, it is not important that the nation or the state should incorporate a single culture or civilization or religion.[35] In other words, if neoliberalism has aimed at contractualizing the (political) community then the differences based on culture or religion become irrelevant in the face of an emphasis on efficiency and rationalization in the globalized market. There has been consensus in Estonia that there is one law for all religious associations to regulate the founding and termination of religious associations as legal entities, and the legal entities have the same rights, privileges and responsibilities.[36] The basic principle that there is no state church in Estonia, as stipulated in the Article 40 of the Constitution, has been interpreted by the Estonian legal experts as a principle of neutrality and equality.[37] Equality and (positive) neutrality have also characterized the practice of governmental agencies as regards religion.[38] Since the early 1990s there has been political consensus that there are areas of common interest between the state and religious associations. In this the Estonian Council of Churches (ECC) has had a special role as it represents the majority of denominations in Estonia.[39]

The relations between the state and the ECC experienced tensions during the mid-1990s as the Council tried to act as a mediator between the Russian Orthodox

[35] Scott M. Thomas, *The Global Resurgence of Religion and the Transformation of International Relations: The Struggle for the Soul of the Twenty-First Century* (New York, 2005), p. 66.

[36] On Estonian legislation concerning religion, see: Merilin Kiviorg, *Law and Religion in Estonia* (Alphen aan den Rijn, 2011); see also Ringo Ringvee, 'State, Religion and the Legal Framework in Estonia' *Religion, State and Society*, 36 (2008): pp. 181–96.

[37] Rait Maruste, *Konstitutsionalism ning põhiõiguste ja -vabaduste kaitse* [Constitutionalism, and the Protection of Basic Rights and Freedoms] (Tallinn, 2004), p. 522; Kiviorg, 'Law and Religion in Estonia', p. 33.

[38] Besides not practising differential treatment of religious associations in the legislation, the principle of equality became evident in 2008 when the Estonian Government adopted a governmental development plan on historical natural holy places (for example, sacred groves, holy springs and so on). In 2003 a similar governmental programme on places of worship (churches and so on) was adopted. The initiative for this programme came from a joint commission of the Estonian Government and the EELC. The main initiator for the development plan for natural holy sites was the House of Taara and Native Religions (*Maavalla Koda*) which represents a (neopagan) indigenous religiosity. The idea in both cases has been the protection and restoration of sites and buildings or natural objects that are important for indigenous identity, or which are culturally valuable.

[39] Ecumenical relations are one of the particularities of the religious life in Estonia. On ecumenical relations in Estonia, see: Riho Altnurme (ed.), *History of Estonian Ecumenism* (Tartu, 2009); Huub Vogelaar, 'Ecumenical Relationships in Estonia', *Exchange. Journal of Missiological and Ecumenical Research*, 37 (2008): pp. 190–219. Member churches of the ECC are currently the Estonian Evangelical Lutheran Church, the Estonian (Apostolic) Orthodox Church, the Estonian Orthodox Church of the Moscow Patriarchate, the Union of Evangelical Christian and Baptist Churches of Estonia, the Estonian Methodist Church, the Roman Catholic Church, the Estonian Christian Pentecostal Church, the Estonian Conference of Seventh-day Adventists Church, the Estonian Congregation of St Gregory of the Armenian Apostolic Church and the Charismatic Episcopal Church of Estonia.

Church (ROC) and the Estonian State on the issue of registration of the diocese of ROC in Estonia as a legal successor of the pre-Soviet Orthodox Church. The ECC represented the view of the ROC, one of the founding churches of the Council, that the issue of the registration of the diocese should be resolved by political means and not through the courts.

In 1994 the last military troops of the former Soviet Union left Estonia. In the same year religion became an important issue for Estonia in the context of international relations, and involved the religious freedom and other human rights issues of the Russian minority as Estonia refused to recognize the diocese of the ROC in Estonia as the legal successor of the pre-Soviet Orthodox Church. In 1991 the Supreme Council had adopted the *Basics of Property Reform Act*, and the subjects of the property reform were the owners of the property before 16 June 1940. The diocese of the ROC was recognized as the subject of the property reform in 1991 shortly after it was entered in the business register as a legal entity. However, as the *Churches and Congregations Act* was signed by the President in 1993, the religious associations had to register their statutes at the Estonian Register of Churches and Congregations at the Ministry of the Interior in order to maintain their legal continuity. The Register was kept by the Board of Religious Affairs which was moved from the Ministry of Culture to the Ministry of the Interior. In 1993 the statute of the Estonian Apostolic Orthodox Church (EAOC) from 1935 was registered by the authorized representatives of the Synod of the EAOC which had maintained continuity in exile. The following application from the bishop of the diocese for registration under the same statute and name as an already registered church was denied by the state. In the following court cases the EAOC was recognized as subject to the property reform. From 1994 onward, religion-related questions emerged in the politically sensitive atmosphere. While for the Estonian state it was a legal question which had already been resolved by court decisions, it was a political question for the administration of the Russian Federation, and for the ROC the conflict in Estonia was part of larger rearrangements taking place in the post-Soviet Orthodox world.[40]

In spite of changing coalitions in the Estonian Government, the approach remained unchanged. Finally, in 2002 the diocese was registered as the Estonian

---

[40]   The conflict in Estonia concerning the Orthodox Church in Estonia should be seen in the wider context of the tensions between the ROC and the Ecumenical Patriarchate. From the 1990s onward, the biggest problem for the ROC has been the situation in the Ukraine. See also Leslie L. McGann, 'The Russian Orthodox Church under Patriarch Aleksii II and the Russian State: An Unholy Alliance?', *Demokratizatsiya. The Journal of Post-Soviet Democratization* 7 (1999): pp. 12–27. On the Ukraine, see: Andrij Yurash, 'Orthodoxy and the 2004 Ukrainian Presidential Electoral Campaign', *Religion, State and Society*, 33 (2005): pp. 367–86; Nikolay Mitrokhin, 'Orthodoxy in Ukrainian Political Life 2004–2009', *Religion, State and Society*, 38 (2010): pp. 229–51. On the Orthodox churches in Moldova, see: Lucian Turcescu and Stan Lavinia, 'Church-State Conflict in Moldova: The Bessarabian Metropolitanate', *Communist and Post-Communist Studies*, 36 (2006): pp. 443–65.

Orthodox Church of the Moscow Patriarchate. It could be claimed that the process concerning the registration reflected the neoliberal theory that conflict and opposition must be mediated through the courts. The proposals from the ECC and also from the businessmen to resolve the conflict between the state and the ROC outside courtrooms were turned down by the representatives of the state to whom the conflict, despite its political connotations, remained a judicial question.[41]

While the ECC had distanced itself from tensions in the Orthodox Church by 1996, the relations between the state and the Council have been pragmatic on both sides. For the state the ECC represents the majority of adherents of religious traditions in Estonia. Thus it became the main partner for the state in organizing chaplaincy in the defence forces as well as in prisons. This approach illustrates well Anthony Gill's notion that the state and politicians tend to minimize the cost of governance.[42] The minimizing of the cost of governance takes place often by delegating certain functions to a third sector, which includes religious associations, and which follows the general neoliberal assumption that the third sector or private sector are more efficient than the public sector in providing certain services to the people. In 2002 the Estonian Government and the ECC signed the protocol of common interests that noticed the areas of these interests and responsible ministries of the areas without any notion on the financial duties or responsibilities for the state to achieve the interests mentioned in the protocol. The document was signed mostly due to the lobby work from the ECC, and it has been used as a policy framework, for example in introducing chaplaincy into the police force in 2007. There have been tensions between religious and non-religious organizations concerning the availability of public money for different programmes. This became evident in 2007 when the National Foundation of Civil Society started to allocate public funding for non-governmental organizations. The question emerged from the non-religious NGOs concerning eligibility for the allocations as the religious organizations related to the member churches of the ECC receive public money through an annual allocation from the state budget. However, as the religious associations are technically non-profit-making associations, then from the equality principle there was no justification for excluding the religious associations and other religious organizations.

Although there have been unofficial initiatives from the EELC over the years to have special legal status in relations with the state, these efforts have not gained support either from other religious associations or from the state institutions. On the other hand, a certain special status of the EELC was recognized in 1995 when a joint commission between the Estonian Government and the EELC was established. For the traditional churches the implementation of neoliberal policy

---

[41] Priit Rohtmets, 'Development of the Membership', in Riho Altnurme (ed.), *History of Estonian Ecumenism* (Tallinn, 2009), pp. 285–8; Ringo Ringvee, *Riik*, pp. 141–2, 158. On the Orthodox churches in Estonia, see also: Ringo Ringvee, 'Orthodox Churches in Estonia', *Estonian Culture* 1 (2003): pp. 34–7, <www.estinst.ee/publications/estonianculture/index3.html>.

[42] Anthony Gill, *The Political Origins of Religious Liberty* (New York, 2008), p. 47.

could be considered to have had a rather negative effect. When looking at the transition period from 1989 to 1991 it becomes apparent that as the restrictions on religion by the Soviet system were gradually abolished, there was also a general trend at the changing administrative and governmental levels to compensate religious associations for the injustices done during the Soviet period. This approach resonated with the positive attitude towards religion in society in general. In 1991 the practice of allocations of funds from the state budget to the ECC was established. Although in theory the traditional churches would have had an advantage on the free market by virtue of having existing structures and being already familiar to potential consumers, the situation in fact turned out to be more complicated. This has been true especially in the case of the EELC, which had been the majority church for centuries and had identified itself as the people's church from 1917 onwards. Since the church boom of the transition period began to wane 1993, membership has been declining for the EELC. There are also ageing factors concerning the membership as the majority of the Lutherans are represented by older generations of Estonians. The so-called traditional churches have not been so much socially proactive as reactive.[43]

Most probably, the traditional churches would have gained a special status and some form of differential treatment of religious associations would have been introduced if the initial elections in 1992 had not given political power to the neoliberals, accompanied by a change from Soviet-period civil servants to new, non-Soviet ones. The new political elite and new Civil Service did not feel personal guilt or responsibility for Soviet wrongdoings. The situation was thus changed and religious associations were able to operate freely in society.

Although implementing neoliberal policy and state neutrality on religion did not have the most positive results for the traditional majority church, the effect of this process definitely had a positive effect on minority religions, both old and new ones, as well as on alternative spiritualities. For them the free market situation provided an environment where confrontation with governmental bodies did not become an issue. The governmental agencies did not have a comprehensive overview of the religious groups active in Estonia before the 1993 CCA was adopted, and the Estonian Register of Churches, Congregations and Associations of Congregations was established.[44] Before that the registration of religious organizations as legal entities took place at the municipal business registers on the same legal basis as other civic societies.

Although there was a certain amount of suspicion from the state towards new religious movements in the early 1990s, which reflected the general trends in Europe at that time, the situation had stabilized by the mid-1990s as the real situation was

---

    [43]   Allan Laur, the Senior Pastor of the Estonian Christian Pentecostal Church, in a personal communication of April 2001.

    [44]   RT L 1993, 16, 442, *Eesti kirikute, koguduste ja koguduste liitude registri põhimäärus* [Statute of the Estonian Register of Churches, Congregations and Associations of Congregations] (1993).

not as serious as expected. However, in 1993 the Minister of the Interior had to close the prisons for a week in order for religious workers to ascertain who were the religious groups and individuals who were providing spiritual care for the inmates.[45] It should be taken into account that several new religious movements active in Estonia were unfamiliar to the governmental agencies, and the expert opinions on new religious movements were provided in most cases by the EELC. This practice changed from the mid-1990s onwards.

However, in the cases where the law has been violated by representatives or members of religious traditions, the responsibility has been individual and not collective. There is only one exception, where a registration of religious association was denied. This case involved Satanism, and raised questions as to how neoliberal policy is practised in a changing society.[46]

Conclusion

In a neoliberal state the idea that the religious market should be self-regulating is considered to be natural and is practised as a governance policy. The state's approach to religious associations in Estonia has been pragmatic and situational over the years, reflecting to some extent the prevailing *zeitgeist*. The state has maintained a tolerant attitude towards different forms of religion and religious traditions. At least implicitly this practice of governance was affected in the 1990s by the controversy on the registration of the diocese of the ROC. A situation where interference in religious affairs could be interpreted as a violation of the religious freedom of ethnic minorities was avoided by the Estonian authorities by stressing the rule of law and letting the religious associations operate in the free market of religions as long as they did not violate the law.

Although there was an increase in official religious associations and alternative spiritual practices from the 1990s onwards in Estonia, religions and different forms of spirituality have not had such an impact on society as was expected back then.[47] Only a few of the religious associations have more than a thousand members, and the majority of the population do not consider themselves to be adherents of any religious or spiritual tradition.

There have been several reasons for the adoption of a neoliberal approach to the religious economy in Estonia. Religion had been privatized and pushed to the margins during the Soviet period, and the majority of the population became

---

[45]   Silvester Jürjo, 'Chaplaincy', in Altnurme (ed.), *History of Estonian Ecumenism*, p. 405.

[46]   On the Satanism scare in Estonia, see: Ringo Ringvee, 'Satanism in Estonia', in Jesper A. Petersen (ed.), *Contemporary Religious Satanism: A Critical Anthology* (Aldershot, 2009), pp. 129–40.

[47]   See also Frans Hoppenbrouwers, 'Romancing Freedom: Church and Society in the Baltic States since the End of Communism', *Religion, State and Society*, 27 (1999): p. 161.

de-churched. The connection between national and religious (Lutheran) identities was weak among native Estonians and this continues to be the case in the current situation.

Most native Estonians tend to be either religiously indifferent or undefined. Religion is unimportant in Estonian society, though among non-Estonians, religion has connections with national identity. Religion and religiosity are considered to be private matters. These tendencies are also reflected in the policy on religion and the governmental practice of religion. Informal norms of privacy and secularity are not directly enforced by the state, but rather shared by the majority of the population. Thus it could be claimed that the neoliberal policy practised with respect to religion in Estonia since the early 1990s has been possible due to several different historical, social and political factors. It is difficult to guess whether policy and regulations will change in the future as the religious landscape changes. In other words, how would the highly secular and religiously unaffiliated Estonians relate to religion and its institutions in a context of emergent immigrant communities in their midst, where religion often has a different role in forming communal and individual identities? The possible change to a more strict regulatory policy, or to closer cooperation, however, requires political decision-making and consensus and also an acknowledgement of the necessity for this by society at large. How this could take place in a society where religious influence on public life and the public presence of religion has been traditionally rather minimal, and where the neoliberal approach to religion is considered to be part of the natural order of things and nothing extraordinary, is another question.

Chapter 9
Neoliberalism and Counterterrorism Laws: Impact on Australian Muslim Community Organizations

Agnes Chong

Introduction

Australia's second longest-serving Prime Minister and former Treasurer John Howard ushered in an era of neoliberal restructuring that successfully combined 'deregulationist economics' and 'interventionalist social policy'.[1] Howard's neoliberal agenda included restructuring the public service and funding arrangements, privatization of the job search sector, outsourcing welfare services to non-governmental organizations and reduction in or non-investment in social capital.[2] As with the investment in faith-based initiatives by both the US and UK governments, Australia also decided that religious organizations, particularly churches, were better placed than private companies to provide services due to their grassroots connection to the community, reliance on volunteerism and minimal unionization. While some of these changes were ostensibly intended to increase community activity and to encourage professionalism, it has been suggested that neoliberal restructuring poses a threat to the autonomy of not-for-profit organizations,[3] quashes the capacity of organizations to conduct advocacy on behalf of the community[4] and, ironically, allows the government to retain control over the sector.[5]

---

[1] Marion Maddox, *God Under Howard: The Rise of the Religious Right in Australian Politics* (Sydney, 2005), pp. 196–7.

[2] Bernadine Van Gramberg and Penny Bassett, 'Neoliberalism and the Third Sector in Australia', Working Paper Series, Victoria University of Technology School of Management (2005).

[3] Donna Baines, 'Neoliberal Restructuring, Activism/Participation, and Social Unionism in the Nonprofit Social Services', *Nonprofit and Voluntary Sector Quarterly*, 39/1 (2010): pp. 10–28.

[4] Ruth Phillips, 'The Role of Nonprofit Advocacy Organizations in Australian Democracy and Policy Governance', *Voluntas: International Journal of Voluntary and Nonprofit Organizations*, 17/1 (2006): pp. 59–75.

[5] Van Gramberg and Bassett, 'Neoliberalism and the Third Sector in Australia'.

These are not the Howard government's only legacy. On fateful 11 September 2001, Howard was on a visit to the United States and personally witnessed the third plane flying into the Pentagon. Over the next six years, his government oversaw the implementation of an extensive series of counterterrorism laws and policies. While not ostensibly part of the neoliberal restructuring, in this chapter I argue that, in practice, counterterrorism laws and policies reflect the agenda and continue these globalized trends. The ways in which counterterrorism laws are communicated and perceived and how Muslim organizations respond to the imposition of these obligations illuminate the intimate processes by which neoliberal globalization is actualized. This case study of Muslim community organizations shows how the laws have led to the legitimization of neoliberalism through an increase in economic rationalization and risk evaluation by organizations. In the face of rising conservatism on the part of donors and the community, organizations that would traditionally rely on social bonds and trust have become more contractualized and commercialized as they are forced to compete with one another for support, and their practices and procedures have become bureaucratized beyond what is actually mandated by the laws.

Scholars have suggested that counterterrorism financing laws' risk-based approach to policing accords the neoliberal understanding of minimal interference with financial markets[6] and operate within a framework of neoliberal globalization by undermining civil society and NGOs.[7] At an international level, despite the global nature of terrorism and the universal recognition of the need to counter it, the lack of a consistent and agreed-upon framework for measures such as Security Council Resolution 1373, 'effectively outsourc[es] the definition of terrorism to members states ... domestically without limitation', and leads to 'dangerous' consequences for the right to self-determination.[8] In a similar vein, the lack of a consistent understanding of the obligations imposed by Australian counterterrorism financing laws effectively outsources the risk to relevant actors and leads to undesirable and potentially counter-productive consequences.

Based on my analysis of empirical data collected in 2009–10, this chapter presents two main findings. First, I describe the process through which laws imposing substantial penalties for financing broadly defined 'terrorist organizations' has led to a form of restrictive self-governance – Australian Muslim organizations internalize risk and adopt excessive policies and practices that minimize their exposure. How organizations govern and regulate their conduct is very much a product of 'their knowledge about legal standards, possibilities

---

[6]   Louise Amoore and Marieke De Goede, 'Governance, Risk and Dataveillance in the War on Terror', *Crime, Law & Social Change*, 43 (2005): pp. 149–73, pp. 152–3.

[7]   Jude McCulloch and Sharon Pickering, 'Suppressing the Financing of Terrorism: Proliferating State Crime, Eroding Censure and Extending Neo-colonialism', *British Journal of Criminology*, 45 (2005): pp. 470–86.

[8]   Mark Muller, QC, 'Terrorism, Proscription and the Right to Resist in the Age of Conflict', *Denning Law Journal*, 20 (2008): pp. 111–31, p. 115.

and constraints'.[9] In this context, due to the sparse and ineffective communication of the laws and the ambiguities inherent in them, organizations rely on their 'common sense' interpretation of the law, leading to behaviour that is overly cautious. Organizations' implementation of concrete and stringent rules beyond what is strictly required appears to be the inevitable result of the government's effective outsourcing of risk and responsibility of policing to the organizations and communities themselves. A noteworthy consequence is that this has led to erosion of trust and social cohesion, which would likely have the effect of stunting community development in the long term.

Second, counterterrorism laws have continued the neoliberal march towards market-driven consumerism as donation patterns have changed, and Muslim community organizations have adopted elements of market-driven policies. In view of government scrutiny into Islamic charity habits, there appears to be a trend towards a 'flight to safety' where the self-restrictive patterns seen in organizations are also reflected in the behaviour of donors, who shop around and evaluate charities. Counterterrorism laws thus have become another criterion used by donors when considering charity. This results in a reluctance to support sensitive or controversial causes that would have been otherwise supported, and a generally inefficient distribution of resources. In order to survive, organizations have had to become more transparent, leading to increased competition and a redistribution of funds.

Yet, paradoxically, an interesting pattern emerges: while the distribution has been consumerized, the act of charity itself, and the level of charity, does not appear to have decreased. Instead, there seems to be a stripping down to the traditional values of charitable giving by the enduring commandment of *zakat* (charitable giving). My findings support a conclusion that there has been a revival of traditional religious teachings, despite the relentless rise of consumerism.

This chapter is based on analysis of data from original empirical research – the publicly articulated views of Muslim organizations as expressed in parliamentary and other governmental inquiries, as well as the private opinions of those who run the organizations in a series of in-depth interviews conducted in 2009 and 2010. The methodology allows for the development of key themes in this exploratory study of Muslim organizations and their experience with counterterrorism law and policy. These research methods do not seek to enable representative or generalized claims about the data. Rather, I have used a qualitative analysis approach in which I find interpretations of data that are actively constructed through social processes[10] by focusing on the 'meanings that people give to their environment', or, in other words, their understandings and interpretations of their social environments.[11]

---

[9] Marc Galanter, 'Presidential Address: The Legal Malaise; Or, Justice Observed', *Law and Society Review*, 19/4 (1985): pp. 537–56, p. 545.

[10] Douglas Ezzy, *Qualitative Analysis: Practice and Innovation* (London, 2002), p. 73.

[11] Tim May, *Social Research: Issues, Methods and Process* (Great Britain, 2001), pp. 13–14.

Counterterrorism Laws in Australia

The imposition of substantial penalties by ambiguous laws to counter terrorism financing has continued the trends of neoliberal restructuring by undermining civil society. Charitable organizations, especially Muslim charities, are often the subject of counterterrorism scrutiny. At an international level, the United Nations Counter-Terrorism Implementation Task Force (UN CTITF) devotes attention to non-profit organizations, stating that they 'provide possible opportunities for terrorism financing and as such pose a potential risk, yet at the same time they play a crucial part in fighting conditions conducive to terrorism'.[12] The Financial Action Task Force's (FATF) Special Recommendations on Terrorist Financing (2001), which set the international standards for counterterrorism financing, called on countries to review the adequacy of laws and regulations with respect to non-profit organizations to ensure against terrorist abuses.

In Australia,[13] the law imposes a life imprisonment penalty for directly or indirectly receiving funds for, making funds available to, or collecting funds for terrorist organizations as proscribed by the government. It is also an offence to provide or collect funds where the person is reckless as to whether the funds will be used to facilitate or engage in a 'terrorist act'.

Further, it is an offence punishable by ten years' imprisonment for a person holding a freezable asset (as determined by the Minister for Foreign Affairs) to use or deal with it, to allow or facilitate it to be used or dealt with, or to directly or indirectly make an asset available to any of the listed individuals or organizations.

Finally, the law imposes obligations on the financial sector to identify their customers and the nature of their business, and to monitor all customer transactions and report suspicious matters. This calls on financial institutions to monitor activities and look out for 'financial transactions for which there appears to be no logical economic purpose or in which there appears to be no link between the stated activity of the organization and the other parties in the transaction',[14] which Tham has interpreted as encouraging financial institutions to view charitable donations as suspect.[15] Taking it one step further, Liberty Victoria submitted in relation to the *Anti-Money Laundering and Counter-Terrorism Financing Bill 2006 (Cth)* that 'the risk of Muslims donating to "terrorist organizations" ... even

---

[12] Counter-Terrorism Implementation Task Force, 'CTITF Working Group Report: Tackling the Financing of Terrorism', United Nations, New York (2009), p. 16.

[13] A full legal analysis of the law is beyond the scope of this chapter. See Agnes Chong, *Alms or Arms?: Communication of Counter-Terrorism Financing Laws and the Consequences for Australian Muslim Organizations*, Master's Thesis, Stanford University, Stanford (2010).

[14] Financial Action Task Force on Money Laundering, 'Guidance for Financial Institutions in Detecting Terrorist Financing' (2002), paragraph D(4).

[15] Joo-Cheong Tham, 'A Risk Analysis of Australia's Counter-Terrorism Financing Regime', *Social Justice*, Summer 34 (2007).

for purely humanitarian purposes, becomes the target of the Bill's provisions'.[16] The requirement that non-trained staff in the financial sector should look out for suspicious transactions increases the potential, or serious 'danger', for discrimination against Australian Arabs and Muslims.[17]

From Ambiguity to Restrictive Self-governance

My first finding describes the process through which counterterrorism financing laws have led Muslim organizations to a form of restrictive self-governance. The lack of effective communication as to the meanings of complex and ambiguous laws leave organizations with little choice but to use their 'common sense' interpretation that errs on the side of caution. The consequences of the limiting self-governance pose challenges for the development of Muslim communities.

Academics, human rights advocates and legal experts have raised a number of concerns about the complexity, breadth and uncertainty regarding definitions of 'terrorist act', 'terrorist organization' and related offences. The breadth of the definition of 'terrorist act' is often criticized for covering a wide range of behaviour unintended by the legislature,[18] and the proscription of terrorist organizations as inconsistent, discretionary and arbitrary.

The aftermath of the 2004 tsunami in Indonesia, for example, posed difficult challenges for organizations wishing to help with recovery efforts. While the Acehnese resistance movement was not on the proscribed list of terrorist organizations, it was arguable that its actions would fall within the broad definition of a 'terrorist act', and therefore any assistance provided to or through them could be interpreted as providing funds to an organization which might become a 'terrorist organization' in a court of law.

Moreover, the law penalizes behaviour where the person providing the funds was *reckless* as to whether the funds would be used for terrorist purposes. This broadens the scope of the offence,[19] yet, at the same time, increases the confusion surrounding its application. An interviewee described the concept of recklessness

---

[16] Liberty Victoria, 'Submission to the Senate Legal & Constitutional Affairs Committee Inquiry into the Provisions of the Provisions of the Anti-Money Laundering and Counter-Terrorism Financing Bill 2006, and the Anti-Money Laundering and Counter-Terrorism Financing (Transitional Provisions and Consequential Amendments) Bill' (2006), p. 3.

[17] Tham, 'A Risk Analysis'.

[18] See for example, Patrick Emerton, Australia's Terrorism Offences – a Case Against, in Andrew Lynch and George Williams (eds), *Law and Liberty in the War on Terror* (Sydney, 2007), pp. 75–86.

[19] Parliamentary Joint Committee on Intelligence and Security, Report on 'Review of Security and Counter Terrorism Legislation', The Parliament of the Commonwealth of Australia, Canberra, Australia (2006), p. 88.

as 'un-understandable', which made it impossible for the organization to continue the flow of donations even to orphans in its target country, as the authorities could interpret this charitable act as recklessly and indirectly supporting terrorists.

The complexity of the legislation and the inherent ambiguities provide little guidance. Moreover, it has been argued that a combination of these factors make counterterrorism legislation 'poor laws': the high risks of terrorism, the inability of parliamentarians to know the true extent of the threat to national security, a repeated failure to commit to consultative and deliberative law-making, the expansive scope of counterterrorism laws and finally the move towards a precautionary or pre-emptive paradigm.[20] As a result:

> It becomes difficult for people to understand their potential liability which is increasingly a matter of discretionary enforcement given the breadth of offences. Laws in the area lack clarity and communicability. This can actually be counterproductive if sectors of the community feel that the laws unfairly target them.[21]

Australian Muslim communities feel the weight of the laws as they view that other broad provisions of counterterrorism laws have been applied to them disproportionately, despite there being no substantial links between terrorist groups and non-profit organizations in Australia,[22] and the fact that no local Muslim organization has been prosecuted for terrorism-related financing offences.[23] This is better understood when viewed against the background of the Howard government's dog-whistle politics that constructed Muslims as 'them' and indirectly, implicitly yet persistently, questioned their loyalty in the public discourse of government and in the media.[24]

Counterterrorism financing laws further fuelled concerns by lawyers, academics and non-governmental organizations about the likely disproportionate effects on Australian Muslims. There is some evidence to suggest that the obligation of the laws falls almost exclusively on Muslim charities.[25] Of the 17

---

[20]   Andrew Lynch, 'Legislating with Urgency – the Enactment of the Anti-Terrorism Act [No. 1] 2005', *Melbourne University Law Review*, 31 (2006): pp. 747–81.

[21]   Ibid., pp. 780–81.

[22]   Australian Government, *Letter dated 11 October 2005 from the Permanent Representative of Australia to the United Nations addressed to the Chairman of the Counter-Terrorism Committee* (2005).

[23]   There have been prosecutions of non-Muslim individuals, however, for making funds available to proscribed organization Liberation Tigers of Tamil Eelam while knowing it was a terrorist organization: Kate Hagan, 'Tamil trio accused of terrorism free on bonds', *The Age*, 1 April 2000.

[24]   Maddox, *God Under Howard*, pp. 166–92.

[25]   Jeroen Gunning, Terrorism, Charities, and Diasporas: Contrasting the Fundraising Practices of Hamas and Al-Qaeda among Muslims in Europe, in Thomas Biersteker and

terrorist organizations proscribed by the Attorney-General, 16 are self-identified as Muslim groups.[26] Commentators have pointed out that the proscription regime has been primarily applied to Muslim organizations:

> It is our concern, that the acts of a Muslim organization may be more likely to render it labelled a 'terrorist organization' than the same acts would if they were committed by a non-Muslim organization. For example, where a Muslim organization somehow indirectly fosters the doing of a terrorist act it is more likely to be viewed as a terrorist organization itself than would, for example, a secular or a Christian organization which did the same thing.[27]

These perceptions of the laws have sparked concerns that individual Muslims may self-limit their behaviour, overestimating the reach of counterterrorism financing laws and becoming unnecessarily cautious,[28] and that the laws 'may undermine the ability of legitimate organizations to operate effectively in addition to curtaining their political independence'.[29] Regarding the introduction of the laws, the Law Council of Australia, the peak national representative body of legal practitioners, submitted:

> ... the proposed measure is likely to lead to a number of unintended results including discouraging donations to charitable organizations ... the Bill's provisions are likely to exacerbate community, and possibly racial, tensions as members of the public who propose to donate funds to seemingly needy groups or causes decide which recipients should be questioned, and to what extent, about how they propose to use the donated funds.[30]

Given the complexity of the laws, and the potential negative concerns surrounding their enactment, the government's communication efforts of the meanings appear

---

Sue Eckert (eds), *Countering the Financing of Terrorism* (Milton Park, 2008), pp. 93–125, pp. 93–4.

[26]   The only exception being the Kurdish Workers Party (PKK) (as of September 8, 2012).

[27]   Federation Of Community Legal Centres (Victoria) Inc., 'Submission To The Parliamentary Joint Committee On Intelligence And Security Review Of The Listing Provisions Of The Criminal Code Act 1995' (2007).

[28]   PJCIS, 'Review of Security and Counter Terrorism Legislation', pp. 27–8.

[29]   Jude McCulloch, Sharon Pickering, Rob McQueen, Joo-Cheong Tham and David Wright-Neville, 'Suppressing the Financing of Terrorism', *Current Issues in Criminal Justice*, 16 (2004): pp. 71–8; McCulloch and Pickering, 'Suppressing the Financing of Terrorism', pp. 470–86.

[30]   Law Council of Australia, 'Submission To The Senate Legal & Constitutional Affairs Committee Inquiry Into The Provisions Of The Anti-Terrorism (No. 2) Bill 2005' (2005), p. 19.

disproportionately slim. While the obligations are complex, very little guidance has been provided to charities and non-profits as to what they entail, despite repeated calls by parliamentary and other review bodies for more effective and responsive communication to Muslim and Arab communities,[31] or to commit additional funds to specific education campaigns for Muslim and Arab communities so that they may become better informed about their rights and obligations under the counterterrorism laws.

While the Australian government has conducted some outreach activities and legal workshops with non-government organizations involved in international aid delivery to explain their responsibilities under counterterrorism financing legislation, and some efforts have been made to reach out to Muslim communities, these consultations tended 'to be compartmentalized and could be more effective in reaching those citizens who least understand and are most fearful of the operation of the legislation'.[32] In practice, this leaves donors and organizations alike with little guidance about how to direct or distribute their funds in a way that minimizes the risk of committing these offences.

Compared with the comprehensive compliance toolkit on how to manage terrorism and other risks provided by the Charity Commission in England and Wales, or the *Anti-Terrorist Financing Guidelines: Voluntary Best Practices for US-Based Charities* released by the United States Treasury in November 2005,[33] the Australian government's two-page guidance for non-profit organizations seems woefully inadequate. The overarching principle is simply: '[Non-profit organizations] must make all reasonable efforts to ensure that funds are not being directed to terrorist activities', and that they 'must comply with Commonwealth, State and Territory laws'.[34] The burden again falls squarely on organizations to find out what their obligations are under these laws, effectively outsourcing the

---

[31]   Security Legislation Review Committee, Report of the Security Legislation Review Committee, Commonwealth of Australia, Barton, Australia (2006); PJCIS, 'Review of Security and Counter Terrorism Legislation'; Parliamentary Joint Committee on Intelligence and Security, 'Inquiry into the Proscription of "Terrorist Organizations" under the Australian Criminal Code', The Parliament of the Commonwealth of Australia, Canberra, Australia (2007).

[32]   SLRC, 'Report of the Security Legislation Review Committee', p. 143.

[33]   The guidelines were '[i]ntended to assist charities in developing a risk-based approach to guard against the threat of diversion of charitable funds for use by terrorists and their support networks.' United States Government, 'Response of the United States to the Counter-Terrorism Committee, Security Council Resolution 1373 (2001)' (2006). However, concerns have been raised about the Guidelines' chilling effect specifically on Muslim charities in the United States: Barnett F. Baron, 'The Treasury Guidelines Have Had Little Impact Overall on US International Philanthropy, But They Have Had a Chilling Impact on US-Based Muslim Charities,' *Pace Law Review*, 25 (2004): pp. 307–20.

[34]   Australian Government, *Safeguarding Your Organization Against Terrorism Financing: A Guidance for Non-Profit Organizations*, Attorney-General's Department, Canberra, (2009), <http://www.nationalsecurity.gov.au/npo>, accessed 23 March 2010.

responsibility for interpreting the criminal law to organizations and creating an environment in which organizations have little option but to conduct their own risk assessment based on their limited understanding of the law:

> Most people know that what they are doing is either right or wrong. With this ...
> anti-terrorism legislation ... we do not know what, how or when these laws can
> apply to an individual, or organization or a group.[35]

Organizations have correspondingly ineffective reception channels, relying very little on formal legal advice, but instead upon intermediaries and informal yet highly unreliable sources. Some interviewees would go straight to the 'source', meaning the laws themselves; another admitted they 'wouldn't know where to look'; while most others simply relied on their 'common sense'. This common sense was a combination of 'rumour and fear', reliance on word of mouth, controversial, sensationalist and often itself confused and highly unreliable media reporting at the time of the proposed introduction of the laws, as well as individual understandings and interpretations of what was 'safe' under the laws:

> We do ... we use our common sense. To some extent, you can't be 100%
> sure, because we don't have the time to read all the laws, and we are not an
> organization to hire a lawyer every time we need to do something, to check with
> the lawyer, and to get legal advice, and spend so much money.

The lack of appropriate communication of the laws exacerbates the ambiguity and uncertainty in Muslim organizations' self-guided 'common sense' interpretation of counterterrorism laws. 'Common sense' told the interviewees that they had to be 'careful with distribution of their funds'; that it might be acceptable if it was for a 'humanitarian purpose', if it was only a small part of their activities, or if the donation had nothing to do with 'building a mosque, or a school'. One aid organization felt that it was protected from scrutiny because the donations were only directed at women and children in the war-torn country, as the 'safest thing in the world is to focus on girls'. None of these, however, were safe assumptions.

This potent mix of the lack of specific knowledge of the laws combined with a reliance on 'common sense' ultimately resulted in a self-governance that was limiting. This self-governance was particularly restrictive. As organizations tended to conflate counterterrorism financing laws with other aspects of counterterrorism laws, their common sense was distorted, tending to err on the side of extreme caution, altering behaviour by devising stringent rules beyond what is actually required by the laws for self-protection. Three features are worthy of note: first, this behaviour was not externally imposed, or demanded by the laws, community

---

[35]   Islamic Information and Support Centre of Australia 2006, Testimony at Public Hearing, Parliamentary Joint Committee on Intelligence and Security, Review of Security and Counter-Terrorism Legislation, 31 July 2006: p. 45.

partners or donors; second, this behaviour was purely for the purpose of perceived self-protection, as organizations placed emphasis on the need to avoid unfair scrutiny from the government or the police; and third, despite the significant level of caution in their work, it did not override the deep-seated mistrust of authorities.

Organizations reported that they had to be more careful with all aspects of their operations than was necessary: 'A strict interpretation [of the law] can possibly criminalize a lot of acts so there is no room for error.' One interviewee said, 'We have to be constantly looking over the shoulders', while another said they had to be 'extremely careful and very transparent':

> After September 11, we have become more cautious, more cautious, in obtaining any funds. We have been very, very careful … to the most of our ability and common sense, that we are careful, when we ask people for money.

This caution had a number of concrete negative consequences for organizations' administration and in their service provision. In one extreme case, the organization stopped fundraising altogether because it was 'too hard' to get all their records to satisfy the laws, as interpreted by them. Prior to the laws' introduction in 2002, all they needed in order to fundraise was documentation from the university stating that the students were raising money to build a residential college on campus. After the financing laws were introduced, however, they felt they needed more evidence of credentials before approaching potential donors for support. Whereas, previously, an independent bank account was sufficient to establish credibility in the community, they now needed much more:

> We want something that, when people send the money from overseas, is to come to a certain bank account recognized by the university and so the government cannot come and say this project is for this or that. Til we get this stuff clear in black and white, we will not be doing the fundraising.

Caution also manifested in other self-regulating ways with respect to providing assistance downstream. Many organizations were repeatedly approached by members of the community for financial assistance. Some of the organizations interviewed decided to apply more stringent criteria in assessing assistance requests. Requesters were required to bring in wage receipts, letters of demand from creditors, other documented proof of need or debt, and even character references. Two organizations decided to disburse monies only through personal contacts, or at the recommendation of trusted members of the organization. Financial assistance to tsunami victims was substantially delayed. Another organization decided that it should completely avoid sending any money overseas, while another felt comfortable only in providing in-kind support to other groups such as catering for events.

These restrictive self-governance practices are a concern. At its best, it means that the organizations are devoting often scarce resources to unnecessary administrative overheads. At its worst, it may mean a reluctance to engage in projects that other communities not as directly affected by counterterrorism laws would have no qualms about undertaking. The effective outsourcing of risk has a substantial unintended consequence of disadvantaging Muslim communities relative to others, and reflects the neoliberal undermining of civil society while allowing the government to retain a sense of control over the activities of the organizations.

Effects on Trust

Counterterrorism laws' effective outsourcing of risk to Muslim organizations has continued the erosion of trust brought on by neoliberal restructuring in the myriad ways that organizations and individuals relate to each other. Since the laws were enacted, organizations began to move towards sets of concrete rules and policies rather than rely entirely on interpersonal relationships and social bonds, as they had done previously. Instead, their translation of the laws into practice was influenced by rationalization and desire to distance themselves from any suspect activity or behaviour, including supporting other organizations whose intentions and objectives may not have always been clear from the outset.

As non-profit organizations, these entities need trust from and in the communities in order to fulfil their expected functions.[36] Equally important, the existence of trust within communities has implications for political trust upwards – trust in authorities and governments.[37] In practical terms, increased trust facilitates cooperation and partnerships for greater impact projects, maximises economies of scale as organizations share resources and skills, and allows some organizations to develop specialized expertise in certain areas. Trust functions as an inter-organizational lubricant that is crucial for the development of communities.

Muslim organizations have numerous opportunities for formal and informal partnerships, place great weight on trust as a factor in interactions with others in the community and interact in an intricate web of relationships. Organizations raise funds from individuals, and they may also raise funds for other organizations, especially aid organizations, to send money overseas. Smaller, less formal groups often approach larger, more established organizations, such as mosques or community centres, for assistance, connections or in-kind support. The concept of trust, however, was not simply blind faith:

---

[36] René Bekkers, 'Trust, Accreditation, and Philanthropy in the Netherlands', *Nonprofit and Voluntary Sector Quarterly*, 32/4 (2003): pp. 596–615; Kathryn Chinnock and Lester Salamon, 'Determinants of Nonprofit Impact: A Preliminary Analysis', paper presented at the panel session on *Nonprofit Impacts: Evidence from Around the Globe*, at the fifth International Society for Third Sector Conference, Cape Town, South Africa (2002): p. 15.

[37] See generally Meindert Fennema and Jean Tillie, 'Civil Community, Political Participation and Political Trust of Ethnic Groups', *Connections*, 24/1 (2001): pp. 26–41.

> What we really cared about was knowing the people, we had to understand the people who were collecting were upstanding members of the community with a high reputation, did not have a reputation for militant or extremist or whatever you want to call it, outspoken views. They have to be trusted members of the community. And only when you know people have been in the community for a long time, they have had a long record of contribution, would we be willing to give for them, not just someone with the latest project.

As a result of their restrictive self-governance, organizations spent more time scrutinizing requests for assistance from other organizations instead of relying on trust. Of those interviewed, two organizations instituted a new policy whereby any project or organization wishing to use their facilities as a platform or to fundraise from their members had to be vetted first to ensure project authenticity. Organizations seeking assistance were required to produce official documentation to prove the existence and legitimacy of the project, for example land titles, building application approval from the local council or municipality, any legal advice received as to the suitability of the project for that particular local government area and any other documentation that would give the assisting organization 'some assurance that this is … a genuine [project], with enough reason to believe that this will be carried on'.

Organizations also experienced less trust from the donor community: there were more questions about the motivations and intent of organization leaders as well as their religious ideologies; more demanding requests about the activities and history of the organization; magnified scrutiny about the religious ideology of the organization leaders; reduced support in terms of membership and attendance; and a tendency for donors or members to shy away from organizations in certain times of perceived high public scrutiny.

Before the laws were introduced, the primary concern of donors had been about the potential personal abuse of the funds: whether the organizations would use funds for their own benefit or whether the mosque or the school would actually be completed and when. After the laws were passed, the concerns seemed to have shifted towards whether the organization would use the funds for any ulterior motives. The crucial question, however, appeared not to be any ulterior motives in and of themselves, but whether they were 'suspect in the eyes of the authorities':

> The terrorism laws would have added one extra little facet to that, before they would have had to have trusted you, on a character basis where, okay, are you going to use the money to build the house or something, but now you've also got the one extra little facet that's saying okay we know these are good people but what if they get caught up with something, what if the government freezes the funds of this organization then nothing's going to happen and the money is going to get wasted.

It would seem that ambiguity in the law and the government's ineffective communication of what it demands amplifies the perceived need to anticipate not what the person themself might consider suspicious, but rather what the *authorities* might consider to be suspicious behaviour.

Market-driven Consumer Behaviour

While the above analysis demonstrates shifts in the level of trust between Muslim organizations and their donor communities, it is also possible to interpret these findings as an indication that donors (individuals and other donor organizations) were demanding more accountability from organizations as in any other market. Just as neoliberal restructuring and outsourcing has led to non-profit organizations becoming more professional and managerial,[38] so too have counterterrorism law and policy demanded increased professionalism, transparency and accountability from Muslim community organizations. For them to remain healthy they need to adapt and become better able to demonstrate their legitimacy to their donors and members. Organizations reported a new awareness of the need to become a legal entity, establish policies and procedures, create structure and board oversight, keep meticulous records, obtain letters of recommendation from the authorities and generally be very open about their financial activities.

As a direct result of the fear and uncertainty about counterterrorism laws, donors exhibited behaviour akin to 'flight-to-safety' trends in a market. Potential donors looked to 'safe' options and avoided what they regarded as 'controversial' projects or organizations. More 'controversial' projects and organizations that fell on the conservative or orthodox end of the spectrum reported experiencing a dramatic decrease in donations as a result of counterterrorism laws. Their portrayal as 'extremist' in the media may well have been a factor in the reduction of donations received. One of these organization interviewees recounted:

> Historically we used to get tens of thousands of dollars in the donation buckets after *jumuah* (Friday prayers), just in cash. People used to have hundreds in their pocket and they put it in the donation bucket. But now, even a month's worth of *jumuah*, that's four Fridays, we still don't get enough to cover the rent for our hall, which is $1,500 a month. Before, the leftover money was used to help poor families, now we can't do that.

Organizations working in conflict-ridden countries also experienced a similar decline in support. One organization's donations 'almost dropped off totally' when two Somali men were arrested on charges of conspiracy to attack an army base.

---

[38]   B. Mitchell Evans and John Shields, 'Neoliberal Restructuring and the Third Sector: Reshaping Governance, Civil Society and Local Relations', Working Paper Series, Centre for Voluntary Sector Studies, no. 13 (2000).

The organization was bombarded with questions from members of the community about where donations were going, whether the money was for terrorists, and was confronted with rumours that people could get in trouble for donating to the organization. A similar organization encountered numerous donor questions about how the money would be sent overseas, and whether the money was going straight to the children.

The challenges faced by the more religiously conservative organizations and those specifically targeting conflict-ridden countries, however, did not seem to extend to other organizations. Nearly all of the interviewees made a distinction between the different types of projects that they thought would be affected by a drop in donations. Projects for tangible results or practical needs were thought to have remained steady in the amount of donations received, and, in fact, one interviewee observed that a number of new mosque building projects had sprung up over the last few years, each raising substantial amounts of money. Many interviewees agreed that mosques and schools in the local community would always be popular donation projects, not least because of religious teachings extolling the virtues of building places of worship and learning. This interviewee recounted the recent boom in new mosque/school building projects:

> Just last week, there's another one in Granville, by another group, and it's costing half a million dollars just to get the land they want. It's something that they probably wouldn't even have attempted five or six years ago, that's too much money. But they're attempting it, and will probably get it. In Parramatta there was a fundraising effort for $1.7 million, they collected a lot of it in donations and the rest of it has been in *qard el-hassan*, as loans. In Belmore, about five or six years ago, they collected over one million dollars. [Organization A], almost at the same time that we were collecting, collected around $6,000; [Organization B] has collected over one million dollars for their project. There's a mosque in Punchbowl that's going to push now for a school that they are building. [Organization C] at Liverpool, they also collected a reasonable amount of money.

This boom in school and mosque funding may at first glance appear to contradict the predicted effects of counterterrorism financing laws, but it is consistent with contemporary analysis regarding the revival of religiosity amongst Muslims as a result of the dynamics of globalization and deterritorialization[39] despite the increasing 'consumerization' of Islam.[40] It is also internally consistent with the idea that Muslim organizations, and by extension, the general Muslim population, use a 'common sense' interpretation of the laws. Project type is intimately relevant to the question of changes in donation patterns: donations that were no longer

---

39   See Olivier Roy, *Globalized Islam: The Search for a New Ummah* (New York, 2004).

40   Patrick Haenni, Economic Politics of Muslim Consumption, in Johanna Pink (ed.), *Muslim Societies in the Age of Mass Consumption: Politics, Culture and Identity between the Local and the Global* (Newcastle Upon Tyne, 2009), pp. 327–42, p. 341.

being made to more religiously conservative organizations were simply being redirected to 'safe' projects, as defined by Muslims themselves.

While one might have expected that high levels of fear and uncertainty would dampen charitable giving, that organizations appeared to have become more transparent and accountable in order to compete for donations in an environment of high risk endeavour, paradoxically the level of charitable giving itself had not decreased. Adherence to the religious obligation of *zakat*, or almsgiving, acted as a tempering or mediating effect on the laws.

A community centre, for example, noticed a jump from the projected growth figures after 9/11, which was maintained for at least three subsequent years. When asked why this was the case, a representative of the organization said he was a strong believer in the *zakat* factor as a neutralizer against fears and uncertainty regarding the laws in the community. Because of the religious obligation for all Muslims to give to charity, the overall amount of donations from the Muslim community was more or less a fixed amount. Another interviewee suggested that it was much more difficult to fundraise but *not* because people were unwilling to pay: 'It's the organization who has to be more careful, not the donor – especially if all they have to do is put money in a donation box.' What it meant, however, was a redistribution of funds to better organized entities:

> Better organized organizations were beneficiaries of this, whereas the more informal smaller organizations wouldn't have kept good records, and wouldn't have worked in a more systemical sort of way to ensure that they did not suffer from a drop of donations.

This view was echoed by some of the interviewees from smaller organizations, who also saw the *zakat* factor as a counterbalance to the effect of the laws in reducing donations. Any donor fears about the laws would have simply caused a redistribution to the more reputable or 'legitimate' organizations and away from smaller organizations, student bodies or 'controversial' projects. An interviewee representing a large community centre cited a few instances when these other organizations approached his centre for assistance instead, complaining that they were not able to collect as much money as they could before 9/11. His centre would then provide some financial assistance to support these smaller groups, redistributing the funds.

Despite the stabilizing effects of *zakat*, the implications of the redistribution of funds may be serious in the long term. Donors' flight-to-safety preferences for traditional institutions such as mosques or schools is likely to stifle less mainstream organizations and projects, such as those serving the needs of Muslim women, the more religiously conservative groups in the community or those organizations targeted at delivering aid to high-risk countries. There is also a risk that the work of smaller, more vulnerable organizations may be shaped by political and foreign policy considerations rather than security issues. Most importantly, the long-term effect of the counterterrorism laws is that donors may likely avoid more innovative institutions, such as media and arts, youth leadership, scholarship funds, public relations, think tanks or political and legal advocacy organizations which are necessary for the Muslim community, as in any other community, to develop.

Conclusion

The introduction, communication and application of counterterrorism financial laws have continued the effects of neoliberal restructuring that was set in motion in the 1980s. As a result of the fear and uncertainty created by the ineffective communication of the laws, Australian Muslim organizations have adopted governance strategies that are restrictive and self-limiting, resorting to overly cautious behaviour beyond what is strictly required by the laws and moving away from the traditional reliance on trust. Whereas once trust was a central element in social dealings in the Muslim community, in that vacuum, organizations have turned to formalizing and professionalizing their practices in order to compete for donations and support and are becoming increasingly managerial in their approach to governance. The result has been a shift from trust-based rapports and relationships towards more formal, bureaucratized, contractual types of socialities which have tended to erode community and social bonds.

The reduction in social capital has been exaggerated by the need to be more transparent and accountable in view of increased demands of the donor community which also exhibits 'flight-to-safety' market behaviour. This has resulted in a change in donation patterns along two axes: the nature of the organization and the nature of the charitable activity. Organizations that were more religiously conservative and hence seen as 'high risk' and organizations working in conflict-ridden parts of the world received considerably less as a result of donors exercising caution. The flight from risk was also seen in a shift towards funding traditional local charitable activities, such as building of mosques and schools, rather than international charity or new projects. Surprisingly there did not appear to be significant drops in donations across the board, and the overall quantity of funds remained approximately the same. Despite increased consumer demands and scrutiny on Muslim organizations, the market-driven nature of charitable giving and the pressure placed upon donors due to fear and uncertainty about the laws, paradoxically, the level of charitable giving had not decreased, indicating a strengthening of religious traditions in the form of *zakat* obligation.

Chapter 10
From Implicitly Christian to Neoliberal: The Moral Foundations of Canadian Law Exposed by the Case of Prostitution

Rachel Chagnon and François Gauthier[1]

Law is a social construct. As such it is the result of a process that begins either in civil society or in political institutions, but which in the end engages all of these actors. The study of law has for a long time been guided by the positivist principle according to which law is neutral – a claim of neutrality that underlies the very functioning of modern judicial institutions. However, a growing number of authors today do recognize the falsity of this positivist proposition. As Jürgen Habermas writes, 'the law is not a narcissistic system closed in upon itself, but is rather irrigated by the democratic social morality of citizens and by a liberal political culture that favours its development'.[2] According to the jurist Pierre Noreau, the law is 'the expression of a social transaction',[3] made possible by a complex process of objectification and subjectification of the judicial norm.

Hence the dominant social ideologies of a given society impact greatly on the law it produces as well as on the way the legal system interprets legislation. A society's moral foundations are thus also those of the law, while a legal norm survives its authors and continues to shape the regulation of society. As such, the law as a social institution is a locus of tensions between inherited moral foundations and new social ideologies, which can be analysed through changes in legislation, procedures and interpretations of the law. Once incorporated into the law, social ideologies have a notable and durable structuring effect.

We can still measure the effects of liberal principles as they were formulated in the eighteenth and nineteenth century in Canadian law. This influence is visible

---

[1]   The authors wish to thank Ariane Lajoie for her contribution to this chapter. Her extensive research on the subject of prostitution was very insightful.

[2]   '[l]e droit n'est pas un système narcissiquement fermé sur lui-même, mais se nourrit à la fois de la "morale sociale démocratique" des citoyens et d'une culture politique libérale qui en favorise le développement', *Droit et démocratie* (Paris, 1997), p. 492, our own translation. For the English version refer to: *Between Facts and Norms* (Cambridge, 1998).

[3]   Pierre Noreau, 'Comment la législation est-elle possible? Objectivation et subjectivation du lien social', *Revue de droit McGill/McGill Law Journal*, 47/1 (2001): pp. 195–236, par 3.

in civil as well as criminal law, be it the rules related to the institution of marriage, or those related to matters of crimes of a sexual nature, such as prostitution. Canadian criminal law maintains and actualizes interdictions formulated by the political actors who voted in the first version of the *Criminal Code* in 1892. These interdictions, which were founded on liberal principles impregnated with Christian notions relating to good and evil, survived relatively well up to the end of the twentieth century. However, many of these principles have been challenged and significantly altered since the early 2000s.

This chapter examines how this change has come about by tracking the morphing moral foundations of Canadian law and distinguishing between four historical periods, corresponding to as many moments in our argumentation. The overarching argument is that the Canadian case exemplifies, in a rather stark manner, how egalitarian liberalism's foundations in Christian morality were gradually eroded, leading to a shift within criminal law that puts it in accord with neoliberal principles and their radical dissolution of any notion of a common good. This chapter examines these issues through the case of sexual offences, namely prostitution, for which the traditional associations with Christian morality are obvious.

The Canadian case is interesting for this discussion for many reasons; the first being that it is relatively under-represented in international discussions compared with European countries and its southern neighbour, the United States. While Canada has developed a strong welfare system, as have many European countries, the specificities of its short history and its division between French and English-speaking populations explains in part why there is no Canadian national Church as such (although the Catholic Church has played that type of role in Quebec). Furthermore, Canada has committed very strongly to multiculturalism, to the extent that the preservation and even promotion of immigrant cultures are inscribed within the Constitution of 1982. Perhaps more importantly for our discussion, while the legal system in the US continues to be highly political in nature (judges are elected according to their political positions, for instance), Canadian law is constituted as politically neutral, and because of this has been progressively handed significant powers. As we will argue, Canada's judicial history can be read as exemplifying the quite pure application of liberal ideas, which allows us to track how in this case neoliberalism has emerged as an unintended yet direct effect of Rawlsian liberalism, once its moorings in Christian morality have been dissolved.

1892–1964: Morality in Support of the Law

The tension between liberty and responsibility is inherent to the evolution of liberal ideology, which produces a philosophy of reasonable liberty as a consequence. Such a moral liberalism was defined by John Stuart Mill (1806–1873) and is supported by the idea of a large social consensus – or the supposition of such a consensus – concerning the notions of good and evil. In Canada, such a consensus was formulated within a Christian moral worldview which distinguished between good and evil, morality and immorality. While the Canadian state was secular from the outset, as it enforced a separation of powers between the political and the religious and did not explicitly favour any religion in particular, the authors of legislation and policy were, of course, products of their culture, while religion (which is to say, Christianity) was perceived as being the best resource for providing conditions for the emergence of morally and socially responsible individuals.[4] There is an undeniable influence of Christianity in judicial concepts such as the presumption of innocence or the *mens rea*.[5]

The concern of Christian morality with respect to issues related to sexuality is well known. The idea that prostitution involves a notion of collective and moral evil is a phenomenon that exceeds Canadian frontiers, and that was amply developed throughout the nineteenth century and beyond.[6] The social attitude towards prostitution at this time was a reflection of social aspirations and actualizations of moral codes, namely of the bourgeois society. These are elements which had repercussions on the laws adopted by the Canadian state and enforced by the tribunals.

Two constructs emerge regarding prostitution and form the basis from which moral reprobation is articulated in social discourse. The first is that of the destitute woman: an object of temptation, laying out her charms in suggestive ways, corrupting young men and leading them away from virtue. She is the incarnation of evil; deceitful and sensual, a vehicle of impurity. The second is a mirror image of the first, with the gender roles inverted; that of the woman as a victim of male desire, the young innocent girl who has been precipitated into vice by miscreant, malevolent men. Both of these figures had an enduring life in the social imaginary and popular iconography, and their roots in Christian morality call on notions of good and evil, pure and impure, life and death and the ambivalent view of women in Christianity, synthesized by the contrasting figures of Eve and Mary (be she believed to be a virgin or not).

Prostitution, understood as the acceptance of goods or services in exchange for a sexual act, has never been a crime in Canada; nor has it been legal. Rather than criminalizing prostitution *per se*, legislators throughout the nineteenth century targeted many of the activities surrounding prostitution. These interdictions were brought together in 1892 as part of the first Canadian Criminal Code in the

---

[4]   Élizabeth Campos, 'Contrôle social, religion et délinquance', *Religiologiques*, no 31 (2005): pp. 15–24, 16.

[5]   Marie-Pierre Robert, 'Des crimes religieux : aux confluents du droit pénal et de liberté de religion', *Les Cahiers de droit*, 50 (2009): pp. 663–90, by 24. *Mens rea* is best translated by 'guilty mind'; it is invoked as proof of a true intention to commit a crime.

[6]   Alexandre Jean-Batiste Parent Duchâtelet, *De la prostitution dans la ville de Paris*, 2 volumes (Paris, 1836); Pierre Dufour, *Histoire de la prostitution chez tous les peuples du monde depuis l'antiquité la plus reculée jusqu'à nos jours*, 6 volumes, (Paris, 1851–53; Brussels, 1853–54); Lombroso, Cesare, Ferrero, *La femme criminelle et la prostituée*, (Paris, 1896); Malika Nor, *Idées reçues: La Prostitution* (Paris, 2001).

section headed 'Title IV, Crimes against religion, morals and public order'. The amalgamation of religion, mores and social regulation can hardly be stated in a clearer fashion.

The following 'crimes' are listed in this section:[7] it is criminal to prostitute 'Indian' women, as it is to not be able to account for one's nightly errings when asked by a policeman. Similarly, it is forbidden by law to lead an innocent woman into prostitution, as it is forbidden for a woman who is prostituting herself, to be too 'visible'. Brothels, rather than prostitution itself, are forbidden. From the early twentieth century onwards, legislators have also targeted street solicitation.[8] Legislators have sought to control behaviours that are socially understood to be vices. This is why it was the most visible and shocking manifestations that became the objects of legal reproof. More profoundly, the measures adopted in 1892 aimed at protecting women and young girls from the 'wiles of procurers, brothel keepers and other sexual exploiters, including parents and guardians'.[9] One also notices that the legislation put in place at the time was especially directed at the commercial exploitation of sexual acts, and thus at sexuality conceived of in contractual and economic terms.

This conception of prostitution, grounded in a profoundly Christian and collective understanding of the common good, was assimilated by the contemporary liberal ideology, especially through its formulation by John Stuart Mill. The influence of Stuart Mill's writings on the Canadian political intelligentsia at the end of the nineteenth century was widespread.[10] A significant portion of legislation with respect to prostitution and other moral 'crimes' involving women was argued, debated and justified in the terms of Mill's writings.

Influenced by Romanticism and not at all as hostile to religion as was Bentham,[11] Stuart Mill inaugurated a more egalitarian brand of liberalism in which liberty was not primarily economic, and equality was not purely formal. Stuart Mill thus amended classical liberalism by emphasizing the need for state regulation

---

[7]   55–56 Victoria, Chap. 29 (1892). Note that these articles have since been removed.

[8]   The development of the municipal arterial roads, the arrival of the car and the abolitionist discourse contributed to making the prostitute a *persona non grata* on the streets. The first measures against soliciting on the street date back to the 1930s.

[9]   John McLaren, 'Recalculating the Wages of Sin: The Social and Legal Construction of Prostitution, 1850–1920', *Manitoba Law Journal*, 23 (1996): pp. 524–55, by 22.

[10]   See for example Matthew Godwin, 'Awaiting the Watershed: Women in Canada's Parliament', *Canadian Parliamentary Review*, 33 (2010). Mill also had attracted interest in the British colonies of North America: J.S. Mill, Radical Party and Canada: 'Lord Durham and the Canadians January 1838', *London and Westminster Review*, VI & XXVIII, pp. 502–33.

[11]   Jeremy Bentham's radical philosophy, utilitarianism, stressed the need for political regulation guided by the 'utility' principle, defined as the greatest sum of quantifiable pleasure for the greatest number of individuals. See Catherine Audard, *Anthologie historique et critique de l'utilitarisme. II. L'utilitarisme victorien (1838–1903)*, (Paris, 1999).

in favour of equality, supported by a valuing of qualitative differentiation that refrained from Bentham's arid conception of social life. In many ways, Stuart Mill provided the template for the egalitarian liberalism of the twentieth century; in other words, liberalism's compromise with the ideals of the welfare state, which was to be targeted by neoliberalism.

In his *avant-garde* book *The Subjection of Women*,[12] Stuart Mill defended women's rights to equality and argued that the inferiority of women was the result of a long, drawn out, yet inexorable, social construction. This analysis resonated with the second of the two constructions of the prostitute described here; that of the victim; the woman who is forced to sell sexual services under the pressures of her social and economic circumstances. Stuart Mill's argument joined with Christian morality in valuing the purity and moral supremacy of the domestic virtues. Beyond the debates around what his true beliefs were about the equality of men and women,[13] or about his political strategies,[14] Stuart Mill's ideas were perfect expressions of the moral liberalism of the times in which the role of the family and the mother were central.[15]

Stuart Mill was nonetheless obliged to justify his position within the liberal paradigm which stresses individual liberty over and against the intervention of the state. In *On Liberty*, he writes that 'the sole end for which mankind are warranted, individually or collectively, in interfering with the liberty of action of any of their number, is *self-protection*. That the only purpose for which power can be rightfully exercized over any member of a civilized community, against his will, is to prevent harm to others.'[16] This reformulation of the principle of utility allowed Stuart Mill to justify what is essentially a social conception of morality within the individualistic perspective of liberalism. Translated into the Canadian legal context, the *Criminal Code* enacted this principle by legitimizing prejudicial state sanctions against individuals – in this case, female 'victims'.

The works of John Stuart Mill provided nineteenth-century liberalism with a framework within which a socially shared Christian morality, be it explicit or implicit in the thought process of the legislators, was reconciled with the empirical and rational pretences of liberalism. Stuart Mill and the legislation he inspired reconcile individual liberties and Christian ethics concerned with the wellness of others. It is important for what follows to note how the law is at the centre of this reconciliation: it is the very instrument of this reconciliation. This alliance of rational, philosophical and scientific discourse with the sacralization of the family and the emphasis on role of the mother for women which is typical of Christian morality made it virtually impossible to consider prostitution from a non-social,

---

[12]   John Stuart Mill, *The Subjection of Women* (Dover, 1997; original 1869).

[13]   Elizabeth S. Smith, 'John Stuart Mill's "The Subjection of Women": a Re-Examination', *Polity*, 34/2 (2010), pp. 181–203.

[14]   Ibid.

[15]   Ibid, p. 40.

[16]   John Stuart Mill, *On Liberty*, re-edition, (Kitchener, 2001), p. 13.

non-moralistic perspective which would take into account the perspective of the person who is prostituting herself – of the prostitute as an individual expressing a personal choice. The agency of the prostitute is almost non-existent in these writings. Whether the cause of prostitution be biological, economic or social, it is an activity which incarnates social evil and vice. The search for optimal social regulation that is the function of legislation on both political and judicial levels is still expressed in terms of a collective-bound morality. In this context, the prostitute also represents a potential collective prejudice if her presence is too public and casts a shadow on this morality. The Christian conception of the common good is the substrate of the legal system. On these grounds, the law realizes the common good by protecting virtuous women and women at risk from the dangers of prostitution, thereby protecting the social institution of the family on the one hand while protecting social morals from being soiled by visible impudence on the other.

In a nutshell, then, the period that stretches from the foundation of the Canadian *Criminal Code* in 1892 into the first decades of the twentieth century is one in which morality acts as the support for the law. Social cohesion rests on a shared conception of good and evil, as a collectively based conception of morality legitimizes the law through the mediation of politics.

1964–1982: The Community Standard of Tolerance Test

This situation prevailed from the adoption of the Canadian *Criminal Code* in 1892 until well into the 1900s. The corpus of Canadian values which served to interpret *Criminal Code* prohibitions was re-evaluated in the 1960s, a period of intense social and cultural change following the post-war baby boom and the advent of media and consumer culture. A case involving pornography – and therefore also involving sexual activity and morality – institutionalized a shift in the law which prepared the way for changes that affected legal rights in relation to prostitution. Two magazines, *The Dude* and *Escapade*, were banned from publication by a court of first instance in the province of Manitoba. In the 1964 court case known as *Dominion News & Gifts Ltd. v. The Queen*, the publisher admitted that the publications had no artistic value and thus that the material was purely pornographic. He was thus convicted by virtue of Article 150(8) of the *Criminal Code* banning the dissemination of material promoting 'unduly' explicit sexual activity. This decision was upheld on appeal, but was overturned by a Supreme Court ruling. The Supreme Court adopted the argument of the dissent appeal court Justice Freedman, who held that a prejudice that merited a criminal sanction was one that trespassed 'community standards of tolerance'. Justice Freedman wrote: 'Those [moral] standards are not set by those of the lowest taste or interest. Nor are they set exclusively by those of rigid, austere, conservative, or puritan taste and habit of mind. Something approaching a general average of community thinking and feeling has to be discovered'.[17] A prejudice involving issues of morality was therefore to be analysed with respect to the mean average of the feelings and sentiments of those forming the community. This was called the 'community standard of tolerance test' and became employed with respect to the legality of pornographic content as well as other issues touching on sexual morality, following its adoption by the Supreme Court.

The evolution of the 'community standard of tolerance test' (CSTT) had a major impact on the maintenance of the notion of morality in the *Criminal Code*. The CSTT enabled the courts to maintain the possibility of repressing a given behaviour, not with respect to the prejudice caused (and so to a substantive definition of morality), nor its inherent harmfulness, but rather because it was simply not tolerated by the mainstream of society.

The CSTT emerged in the context of a moral liberalization and democratization of society in general. It was a response to the courts' wish to 'objectify' the limits of socially acceptable behaviour so as to not be dependent on the 'arbitrariness' of the legislator – which is to say the political sphere.[18] In so doing, the courts created a precedent of the utmost importance by which the moral foundations of society were withdrawn from the political arena and handed to the judiciary. This amounted to a first step in a process of de-politicization. The reasoning of the Supreme Court was that the CSTT guarded against a minority (whether conservative or permissive) defining morality for the whole of society. Hence what could be considered immoral was no longer so because of the intrinsic nature of the act, but because it was considered immoral from the standpoint of the 'average citizen'. Yet what was considered morally tolerable and intolerable by this 'average citizen' was decided in the end by the judge, considered as a neutral and objective party.

With the CSTT, we see how the (Christianity-originating) moral foundations are forwarded and actualized by the courts in order to implicitly legitimize a ruling. Thus the moral foundations of the law were still social in nature and still beheld a conception of the common good, yet they had started to become de-substantiated, objectified, abstracted and neutralized within the judicial process. While a communal conception of morality still supported the exercise of law, the balance of power between the political and judicial spheres had changed. The judicial now defined and gave substance to the social, moral norm, bypassing the mediation of the political sphere.

---

[17] *Dominion News & Gifts Ltd. Vs. The Queen* [1963] M.J. No. 542; W.W.R. 65; [1963] 2 C.C.C. 103 (C.A. Manitoba), by 60.

[18] Tristan Desjardins, 'Échanger est-il péché ? Analyse de la norme de tolérance de la société canadienne contemporaine à la lumière de l'arrêt R. c. Labaye', *Les Cahiers de Droit* 45/4 (2004), pp. 767–90.

1982–2005: The Canadian Charter of Rights and Freedom

Politics in Canada post Second World War and until the turn of the millennium were dominated by the Liberal Party of Canada, with periods of government under the Progressive-Conservatives whom, as their name attests, did share with their Liberal counterparts significant portions of their political orientation. A prominent figure of this period was Pierre Elliott Trudeau (1919–2000), a Quebec-born flamboyant intellectual of bourgeois descent, who became Prime Minister of Canada at the head of the Liberal party from 1968–79, and 1980–84. Trudeau had a considerable effect on Canadian politics and left an enduring imprint on Canadian institutions. His political life was intricately tied to the emergence of Quebec's Independence Movement, against which he led an incessant and all-out battle. For Trudeau as for many liberals, nationalisms were intrinsically tribal and regressive, and therefore any substantive notion of the political body had to be fought against and replaced with a procedural conception of citizenship.

Following the Quebec Referendum of 1980 (in which the 'No' to independence vote gathered 60 per cent of the total), Trudeau began to work towards a far-reaching reform of Canadian institutions, commencing with the project of the Patriation of the Constitution which was realized in 1982 (without the signature of the Province of Quebec). Prior to this, Canada's constitution was contained in the imperial *British North American Act*, kept in London. The patriation of the founding text of Canada included the enshrinement of a *Canadian Charter of Rights and Freedom*, which would have a major structuring effect on the law and Canadian society in general. The *Charter* is a pure product of liberal thought, in line with the American Bill of Rights[19] and the French Declaration of Human and Citizens' Rights. The rights enshrined in the *Charter* reflect the values defended by Locke, Stuart Mill and others, starting with individual rights to freedom of expression, religion and association (Article 2; Article 1 being an introductory clause).

While incorporating the liberal values that had emerged during the eighteenth century and onwards in Britain, the *Charter* also accomplished a significant transfer of power from the political to the judiciary, as the legal system, and in last instance, the Supreme Court, became the institution whose responsibility it was to enforce these rights. While the judiciary had formerly been subject to the legislature, the enshrinement of the *Charter* into the Canadian Constitution resulted in the submission of the legislative products of the elected parliament to approval by the courts with respect to its content. This *Charter* is what the courts refer to when there is a need to define core Canadian values.[20] The *Charter* is a judiciary incarnation of the common good, which substitutes the former collective-

---

[19]   Pierre Mackay, 'La *Charte canadienne des droits et libertés* de 1982 ou le déclin de l'empire britannique', in R. Bureau and P. Mackay, *Le droit dans tous ses états* (Montréal, 1987).

[20]   Charles Taylor, 'Can Canada Survive the Charter?', *Atlanta Law Review*, 30 (1992), pp. 427–47.

bound notion of morality. Since the role of the courts is to arbiter the defence of individual interests, the adoption of the *Charter* has resulted in a prioritization of 'the individual dimension of personal rights over their collective dimension'.[21] For Trudeau, justice was to be best addressed through the prism of individual liberties.[22]

As such, the *Charter* corresponds to the conceptualization of liberty and equal rights as redefined by John Rawls. If John Stuart Mill exemplified the thought of late nineteenth-century Canadian liberals, the contents of the *Charter* come close to the conceptions put forward by Rawls. Trudeau's writings and the debates of this period do attest to a close proximity with the theses of Rawls, who is believed to be one of the influences in the elaboration of his model of a society based on a charter of rights.[23] With the *Charter*, Canada is characterized by the 'primacy of the person' as much as by the sovereignty of the nation. For Trudeau, the *Charter* constituted the purest form of liberalism. In his *Theory of Justice* (1974), Rawls pleaded for a de-politicization of the notion of justice in favour of a judicial re-enforcement of individual rights and liberties.[24] For Rawls, the law, rather than politics, must be the vehicle for social justice. Justice is thus what is left of notions such as morality and the common good once they have been de-substantivized, de-collectivized and de-politicized.[25] The notion of procedure is fundamental for theories of justice such as that of Rawls, as the law becomes a mechanism put in the service of establishing a social consensus about the imperatives of justice:[26] 'thus, for Rawls, fundamental rights are neither absolute nor natural, but rather the result of a procedure that is just and fair'.[27] In the Rawlsian perspective, the foremost vehicle for justice is constitutional law, which represents the product of freely consented choices by all members of society.[28] With the enshrinement of the *Charter* in the constitution, the Canadian model comes close to the 'contractual judicial society' envisioned by Rawls.[29] The constitution becomes an instrument invested with its own moral authority, detached from political will.

Returning to the case of prostitution, the *Charter* was invoked to claim the rights of those practising prostitution to freely solicit clients in what is known as

---

[21]   Henri Brun, Guy Tremblay and Eugénie Brouillet, *Droit constitutionnel*, fifth edn, (Cowansville, 2008), p. 902, our own translation.

[22]   Victor LaSelva, *The Moral Foundations of Canada: Paradoxes, Achievements, and Tragedies of Nationhood* (Toronto, 1996), p. 7.

[23]   Éric Schwimmer, 'La bonne distance. Réflexions sur le phénomène P. E. Trudeau', *Anthropologica*, 50/1 (2008): pp. 31–47, p. 40.

[24]   Catherine Audard, *Qu'est-ce que le libéralisme* (Paris, 2009), ch. VI.

[25]   Philippe Chanial, *Justice, don et association* (Paris: 2001), especially pp. 73–94.

[26]   Steve Sheppard, 'The Perfectionisms of John Rawls', *Canadian Journal of Law and Jurisprudence*, 11 (1998): pp. 383–415.

[27]   Audard, *Qu'est-ce que le libéralisme*, p. 435.

[28]   Ibid., p. 459.

[29]   Schwimmer, p. 40.

Reference re ss. 193 and 195.1(1)(c) of the Criminal Code (Man.).[30] In this case, the Supreme Court was asked to advise as to the constitutionality of two articles of the Canadian *Criminal Code*. The first of these (Article 193) criminalized street solicitation with the objective of prostitution, while the second (Article 195) criminalized residence in a bawdy-house. The plaintiffs pleaded that these articles contravened the right to freedom of personal expression (freedom of expression for commercial aims being guaranteed by the *Charter*), as well as the right to choose one's professional activity and the right to security.

In the Supreme Court's decision, the ban on bawdy-houses was withheld without dissent, while the criminalization of the advertising of sexual commerce gave rise to a debate that attests to the burgeoning of a new logic produced by the introduction of the *Charter*. While the majority of judges re-actualized the CSTT by arguing that prostitution was degrading and that potential entrants needed to be deflected from the profession, the two minority judges observed that the punishment imposed (incarceration) was too severe with respect to the crime of street solicitation. While agreeing that sexual solicitation constituted a social nuisance, they argued that imprisonment for solicitation with the objective of a practice (prostitution) that is not illegal went against the fundamental principles of justice, and signficantly interpreted the notion of prejudice as the transgression of a rule of law, and not as a subversion of more general collective values.

The introduction of the *Charter* had the effect of translating the notions of common good and morality into the procedural language of justice. Yet, as the reference on prostitution attests, the full effect of the *Charter* was not immediate, as a social notion of morality continued to inform the interpretation of the *Criminal Code*, through the survival of the CSTT. Canadian law continued to rest on implicitly Christian moral foundations, and the alliance of Christian ethics with Stuart-Millian liberalism continued to prevail in the interpretation of the law so as to contain the individualistic pulse of the *Charter*.

2005: The Effects of the *Charter*

The examination of significant cases from the last decade shows how, once these foundations are dissolved, Canadian law has refounded itself on procedural and falsely neutral grounds that correspond to the morality of neoliberalism. As we have seen, the evolution of the moral foundations of Canadian law did not affect the issue of prostitution for some time. The notion of indecency was challenged more quickly, as an indecent act is defined as one that is contrary to the moral norms of society as measured by the CSTT. An indecent act is not inherently forbidden. If performed in an inappropriate setting, however, this act can then offend a certain sector of public opinion.

---

30   [1990] 1 S.C.R. 1123.

The Supreme Court of Canada was called on to review what constitutes an indecent act in 2005 in the ruling of the *R. v. Labaye* case. In this case, Mr Labaye was accused of owning and operating a bawdy-house. In fact, Mr Labaye was the owner of a private Montreal club in which adepts of 'swinging' (the practice, between consenting adults, of exchanging sexual partners) could meet and indulge in the activity. In the court's decision, the judges ruled that the social standard of tolerance for indecency (as well as obscenity) was equal to a harm incompatible with the proper functioning of society, and defined, in the words of Justice McLachlin, as follows:

> Two general requirements emerge from this description of harm required for criminal indecency to be established. First, the words 'formally recognize' suggest that the harm must be grounded in *norms which our society has recognized in its Constitution or similar fundamental laws*. This means that the inquiry is not based on individual notions of harm, *nor on the teachings of a particular ideology*, but on what society, through its laws and institutions, has recognized as essential to its proper functioning. Second, the harm must be serious. It must not only detract from proper societal functioning, but must be *incompatible* with it.[31] [Emphasis added.]

The principles put forth by Justice McLachlin in her interpretation of what constitutes a prejudice espoused the individualistic values defended by the *Charter*, without reference to a common morality. In the argument presented above, prejudices involve individuals, while a prejudice caused to society can only be related to the violation of a rule of law, either explicit, or inferred by the constitution. Furthermore, the reality of a prejudice is to be evaluated with respect to individualized circumstances which must be arbitrated.

In these circumstances, could the earlier ruling on the *Reference* on prostitution be withheld? This is the question that lies at the heart of the 2010 ruling of *Bedford v. Canada*.[32] It is too early to know if the decision rendered by Judge Himel of the Superior Court of Ontario will become jurisprudence in Canadian law. However, this decision incorporates the new principles forwarded by the Supreme Court in the Labaye case. In the *Bedford v. Canada* case, three female plaintiffs requested the Superior Court of Ontario to judge the constitutionality of three articles of the *Criminal Code* related to prostitution that dealt with the tenancy of a brothel, procurement and street solicitation with the objective of prostitution.[33] The plaintiffs essentially pleaded that the aforementioned articles adversely affected their freedom of expression, their liberty to choose their professional activity and their security.

---

[31] Ibid., p. 741.

[32] 2010 ONSC 4264.

[33] The articles are 210 (1)(2)a)b)c)), 212 (1)j)) et 213 (1(c)). Article 210 corresponds to the former Article 195, and Article 213 corresponds to Article 193 of Reference in Prostitution.

The three women were all retired prostitutes; one was the owner of a brothel and the two other were militants for the complete decriminalization of prostitution. A number of actors from civil society were permitted to intervene in this debate in court, with many pleading in accordance with the moral principles that have been used since the nineteenth century to support the bans surrounding prostitution.

Making reference to the *R v. Butler* and *R. vs. Labaye* cases, Judge Himel rejected the arguments founded on morality. Himel disagreed that the protection of women against the sexual exploitation represented by prostitution was a responsibility of the state. As she explains in her judgement:

> The conclusion I have reached is that three provisions of the Criminal Code, R.S.C. 1985, c. C-46 that seek to address facets of prostitution (living on the avails of prostitution, keeping a common bawdy-house and communicating in a public place for the purpose of engaging in prostitution) are not in accord with the principles of fundamental justice and must be struck down. These laws, individually and together, force prostitutes to choose between their *liberty interest and their right to security of the person as protected under the Canadian Charter of Rights and Freedoms (the 'Charter')*. I have found that these laws infringe the core values protected by s. 7 and that this infringement is not saved by s. 1 as a reasonable limit demonstrably justified in a free and democratic society. [Emphasis added] (par 3)

The judge's reasoning casts the issue at hand as a paradoxical balance between liberty of choice and personal security within an entirely individualized and entrepreneurial frame, in complete contrast to the manner in which prostitution had been interpreted in Canadian law at the times of the adoption of the *Criminal Code*. Accordingly, by forbidding a person to hire a 'body guard' (a procurer) or to practice her professional activity behind closed doors, the state was seen as 'forcing' that person to exercise her freedom of choice to prostitute on the street, thereby putting herself in danger.

Concerning morality, Judge Himel's argument is clear: 'a law grounded in morality remains a proper legislative objective *so long as it is in keeping with Charter values*'[34] The question of morality is not rejected: it is entirely subjected to the respect of the *Charter* and the values it contains, namely individual rights to liberty and security, according to the criteria developed in the *R. vs. Labaye* case. The implementation of *Charter* rights clearly has precedence over any moral element carried by the political establishment. If morality, mediated by the political establishment, was the support of law a century earlier, it is now law, through the effects of the *Charter*, which legitimates, defines and realizes morality.

Judge Himel does not ponder on whether resorting to prostitution proceeds from a freedom of choice: this is taken for granted. Since prostitution in itself is not an illegal activity, the right to practice is not questioned. Implicitly, the practice

---

[34] *Bedford v. Canada*, by 335, emphasis added.

of prostitution is considered from the point of view of a personal, entrepreneurial choice. This ruling therefore does not so much concern those who resort to prostitution as those who live from the 'industry' of prostitution: brothel owners, escort agency owners and so forth. The decriminilization of their activities acts as a guarantee of the prostitute's right to 'autonomy', understood in a way quite remote from that defended by such modern thinkers as Immanuel Kant as part of the 'Project of the Enlightenment'. Rather, autonomy here refers to an individual's right to engage in enterprise, defined as the pursuit of economic activity with the objective of personal enrichment as the yardstick for success and happiness – in other words, a purely utilitarian conception of self-realization.

The case has been appealed, and it is too early to say if the Himel ruling will stand in a higher court and thus create a precedent.[35] If the same principles are applied as those of the Labaye case, however, we believe that a similar result should ensue. As we have shown, this evolution is coherent with the evolution of Canadian law over the last century, particularly with the unravelling of the effects of the *Charter*.

The Neoliberalization of Canadian Law

At first glance, this portrayal of the evolution of Canadian law and the progressive dissolution of its Christianity-infused communal moral foundations would seem consistent with the framework of secularization theory, whose 'untouchable' core is the differentiation and the emancipation of secular spheres from religious norms.[36] If we interpret this emancipation in a wider, cultural-ideological sense rather than in the more frequent institutional one, this indeed would seem to be the case. Yet the secularization approach in this case fails to account for the direction in which we have seen Canadian law evolve since the year 2000, in particular because it falls short with respect to issues related to economics and the way in which Canadian law has been imbued with a utilitarian and entrepreneurial perspective which is typical of neoliberalism. Attentive to the differentiation and detotalizing of social spheres, the view given by the secularization approach is limited with respect to the growing pull of economics.

This evolution we have charted aligns Canadian law with the principles of neoliberalism in many ways. To start with, recent rulings attest to the complete dissolution of any substantive notion of society. The values of Canadian society – which in reality is heterogeneous, conflicting, multilayered, complex, intangible and fluctuating – have no existence outside their formulation in the *Charter*. There is indeed no such thing as society, only collections of individuals – to

---

35   The Ontario Court of appeal has rendered judgment in March 2012, (Canada (Attorney General) v. Bedford, 2012 ONCA 186). It confirms J. Himel's decision as regard to the decriminalisation of bawdy-house. The decision has been appealed.

36   José Casanova, *Public Religions in the Modern World* (Chicago, 1994), p. 5.

paraphrase Margaret Thatcher's famous saying. As such, the moral foundations of Canadian law have been radically transformed, dechristianized, but also, in so doing, stripped of the communal groundings of egalitarian, Stuart-Mill inspired liberalism. Neoliberalism is a radicalization of liberalism on the individual, as well as a purely economic understanding of social reality and personal aspirations; a purely economic approach to evaluation, including issues of morality. With such a contractual conception of society, neoliberalism pursues (and completes) liberalism's process of depoliticization.

Neoliberalism is often equated with the forefronting of the market as the answer to optimal social regulation and a conception of social life as being the theatre of economically driven pre-social, rational, maximizing individuals (the *homo economicus* of political economy). What the Labaye and Bedford cases attest to is how the radical individualism that has transpired from the *Charter* seems to 'naturally' tend towards an economistic argumentation in which interested parties are cast as entrepreneurial types seeking to maximize costs and benefits[37] without any qualitative distinctions. In Judge Himel's ruling in the Bedford case, the logic underlying the argument self-evidently considers prostitution to be a professional activity like any other, thereby completely reversing the original *Criminal Code*'s dispositions for which prostitution could not be cast as a personal choice and understood in principally economic terms.

The result is the complete dissolution of any working notion of equality, other than a formal right to exercise freedom of choice of one's professional activity within a secure environment. If there is no testimony to the effect of coercion, the state has no business interfering, and so risk is privatized, in agreement with neoliberal principles.[38]

Judge Himel's ruling rejects any argument founded on the idea of a moral prejudice while retaining as determining all arguments linked to the rights to security in the exercise of a professional activity. Judge Himel writes, referring to the Labaye case: 'While indecency was historically inspired and informed by the moral views of the community, courts increasingly came to recognize that morals and taste were subjective, arbitrary and unworkable in the criminal context, and that a diverse society could function only with a generous measure of tolerance for minority mores and practices'.[39] The judge substitutes the benevolent neutrality of the courts to the particularistic and subjective morality of the legislator. Hence all moral considerations are pushed aside in favour of a cost/benefit analysis in which the only enduring social dimensions that must be taken into account have to do with state/public security. This evolution of the law towards issues of security is a main feature of neoliberalism's effect on politics, social life and the law, as the chapters in this volume attest.

---

[37]   See also Chapter 11 (Lori Beaman).

[38]   Amanda Glasbeek, '"My wife has endured a torrent of abuse": Gender, safety, and anti-squeegee discourses in Toronto, 1998–2000', (2006) 24 Windsor Y.B. Access Just. 55.

[39]   *Bedford v. Canada*, by 241.

Conclusion

The evolution of the moral foundations of Canadian law shows a tendency towards the incorporation of neoliberal principles in the practice of law and the very definition of justice. How are we to explain this phenomenon? By analysing the case of sexual offences, we have seen how this development follows a coherent trend involving a radicalization on the grounds of individualization, depoliticization and the disappearance of the social, with an end-point drenched in economic ideology. Yet this influence of new political economy concepts is not the result of an intentional imposition from above. Nor have Canadian judges become, all of a sudden, militant neoliberals. The neoliberalization we are hinting at has emerged out of the very process of 'secularization' and has colonized the judiciary through the liberal proceduralism that seems to have resulted from the application of the Canadian *Charter* as entrenched in the 1982 Constitution. This supports the claim according to which the structuration of contemporary societies by an economic ideology (that of neoliberalism) is the product of a deep and transversal process that involves culture as well as society's political institutions.

The specificity of Canada lies in its fairly pure application of liberal principles, starting with John Stuart Mill and continuing with John Rawls. Incidentally, the neoliberalization of Canadian law can be read as the logical outcome of the application of a depoliticized conception of justice that relies heavily on proceduralism and claims of judicial neutrality. To state things bluntly, the Canadian case tends to show that applied Rawlsian liberalism ends up scrapping its egalitarian pretentions in favour of the enactment of neoliberal principles. Similarly, it seems that the egalitarian principles of liberalism such as those deployed by Stuart Mill and Rawls and actualized in Canadian law were effective on the condition of their support by implicitly Christian and community-bound moral foundations, which is precisely what the application of Rawlsian proceduralism finished the job of undermining. What subsists of this translation of 'the common good' into procedural justice is the institutionalization of new moral foundations that share more than a family resemblance with utilitarianism and neoliberalism.

Chapter 11
Religious Freedom and Neoliberalism:
From Harm to Cost-benefit

Lori G. Beaman

Introduction

Although much attention has been paid to neoliberalism and the shifts and declines in welfare states, and the implications for religion in European contexts, there has been comparatively little discussion about North America's welfare stalwart, Canada. Sometimes referred to by Americans as 'our Commie neighbour to the north', Canada has maintained a relatively strong social safety net that has included state-funded medical care, education, employment benefits, pension benefits and so on. In this way, Canada has resembled its European counterparts more than its large neighbour to the south. Yet, like Europe, Canada seems to be in the midst of a neoliberal transformation, with state support for social programmes eroding and a language of securitization and free markets emerging as important state (and Canadian) values, particularly under the present federal conservative government.

Canada has distinguished itself from both its American and European counterparts to some extent by its strong commitment to multiculturalism, which has been identified as an important export and contribution to the international community.[1] The extent to which multiculturalism as a value has been embraced

[1] Will Kymlicka, *Multicultural Odyssey: Navigating the New International Politics of Diversity* (Oxford, 2007). The situation in Quebec is arguably somewhat different on both welfare and commitment to multiculturalism issues. Quebec has an even stronger social safety net in that it offers more state-sponsored programmes, such as state-sponsored daycare, for example. Resource shortage means that how this plays out in practice does not always meet the ideal (because of not enough daycare spaces or sometimes poor delivery of medical services), but state rhetoric of commitment is strong. Further, particularly among academic elites, the discourse of multiculturalism has been dismissed as 'Canadian' and not as representative of Quebec, which, some argue, is better understood through the concept of interculturalism. See Gérard Bouchard and Charles Taylor, 'Building The Future. A Time for Reconciliation'. Abridged Report, Commission de consultation sur les pratiques d'accommodement reliées aux différences culturelles, Gouvernement du Quebec (Quebec, 2008). Downloadable at http://www.accommodements.qc.ca/. See also Gérard Bouchard, *Interculturalism and the Management of Ethno-Cultural Diversity in Quebec*. Paper presented at Critical Thinkers in Law, Religion and Social Theory lecture series. University of Ottawa, Ottawa, ON, 2011 September 23.

is illustrated by the inclusion of its mention in the *Canadian Charter of Rights and Freedoms*, which states that the provisions of the *Charter* are to be interpreted in keeping with Canada's multicultural heritage (section 27). Public policy and public discourse have, until recently, been intimately tied to the notion that Canada is not only demographically multicultural, but ideologically committed to this task as well. To be sure, the exact meaning of the multiculturalism programme has been contested[2] but it is widely acknowledged that integration rather than assimilation or *pillarization* (segregation) has been its goal.[3] Canada's constitutional commitment means that, unlike the British and European contexts, it is much more difficult for politicians and policymakers to simply jettison multiculturalism as a value or programme, although the language of multiculturalism has somewhat disappeared from public discourse in the current context. This interesting intersection of similarity and difference from Europe means that Canada is a unique case study for reflecting on neoliberalism and the global order. In particular, because of its strong constitutional protection of human rights such as freedom of religion, its emphasis on equality based on membership in historically disadvantaged groups (section 15 of the *Charter* guarantees that every individual has equal right to protection without discrimination based on race, national or ethnic origin, colour, religion, sex, age or mental or physical disability), combined with its relatively strong welfare state, the Canadian context offers a unique opportunity for exploration of the processes of neoliberalism as they relate to the law and religion.

In the following discussion I am interested in the ways that market logic and securitization have infiltrated legal decisions in relation to religion. In this chapter I have chosen to focus on the most recent Supreme Court of Canada decision related to religion, that of *Alberta v. Hutterian Brethren of Wilson Colony*,[4] in order to explore the emergence of an explicitly neoliberal language and approach. I had read this case numerous times for other sorts of analyses, and it was not until the editors of this book invited me to contribute a piece on law that I re-read the case in this light. A systematic coding for cost-benefit analysis and discussion of securitization across three recent cases revealed a surprising shift that is reported in this chapter.

In short, the analysis of the decision in the *Hutterian Brethren* case suggests that there is an emerging market logic in law that has implications for the ways in which the limits of religious freedom are constructed. Specifically, the market logic takes the form of cost-benefit analysis that differs from the Court's previous

---

²   See Richard Day, *Multiculturalism and the History of Canadian Diversity* (Toronto, 2000); Himani Bannerji, *The Dark Side of the Nation: Essays on Multiculturalism, Nationalism and Gender* (Toronto, 2000); Gerald Kernerman, *Multicultural Nationalism: Civilizing Difference, Constituting Community* (Vancouver, 2005); and Kamala Nayar, *The Sikh Diaspora in Vancouver: Three Generations amid Tradition, Modernity, and Multiculturalism* (Toronto, 2004).

³   Phil Ryan, *Multicultiphobia* (Toronto, 2010).

⁴   *Alberta v. Hutterian Brethren of Wilson Colony*, 2009 SCC 37, [2009] 2 S.C.R. 567.

harm-based approach. The emerging cost-benefit assessment is accompanied by a shift from the language of diversity to the language of pluralism; from an understanding of multiculturalism as a programme and an expression of Canadian values to demographic description; a regression from substantive equality to formal equality; and a valorization of security and securitization.

In this chapter I am especially interested in how cost-benefit analysis is coalescing in legal decisions to frame the limits of religious freedom. While the law has been widely recognized as necessary to the neoliberal project of ensuring the operation of free markets, the neoliberal impulse in law in relation to cases that are not directly related to the market has not been adequately explored.[5] There is an emerging neoliberal resonance in law that is accompanying a contraction of the boundaries of religious freedom in the Canadian context resulting in a shift in the substance of religious freedom. The *Hutterian Brethren* case marks the first time that neoliberal reasoning intersects with freedom of religion at the Supreme Court level. Previous to the decision, the Court had embarked on an expansive interpretation of religious freedom which had been much more inclusive of minority religious groups. How this is interwoven with neoliberal discourse will be explored in the following sections. First, though, I will turn to a broader discussion of neoliberalism and the law.

The Neoliberal Theme

In her 2010 book *Walled States, Waning Sovereignty*, Wendy Brown argues powerfully and provocatively that walls such as those in Israel and the United States southern border are paradoxical representations of waning state sovereignty rather than strength. Linking increased securitization (policing and blockading) to what she calls ungovernability in the rise of the God-like status of capital, Brown argues that 'states increasingly shoulder the task of protecting national populations against the ravaging effects of open markets on everything, including the national imaginary.'[6] There are three specific observations Brown makes that I draw on to consider the ways in which the neoliberal order impacts on law:

---

[5]   Hester Lessard, 'The Empire of the Lone Mother: Parental Rights, Child Welfare Law, and State Restructuring', *Osgoode Hall Law Journal*, 39/4 (2002): pp. 717–70; Shelley A.M. Gavigan and Dorothy E. Chunn, 'From Mothers' Allowance to Mothers Need Not Apply: Canadian Welfare Law as Liberal and Neo-Liberal Reforms', *Osgoode Hall Law Journal*, 45/4 (2007): pp. 733–71; Owen M. Fiss, 'The Autonomy of Law', *Faculty Scholarship Series, Yale Law School*, Paper 1316 (2001), <http://digitalcommons.law.yale.edu/fss_papers/1316>.

[6]   Wendy Brown, *Walled States, Waning Sovereignty* (Cambridge, 2010), p. 68.

1. 'Foucault reminds us that neoliberal rationality, which exceeds the economic sphere and permeates the political and the social with market values, has a corrosive effect on the rule of law as this rationality moulds both individual and state activity to entrepreneurial criteria';[7] and
2. Under neoliberalism, commitments to universal equality and liberty cede the field to utilitarian cost-benefit accounting in political and legal life.[8]
3. That the 'figure of alien danger is thus literally overdetermined today, comprising economic, political, security and cultural effects of globalization. These disparate elements are fused into one, producing "the alien" as a many-headed dragon.'[9]

Brown's first point goes to the authority of neoliberal rationality, including cost-benefit analysis, and the ways in which it has permeated political and social spheres, including the law. Cost-benefit analysis has a certain seductive sway, in part because it seems to be positioned within the realm of the rational, with certainty and truth on its side. The costs of a particular course of action are weighed against the benefits. In the neoliberal world, these assessments are conducted against the backdrop of security and an emphasis on individual choice. The illusion of measurability permeates, and this, along with the law's claim to truth, presents a compelling narrative for legal decisions.[10] The erosion of the rule of law, or the idea that the law applies to everyone, equally, and that everyone has access to justice, is facilitated by a rationality which only accepts reasoning framed in terms of costs and benefits.[11] Of course, for religious groups, the benefit and cost will only be framed in terms of what the particular measure or practice does for the group. Thus the benefits will almost always be framed narrowly. For the state, the benefits and costs will be framed in terms of society. The deck is stacked from the outset in such analyses (societal costs can be invoked to offset or outweigh individual benefits) unless one refuses to engage with the cost-benefit framework.

Brown's emphasis on the individual is important. Individuals are imagined to make choices rationally, weighing the costs and benefits and making decisions based on a measured assessment that calculates a favourable outcome. This tautological reasoning has come to dominate certain theories of religion and leaves no room for exception. If we think about a tautology as a formula which is always true, then everything is imagined to fit within the explanation, a criticism that has been levelled against rational choice theory in relation to religion. The nuance of relationality, which feminist theorists in particular had hoped created an alternative way of understanding choice and agency, disappears, or is again

---

7   Brown, p. 96.
8   Brown, p. 101.
9   Brown, p. 117.
10   Carol Smart, *Feminism and the Power of Law* (London, 1989).
11   Annie Bunting, 'Feminism, Foucault and Law as Power/Knowledge', *Alberta Law Review*, 30/3 (1992): pp. 829–42.

stuffed into the model of rationality, with people making 'rational' choices that maximize benefit.[12] A sociology of emotion also disappears from this modelling, except as it relates to the calculation of cost.[13] Economic models of explanation can contain valuable modes of assessing social life, but their use as total explanations are problematic.

In the neoliberal model, equality disappears from discourse and in particular from legal discourse. Moreover, the abandonment of equality comes from a number of sites, and there is a disconcerting fusion of neoliberalism and feminism, the latter having grown tired of equality's failure to deliver in the legal realm.[14] In a recent panel I sat on at a Canadian academic conference I lamented the disappearance of equality in the adjudication of religious freedom claims and in public discourse around religious diversity, or any diversity for that matter, and worried about the rise of accommodation as the framework within which diversity was being positioned. I met with a surprising amount of resistance to the idea of the reintroduction or reinvigoration of equality, rooted mostly, I think, in equality's failure to deliver, combined with the colonization of equality by ideas like *laïcité*, particularly as it has developed in the French context, which is based on a formal definition of equality that fails to deliver substantive equality or justice for those who find themselves in the minority.[15]

Finally, Brown's third point about the overdetermination of the alien other and the danger presented by them marks the culture of fear and securitization. How, we might ask, does a small group of Hutterites in Alberta figure in this picture of the alien other? This was in fact the question asked by one of the minority judgments in the case itself, but it might also be useful to reflect for a moment on the broader social and legal context of the case. As will be discussed in more detail below, the Court framed the exemption of the Hutterian Brethren as posing a threat to the entire system, a framing which is, again, challenged by one of the justices themselves. It is important to understand the broader context of 'us' and 'them' within which the battle over this small religious group takes place. Looming on the horizon at the time of the case was a case over the legality of polygamy in Canada, a case that was linked not only to the Fundamentalist Latter-day Saints who publicly practice polygamy, but to Muslim immigrants to Canada. Also working its way through the courts was a case dealing with the issue of whether a Muslim

---

[12]   Robin West, 'Jurisprudence and Gender', *Chicago Law Review*, 55/1 (1988): pp. 1–72; Rebecca Johnson, *Taxing Choices: The Intersection of Class, Gender, Parenthood, and the Law* (Vancouver, 2002).

[13]   Ole Riis and Linda Woodhead, *A Sociology of Religious Emotion* (New York, 2010).

[14]   See for example Rosemary Hunter (ed.), *Rethinking Equality Projects in Law: Feminist Challenges* (Portland, 2008).

[15]   Jean Baubérot, *Les Laïcités dans le monde* (Paris, 2007); Jean Baubérot, *L'intégrisme républicain contre la laïcité.* (Paris, 2006); Jean–Paul Martin (ed.), 'Laïcité, Croyances et Éducation', *Spirale* 39 (2007); Alain Renaut and Alain Touraine, *Un débat sur la laïcité* (Paris, 2005).

woman should be allowed to wear her *niqab* (full-body and full-face veil) while giving evidence in criminal court. By casting such practices as 'exemptions', the public and the courts are able to maintain a distance between 'us' and 'them', the latter being the alien other Brown refers to. In the cost-benefit analysis, then, the overdetermination of the alien other and the threat posed by them becomes an exaggerated cost.

The Legal Context

Although religious freedom has always been part of the Canadian legal landscape, its precise contours have shifted over the past century, moving largely from diversity within Christianity to a broader diversity that includes religious variety of many types. A series of cases emerging mostly from Quebec during the 1940s and 1950s, related to discrimination against Jehovah's Witnesses form the backbone of jurisprudence on religious freedom prior to the enactment of the *Charter*.[16] Of particular importance are *Boucher v. the King* and *Saumur v. City of Quebec*,[17] in these cases, which supported the right of Jehovah's Witnesses to proselytize publicly and condemned attempts to exclude them from business-related activities, the Supreme Court laid the groundwork for the idea of religious freedom which was later to become enshrined in the *Charter of Rights and Freedoms*.

A significant marker in the religious freedom landscape has been the enactment of the *Canadian Charter of Rights and Freedoms* in 1982. Perhaps contrary to common perception, and very much unlike the United States, there is no explicit separation of Church and state in the *Charter*, and indeed, the preamble states: 'Whereas Canada is founded upon principles that recognize the supremacy of God and the rule of law'. Two clauses that specifically mention religion that are relevant to the present discussion are sections 2 and 15. Section 2, which is the clause used most frequently in religious freedom cases, states:

2. Everyone has the following fundamental freedoms:
   (a) freedom of conscience and religion;
   (b) freedom of thought, belief, opinion and expression, including
       freedom of the press and other media of communication;
   (c) freedom of peaceful assembly; and
   (d) freedom of association.

Religion is also mentioned in section 15, which states:

---

[16]   Lori G. Beaman, 'Assessing Religious Identity in Law: Sincerity, Accommodation and Harm,' in Avigail Eisenberg and Will Kymlicka (eds), *Identity Politics in the Public Realm: Bringing Institutions Back In* (Vancouver, 2011), pp. 238–59.

[17]   *Boucher v. the King*, [1949] 96 C.C.C. 48; *Saumur v. City of Quebec*, [1953] 2 S.C.R. 299.

15. (1) Every individual is equal before and under the law and has the right to the equal protection and equal benefit of the law without discrimination and, in particular, without discrimination based on race, national or ethnic origin, colour, religion, sex, age or mental or physical disability.

The freedoms set out in the *Charter* are limited by section 1, which states: 'The *Charter of Rights and Freedoms* guarantees the rights and freedoms set out in it subject only to such reasonable limits presented by law as can be demonstrably justified in a free and democratic society.'

The court has tended to give a wide read to section 2a and has left the limiting of freedom of religion to the section 1 analysis. So, for example, in a religious freedom claim the courts will be reluctant to impose what they refer to as 'internal limits' on the right or freedom. For religion, this has meant a fairly expansive definition of religion. The test or process by which courts are to make the section 1 determination has been laid out in an early post-*Charter* case known as the *Oakes* case[18] (and hence has become known as the Oakes test). Under the Oakes test, as set out in that case, in order to determine whether a practice or piece of legislation by the state violates freedom of religion, the court must ask:

1. Is the legislative objective being pursued sufficiently important to warrant limiting a constitutional right?
2. Are the means chosen by the state authority proportional to the objective in question? This includes: a) a determination of whether the decision, law, measure has a rational connection with the objective; b) whether the limit minimally impairs the right or freedom in question.

The balancing required by section 1 has often been couched in the language of harm and has been used when so-called competing rights need to be reconciled. Harm to the rights of others (and sometimes to self) has been a gauge by which the courts have justified limiting religious freedom. While harm has its own limitations, about which I have written elsewhere,[19] it has allowed the court to ask questions about the place of particular religious practices in a society, and, occasionally, to ask questions about majoritarian practices and their effects on religious minorities. The analysis under section 1, at least in relation to religious freedom, has not been framed as a cost-benefit analysis, even though some might argue that this is mere semantics when one talks about balancing and harm. There is something qualitatively different, though, between asking about the harm done by a particular religious belief/practice and the cost of it, which I will examine below in the analysis of the *Hutterian Brethren* case.

It is impossible to give an overview in the present chapter of all of the case law related to religious freedom. However, the years previous to the 2009 *Hutterian*

---

18   *R. v. Oakes*, [1986] 1 S.C.R. 103.

19   Lori G. Beaman, *Defining Harm* (Vancouver, 2008).

Brethren case were especially promising. The Supreme Court broadened its understanding of religion, and demonstrated an openness to religious practices with which it was not especially familiar. The following is a quick overview of two religious freedom cases preceding that of the *Hutterian Brethren.*[20]

In the *Amselem*[21] case the claimant was an Orthodox Jew who lived in a condominium building in Montréal. Under the terms of the by-laws in the declaration of co-ownership, decorations, alterations and constructions on the balconies were prohibited. During the festival of *Succot* Mr. Amselem wished to build a *succah* on his own balcony, a structure resembling a tent that was prohibited by co-ownership by-laws. During *Succot* some Jews eat, sleep and live in the *succah*. Although there was some evidence that a communal *succah* would fulfill the requirements of his religion, the claimant's interpretation was that he should build his own *succah* on his balcony. The Supreme Court accepted this argument, noting that aesthetic concerns should not outweigh religious commitment.

The *Amselem* case represented a significant turn in post-*Charter* case law on religious freedom for three reasons: 1) it solidified the formal requirement for an inquiry into sincerity of belief in religious freedom claims; 2) it explicitly recognized the importance of the religious subject in determining the importance and validity of religious beliefs/practices; and 3) it included a specific consideration of the definition of religion and acknowledged the relationship between the individual beliefs/practices and a 'nexus' to religion. The case is an affirmation of a broad interpretation of religion and an acknowledgement of the courts that religious freedom is important. For the purposes of this discussion, perhaps the most relevant point about the *Amselem* case is that it returned to the expansive approach adopted by Justice Dickson in a case involving Big M Drug Mart,[22] in which the Supreme Court struck down a Sunday closing law on the basis that it enforced a majoritarian Christian practice on religious minorities. That early post-*Charter* case presented a broad interpretation of religious freedom with a relatively unfettered section 1 or limits position.

Although the *Amselem* decision has been sometimes interpreted as meaning that religion is reduced purely to individual belief, this is not accurate. The Court maintained that the belief or practice must retain a nexus to religion, thus implicitly recognizing the communal aspects of religious belief and belonging. While the court held that expert evidence on this was not required, it is obvious that convincing the courts that one's practice is 'religious' under the religious freedom section requires some evidence that this is the case. Thus, in the subsequent case to

---

[20]   *Bruker v. Marcovitz* also dealt with religion, but involved a husband's refusal to give his wife a *get* (Jewish divorce), thus prohibiting her from remarrying. He had contractually agreed to give her the *get* (*Bruker v. Marcovitz*, [2007] 3 S.C.R. 607, 2007 SCC 54). This case involves private law which renders it qualitatively different from especially *Multani v. Commission Scolaire Marguerite-Bourgeoys* and the *Hutterian Brethren.*

[21]   *Syndicat Northcrest v. Amselem*, [2004] 2 S.C.R. 551, 2004 SCC 47.

[22]   *R. v. Big M Drug Mart Ltd.*, [1985] 1 S.C.R. 295.

come before the court on religious freedom, brought by Multani,[23] expert evidence about Sikh practices was in fact led. The case was significant, however, in its recognition of the subjective interpretation of religion and its practices.

In the *Multani* case a Sikh schoolboy sought to have his right to wear his *kirpan* to school protected under the religious freedom provisions of the *Charter*. The *kirpan* is a ceremonial sword or dagger carried by orthodox or fully-observant Sikhs. The Supreme Court's decision, which supported the boy's right to wear his *kirpan* to school, was highly controversial and is largely recognized as having the effect of sparking the formation of the Bouchard-Taylor Commission[24] which examined what have become known as the reasonable accommodation debates in Quebec. Although the Court's reasoning was at the time problematic (the majority judgment drew an analogy of reasonable accommodation from employment law in the process of conducting its section 1 balancing, a move that was rejected in the *Hutterian Brethren* case), the fact that the Court supported the wearing of the *kirpan* in the school context was a significant decision in the history of religious freedom in Canada.

The combined effect of the *Amselem* and *Multani* cases was significant: religious freedom received a broad interpretation from the Court, and the Court was clearly employing a substantive understanding of equality. Both decisions highlighted multiculturalism as a Canadian value, and neither used the language of costs and benefits when engaged in the balancing required by section 1 of the *Charter*. Given the *Charter* guarantees, the commitment to multiculturalism, and the history of communal thinking both within and outside of the law in the Canadian context, none of this should be especially surprising.

Hutterian Brethren and the Turn to Neoliberal Logic

The most recent Supreme Court decision on religion is the one in *Alberta v. Hutterian Brethren of Wilson Colony*. The Hutterian Brethren are an Anabaptist group who came to North America from Europe in the 1870s. Resistance to military participation in the First World War led to a large exodus from the United States to Canada. Their relationship with the state has not been completely unproblematic in Canada, with their resistance to military service and communal living distinguishing them. In an attempt to control the amount of land they owned, the province of Alberta enacted the *Communal Property Act* (in force from the 1940s until the early 1970s), which restricted the property holding of Hutterites. Their primary focus has been agriculture, which has resulted in the creation of

---

[23] *Multani v. Commission Scolaire Marguerite-Bourgeoys*, 2005 SCC 6, [2006] 1 S.C.R. 256.

[24] Gérard Bouchard and Charles Taylor, 'Building the Future: A Time for Reconciliation', *Commission de consultation sur les pratiques d'accommodement reliées aux différences culturelles* (2008).

relative wealth for the communities. They are quite readily distinguishable by their dress when they interact with surrounding communities, which they regularly do, usually by vehicle,[25] which brings us to the case that came before the Supreme Court of Canada in 2008.

Known as the 'drivers' licence case', the *Hutterian Brethren* case involved a small group – of 250 – Hutterites who believe that having their pictures taken contravenes their religious beliefs. This brought them head to head with an Alberta provincial statute which requires individuals' photographs to appear on their driving licences. The Hutterites had enjoyed a long-standing exemption from the law. They live a rural lifestyle which is agriculturally based, and depend on their driving licences to do related business. Nonetheless, the Court holds that the requirement to have their pictures taken is not an unreasonable requirement, and that, if they wish to refrain from having their pictures taken they can find other ways to do their business, such as hire someone to drive them.

The *Hutterian Brethren* case is important because it marks a dramatic shift in the approach of the Supreme Court for a number of reasons, including its minimization of the importance of a particular practice (through refusal and avoidance of having pictures taken) to a religious group. For the purposes of this chapter it further circumscribes the 'type' of religion which is imagined as 'universal' religion and thus protected under the *Charter of Rights and Freedoms*. The Court emphasizes the idea that groups cannot expect to have exemption from laws of general application, thus reverting from a more substantive vision of equality it adopts in previous post-*Charter* decisions to a much more formal interpretation of equality in this case. The context in which the case occurs, which is about securitization, identity theft and so on, shifts the boundaries of religious freedom and acceptable religious practice. As one of the dissenting judgments notes, there are some 700,000 Albertans whose faces do not appear in the central data bank, so why is it that 250 Hutterites are imagined to pose such a threat? A cost-benefit analysis forms the basis on which the Hutterian Brethren are denied protection under the *Charter*.

Costs   There is a marked shift in the *Hutterian Brethren* case to a usage of market language, with an emphasis on cost and benefit. The cost-benefit language is authoritative in tone, using a logic of self-evidence rather than measurable data:

> However, in many cases, the incidental effects of a law passed for the general good on a particular religious practice may be less serious. The limit may impose costs on the religious practitioner in terms of money, tradition or inconvenience. However, these costs may still leave the adherent with a meaningful choice concerning the religious practice at issue. The Charter guarantees freedom of religion, but does not indemnify practitioners against all costs incident to the

---

[25]   Alvin Esau, *The Courts and the Colonies: The Litigation of Hutterite Church Disputes* (Vancouver, 2005).

practice of religion. Many religious practices entail costs which society benefits or privileges conferred by law may be among such costs. A limit on choice about religious practice at issue will be less serious than a limit that effectively deprives the adherent of such choice.[26]

In the paragraph above the Court weighs the costs – the compromise of a security measure that allegedly provides protection against identity theft for all of society – against the benefits to the Hutterian Brethren, a small religious group who can, notes the Court, carry on business as usual by hiring a driver. That the cost to the group is more than the cost regarding business practices is minimized in the majority decision, but taken up on the dissent by Justice Abella, who states:

> The harm to the constitutional rights of the Hutterites, in the absence of an exemption, is dramatic. Their inability to drive affects them not only individually, but also severely compromises the autonomous character of their religious community.[27]

The dissenting judgment takes issue with the failure to consider cost beyond the business concerns, noting that motor vehicles are used to attend medical appointments for the 48 children and 8 diabetics in the community, for community firefighting and for commercial activity to sustain business.

For the majority, cost is linked with individual choice in a context which imagines people as freely choosing to engage in this or that behaviour with full knowledge of the costs associated with those choices. The failure to embed the 'choice' in the communal context in which the Hutterian Brethren live allows the Court to ignore the costs to the community, or, as the dissenting judgment frames it, the harm caused to the communal way of life of the Hutterian Brethren.

Costs and benefits are, like harm, situated in a social context which allows them to be constructed in particular ways. They are not neutral, or valueless or norm free. Contrasting the approaches of the majority and dissenting judgments illustrates the result of cost-benefit analysis and reveals the neoliberal preoccupation with cost to business. But even the majority judgment itself shows cracks in the façade of calculated certainty in the assessment of cost and benefit, as we can see from the statements below:

> Though it is difficult to quantify in exact terms how much risk of fraud would result from permitted exemptions, it is clear that the internal integrity of the system would be compromised. In this respect, the present case may be contrasted with previous religious freedom cases where this Court has found that the potential risk was too speculative.[28]

---

[26]   *Hutterian Brethren*, SCC 37, p. 95.

[27]   Ibid., p. 114.

[28]   Ibid., p. 81.

Yet another salutary benefit may flow from eventual harmonization with other licensing systems. This benefit, however, remains to be realized.[29]

As discussed earlier, a government enacting social legislation is not required to show that the law will in fact produce the forecast benefits. Legislatures can only be asked to impose measures that reason and the evidence suggest will be beneficial. If legislation designed to further the public good were required to await proof positive that the benefits would in fact be realized, few laws would be passed and the public interest would suffer.[30]

Despite the recognition of the importance of freedom of religion in the *Charter* under section 2(a), and the guarantee of equality under section 15 (specifically that one cannot be discriminated against on the basis of religion), the Court is willing to sacrifice these constitutionally recognized protections (which are also recognized by a wide range of international human rights conventions and by other nation-states) in favour of a security regime whose benefits are unproven.

Part of the neoliberal approach is an emphasis on security.[31] The demarcation of security as the framework within which the claim to religious freedom must be assessed thus excludes other discursive possibilities. So, for example, equality, freedom and justice disappear. Any analysis of harm to the group in question is displaced by a discussion of the costs of doing business without a driver's licence, which as mentioned above, the Court resolves by suggesting that the community can simply hire drivers to take their goods to market. The Court states:

> The Hutterian claimants argue that the limit presents them with an invidious choice: the choice between some of its members violating the Second Commandment on the one hand, or accepting the end of their rural communal life on the other hand. However, the evidence does not support the conclusion that arranging alternative means of highway transport would end the Colony's rural way of life. The claimants' affidavit says that it is necessary for at least some members to be able to drive from the Colony to nearby towns and back. It does not explain, however, why it would not be possible to hire people with driver's licences for this purpose, or to arrange third party transport to town for necessary services, like visits to the doctor. Many businesses and individuals rely on hired persons and commercial transport for their needs, either because they cannot drive or choose not to drive. Obtaining alternative transport would impose an additional economic cost on the Colony, and would go against their traditional self–sufficiency. But there is no evidence that this would be prohibitive.[32]

---

29   Ibid., p. 84.
30   Ibid., p. 85.
31   See Brown 2010.
32   *Hutterian Brethren*, SCC 37, p. 97.

Equality   Although equality discourse has often entered into religion cases, it is rather rare to see the equality provision of the *Charter* explicitly used to construct arguments in religious freedom cases. Unusually in the *Hutterian Brethren* case there is an argument that raises section 15 of the *Charter*, which prohibits discrimination on the basis of religion.

The court dismisses the equality argument summarily:

> Assuming the respondents could show that the regulation creates a distinction on the enumerated ground of religion, it arises not from any demeaning stereotype but from a neutral and rationally defensible policy choice [...] The Colony members' claim is to the unfettered practice of their religion, not to be free from religious discrimination. The substance of the respondents' s. 15(1) claim has already been dealt with under s. 2(a). There is no breach of s. 15(1).[33]

Cost in the Court's view is in turn linked with choice – in the context of the market, people are imagined as freely choosing to engage in this or that behaviour with a full knowledge of the costs associated with those choices. The 'neutrality' of the policy choice as articulated by the Court is language used in the context of formal equality arguments. In short, the Hutterian Brethren are free to choose, just like everybody else, to comply with the law, and can choose to offset the choice to deny themselves a driving licence. The effect of neoliberal reasoning in this case is dramatic in that it effectively positions the impact on the Hutterian community as trivial.

There is a broader issue of equality as a principle rather than as an explicitly constitutional claim that emerges in religious freedom cases. The promise of equality under the *Charter* establishes what might be called (and has been in numerous contexts) a '*Charter* value'. This is of course not unique to the Canadian context, but rather draws from a 'universal' ideal of equality of all citizens, including in various pieces of international law, such as the Universal Declaration of Human Rights.[34]

Discussions about the meaning of equality have produced volumes of academic and policy literature, perhaps the most important in recent decades being feminist scholarship and more recently in the context of queer theory.[35] The precise meaning

---

[33]   Ibid., p. 108.

[34]   Article 1: All human beings are born free and equal in dignity and rights. They are endowed with reason and conscience and should act towards one another in a spirit of brotherhood. Article 7: All are equal before the law and are entitled without any discrimination to equal protection of the law. All are entitled to equal protection against any discrimination in violation of this declaration and against any incitement to such discrimination.

[35]   Brenda Cossman, *Sexual Citizens: The Legal and Cultural Regulation of Sex and Belonging* (Stanford, 2007); Brenda Cossman, 'Sexuality, Queer Theory, and "Feminism After": Reading and Rereading the Sexual Subject', *McGill Law Journal*, 49 (2004): pp. 847–76; Annamarie Jagose, 'Queer Theory', *Australian Humanities Review*, (1996) <http://www.australianhumanitiesreview.org/archive/Issue–Dec–1996/jagose.html>.

of equality has remained contested, and certainly the legal interpretation of it has come under fire, so much so that many feminist theorists have backed away from it as a useful category for engagement with diversity.[36]

The post and even pre-*Charter* decisions on religious freedom have incorporated, generally speaking, an ethos of equality that has shown concern for religious minorities and the consequences of majoritarian practices as well as living in societies with shadow establishments, to use the words of David Martin.[37] This has certainly been the case in the *Multani* and *Amselem* cases, but perhaps even more explicitly in the early case of *Big M Drug Mart*, which struck down Sunday closing laws as violating religious freedom. In that case Justice Dickson invoked the idea that there exists an ethic of equality that extends beyond legal discussions about equality:

> 94. A truly free society is one which can accommodate a wide variety of beliefs,
> diversity of tastes and pursuits, customs and codes of conduct. A free society is
> one which aims at equality with respect to the enjoyment of fundamental freedoms
> and I say this without any reliance upon s. 15 of the *Charter*. (at para 94)

He also emphasized the links between majoritarian religions, states and the need for protection of religious minorities: 'What may appear good and true to a majoritarian religious group, or to the state acting at their behest, may not, for religious reasons, be imposed upon citizens who take a contrary view. The *Charter* safeguards religious minorities from the threat of "the tyranny of the majority"' (at para 96).

The discussion in the *Hutterian Brethren* case shifts the conversation from one which imagines religious minorities as equals and reshapes the analysis to one of cost and benefit. The security of the state is invoked to displace any remaining doubt about the possibility of allowing the Hutterites an 'exemption'. By refusing to allow exceptions to laws of general application, the Court by implication adopts

---

[36]   See, Sophia Moreau, 'The Wrongs of Unequal Treatment,' *University of Toronto Law Journal*, 54/3 (2004): pp. 291–326; Sophia Moreau 'The Promise of *Law V. Canada*', *University of Toronto Law Journal*, 57/2 (2007): pp. 415–30; Denise Réaume, '*Law v. Canada* (Minister of Employment and Immigration)', *Canadian Journal of Women and Law*, 18/1 (2006a): pp. 143–88; Denise Réaume, 'The Relevance of Relevance to Equality Rights', *Queen's Law Journal* 31 (2006b): pp. 695–730; Emily Grabham, '*Law v Canada*: New Directions for Equality Under the Canadian Charter?' *Oxford Journal of Legal Studies*, 22/4 (2002): pp. 641–61; Daphne Gilbert, 'Substance Without Form: The Impact of Anonymity on Equality-Seeking Groups', *University of Ottawa Law & Technology Journal* 3/1 (2006): pp. 225–47.

[37]   David Martin, *On Secularization: Towards a Revised General Theory* (London, 2005); David Martin, 'Canada in Comparative Perspective', in David Lyon and Marguerite Van Die (eds), *Rethinking Church, State and Modernity: Canada between Europe and America* (Toronto, 2000), pp. 23–33.

a model of formal equality that gives superficial lip service to equality while blocking any move to a deeper or more substantive development of that concept.

Security The security emphasis in neoliberalism can have the effect of excluding other types of discussions, or of making other concerns or considerations seem to be trivial.[38] The demarcation of security as the framework within which the claim to religious freedom must be assessed thus excludes other discursive possibilities. So, for example, equality, freedom and justice disappear from the analysis. In this sort of reasoning, analysis of harm in the *Hutterian Brethren* is displaced by a discussion of the costs of doing business. How have security discussions emerged in other contexts? When the neoliberal cost-benefit emphasis disappears, risk can be considered in context.

So, for example, in the *Amselem* case, the 'security concern' posed by the construction of personal *succahs* was purely speculative because there was no evidence that emergency exits were actually being blocked. The appellants had offered to set up their *succahs* 'in such a way that they would not block any doors, would not obstruct fire lanes, [and] would pose no threat to safety or security in any way.'[39] The Court noted that 'security concerns, if soundly established, would require appropriate recognition in ascertaining any limit on the exercise of the appellants' religious freedom.'[40] In the case of the *Hutterian Brethren*, by contrast, it is established that exempting people from the photo registry creates a real risk to security because it undermines the integrity of the system.

One might think that if ever there was a case that emphasized security it might be the *Multani* case, discussed above, in which the Sikh student sought to wear his *kirpan* to school. However, a comparison of the use of security language in the two cases reveals an interesting result – while security is invoked 17 times in the *Hutterian Brethren* case, it is used only 3 times in *Multani*. In the latter case the Court considers the safety of the students, emphasizing the specific context and the specific arrangements of the Multani family, the record of the student and so on. The Court concluded that safety does not mean absolute safety, but rather on the continuum of minimum safety and no concern for safety, the standard of reasonable safety in schools was a pressing and substantial objective. The success of securitization in framing the cost-benefit analysis depends on an imagined, pervasive, dangerous, alien other.[41] We might ask how it is that the Hutterian Brethren, a small Christian community living in rural Alberta, can possibly be construed as a dangerous, threatening, alien other? But the social and legal context contributes to how a group such as this is construed as threatening. As mentioned at the beginning of this discussion, other cases on the horizon, as well as the ongoing post-9/11 construction of Muslims as a threat, have allowed

---

[38] See Brown 2010.

[39] *Amselem*, SCC 47, p. 89.

[40] Ibid., p. 88.

[41] See Brown 2010.

for the successful integration of securitization into multiple social frameworks, including law. The *N.S*[42] case, a criminal case in which a Muslim woman wishes to give evidence wearing her *niqab*, has now been heard by the Supreme Court of Canada and the decision is pending. Whether that case is framed in the language of security remains to be seen, as it has been argued primarily around the issue of the rights of an accused to make fair answer and defence.

The Court was no doubt acutely aware, as it made its decision in the *Hutterian Brethren* case, that whatever it decided in relation to the so-called 'exemption' of the Hutterites will form part of the precedent that shapes the decision in these other cases. That the threat of the alien other is not far from that Court's mind is evidenced by the particular approach it takes in relation to multiculturalism. In previous cases, multiculturalism undergoes a metamorphosis, becoming a sword to attack those who would threaten the security of the state, slicing the bonds that form the fabric of the Hutterite community. The diverse society that is so celebrated in previous decisions becomes a plural society with multiple groups (including atheists) which the state has a duty to *manage*. Multiculturalism shifts from being a cherished Canadian value to a statement of demographic reality which presents almost as a burden for the state.

Conclusion

The departure in *Hutterian Brethren* from the open approach of the Supreme Court to religious freedom during most of the post-*Charter* era marks a shift in the ways in which religious freedom is imagined by the Supreme Court of Canada. Relying on a cost-benefit analysis which displaces considerations of equality, harm, fairness and justice, the Court enters a new era in that neoliberal logic overtakes a previous commitment to an expansive definition of religion and the fledgling promise of religious freedom, and substantive equality, for religious minorities.

The decision moves away from an approach that recognized the values of religious communities, to a cost-benefit analysis which emphasizes individual choice as the defining characteristic of religious commitment. Commitment to community, except to identify the alien other, threatens market logic by introducing the possibility that there is a priority other than capital. The commitment of the Hutterian Brethren to community property, for example, is directly contrary to market logic. If we understand neoliberalism as a move away from communal thinking, which would include socialism and the welfare state, to a free market ethos, the decision to reject a claim from a group whose existence is fundamentally marked by a communal approach becomes more comprehensible.

Why, though, the seemingly sudden shift? There was not, for example, a dramatic change in the make up of the Supreme Court, which may or may not have offered a possible explanation. It is likely, however, that the shift was not as

---

42   *R. v. N.S.*, [2009] O.J. 1766.

sudden as it may appear to be. Although it lacked visibility in law, it was perhaps foreshadowed. The *Amselem* decision may have made more possible a rejection of an acknowledgment of the importance of religious communities through its emphasis on the individual subjectivity in relation to religious practices.[43] The explanation is found less in a single cause than a coming together of factors that have already been noted, including the cases the court could see on the horizon, the re-emergence of religion as a public factor (and the fear of certain religious groups and religions) and the entrenchment of neoliberal reasoning that seems to have been a bit slow to come to Canada, in part because of the strong welfare state and in part because of the *Charter*'s emphasis on equality.

---

[43] This argument was suggested by Louise Tardif, 'Religious Freedom in Canada: Whither the Community?' (unpublished, 2010).

Bibliography

2000 Population and Housing Census IV. Education. Religion (Tallinn: Statistical Office of Estonia, 2002).

2009 Estonian Human Development Report 2009 (Tallinn: Eesti Koostöö Kogu, 2011), <www.kogu.ee/public/eia2009/EIA2009_engredis.pdf>.

Aberle, David F., *The Peyote Religion Among the Navajo* (New York: Viking Fund, 1966).

Alexander, Jeffrey C., *The Civil Sphere* (New York: Oxford University Press, 2006).

Almeida, Ronaldo Rômulo M. de, 'A expansão pentecostal: circulação e flexibilidade', Centro de Estudos da Metrópole (2006), <www.centrodametropole. org.br/v1/pdf/2007/ronaldo_pentecostalismo.pdf>, accessed 10 April 2011.

Almond, Gabriel A. and Sidney Verba, *The Civic Culture: Political Attitudes and Democracy in Five Nations* (London: Sage, 1989).

Almond, Gabriel A., R. Scott Appleby and Emmanuel Sivan, *Strong Religion: The Rise of Fundamentalisms Around the World* (Chicago: University of Chicago Press, 2003).

Altnurme, Lea, Kristlusest oma usuni: Uurimus muutustest eestlaste religioossuses 20. sajandi II poolel [From Christianity to Personal Belief: A Study of Changes in the Religiosity of the Estonians in the Second Half of the Twentieth Century]. *Dissertationes Theologiae Universitatis Tartuensis*, 9 (Tartu: Tartu Ülikooli Kirjastus, 2005).

Altnurme, Lea, 'Changes in Mythic Patterns in Estonian Religious Life Stories', *Social Compass*, 58/1 (2011): 77–94.

Altnurme, Riho, 'Relations with the State', Riho Altnurme (ed.), *History of Estonian Ecumenism* (Tallinn, Tartu: Estonian Council of Churches, University of Tartu, 2009).

American Civil Liberties Union, 'ACLU Calls on Congress to Reject Funding of Religious Activities' (21 June 2005).

Amoore, Louise and Marieke De Goede, 'Governance, Risk and Dataveillance in the War on Terror', *Crime, Law & Social Change*, 43 (2005): 149–73.

Anderson, Brian C., 'How Catholic Charities Lost its Soul,' *City Journal*, Winter (2000).

Annus, Taavi, *Governance and Law in Transition States* (Tartu: Tartu University Press, 2004).

Archer, Toby and Leena Malkki, 'Terrorismin- ja radikalisaation vastaisuuden nousu Suomessa', in Tuomas Martikainen and Marja Tiilikainen (eds), *Islam, hallinta ja turvallisuus* (manuscript in review).

Audard, Catherine, *Anthologie historique et critique de l'utilitarisme. II. L'utilitarisme victorien (1838–1903)* (Paris: Presses universitaires de France, 1999).

Audard, Catherine, *Qu'est-ce que le libéralisme* (Paris: Édition Gallimard, Coll. Folio essais, 2009).

Audier, Serge, *Le colloque Lippmann* (Paris: Le Bord de l'Eau, 2008).

Australian Government, Letter dated 11 October 2005 from the Permanent Representative of Australia to the United Nations addressed to the Chairman of the Counterterrorism Committee (2005).

Australian Government, Safeguarding Your Organisation Against Terrorism Financing: A Guidance for Non-Profit Organisations, Attorney-General's Department, Canberra (2009), <www.nationalsecurity.gov.au/npo>, accessed 23 March 2010.

Bache, Ian and Matthew Flinders, 'Themes and Issues in Multi-level Governance', in Ian Bache and Matthew Flinders (eds), *Multi-level Governance* (Oxford: Oxford University Press, 2004).

Backhouse, Constance, 'Nineteenth Century Prostitution Law: Reflection of a Discriminatory Society', *Social History*, 35/8 (1985): 387–423.

Bäckström, Anders and Grace Davie with Ninna Edgardh and Per Pettersson (eds), *Welfare and Religion in 21st Century Europe: Volume 1: Configuring the Connections* (Farnham: Ashgate 2010).

Bäckström, Anders, Grace Davie, Ninna Edgardh and Per Pettersson (eds), *Welfare and Religion in 21st Century Europe: Volume 2: Gendered, Religious and Social Change* (Farnham: Ashgate, 2011).

Bacon, Margaret Hope, *Mothers of Feminism: The Story of Quaker Women in America* (San Francisco: Harper & Row, 1986).

Bader, Veit, *Secularism or Democracy? Associational Governance of Religious Diversity* (Amsterdam: University of Amsterdam Press, 2007).

Baines, Donna, 'Neoliberal Restructuring, Activism/Participation, and Social Unionism in the Nonprofit Social Services', *Nonprofit and Voluntary Sector Quarterly*, 39/1 (2010): 10–28.

Bannerji, Himani, *The Dark Side of the Nation: Essays on Multiculturalism, Nationalism and Gender* (Toronto: Canadian Scholars' Press, 2000).

Barber, Benjamin R., *Jihad Vs McWorld: Terrorism's Challenge to Democracy* (New York: Ballentine Books, 2001).

Baron, Barnett F., 'The Treasury Guidelines Have Had Little Impact Overall on US International Philanthropy, But They Have Had a Chilling Impact on US-Based Muslim Charities', *Pace Law Review*, 25 (2004): 307–20.

Baubérot, Jean, *L'intégrisme républicain contre la laïcité* (Paris: Aube, 2006).

Baubérot, Jean, *Les Laïcités dans le monde* (Paris: PUF, 2007).

Beaman, Lori. G., *Defining Harm: Religious Freedom and the Limits of the Law* (Vancouver: University of British Columbia Press, 2008).

Beaman, Lori. G., 'Assessing Religious Identity in Law: Sincerity, Accommodation and Harm', in Avigail Eisenberg and Will Kymlicka (eds), *Identity Politics in the Public Realm: Bringing Institutions Back In* (Vancouver: UBC Press, 2011).

Beaumont, Justin, 'Faith Action on Urban Social Issues', *Urban Studies*, 45/10 (2008): 2019–34.

Beaumont, Justin, and Candice Dias, 'Faith-based Organizations and Urban Social Justice in the Netherlands', *Tijdschrift voor Economische en Sociale Geografie*, 99/4 (2008): 382–92.

Becker, Gary S., 'A Theory of Social Interaction', *Journal of Political Economy*, 82/6 (1974): 1063–93.

Becker, Gary S., *The Economic Approach to Human Behavior* (Chicago, 1976).

Bedford-Strohm, Heinrich (ed.), *Von der „Barmherzigkeit" zum „Sozial-Markt". Zur Ökonomisierung der sozialdiakonischen Dienste. Jahrbuch Sozialer Protestantismus* (2 vols, Gütersloh: Gütersloher Verlagshaus, 2008).

Bekkers, René, 'Trust, Accreditation, and Philanthropy in the Netherlands', *Nonprofit and Voluntary Sector Quarterly*, 32/4 (2003): 596–615.

Belien, Paul, 'Walking on Water: How to Do It', *The Brussels Journal*, 27 August (2005), <www.brusselsjournal.com/node/202>, accessed 4 October 2011.

Bell, Daniel, *The Cultural Contradictions of Capitalism* (New York: Basic Books, 1976).

Benson, Bruce E. and Peter G. Hetzel (eds), *Evangelicals and Empire: Christian Alternatives to the Political Status Quo* (Grand Rapids: Brazer, 2008).

Berger, Julia, 'Religious Nongovernmental Organizations: An Exploratory Analysis', *Voluntas: International Journal of Voluntary and Nonprofit Organizations*, 14/1 (2003): 15–39.

Berger, Peter L., *The Sacred Canopy: Elements of a Sociological Theory of Religion* (Garden City: Doubleday, 1967).

Berger, Peter L., *Heretical Imperative: Contemporary Possibilities of Religious Affirmation* (New York: Doubleday, 1980).

Berger, Peter L. (ed.), *The Desecularization of the World: Resurgent Religion and World Politics* (Grand Rapids: William B. Eerdmans Publishing Company, 1999).

Berlin, Isaiah, *Four Essays on Liberty* (London: Oxford University Press, 1969).

Biebricher, Thomas, 'Faith-based Initiatives and Pastoral Power', *Economy and Society*, 40/3 (2011): 399–420.

Bigelow, Gordon, 'Let There Be Markets: The Evangelical Roots of Economics', *Harper's Magazine*, 310/1860 (2005): 33–8.

Binkley, Sam, 'The Work of Neoliberal Governmentality: Temporality and Ethical Substance in the Tale of Two Dads', *Foucault Studies*, 6 (2009): 60–78.

Black, Amy, Douglas Koopman, and David Ryden, *Of Little Faith: The Politics of George W. Bush's Faith-based Initiatives* (Washington: Georgetown University Press, 2004).

Bobineau, Olivier, *Dieu change en paroisse. Une comparaison franco-allemande* (Rennes: Presses universitaires de Rennes 2005).

Boleyn-Fitzgerald, Patrick, 'Misfortune, Welfare Reform, and Right-wing Egalitarianism', *Critical Review*, 13/1–2 (1999): 141–63.

Boltanski, Luc and Ève Chiapello, *Le nouvel esprit du capitalisme* (Paris, 1999).

Boston Consulting Group, 'Shaping a New Tomorrow: How to Capitalize on the Momentum of Change', 31 May (2011), <www.bcg.com/media/PressReleaseDetails.aspx?id=tcm:12-77753>, accessed 23 July 2011.

Bouchard, Gérard and Charles Taylor, *Building the Future: A Time for Reconciliation* (Commission de consultation sur les pratiques d'accommodement reliées aux différences culturelles, 2008).

Bouchard, Gérard, *Interculturalism and the Management of Ethno–Cultural Diversity in Québec*. Paper presented at Critical Thinkers in Law, Religion and Social Theory lecture series (University of Ottawa, September 23, 2011).

Boucher, Gerry, 'Ireland's Lack of a Coherent Integration Policy', *Translocations*, 3/1 (2008): 5–28.

Bramadat, Paul and Matthias Koenig (eds), *International Migration and the Governance of Religious Diversity* (Montreal: McGill-Queen's University Press, 2009).

Bresser Pereira and Luiz Carlos, *Development and Crisis in Brazil, 1930–1983* (Boulder: Westview, 1984).

Broder, John M., 'Obama Courting Evangelicals Once Loyal to Bush', *The New York Times*, 1 July (2008).

Brown, Wendy, *Edgework: Critical Essays on Knowledge and Politics* (Princeton: Princeton University Press, 2005).

Brown, Wendy, 'American Nightmare: Neoliberalism, Neoconservatism, and De-democratization', *Political Theory*, 34/6 (2006): 690–714.

Brown, Wendy, *Walled States, Waning Sovereignty* (Cambridge: The MIT Press, 2010).

Bruce, Steve, 'Modernisation, Religious Diversity and Rational Choice in Eastern Europe', *Religion, State and Society* 27/3–4 (1999): 265–75.

Bruce, Steve, *Choice and Religion: A Critique of Rational Choice* (Oxford: Oxford University Press, 1999).

Bruce, Steve, 'The Supply Side Model of Religion: The Nordic and Baltic States', *Journal for the Scientific Study of Religion*, 39/1 (2000): 32–46.

Bruce, Steve, *God is Dead: Secularization in the West* (Oxford: Blackwell, 2002).

Brun, Henri, Guy Tremblay and Eugénie Brouillet, *Droit constitutionnel*, 5th ed. (Cowansville: Yvon-Blais, 2008).

Bunting, Annie, 'Feminism, Foucault and Law as Power/Knowledge', *Alberta Law Review*, 30/3 (1992): 829–42.

Burchell, Graham, Colin Gordon and Peter Miller (eds), *The Foucault Effect: Studies in Governmentality with Two Lectures by and an Interview with Michel Foucault* (Chicago: University of Chicago Press, 1991).

Burity, Joanildo, 'Reform of the State and the New Discourse on Social Policy in Brazil', *Latin American Perspectives*, 33 (2006): 67–88.

Burity, Joanildo, *Redes, parcerias e participação religiosa nas políticas sociais no Brasil* (Recife: Massangana, 2006).

Burity, Joanildo, 'Inequality, Culture and Globalization in Emerging Societies: Reflections on the Brazilian case', in Jan Nederveen Pieterse and Boike Rehbein (eds), *Globalisation and Emerging Societies: Development and Inequality* (Basingstoke: Palgrave Macmillan, 2009).

Burns, Jennifer, *Goddess of the Market: Ayn Rand and the American Right* (Oxford: Oxford University Press, 2009).

Byrnes, Timothy A. and Peter J. Katzenstein (eds), *Religion in an Expanding Europe* (Cambridge: Cambridge University Press, 2006).

Cadge, Wendy and Elaine Howard Ecklund, 'Immigration and Religion', *Annual Review of Sociology*, 33 (2007): 359–79.

Caillé, Alain, *Dé-penser l'économique. Contre le fatalisme* (Paris: La Découverte 2005).

Campos, Élizabeth, 'Contrôle social, religion et délinquance', *Religiologiques*, 31/printemps (2005): 15–24.

Carrette, Jeremy, *Foucault and Religion: Spiritual Corporality and Political Spirituality* (London: Routledge, 2000).

Carrette, Jeremy (ed.) *Religion and Culture, Michel Foucault*, selected and edited, with introduction (Manchester: Manchester University Press, 1999).

Carrette, Jeremy and Richard King, *Selling Spirituality: The Silent Takeover of Religion* (Abingdon: Routledge, 2005).

Casanova, José, *Public Religions in the Modern World* (Chicago: University of Chicago Press, 1994).

Casanova, José, 'Religion, European Secular Identities, and European Integration', in Timothy A. Byrnes and Peter J. Katzenstein (eds), *Religion in an Expanding Europe* (Cambridge: Cambridge University Press, 2006).

Casanova, José, 'Immigrants and the New Religious Pluralism: A European Union/United States Comparison', in Thomas Banchoff (ed.), *Democracy and the New Religious Pluralism* (Oxford: Oxford University Press, 2007).

Central Statistics Office, *Census 2006: Non-Irish Nationals Living in Ireland* (Dublin: The Stationery Office, 2008).

Chambers, Simone, 'A Critical Theory of Civil Society,' in Simone Chambers and Will Kymlicka, *Alternative Conceptions of Civil Society* (Princeton University Press, 2002).

Chambers, Simone and Jeffrey Kopstein, 'Bad Civil Society', *Political Theory*, 29/6 (2001): 838–66.

Chambers, Simone and Will Kymlicka (eds), *Alternative Conceptions of Civil Society* (Princeton: Princeton University Press, 2002).

Champion, Françoise and Danièle Hervieu-Léger (eds), *De l'émotion en religion. Renouveaux et traditions* (Paris: Le Centurion, 1990).

Chang, Ha-Joon, *Bad Samaritans: The Myth of Free Trade and the Secret History of Capitalism* (New York: Bloomsbury Press, 2007).

Chanial, Philippe, *Justice, don et association* (Paris: La Découverte/MAUSS, 2001).

Chaves, Mark and William Tsitsos, 'Congregations and Social Services: What They Do, How They Do It, and With Whom', *Nonprofit and Voluntary Sector Quarterly*, 30/4 (2001): 660–83.

Chaves, Mark and William Tsitsos, 'Six Myths About Faith-Based Initiatives', *The Christian Century*, 12–19 September (2001): 20–23.

Chinnock, Kathryn and Lester Salamon, 'Determinants of Nonprofit Impact: A Preliminary Analysis', paper presented at the panel session on *Nonprofit Impacts: Evidence from Around the Globe*, at the fifth International Society for Third Sector Conference, Cape Town, South Africa, July 2002.

Chong, Agnes, *Alms or Arms?: Communication of Counter-Terrorism Financing Laws and the Consequences for Australian Muslim Organizations*, Master's Thesis (Stanford: Stanford University, 2010).

Christoffersen, Lisbet, Kjell Å Modéer and Svend Andersen (eds), *Law & Religion in the 21st Century – Nordic Perspectives* (Copenhagen: Djøf Publishing, 2010).

Clarke, Gerald and Michael Jennings (eds), *Development, Civil Society and Faith-Based Organizations: Bridging the Sacred and the Secular* (Basingstoke: Palgrave Macmillan, 2008).

Clarkson, Frederick (ed.), *Dispatches from the Religious Left* (New York: IG Publishing, 2009).

Cloke, Paul, 'Deliver us from Evil? Prospects for Living Ethically and Acting Politically in Human Geography', *Progress in Human Geography*, 26/5 (2002): 587–604.

Cloke, Paul, Andrew Williams and Samuel Thomas, 'FBOs and Social Exclusion in the United Kingdom', in Danielle Dierckx, Jan Vranken and Wendy Kerstens (eds) *Faith-based Organisations and Social Exclusion in European Cities. National Context Reports* (Leuven: Acco, 2009).

Cnaan, Ram, Stephanie Boddie, Femida Handy, Gaynor Yancey and Richard Schneider, *The Invisible Caring Hand: American Congregations and the Provision of Welfare* (New York: New York University Press, 2002).

Cnaan, Ram, Stephanie Boddie, Charlene McGrew and Jennifer Kang, *The Other Philadelphia Story: How Local Congregations Support Quality of Life in Urban America* (Philadelphia: University of Pennsylvania Press, 2006).

Cnaan, Ram, Stephanie Boddie, and Robert Wineburg, *The Newer Deal: Social Work and Religion in Partnership* (New York: Columbia University Press, 1999).

Cole, Stewart, *History of Fundamentalism* (Hamden, CT: Archon Books, 1931, reissued 1963).

Coleman, John A., 'Catholic Social Thought and Civil Society', paper delivered, Hong Kong 18 May (2006), <www.cuhk.edu.hk/crs/catholic/CCS/download/Civil%20Society_Coleman.doc>, accessed 12 September 2011.

Coleman, Simon, *The Globalisation of Charismatic Christianity: Spreading the Gospel of Prosperity* (Cambridge: Cambridge University Press, 2000).

Comaroff, John L. and Jean Comaroff, *Ethnicity Inc.* (Chicago: The University of Chicago Press, 2009).

Comaroff, John L. and Jean Comaroff (eds), *Millenial Capitalism and the Culture of Neoliberalism* (Durham: Duke University Press, 2001).

Connolly, William, 'The Evangelical-capitalist Resonance Machine', *Political Theory*, 33/6 (2005): 869–86.

Connolly, William E., *Capitalism and Christianity, American Style* (Durham: Duke University Press, 2008).

Conradson, David, 'Expressions of Charity and Action towards Justice: Faith-based Welfare Provision in Urban New Zealand', *Urban Studies*, 45/10 (2008): 2117–41.

Cooperman, Alan, 'Faith-Based Charities May Not Be Better, Study Indicates', *The Washington Post*, 25 May (2003): A07.

Cooperman, Alan and Thomas B. Edsell, 'Evangelicals Say They Led the Charge for the GOP,' *Washington Post*, 7 November (2004): A1.

Cossman, Brenda, 'Sexuality, Queer Theory, and "Feminism After": Reading and Rereading the Sexual Subject', *McGill Law Journal*, 49 (2004): 847–76.

Cossman, Brenda, *Sexual Citizens: The Legal and Cultural Regulation of Sex and Belonging* (Stanford: Stanford University Press, 2007).

Counter-Terrorism Implementation Task Force, *CTITF Working Group Report: Tackling the Financing of Terrorism* (New York: United Nations, 2009).

Cox, Harvey, 'Old-time religion', *The Boston Globe*, 10 July (2006), <www.boston.com/news/globe/ideas/articles/2006/07/09/old_time_religion>, accessed 10 March 2011.

Crittenden, Ann, *Sanctuary: A Story of American Conscience and the Law in Collision* (New York: Weidenfeld & Nicholson, 1988).

Crossley, Nick and John Michael Roberts, *After Habermas: New Perspectives on the Public Sphere* (Oxford: Blackwell, 2004).

Dagnino, Evelina, 'Participation, Citizenship and Democracy: Perverse Confluence and Displacement of Meanings', in Catherine Neveu (ed.), *Cultures et Pratiques Participatives: Perspectives Comparatives* (Paris: L'Harmattan, 2007).

Davie, Grace, 'Believing without Belonging: Is this the Future of Religion in Britain?', *Social Compass*, 37/4 (1990): 455–69.

Davie, Grace, *Religion in Britain Since 1945: Believing Without Belonging* (Oxford: Blackwell, 1994).

Davie, Grace, *Religion in Modern Europe: A Memory Mutates* (Oxford: Oxford University Press, 2000).

Dawkins, Richard, *The God Delusion* (New York: Houghton Mifflin, 2006).

Day, Richard, *Multiculturalism and the History of Canadian Diversity* (Toronto: University of Toronto Press, 2000).

De Tocqueville, Alexis, *Democracy in America* (2 vols, New York: Knopf, 1945).

Dean, Mitchell, *Governmentality: Power and Rule in Modern Society* (London: Sage, 1999).

Dean, Mitchell, *Governing Societies* (Maidenhead: Open University Press, 2007).

Debord, Guy, *The Society of the Spectacle* (New York: Zone Books, 1994).

DeHaven, Mark J., Irby B Hunter, Laura Wilder, James W. Walton and Janet Berry, 'Health Programs in Faith-Based Organizations: Are They Effective?', *American Journal of Public Health*, 94/6 (2004): 1030–36.

Delanty, Gerard, 'The Foundations of Social Theory', in Bryan S. Turner, *The New Blackwell Companion to Social Theory* (Oxford: Blackwell 2009).

Department of Social, Community and Family Affairs, *White Paper on a Framework for Supporting Voluntary Activity and for Developing the Relationship between the State and the Community and Voluntary Sector* (Dublin: Government Publications, 2000).

Desjardins, Tristan, 'Échanger est-il péché ? Analyse de la norme de tolérance de la société canadienne contemporaine à la lumière de l'arrêt R. c. Labaye', *Les Cahiers de Droit*, 45/4 (2004): 767–90.

Devereux, Eoin, 'Saving Rural Ireland – Muintir na Tire and Its Anti-Urbanism 1931–1958', *The Canadian Journal of Irish Studies*, 17/2 (1991): 23–30.

Dewey, John, *Liberalism and Social Action* (Amherst, NY: Prometheus Books, 1991).

Dilulio, John, 'Getting Faith-based Programs Right', *Public Interest*, 155/Spring (2004): 75–88.

Dinham, Adam, *Faiths, Public Policy and Civil Society: Problems, Policies, Controversies* (Basingstoke: Palgrave Macmillan, 2009).

Dionne, E.J., *Souled Out: Reclaiming Faith and Politics after the Religious Right* (Princeton: Princeton University Press, 2008).

Dobbelaere, Karel, *Secularization: A Multidimensional Concept* (London: Sage, 1982).

Dolgoff, Ralph, 'What does Social Welfare Produce?', *International Social Work*, 42/3 (1999): 295–307.

Domhoff, G. William, *Who Rules America? Challenges to Corporate and Class Dominance*, 6th ed. (New York: McGraw-Hill, 2009).

Donnelly, Susie and Tom Inglis, 'The Media and the Catholic Church in Ireland: Reporting Clerical Child Sex Abuse', *Journal of Contemporary Religion*, 25/1 (2010): 1–19.

Donzelot, Jacques, 'Michel Foucault and Liberal Intelligence', *Economy and Society*, 37/1 (2008): 115–34.

Douglas, Ann, *The Feminization of American Culture* (New York: Knopf, 1977).

Duchastel, Jules, 'Du gouvernement à la gouvernance. Crise ou ajustement de la régulation néolibérale', in Raphaël Canet and Jules Duchastel, *La régulation néolibérale. Crise ou ajustement ?* (Montréal: Athéna 2004).

Dufour, Pierre, *Histoire de la prostitution chez tous les peuples du monde depuis l'antiquité la plus reculée jusqu'à nos jours* (6 vols, Paris: Séré, 1851–53; Brussels: Librairie Encyclopedique de Perichon, 1851–54).

Dumont, Louis, *Homo aequalis I. Genèse et épanouissement de l'idéologie économique* (Paris: Gallimard, 1985).

Duvall, Tim, 'The New Feudalism: Globalization, the Market and the Great Chain of Consumption', *New Political Science*, 25/1 (2003): 81–97.

Ebaugh, Helen Rose, Paula F. Pipes, Janet Saltzman Chafetz and Martha Daniels, 'Where's the Religion? Distinguishing Faith-Based from Secular Social Service Agencies', *Journal for the Scientific Study of Religion*, 42/3 (2003): 411–26.

Ecklund, Elaine Howard, *Science Vs. Religion: What Scientists Really Think* (New York: Oxford University Press, 2010).

Edwards, Michael, *Civil Society* (Cambridge: Polity, 2004).

Ehasalu, Vallo, *EELK Valga praostkonna sõnaline aruanne 2006* [Report on 2006 of the Valga Deanery of the EELC] (31 March 2007).

Eisenstadt, Shmuel N., *Fundamentalism, Sectarianism, and Revolution* (Cambridge: Cambridge University Press, 1999).

Elisha, Omri, 'Moral Ambitions of Grace: The Paradox of Compassion and Accountability in Evangelical Faith-based Activism', *Cultural Anthropology*, 23/1 (2008): 154–89.

Elust, usust, usuelust 2010 [On Life, Faith, Religious Life], a sociological survey conducted by social and market research company Saar Poll from 25 March to 11 April 2010.

Emerton, Patrick, 'Australia's Terrorism Offences – A Case Against', in Andrew Lynch and George Williams (eds), *Law and Liberty in the War on Terror* (Sydney: Federation Press, 2007).

ENSV Teataja, *Eesti NSV Valitsuse määrus nr 67 Eesti NSV Riikliku Usuameti moodustamise kohta* [Governmental Regulation No 67 of the Estonian SSR on establishing the Board of Religion] (Tallinn, 1990).

Esau, Alvin, *The Courts and the Colonies: The Litigation of Hutterite Church Disputes* (Vancouver: UBC Press, 2005).

Escobar, Arturo, 'Beyond the Third World: Imperial Globality, Global Coloniality and Anti-globalisation Social Movements', *Third World Quarterly*, 25/1 (2004): 207–30.

Esperandio, Mary Ruth Gomes, 'Subjetividade, religiosidade contemporânea e globalização: o caso da Igreja Universal do Reino de Deus', *Protestantismo em Revista*, 9 (2006): 31–47, <www3.est.edu.br/nepp>, accessed 10 May 2011.

Esping-Andersen, Gøsta, *The Three Worlds of Welfare Capitalism* (Princeton: Princeton University Press, 1990).

Evangelische Kirche in Deutschland, *Evangelische Kirche gegen Ökonomisierung des Sozialen* (1998), <www.ekd.de/presse/1831.html>, accessed 28 December 2011.

Evangelische Kirche in Deutschland, *Kirche der Freiheit: Perspektiven für die Evangelische Kirche im 21. Jahrhundert* (2006), <www.ekd.de/download/kirche- der-freiheit.pdf>, accessed 28 December 2011.

Evans, B. Mitchell and John Shields, 'Neoliberal Restructuring and the Third Sector: Reshaping Governance, Civil Society and Local Relations', Working Paper Series, Centre for Voluntary Sector Studies, no. 13 (Toronto: Ryerson University, Faculty of Business, 2000).

Ezzy, Douglas, *Qualitative Analysis: Practice and Innovation* (London: Routledge, 2002).

Falwell, Jerry, *Listen America* (Garden City: Doubleday, 1980).

Federation of Community Legal Centres (Victoria) Inc., 'Submission To The Parliamentary Joint Committee On Intelligence And Security Review Of The Listing Provisions Of The Criminal Code Act 1995' (2007).

Feldman, Alice, Deo L. Ndakengerwa, Ann Nolan and Carmen Frese, *Diversity, Civil Society and Social Change in Ireland: A North-South Comparison of the Role of Immigrant/'New' Minority Ethnic-led Community and Voluntary Sector Organisations* (Dublin: University College Dublin, Geary Institute, 2005).

Fenn, Richard K., *Key Thinkers in the Sociology of Religion* (New York: Continuum, 2009).

Fennema, Meindert and Jean Tillie, 'Civil Community, Political Participation and Political Trust of Ethnic Groups', *Connections*, 24/1 (2001): 26–41.

Fetzer, Joel and Christopher Soper, *Muslims and the State in Britain, France, and Germany* (Cambridge: Cambridge University Press, 2005).

Financial Action Task Force on Money Laundering, 'Special Recommendations on Terrorist Financing' (2001).

Financial Action Task Force on Money Laundering, 'Guidance for Financial Institutions in Detecting Terrorist Financing' (2002).

Finke, Roger, 'The Consequences of Religious Competition: Supply-side Explanations for Religious Change', in Lawrence A. Young (ed.), *Rational Choice Theory and Religion: Summary and Assessment* (New York: Routledge, 1997).

Fiss, Owen M., 'The Autonomy of Law', *Faculty Scholarship Series, Yale Law School,* Paper 1316 (2001), <digitalcommons.law.yale.edu/fss_papers/1316>.

Foner, Nancy and Richard Alba, 'Immigrant Religion in the U.S. and Western Europe: Bridge or Barrier to Inclusion?', *International Migration Review*, 42/2 (2008): 360–92.

Foucault, Michel, *Discipline and Punish: The Birth of the Prison* (New York: Vintage, 1977).

Foucault, Michel, *The History of Sexuality, vol. 1. An Introduction* (London: Allen Lane, (1979).

Foucault, Michel, 'The Subject and the Power', in Hubert Dreyfus and Paul Rabinow, *Michel Foucault: Beyond Structuralism and Hermeneutics* (Brighton: Harvester, 1982).

Foucault, Michel, 'Governmentality', in Graham Burchell, Colin Gordon and Peter Miller (eds), *The Foucault Effect: Studies in Governmentality* (Hemel Hempstead: Harvester Wheatsheaf, 1991).

Foucault, Michel, 'Security, Territory, and Population', in Paul Rabinow (ed.), *Michel Foucault, Ethics: Subjectivity and Truth* (New York: The New Press, 1991).

Foucault, Michel, *Sécurité, territoire, population: Cours au Collège de France (1977–1978)*, edited by M. Senellart (Paris: Gallimard/le Seuil, 2004).

Foucault, Michel, *Security, Territory, Population. Lectures at the College de France 1977–78*, translated by Graham Burchell (Basingstoke: Palgrave Macmillan, 2007).

Foucault, Michel, *The Birth of Biopolitics Lectures at the College De France 1978–79*, translated by Graham Burchell (Basingstoke: Palgrave Macmillan, 2008).

Frank, Thomas, *What's the Matter with Kansas? How Conservatives Won the Heart of America* (New York: Henry Holt, 2004).

Freston, Paul, 'The Transnationalisation of Brazilian Pentecostalism: The Universal Church of the Kingdom of God', in Andre Corten and Ruth Marshall-Fratani (eds), *Between Babel and Pentecost: Transnational Pentecostalism in Africa and Latin America* (Bloomington: Indiana University Press, 2000).

Freston, Paul, *Evangelicals and Politics in Asia, Africa and Latin America* (Cambridge: Cambridge University, 2004).

Friedman, Milton, *Capitalism and Freedom* (Chicago: University of Chicago Press, 1962).

Friedman, Thomas L., *The World Is Flat: A Brief History of the Twenty-First Century*. Expanded and updated edition (New York: Farrar, Strauss, and Giroux, 2006).

Fukuyama, Francis, 'The End of History', *National Interest*, 16 (1989): 3–18.

Fuller, Robert C., *Spiritual, but not Religious: Understanding Unchurched America* (New York: Oxford University Press, 2001).

Galanter, Marc, 'Presidential Address: The Legal Malaise; Or, Justice Observed', *Law and Society Review* 19/4 (1985): 537–56.

Gaudreault-DesBiens, Jean-François, 'Identitarisation du droit et perspectivsme épistéologique. Quelques jalons pour une saisie juridique complexe de l'identititaire', *Canadian Journal of Law and Jurisprudence*, 13/1 (2000), 33–74.

Gaulejac, Vincent de, *La société malade de la gestion. Idéologie gestionnaire, pouvoir managérial et harcèlement social* (Paris: Seuil, 2005).

Gauthier, François, 'Religion in Contemporary Consumer Societies, In Search of a Global Comprehensive Analytic', *Revue du MAUSS permanente*, 1st September (2009), <www.journaldumauss.net/spip.php?article539>.

Gauthier, François, Tuomas Martikainen and Linda Woodhead, 'Introduction: Religion in Consumer Society', *Social Compass*, 58/3 (2011): pp. 291–301.

Gavigan, Shelley A. M. and Dorothy E. Chunn, 'From Mothers' Allowance to Mothers Need Not Apply: Canadian Welfare Law as Liberal and Neo–Liberal Reforms', *Osgoode Hall Law Journal*, 45/4 (2007): 733–71.

Gaynor, Niamh, 'Associations, Deliberation, and Democracy: The Case of Ireland's Social Partnership', *Politics and Society*, 39/4 (2011): 497–519.

Giddens, Anthony, *The Consequences of Modernity* (Stanford: Stanford University, 1990).

Gilbert, Daphne, 'Substance Without Form: The Impact of Anonymity on Equality-Seeking Groups', *University of Ottawa Law & Technology Journal*, 3/1 (2006): 225–47.

Gilbert, Jeremy, *Anticapitalism and Culture: Radical Theory and Popular Politics* (Oxford: Berg, 2008).

Gill, Anthony, *The Political Origins of Religious Liberty* (New York: Cambridge University Press, 2008).

Gillmor, Desmond A., 'Changing Religions in the Republic of Ireland, 1991–2002', *Irish Geography*, 39/2 (2006): 111–28.

Giroux, Henry, 'Neoliberalism and the Demise of Democracy: Resurrecting Hope in Dark Times,' *Dissident Voice*, 7 August (2004).

Girvetz, Harry, *The Evolution of Liberalism* (New York: Collier, 1963).

Glasbeek, Amanda, '"My Wife Has Endured a Torrent of Abuse": Gender, Safety, and Anti-Squeegee Discourses in Toronto, 1998–2000', *Windsor Yearbook of Access to Justice*, 24/1 (2006).

Glynos, Jason and David Howarth, *Logics of Critical Explanation in Social and Political Theory* (London: Routledge, 2008).

Godwin, Matthew, 'Awaiting the Watershed: Women in Canada's Parliament', *Canadian Parliamentary Review*, 33 (2010), <www.revparl.ca/english/issue. asp?param=198&art=1384>.

Golder, Ben, 'Foucault and the Genealogy of Pastoral Power', *Radical Philosophy Review*, 10/2 (2007): 157–76.

Government Accounting Office, *Faith-based and Community Initiative. Improvements in Monitoring Grantees and Measuring Performance Could Enhance Accountability* (Washington: United States Accountability Office, June 2006).

Grabham, Emily, '*Law v Canada*: New Directions for Equality Under the Canadian Charter?', *Oxford Journal of Legal Studies*, 22/4 (2002): 641–61.

Grassman, Eva Jeppson, 'Welfare in Western Europe: Existing Regimes and Patterns of Change', in Anders Bäckström and Grace Davie with Ninna Edgardh and Per Pettersson (eds), *Welfare and Religion in 21st Century Europe: Volume 1. Configuring the Connections* (Farnham: Ashgate, 2010).

Gray, Breda and Ria O'Sullivan Lago, 'Migrant Chaplains: Mediators of Catholic Church Transnationalism', *Irish Journal of Sociology*, 19/2 (2011): 93–109.

Gray, Breda, 'Governing Integration', in Bryan Fanning and Ronaldo Munck (eds), *Globalization, Migration and Social Transformation* (Farnham: Ashgate, 2011).

Gray, Breda, 'Making Migration a Public Issue: The 'Network-making Power' of the Irish Catholic Church', in Mary Gilmartin and Alan White (eds), *Ireland and Migration* (Manchester: Manchester University Press, 2013).

Greeley, Andrew M. and Michael Hout, *The Truth About Conservative Christians: What They Think and What They Believe* (Chicago: University of Chicago Press, 2006).

Green, John, 'Seeking a Place: Evangelical Protestants and Public Engagement in the Twentieth Century', in Ronald Sider and David Knippers (eds), *Toward and Evangelical Public Policy: Political Strategies for the Health of a Nation* (Grand Rapids: Baker Books, 2005).

Greenberg, James B., 'A Political Ecology of Structural-Adjustment Policies: The Case of the Dominican Republic', *Culture and Agriculture*, 19/3 (1997).

Grillo, Beppe, 'The Pact with the Devil by Joseph E. Stiglitz', January (2007), <http://www.beppegrillo.it/eng/2007/01/stiglitz.html>, accessed 23 July 2011.

Grosfoguel, Ramón, 'Developmentalism, Dependence Theory in Latin America', in Mabel Moraña, Enrique D. Dussel and Carlos A. Jáuregui (eds), *Coloniality At Large: Latin America and the Postcolonial Debate* (Durham: Duke University, 2008).

Gruber, Jonathan, and Hungerman, Daniel, 'Faith-based Charity and Crowd-out during the Great Depression', *Journal of Public Economics*, 91/5–6 (2007): 1043–69.

Gunning, Jeroen, 'Terrorism, Charities, and Diasporas: Contrasting the Fundraising Practices of Hamas and Al-Qaeda among Muslims in Europe', in Thomas Biersteker and Sue Eckert (eds), *Countering the Financing of Terrorism* (Milton Park: Routledge, 2008).

Habermas, Jürgen, *Legitimation Crisis*, trans. Thomas McCarthy (Boston: Beacon Press, 1975).

Habermas, Jürgen, *The Theory of Communicative Action, Vol. 1: Reason and the Rationalization of Society*, trans. Thomas McCarthy (Boston: Beacon Press, 1984).

Habermas, Jürgen, *The Philosophical Discourse of Modernity*, ed. Frederick Lawrence (Cambridge: MIT Press, 1987).

Habermas, Jürgen, *The Theory of Communicative Action, Vol. 2: Lifeworld and System: A Critique of Functionalist Reason*, trans. Thomas McCarthy (Boston: Beacon Press, 1987).

Habermas, Jürgen, *The Structural Transformation of the Public Sphere. An Inquiry Into a Category of Bourgeois Society*, trans. Thomas Burger (Cambridge: MIT Press, 1991).

Habermas, Jürgen, *Between Facts and Norms: Contributions to a Discourse Theory of Law and Democracy*, trans. William Rehg (Cambridge: MIT Press, 1996).

Habermas, Jürgen, *Entre faits et normes*, traduit de l'allemand par Rainer Rochlitz et Christian Bouchindhomme (Paris: Gallimard, nrf essais, 1997).

Habermas, Jürgen, 'Equal Treatment of Cultures and the Limits of Postmodern Liberalism', *The Journal of Political Philosophy*, 13/1 (2005): 1–28.

Hackworth, Jason, 'Local Autonomy, Bond-rating Agencies and Neoliberal Urbanism in the US', *International Journal of Urban and Regional Research*, 26/4 (2002): 707–25.

Hackworth, Jason, *The Neoliberal City: Governance, Ideology, and Development in American Urbanism* (Ithaca: Cornell University Press: 2007).

Hackworth, Jason, 'Compassionate Neoliberalism?: Evangelical Christianity, the Welfare State, and the Politics of the Right', *Studies in Political Economy*, 86 (2010): 83–108.

Hackworth, Jason, 'Neoliberalism for God's Sake: Sectarian Justifications for Secular Policy Transformation in the United States', in Arie Molendijk, Justin Beaumont and Chris Jedan (eds), *Exploring the Postsecular: The Religious, the Political, the Urban* (Leiden: Brill, 2010).

Hackworth, Jason, *Faith Based: Religious Neoliberalism and the Politics of Welfare in the United States* (Athens: University of Georgia Press, 2012).

Haenni, Patrick, 'Economic Politics of Muslim Consumption', in Johanna Pink (ed.), *Muslim Societies in the Age of Mass Consumption: Politics, Culture and Identity between the Local and the Global* (Newcastle Upon Tyne: Cambridge Scholars Publishing, 2009).

Hagan, Kate, 'Tamil Trio Accused of Terrorism Free on Bonds', *The Age*, 1 April (2010).

Harris, Margaret, Halfpenny, Peter and Rochester, Colin, 'A Social Policy Role for Faith-based Organisations? Lessons from the UK Jewish Voluntary Sector', *Journal of Social Policy*, 32/1 (2003): 93–112.

Harris, Sam, *The End of Faith: Religion, Terror, and the Future of Reason* (New York: W.W. Norton & Company, 2004).

Harvey, David, *The Condition of Postmodernity: An Enquiry into the Origins of Cultural Change* (Oxford: Wiley-Blackwell, 1990).

Harvey, David, *A Brief History of Neoliberalism* (Oxford: Oxford University Press, 2005).

Hays, R. Alan, 'Habitat for Humanity: Building Social Capital through Faith Based Service', *Journal of Urban Affairs*, 24/3 (2002): 247–69.

Heikkilä, Markku, Jyrki Knuutila and Martin Scheinin, 'State and Church in Finland', in Gerhard Robbers (ed.), *State and Church in the European Union* (2nd edn, Baden-Baden: Nomos, 2005), 519–36.

Heiskala, Risto, 'Kansainvälisen toimintaympäristö muutos ja Suomen yhteiskunnallinen murros', in Risto Heiskala and Eeva Luhtakallio (eds), *Uusi jako: Miten Suomesta tuli kilpailukyky-yhteiskunta?* (Helsinki: Gaudemus, 2006).

Hervieu-Léger, Danielle, *Vers un nouveau Christianisme?* [Toward a New Christianity?] (Paris: Les Éditions du Cerf, 1996).

Hervieu-Léger, Danielle, *Religion as a Chain of Memory* (Cambridge: Polity, 2000).

Hiemstra, John, 'Government Relations with Faith-based Non-profit Social Agencies in Alberta', *Journal of Church and State*, 44/1 (2002): 19–44.

Hilton, Boyd, *The Age of Atonement: The Influence of Evangelicalism on Social and Economic Thought, 1785–1865* (Oxford: Oxford University Press, 1986).

Hindness, Barry, 'Neo-liberal Citizenship', *Citizenship Studies*, 6/2 (2002): 127–43.

Hitchens, Christopher, *God is not Great: How Religion Poisons Everything* (Toronto: McClelland & Stewart, 2007).

Hofstadter, Richard, *Anti-Intellectualism in American Life* (New York: Knopf, 1962).

Honohan, Iseult and Nathalie Rougier, *Tolerance and Cultural Diversity Discourses in Ireland* (Florence: European University Institute, Florence Robert Schuman Centre for Advanced Studies, 2010).

Hoppenbrouwers, Frans, 'Romancing Freedom: Church and Society in the Baltic States since the End of Communism', *Religion, State and Society*, 27/2 (1999): 162–73.

Hout, Michael and Claude S. Fischer, 'Why More Americans Have No Religious Preference: Politics and Generations', *American Sociological Review*, 67/2 (2002): 165–90.

Hsu, Spencer S., 'Bush Orders DHS to Create Center for Faith-Based Aid', *The Washington Post*, 8 March (2006): A20.

Hudson, Kenneth and Coukos, Andrea, 'The Dark Side of the Protestant Ethic: A Comparative Analysis of Welfare Reform', *Sociological Theory*, 23/1 (2005): 1–24.

Hula, Richard, Cynthia Jackson-Elmoore and Laura Reese, 'Mixing God's Work and the Public Business: A Framework for the Analysis of Faith-based Service Delivery', *Review of Policy Research*, 24/1 (2007): 67–89.

Hungerman, Daniel, 'Are Church and State Substitutes? Evidence from the 1996 Welfare Reform', *Journal of Public Economics*, 89/11–12 (2005): 2245–67.

Hunter, James Davidson, *American Evangelicalism: Conservative Religion and the Quandary of Modernity* (New Brunswick: Rutgers University Press, 1983).

Hunter, Rosemary (ed.), *Rethinking Equality Projects in Law: Feminist Challenges* (Portland: Hart Publishing, 2008).

Huntington, Samuel P., *The Clash of Civilizations and the Remaking of World Order* (New York: Simon & Schuster, 1996).

Iannaccone, Laurence R., 'Why Strict Churches Are Strong', *American Journal of Sociology*, 99/5 (1994): 1180–211.

Ireland, Patrick, *Becoming Europe: Immigration, Integration, and the Welfare State* (Pittsburgh: University of Pittsburgh Press, 2004).

Islamic Information and Support Centre of Australia, Testimony at Public Hearing, Parliamentary Joint Committee on Intelligence and Security, Review of Security and Counter-Terrorism Legislation, 31 July (2006).

Itçaina, Xabier, 'The Roman Catholic Church and the Immigration Issue: The Relative Secularisation of Political Life in Spain', *American Behavioral Scientist Journal*, 49/1 (2006): 471–88.

Jacoby, Susan, 'Keeping the Faith: Ignoring the History', *The New York Times*, 28 February (2009): 11.

Jagose, Annamarie, 'Queer Theory', *Australian Humanities Review* (1996), <www.australianhumanitiesreview.org/archive/Issue-Dec-1996/jagose.html>, accessed 1 February 2012.

Jaworsky, Bernadette Nadya, Peggy Levitt, Wendy Cadge, Jessica Hejtmanek and Sara Curran, 'New Perspectives on Immigrant Contexts of Reception: The Cultural Armature of Cities', *Nordic Journal of Migration Studies*, 2 (2012): 78–88.

Jeavons, Thomas, 'The Vitality and Independence of Religious Organizations', *Society*, Jan./Feb. (2003): 27–36.

Jenkins, Philip, *The Next Christendom: The Coming of Global Christianity* (Oxford: Oxford University Press, 2002).

Jenkins, Philip, 'Believing in the Global South', *First Things*, December (2006), <http://www.firstthings.com/article/2007/01/believing-in-the-global-south-17>, accessed 23 July 2011.

Johannsen, Lars and Karin Hilmer Pedersen, 'Path Making: Democracy in the Baltic States Twenty Years after', *Politics in Central Europe*, 7/1 (2011): 57–73.

Johnson, Rebecca, *Taxing Choices: The Intersection of Class, Gender, Parenthood, and the Law* (Vancouver: UBC Press, 2002).

Juergensmeyer, Mark, *Terror in the Mind of God: The Global Rise of Religious Violence* (3rd ed., Berkeley: University of California Press, 2003).

Jürjo, Silvester, 'Chaplaincy', in Riho Altnurme (ed.), *History of Estonian Ecumenism* (Tartu/Tallinn: University of Tartu/Estonian Council of Churches, 2009).

Jürjo, Villu, 'Kas riigikirik?' [A State Church?], *Eesti Kirik*, 17 December (1992).

Kahl, Sigrun, 'The Religious Roots of Modern Poverty Policy: Catholic, Lutheran, and Reformed Protestant Traditions Compared', *Archives Europeennes de Sociologie*, 46/1 (2005): 91–126, 171.

Karim, Karim H,. *Islamic Peril: Media and Global Violence* (Montreal: Black Rose, 2003).

Katzenstein, Peter J., 'Multiple Modernities as Limits to Secular Europeanization?', Timothy A. Byrnes and Peter J. Katzenstein (eds), *Religion in an Expanding Europe* (Cambridge: Cambridge University Press, 2006).

Kaya, Ayhan, *Islam, Migration and Integration: The Age of Securitization* (New York: Palgrave Macmillan, 2009).

Keane, John, *Civil Society: Old Images, New Visions* (Stanford: Stanford University Press, 1998).

Kearns, Kevin, Chisung Park and Linda Yankoski, 'Comparing Faith-based and Secularly Community Service Corporations in Pittsburgh and Allegheny County, Pennsylvania', *Nonprofit and Voluntary Sector Quarterly*, 34/2 (2005): 206–31.

Kennedy, Duncan, *Legal Reasoning: Collected Essays* (Aurora: The Davies Book Publishers, 2008).

Kernerman, Gerald, *Multicultural Nationalism: Civilizing Difference, Constituting Community* (Vancouver: UBC Press, 2005).

Kersbergen, Kees van and Frans van Waarden, "Governance' as Bridge between Disciplines: Cross-disciplinary Inspiration Regarding Shifts in Governance and Problems of Governability, Accountability and Legitimacy', *European Journal of Political Research*, 43 (2004): 143–71.

Kintz, Linda, *Between Jesus and the Market: The Emotions that Matter in Right-wing America* (Durham, NC: Duke University Press, 1997).

Kintz, Linda, 'Finding the Strength to Surrender: Marriage, Market Theocracy, and the Spirit of America', *Theory, Culture and Society*, 24/4 (2007): 111–30.

Kiviorg, Merilin, *Law and Religion in Estonia* (Alphen aan den Rijn: Kluwer Law International, 2011).

Kjær, Anne Mette, *Governance* (Cambridge: Polity, 2004).

Klein, Naomi, *Shock Doctrine: The Rise of Disaster Capitalism* (Toronto: Random House, 2007).

Kodacsy, Tamas, 'The Church and Democracy in Central Europe', *Religion in Eastern Europe* 1 (2004): 34–9.

Koenig, Matthias, 'How Nation-States Respond to Religious Diversity', in Paul Bramadat and Matthias Koenig (eds), *International Migration and the Governance of Religious Diversity* (Montreal: McGill-Queen's University Press, 2009).

Kõpp, Johan, 'Haridusolud', in August Tammekann, Edgar Kant and Johannes Veski (eds), *Setumaa: Eesti maateaduslik, tulunduslik ja ajalooline kirjeldus III* [Setumaa: A Geographic, Economic and Historical Description of Estonia III] (Tartu: Eesti Kirjanduse Selts, 1928).

Kramer, Martin, 'Coming to Terms: Fundamentalists or Islamists?', *Middle Eastern Quarterly*, Spring (2003): 65–77.

Krugman, Paul, *The Return of Depression Economics and the Crisis of 2008* (New York: W.W. Norton & Company, 2008).

Kuo, David, *Tempting Faith: An Inside Story of Political Seduction* (New York: Free Press, 2006).

Kymlicka, Will, *Multicultural Odyssey: Navigating the New International Politics of Diversity* (Oxford: Oxford University Press, 2007).

L'Estrange, Sean, '"A Community of Communities" – Catholic Communitarianism and Societal Crises in Ireland, 1890s–1950s', *Journal of Historical Sociology*, 20/4 (2007): 555–78.

L'Estrange, Sean, *Catholicism and Capitalist Social Order in Ireland, 1907-1973: An Historical Institutionalist Analysis*. PhD Thesis, School of Sociology, Social Policy, and Women's Studies Queen's University Belfast (Belfast, 2004).

Laclau, Ernesto, 'Identity and Hegemony: the Role of Universality in the Constitution of Political Logics', in Judith Butler, Ernesto Laclau and Slavoj Žižek, *Contingency, Hegemony, Universality: Contemporary Debates on the Left* (London: Verso, 2000).

Laclau, Ernesto, *The Populist Reason* (Verso: London, 2005).

LaSelva, Victor, *The Moral Foundations of Canada: Paradoxes, Achievements, and Tragedies of Nationhood* (Toronto: McGill-Queens University Press, 1996).

Laurence, Jonathan, 'Muslims and the State in Western Europe', in Arianne Chebel d'Appolonia and Simon Reich (eds), *Immigration, Integration, and Security: America and Europe in Comparative Perspective* (Pittsburgh: University of Pittsburgh Press, 2008).

Laurence, Jonathan, *The Emancipation of Europe's Muslims: The State's Role in Minority Integration* (Princeton: Princeton University Press, 2012).

Lauristin, Marju and Peeter Vihalemm, 'The Political Agenda During Different Periods of Estonian Transformation: External and Internal Factors', *Journal of Baltic Studies*, 40 (2009): 1–28.

Law Council of Australia, 'Submission To The Senate Legal & Constitutional Affairs Committee Inquiry Into The Provisions Of The Anti-Terrorism (No. 2) Bill 2005' (2005).

Lehmann, David, *Struggle for the Spirit: Religious Transformations and Popular Culture in Brazil and Latin America* (Cambridge: Polity, 1996).

Lemke, Thomas, '"The Birth of Bio-politics" – Michel Foucault's Lecture at the Collège de France on Neo-liberal Governmentality', *Economy and Society*, 30/2 (2001): 190–207.

Lemke, Thomas, 'Foucault, Governmentality, and Critique', *Rethinking Marxism*, 14/3 (2002): 49–64.

Lemke, Thomas, 'An Indigestible Meal? Foucault, Governmentality and State Theory' (2007), <www.thomaslemkeweb.de/publikationen/IndigestibleMeal final5.pdf>, accessed 10 November 2011.

Lessard, Hester, 'The Empire of the Lone Mother: Parental Rights, Child Welfare Law, and State Restructuring', *Osgoode Hall Law Journal*, 39/4 (2002): 717–70.

Levine, Peter and William M. Galstone, 'America's Civic Condition: A Glance at the Evidence', *Brookings Institute*, 4 January (2012).

Lévy, Chairman, 'Influência e Contribuição: a Igreja Católica Progressista Brasileira e o Fórum Social Mundial', *Religião & Sociedade*, 29/2 (2009): 177–97.

Lewis, Nick, Wendy Larner and Richard Le Heron, 'The New Zealand Designer Fashion Industry: Making Industries and Co-constituting Political Projects', *Transactions of the Institute of British Geographers*, 33/1 (2007): 42–59.

Ley, David, 'The City and Good and Evil: Reflections on Christian and Marxist Interpretations', *Antipode*, 6 (1974): 66–74.

Ley, David, 'The Immigrant Church as an Urban Service Hub', *Urban Studies*, 45/10 (2008): 2057–74.

Liberty Victoria, 'Submission to the Senate Legal & Constitutional Affairs Committee Inquiry into the Provisions of the Provisions of the Anti-Money Laundering and Counter-Terrorism Financing Bill 2006, and the Anti-Money

Laundering and Counter-Terrorism Financing (Transitional Provisions and Consequential Amendments) Bill' (2006).

Liiman, Raigo, *Usklikkus muutuvas Eesti ühiskonnas* [Religiosity in a Changing Estonian Society] (Tartu: Tartu University Press, 2001).

Lim, Wonhyuk, 'Demise of the Anglo-American Model of Capitalism', *Global Asia*, Winter (2008): 58–60.

Lippert, Randy, 'Rationalities and Refugee Resettlement', *Economy and Society*, 27/4 (1998), 380–406.

Lippert, Randy, *Sanctuary, Sovereignty, Sacrifice: Canadian Sanctuary Incidents, Power, and Law* (Vancouver: UBC Press, 2005).

Lockhart, William H., 'Building Bridges and Bonds: Generating Social Capital in Secular and Faith-Based Poverty-to-Work Programs', *Sociology of Religion*, 66/1 (2005): 45–60.

Lombroso, Cesare Ferrero, *La femme criminelle et la prostituée* (Paris: Alcan, 1896).

Lucas, Phillip Charles and Thomas Robbins (eds), *New Religious Movements in the Twenty-First Century: Legal, Political, and Social Challenges in Global Perspective* (London: Routledge, 2004).

Luhmann, Niklas, 'Interaktion, Organisation, Gesellschaft: Anwendungen der Systemtheorie', in Niklas Luhmann, *Soziologische Aufklärung, Vl. 2: Aufsätze zur Theorie der Gesellschaft* (Opladen 1975).

Lynch, Andrew, 'Legislating with Urgency – the Enactment of the Anti-Terrorism Act [No. 1] 2005', *Melbourne University Law Review*, 31 (2006): 747–81.

Mackay, Pierre, 'La *Charte canadienne des droits et libertés* de 1982 ou le déclin de l'empire britannique', in Robert Bureau and Pierre Mackay (eds), *Le droit dans tous ses états* (Montréal: Wilson & Lafleur, 1987).

Macourt, Malcolm, 'Mapping the "New Religious Landscape" and the "New Irish": Uses and Limitations of the Census', in Olivia Cosgrove, Laurence Cox, Carmen Kuhling and Peter Mulholland (eds), *Ireland's New Religious Movements* (Cambridge: Cambridge Scholars Publishing, 2011).

Maddox, Marion, *God Under Howard: The Rise of the Religious Right in Australian Politics* (Sydney: Allen & Unwin, 2005).

Madeley, John, 'Religion and the State', in Jeffrey Haynes (ed.), *Routledge Handbook of Religion and Politics* (London: Routledge, 2009).

Madison, James, *Memorial and Remonstrance Against Religious Assessments* (1785).

Mariano, Ricardo, *Neopentecostais: sociologia do novo pentecostalismo no Brasil* (São Paulo: Loyola, 1999).

Marsden, George M., *Fundamentalism and American Culture: The Shaping of Twentieth-Century Evangelicalism: 1870–1925* (New York: Oxford University Press, 1980).

Marsden, George M., *Understanding Fundamentalism and Evangelicalism* (Grand Rapids: William B. Eerdmans Publishing Company, 1991).

Marti, Gerardo, *Hollywood Faith: Holiness, Prosperity, and Ambition in a Los Angeles Church* (New Brunswick: Rutgers University Press, 2009).

Martikainen, Tuomas, *Immigrant Religions in Local Society: Historical and Contemporary Perspectives in the City of Turku* (Åbo: Åbo Akademi University Press, 2004).

Martikainen, Tuomas, 'The Governance of Islam in Finland', *Temenos* 43/2 (2007): 243–65.

Martikainen, Tuomas, 'Finland', in Göran Larsson (ed.), *Islam in the Nordic and Baltic Countries* (London: Routledge, 2009).

Martikainen, Tuomas, 'The Global Political Economy, Welfare State Reforms, and the Governance of Religion', in Peter Nynäs, Mika Lassander and Terhi Utriainen (eds), *The Post-Secular Society* (London: Transaction Publishers, 2012).

Martikainen, Tuomas, Kathleen Valtonen and Östen Wahlbeck, 'The Social Integration of Immigrants in Finland', in James S. Frideres and John Biles (eds), *International Perspectives: Integration and Inclusion* (Montreal: McGill-Queen's University Press, 2012), pp. 127–46.

Martin, David, *A General Theory of Secularization* (Oxford: Basil Blackwell, 1978).

Martin, David, 'Canada in Comparative Perspective', in David Lyon and Margaret Van Die (eds), *Rethinking Church, State and Modernity: Canada between Europe and America* (Toronto: University of Toronto Press, 2000).

Martin, David, *Pentecostalism: The World Their Parish* (Oxford: Blackwell, 2003).

Martin, David, *On Secularization: Towards a Revised General Theory* (Farnham: Ashgate, 2005).

Martin, Jean–Paul (ed.), 'Laïcité, Croyances et Éducation', Special Issue, *Spirale* 39 (2007).

Marty, Martin E., 'Fundamentalism as a Social Phenomenon', *Bulletin of the American Academy of Arts and Sciences*, 42/2 (1988): 15–29.

Marty, Martin E., 'Too Bad We're So Relevant: The Fundamentalism Project Projected', *Bulletin of the American Academy of Arts and Sciences*, 49/6 (1996): 22–38.

Marty, Martin E. and R. Scott Appleby (eds), *Fundamentalisms Observed*. The Fundamentalism Project Vol 1. (Chicago: University of Chicago Press, 1991).

Marty, Martin E. and R. Scott Appleby (eds), *The Glory and the Power: The Fundamentalist Challenge to the Modern World* (Boston: Beacon Press, 1992).

Maruste, Rait, *Konstitutsionalism ning põhiõiguste ja -vabaduste kaitse* [Constitutionalism, and the Protection of Basic Rights and Freedoms] (Tallinn: Juura, 2004).

Maussen, Marcel, *The Governance of Islam in Western Europe: A State of the Art* (Amsterdam: IMISCOE, 2007).

Maussen, Marcel and Veit Bader, 'Introduction', in Marcel Maussen, Veit Bader and Annelies Moors (eds), *Colonial and Post-Colonial Governance of Religion: Continuities and Ruptures* (Amsterdam: Amsterdam University Press, 2011).

Maussen, Marcel, Veit Bader and Annelies Moors (eds) *Colonial and Post-Colonial Governance of Religion: Continuities and Ruptures* (Amsterdam: Amsterdam University Press, 2011).

May, Tim, *Social Research: Issues, Methods and Process* (3rd ed., Buckingham: Open University Press, 2001).

McClain, Linda, *Unleashing or Harnessing 'Armies of Compassion'?: Reflections on the Faith-Based Initiative*, Boston University School of Law, Working Paper Series. Public Law & Legal Theory Working Paper No.08-11 (Boston, 2008) <www.bu.edu/law/faculty/scholarship/../Faith-based-McClain.html>, accessed 10 May 2011.

McCulloch, Jude and Sharon Pickering , 'Suppressing the Financing of Terrorism: Proliferating State Crime, Eroding Censure and Extending Neo-colonialism', *British Journal of Criminology*, 45 (2005): 470–86.

McCulloch, Jude, Sharon Pickering, Rob McQueen, Joo-Cheong Tham and David Wright-Neville, 'Suppressing the Financing of Terrorism', *Current Issues in Criminal Justice*, 16 (2004): 71–8.

McGuire, Meredith, *Lived Religion: Faith and Practice in Everyday Life* (Oxford: Oxford University Press, 2007).

McLaren, John, 'Recalculating the Wages of Sin: The Social and Legal Construction of Prostitution, 1850–1920', *Manitoba Law Journal*, 23 (1992): 524–55.

McLoughlin, William, 'Is There a Third Force in Christendom?', *Daedalus*, XCVI Winter (1967): 43–68.

McNay, Lois, 'Self as Enterprise. Dilemmas of Control and Resistance in Foucault's *The Birth of Biopolitics*', *Theory, Culture & Society*, 26/6 (2009): 55–77.

Mead, Lawrence, *The New Paternalism: Supervisory Approaches to Poverty* (Washington, DC: Brookings Institution Press, 1997).

Mead, Lawrence, 'A Biblical Response to Poverty', in Mary Bane and Lawrence Mead (eds), *Lifting Up The Poor: A Dialogue on Religion, Poverty and Welfare Reform* (Washington: Brookings Institute Press, 2003).

Melasuo, Tuomo, Matti Pesu and Outi Tomperi (eds), *Impivaarasta pyramideille: Kulttuurienvälinen vuoropuhelu ja suomalainen kansalaisyhteiskunta* (Tampere: Tampereen yliopisto, Rauhan- ja konfliktintutkimuskeskus TAPRI, 2011).

Meyer, Birgit, 'Pentecostalism and Neo-Liberal Capitalism: Faith, Prosperity and Vision in African Pentecostal-Charismatic Churches', *Journal for the Study of Religion*, 20/2 (2007): 5–28.

Meyer, Birgit, 'Pentecostalism and Globalization', in Allan Anderson, Michael Bergunder, André Droogers and Cornelis van der Laan (eds), *Studying Global Pentecostalism: Theories and Methods* (Berkeley: University of California, 2010).

Meyer, David S. *A Winter of Discontent: The Nuclear Freeze and American Politics* (Westport: Praeger, 1990).

Mill, John Stuart, 'Radical Party and Canada: "Lord Durham and the Canadians January 1838"', *London and Westminster Review*, VI & XXVIII, 502–33.

Mill, John Stuart, *On Liberty* (Kitchener: Batoche Books, 2001).

Mill, John Stuart, *The Subjection of Women* (Dover: Thrift Editions, 1997, original 1869).

Miller, Donald E. and Tetsunao Yamamori, *Global Pentecostalism: The New Face of Christian Social Engagement* (Berkeley: University of California Press, 2007).

Miller, Peter, 'Accounting and Objectivity: The Invention of Calculating Selves and Calculable Spaces', *Annals of Scholarship*, 9/1–2 (1992): 61–8.

Miller, Peter and Nikolas Rose, 'Governing Economic Life', *Economy and Society*, 19/1 (1990): 1–31.

Miller, Peter and Nikolas Rose, *Governing the Present: Administering Economic, Social and Personal Life* (Cambridge: Polity, 2008).

Modood, Tariq, 'Their Liberalism and Our Multiculturalism?', *British Journal of Politics and International Relations*, 3/2 (2001): 245–57.

Montero, Federico, 'Reflexiones preliminares sobre discriminación, ciudadanía y políticas públicas en el MERCOSUR', in Federico Montero, Paikin Damián and Makarz Jorge (eds), *Hacia una ciudadanía plena. Los desafíos de las políticas antidiscriminatorias en el MERCOSUR* (Buenos Aires: Instituto Nacional contra la Discriminación, la Xenofobia y el Racismo/Ministerio de Justicia, Seguridad y Derechos Humanos, 2009).

Mooney, Margarita, 'The Catholic Bishops Conferences of the United States and France: Engaging Immigration as a Public Issue', *American Behavioral Scientist*, 49/11 (2006): 1455–70.

Moreau, Sophia, 'The Wrongs of Unequal Treatment', *University of Toronto Law Journal*, 54/3 (2004): 291–326.

Moreau, Sophia. 'The Promise of *Law V. Canada*', *University of Toronto Law Journal*, 57/2 (2007): 415–30.

Mouffe, Chantal (ed.), *Dimensions of Radical Democracy: Pluralism, Citizenship, Community* (London: Verso, 1992).

Muller, Mark, QC, 'Terrorism, Proscription and the Right to Resist in the Age of Conflict', *Denning Law Journal*, 20 (2008): 111–31.

Narits, Raul, 'Seadusloome õigusliku ja regulatiivse mõju hindamine' [An assesment of the Legal and Regulatory Impact of Legislation], in *Riigikogu toimetised* 23. (2011), <http://www.riigikogu.ee/rito/index.php?id=11863>.

Nasr, Seyyed Hossein, *Islam in the Modern World: Challenged by the West, Threatened by Fundamentalism, Keeping Faith with Tradition* (New York: HarperOne, 2011).

National Conference of Catholic Bishops, 'The Challenge of Peace: God's Promise and Our Response', (1983), <www.usccb.org/sdwp/international/TheChallengeofPeace.pdf>, accessed 23 July 2011.

National Conference of Catholic Bishops, 'Economic Justice for All: Pastoral Letter on Catholic Social Teaching and the U.S. Economy', (1986), <www.usccb.org/jphd/economiclife/pdf/economic_justice_for_all.pdf>, accessed 23 July 2011.

Nayar, Kamala, *The Sikh Diaspora in Vancouver: Three Generations amid Tradition, Modernity, and Multiculturalism* (Toronto: University of Toronto Press, 2004).

Newman, Janet and John Clarke, *Publics, Politics & Power: Remaking the Public in Public Services* (London: Sage, 2009).

Nolan, Bruce, 'Obama Narrows, But Doesn't End, Electoral "God Gap"', *Pew Forum on Religion and Public Life*, 13 November (2008).

Nor, Malika, *Idées reçues: La Prostitution* (Paris: Le Cavalier bleu 2001).

Noreau, Pierre, 'Comment la législation est-elle possible? Objectivation et subjectivation du lien social', *McGill Law Journal*, 47/1 (2001): 195–236.

O'Neill, Kevin Lewis, 'But Our Citizenship is in Heaven: A Proposal for the Future Study of Christian Citizenship in the Global South', *Citizenship Studies*, 13/4 (2009): 333–48.

Obstfeld, Maurice and Alan M. Taylor, 'Globalization and Capital Markets', *NBER Working Papers*, Number 8846 (March 2002).

OECD, 'Society at a Glance 2011 – OECD Social Indicators', *OECD* (23 July 2011), <www.oecd.org/els/social/indicators/SAG>.

Office of Faith-Based and Community Initiatives, US Small Business Administration, Welcome Page, 2006.

Olasky, Marvin, *The Tragedy of American Compassion* (Washington: Regnery Gateway, 1992).

Olasky, Marvin, *Compassionate Conservatism: What It Is, What It Does, And How It Can Transform America* (New York: Free Press, 2000).

Olson, Laura R. and John C. Green, 'The Religion Gap', *Political Science and Politics*, 39 (2006): 455–9.

Ong, Aihwa, 'Neoliberalism As a Mobile Technology', *Transactions of the Institute of British Geographers*, 32/1 (2007): 3–8.

Orléan, André, *L'empire de la valeur. Refonder l'économie* (Paris: Seuil 2011).

Oro, Ari Pedro, André Corten and Jean-Pierre Dozon (eds), *Igreja Universal do Reino de Deus: Os Novos Conquistadores da Fé* (São Paulo: Paulinas, 2003).

Pacione, Michael, 'The Ecclesiastical Community of Interest as a Response to Urban Poverty and Deprivation', *Transactions of the Institute of British Geographers*, 15/2 (1990): 193–204.

Parent Duchâtelet, Alexandre Jean-Batiste, *De la prostitution dans la ville de Paris* (2 vols, Paris: J.B. Baillière, 1836).

Parliamentary Joint Committee on Intelligence and Security, Report on 'Review of Security and Counter Terrorism Legislation', The Parliament of the Commonwealth of Australia, Canberra, Australia (2006).

Parliamentary Joint Committee on Intelligence and Security, 'Inquiry into the Proscription of "Terrorist Organisations" under the Australian Criminal Code', The Parliament of the Commonwealth of Australia, Canberra, Australia (2007).

Parsons, Talcott, *Societies: Evolutionary and Comparative Perspectives* (Englewood Cliffs: Prentice Hall, 1966).

Parsons, Talcott, *Politics and Social Structure* (New York: The Free Press, 1969).

Parsons, Talcott, *The System of Modern Societies* (Englewood Cliffs, NJ: Prentice-Hall, 1971).

Passeron, Jean-Claude, 'Introduction', in Max Weber, *Sociologie des religions* (Paris, 1996).

Peck, Jamie, 'Liberating the City: Between New York and New Orleans', *Urban Geography*, 27/8 (2006): 681–713.

Peck, Jamie, 'Remaking laissez-faire', *Progress in Human Geography*, 32/1 (2008): 3–43.

Pedersen, Anne Reff, Karina Sehested and Eva Sørensen, 'Emerging Theoretical Understanding of Pluricentric Coordination in Public Governance', *The American Review of Public Administration*, 41/4 (2011): 375–94.

Peet, Richard, *Unholy Trinity: The IMF, World Bank, and WTO* (Boston: Zed Press, 2003).

Permoser, Julia Mourão, Sieglinde Rosenberger and Kristina Stoeckl, 'Religious Organizations as Political Actors in the Context of Migration: Islam and Orthodoxy in Austria', *Journal of Ethnic and Migration Studies*, 36/9 (2010), 1463–81.

Pessi, Anne Birgitta, Olav Helge Angell and Per Pettersson, 'Nordic Majority Churches as Agents in the Welfare State: Critical Voices and/or Complementary Providers?', *Temenos*, 45/2 (2009): 207–34.

Pew Forum on Religion and Public Life, 'How the Faithful Voted: Political Alignments and the Religious Divide in Election 2004', 17 November (2004).

Pew Forum on Religion and Public Life, 'Religion and Public Life. A Faith-Based Partisan Divide', 26 January (2005).

Pew Forum on Religion and Public Life, 'Tolerance and Tension: Islam and Christianity in Sub-Saharan Africa', *Pew Research Center*, 15 April (2010), <pewforum.org/executive-summary-islam-and-christianity-in-sub-saharan-africa.aspx>, accessed 16 July 2011.

Pew Forum on Religion and Public Life, 'The Future of the Global Muslim Population: Projections for 2010–2030', *Pew Research Center*, 27 January (2011), <pewforum.org/Global-Muslim-Population.aspx>, accessed 16 July 2011.

Phillips, Ruth, 'The Role of Nonprofit Advocacy Organizations in Australian Democracy and Policy Governance', *Voluntas: International Journal of Voluntary and Nonprofit Organizations*, 17/1 (2006): 59–75.

Pierson, Christopher, *Beyond the Welfare State? The New Political Economy of Welfare* (Third edn, Cambridge: Polity, 2006).

Polanyi, Karl, *The Great Transformation: The Political and Economic Origins of Our Time* (Boston: Beacon Press, 1944/2001).

Pollitt, Christopher, Sandra van Thiel and Vincent Homburg (eds), *New Public Management in Europe: Adaptations and Alternatives* (Basingstone: Palgrave Macmillan, 2007).

Powell-Jackson, Timothy et al., 'Democracy and Growth in Divided Societies: A Health-Inequality Trap?', *Social Science and Medicine*, 73/1 (2011): 33–41.

Putnam, Robert D, 'The Strange Disappearance of Civic America', *American Prospect*, 7/Winter (1996): 34–48.

Putnam, Robert D., *Bowling Alone: The Collapse and Revival of American Community* (New York: Simon and Schuster, 2000).

Pyykkönen, Miikka, 'Integrating Governmentality: Administrative Expectations for Immigrant Associations in Finland', *Alternatives*, 32 (2007): 197–224.

Rabataux, Augustin-Philippe Edouard, *De la prostitution en Europe depuis l'antiquité jusqu'à la fin du XVIe siècle* (Paris: Séré, 1851).

Rahvastiku koostis ja korteriolud: 1. III 1934 rahvaloenduse andmed. Vihk II [The Composition of the Population and Housing Conditions. Data from the 1934 Population Census] (Tallinn: Riigi Statistika Keskbüroo, 1935).

Raun, Toivo U., *Estonia and the Estonians* (Updated 2nd edn, Stanford: Hoover Institution Press, 2001).

Réaume, Denise, '*Law v. Canada* (Minister of Employment and Immigration)', *Canadian Journal of Women and Law*, 18/1 (2006): 143–88.

Réaume, Denise, 'The Relevance of Relevance to Equality Rights', *Queen's Law Journal*, 31 (2006): 695–730.

Reingold, David, Maureen Pirog and Brady, David, 'Empirical Evidence on Faith-based Organizations in an Era of Welfare Reform', *Social Service Review*, 81/2 (2007): 245–83.

Renaut, Alain, and Alain Touraine, *Un débat sur la laïcité* (Paris: Stock, 2005).

Report of the Task Force on Active Citizenship (Dublin: Secretariat of the Taskforce on Active Citizenship, 2007).

Richards, Jay, *Money, Greed, and God: Why Capitalism is the Solution and Not the Problem* (New York: Harper One, 2009).

Richardson, James T., 'Religion, Law, and Human Rights', in Peter Beyer and Lori Beaman (eds), *Religion, Globalization and Culture* (Leiden, 2007), 391–405.

Riis, Ole and Linda Woodhead, *A Sociology of Religious Emotion* (New York: Oxford University Press, 2010).

Ringvee, Ringo, *Riik ja religioon nõukogudejärgses Eestis 1991–2008* [State and Religion in Post-Soviet Estonia 1991–2008], Dissertationes Theologiae Universitatis Tartuensis 23 (Tartu: Tartu University Press, 2011).

Ringvee, Ringo, 'Ristiusu kohtumine teiste vaimsete praktikatega – Eestimaa kogemus' [Christianity Encountering other Spiritual Practices – the Estonian Experience], in Eerik Jõks (ed.), *Astu alla rahva hulka* (Tallinn: Eesti Kirikute Nõukogu, 2012).

Robbers, Gerhard (ed.), *State and Church in the European Union* (Second edn, Baden-Baden: Nomos, 2005).

Robert, Marie-Pierre, 'Des crimes religieux : aux confluents du droit pénal et de liberté de religion', *Les Cahiers de droit*, 50/3–4 (2009): 663–90.

Robertson, Roland, *Globalization: Social Theory and Global Culture* (London: Sage, 1992).

Rohtmets, Priit, 'Development of the Membership', in Riho Altnurme (ed.), *History of Estonian Ecumenism* (Tallinn, Tartu: Estonian Council of Churches, University of Tartu, 2009).

Roof, Wade Clark, *Spiritual Marketplace: Baby Boomers and the Remaking of American Religion* (Princeton: Princeton University Press, 1999).

Roof, Wade Clark and William McKinney, *American Mainline Religion: Its Changing Shape and Future* (New Brunswick: Rutgers University Press, 1987).

Rosanvallon, Pierre, *Le libéralisme économique. Histoire de l'idée de marché* (Paris: Seuil, 1989).

Rose, Nikolas, 'Governing 'Advanced' Liberal Democracies', in Andrew Barry, Thomas Osborne and Nikolas Rose (eds), *Foucault and Political Reason: Liberalism, Neo-liberalism and Rationalities of Government* (London: UCL Press, 1996).

Rose, Nikolas, *Powers of Freedom: Reframing Political Thought* (Cambridge: Cambridge University Press, 1999).

Roy, Olivier, *Globalized Islam: The Search for a New Ummah* (New York: Columbia University Press, 2004).

RT L (Riigi Teataja Lisa), *Eesti kirikute, koguduste ja koguduste liitude registri põhimäärus* [Statute of the Estonian Register of Churches, Congregations and Associations of Congregations] (1993).

Ryan, Phil, *Multicultiphobia* (Toronto: University of Toronto Press, 2010).

Ryynänen, Aimo and Asko Uoti, 'Kunnallinen itsehallinto ja uusi hallintotapa', in Ilari Karppi and Lotta-Mari Sinervo (eds), *Governance: Uuden hallintotavan jäsentyminen* (Tampere, 2009).

Saad-Filho, Alfredo and Deborah Johnston, 'Introduction', in Saad-Filho and Johnston (eds), *Neoliberalism: A Critical Reader* (London: Pluto Press, 2005).

Saard, Riho, 'Establishment of the Council of Churches', in Riho Altnurme (ed.), *History of Estonian Ecumenism* (Tartu/Tallinn: University of Tartu/Estonian Council of Churches, 2009).

Sager, Rebecca, *Faith, Politics, & Power: The Politics of Faith-Based Initiatives* (New York: Oxford University Press, 2010).

Sager, Ryan, *The Elephant in the Room: Evangelicals, Libertarians, and the Battle to Control the Republican Party* (Hoboken: John Wiley and Sons, 2006).

Santos, Boaventura de Sousa, 'Para Uma Reinvenção Solidária e Participativa do Estado', in Luis Carlos Bresser Pereira, Jorge Wilheim and Lourdes Sola (eds), *Sociedade e Estado em Transformação* (São Paulo: UNESP, 2001).

Santos, Boaventura de Sousa, 'A crítica da governação neoliberal: O Fórum Social Mundial como política e legalidade cosmopolita subalterna', *Revista Crítica de Ciências Sociais*, 72 (2005): 7–44.

Santos, Boaventura de Sousa and César Rodríguez-Garavito, 'Law, Politics, and the Subaltern in Counter-Hegemonic Globalization', in Boaventura de Sousa Santos and César Rodríguez-Garavito (eds), *Law and Globalization from Below: Towards a Cosmopolitan Legality* (Cambridge: Cambridge University, 2005).

Scharbrodt, Oliver and Sakaranaho, Tuula, 'Islam and Muslims in the Republic of Ireland', *Journal of Muslim Minority Affairs*, 31/4 (2011): 469–85.

Schlamelcher, Jens, 'Unternehmen Kirche? Neoliberale Diskurse in den deutschen Großkirchen', in Walter Otto Ötsch and Claus Thomasberger (eds), *Der neoliberale Markt-Diskurs: Ursprünge, Geschichte, Wirkungen* (Marburg: Metropolis 2009).

Schlamelcher, Jens, 'Kirchliche Vergemeinschaftungsformen im Prozess der Vergesellschaftung', *Evangelische Theologie*, 70/6 (2010): 439–50.

Schwimmer, Éric, 'La bonne distance. Réflexions sur le phénomène P.E. Trudeau', *Anthropologica*, 50/1 (2008): 31–47.

Sckinkel, Willem and Friso van Houdt, 'The Double Helix of Cultural Assimilation and Neo-liberalism: Citizenship in Contemporary Governmentality' *British Journal of Sociology*, 61/4 (2010): 696–715.

Security Legislation Review Committee, Report of the Security Legislation Review Committee, Commonwealth of Australia, Barton, Australia (2006).

Sen, Amartya, *Inequality Reexamined* (Cambridge: Harvard University Press, 1992).

Sen, Amartya, *Develpment as Freedom* (Oxford: Oxford University Press, 1999).

Sheppard, Steve, 'The Perfectionisms of John Rawls', *Canadian Journal of Law and Jurisprudence*, 11 (1998): 383–415.

Sider, Ronald and Knippers, Donald, 'Introduction', in Ronald Sider and David Knippers (eds), *Toward an Evangelical Public Policy: Political Strategies for the Health of a Nation* (Grand Rapids: Baker Books, 2005).

Silva, Vágner Gonçalves da, 'Neo-Pentecostalism and Afro-Brazilian Religions: Explaining the Attacks on Symbols of the African Religious Heritage in Contemporary Brazil', *Mana*, 3/se (2007): 1–24.

Silvestri, Sara, 'Islam and Religion in the EU Political System', *West European Politics*, 32(6) (2009), 1210–39.

Skocpol, Theda, *Diminished Democracy: From Membership to Management in American Civic Life* (Norman: University of Oklahoma Press, 2003).

Smart, Carol, *Feminism and the Power of Law* (London: Routledge, 1989).

Smith, Anne Marie, 'Neoliberalism, Welfare Policy, and Feminist Theories of Social Justice' *Feminist Theory*, 9/2 (2008): 131–44.

Smith, Christian S., *American Evangelicalism: Embattled and Thriving* (Chicago: University of Chicago Press, 1998).

Smith, Elizabeth S., 'John Stuart Mill's *The Subjection of Women:* a Re-Examination', *Polity*, 34/2 (2001), 181–203.

Smith, Steven and Sosin, Michael, 'Varieties of Faith-related Agencies', *Public Administration Review*, 61/6 (2001): 651–70.

Sørensen, Eva and Jacob Torfing, 'The Democratic Anchorage of Governance Networks', *Scandinavian Political Studies*, 28/3 (2005): 195–218.

Spickard, James, 'Narrative versus Theory in the Sociology of Religion: Five Stories of Religion's Place in the Late Modern World', in James Beckford and John Walliss (eds), *Religion and Social Theory: Classical and Contemporary Debates* (Aldershot: Ashgate, 2006).

Springer, Simon, 'Violence Sits in Places? Cultural Practice, Neoliberal Rationalism, and Virulent Imaginative Geographies', *Political Geography*, 30 (2011): 90–98.

Stark, Rodney, 'Secularization R.I.P.', *Sociology of Religion*, 60/3 (1999): 249–73.

Stark, Rodney and William Sims Bainbridge, *The Future of Religion: Secularization, Revival and Cult Formation* (Berkeley: University of California Press, 1985).

Stark, Rodney, and William Sims Bainbridge, *A Theory of Religion* (New York: Peter Lang, 1987).

Stark, Rodney and Roger Finke, *Acts of Faith: Explaining the Human Side of Religion* (Berkeley: University of California Press, 2000).

Stausberg, Michael 'Exploring the Meso-levels of Religious Mappings: European Religion in Regional, Urban, and Local Contexts', *Religion: An International Journal*, 39/2 (2007): 103–8.

Steger, Manfred A. and Ravi K. Roy, *Neoliberalism: A Very Short Introduction* (New York: Oxford University Press, 2010).

Steinberg, Richard, 'Does Government Spending Crowd-out Donations? Interpreting the Evidence', *Annals of Public and Cooperative Economics*, 62/4 (1991): 591–617.

Stiglitz, Joseph E., *Globalization and Its Discontents* (New York: W.W. Norton & Company, 2003).

Stockman, Farah, 'Bush Brings Faith to Foreign Aid,' *The Boston Globe*, 8 October (2006).

Stolz, Jörg (ed.), *Salvation Goods and Religious Markets: Theory and Applications* (Bern: Peter Lang, 2008).

Strathern, Marilyn, 'Introduction: New Accountabilities', in Marilyn Strathern (ed.), *Audit Cultures: Anthropological Studies in Accountability, Ethics and the Academy* (London: Routledge, 2000).

Sullivan, Amy, 'Faith Without Works', *Washington Monthly* (2004).

Sulze, Emil, *Die Reform der evangelischen Landeskirchen nach den Grundsätzen des neueren Protestantismus* (Berlin: Schwetschke, 1906).

Sustaining Progress 2003–2005 (Dublin: Government Publications Office, 2003).

Svanberg, Ingvar and David Westerlund, 'Från invandrarreligion till blågul islam? 50 år av organisered muslimsk närvaro', in Ingvar Svanberg and David Westerlund (eds), *Blågul islam? Muslimer i Sverige* (Nora: Nya Doxa, 1999).

Swan, Samuel Hauenstein and Bapu Vaitla, *Hunger Watch Report 2007–2008: The Justice of Eating* (London: Pluto Press, 2007).

Sziarto, Kristen, 'Placing Legitimacy: Organizing Religious Support in a Hospital Workers' Contract Campaign', *Tijdschrift Voor Economische En Sociale Geografie*, 99/4 (2008): 406–25.

Tadros, Mariz, *Faith-Based Organizations and Service Delivery: Some Gender Conundrums, Gender and Development Programme*, Paper Number 11. (Geneva: United Nations Research Institute for Social Development, 2010), <http://www.unrisd.org/80256B3C005BCCF9/%28httpAuxPages%29/592137 C50475F6A8C12577BD004FB5A0/$file/Tadros.pdf>, accessed 10 May 2011.

Tambiah, Stanley J., *Buddhism Betrayed?: Religion, Politics, and Violence in Sri Lanka* (Chicago: University of Chicago Press, 1992).

Tardif, Louise, 'Religious Freedom in Canada: Whither the Community', (unpublished paper, 2010).

Taylor, Charles, *Sources of the Self: The Making of the Modern Identity* (Cambridge: Harvard University Press, 1989).

Taylor, Charles, *The Malaise of Modernity* (Toronto: Anansi, 1991).

Taylor, Charles, 'Can Canada Survive the *Charter*?', *Atlanta Law Review*, 30 (1992): 427–47.

Taylor, George, *Negotiated Governance and Public Policy in Ireland* (Manchester: Manchester University Press, 2005).

Tezcan, Levent, 'Interreligiöser Dialog und politische Religionen', *Aus Politik und Zeitgeschichte*, 28–9 (2006): 26–32.

Tham, Joo-Cheong, 'A Risk Analysis of Australia's Counter-Terrorism Financing Regime', *Social Justice*, 34/ Summer (2007).

The White House Office on Faith-Based Initiatives and Community Organizations, 'Rallying the Armies of Compassion' (2001).

The White House, '*WHOFBCI Accomplishments in 2006, 2007*'.

Theodossopoulos, Dimitrios, and Elisabeth Kirtsoglou (eds), *United in Discontent: Local Responses to Cosmopolitanism and Globalization* (Oxford: Berghahn Books, 2010).

Thomas, Scott M., *The Global Resurgence of Religion and the Transformation of International Relations: The Struggle for the Soul of the Twenty-First Century* (New York, NY: Palgrave, 2005).

Tormey, Simon, *Anti-Capitalism: A Beginner's Guide* (Oxford: Oneworld, 2005).

Tully, James 'Political Philosophy as a Critical Activity' *Political Theory*, 30(4): 533–55 (2002).

Turner, Bryan S., *Religion and Modern Society: Citizenship, Secularisation and the State* (Cambridge: Cambridge University Press, 2011).

Twombly, Eric C., 'Religious Versus Secular Human Service Organizations: Implications for Public Policy', *Social Science Quarterly*, 88 (2002): 947–61.

United States Government, 'Response of the United States to the Counter-Terrorism Committee, Security Council Resolution 1373 (2001)' (2006).

US Department of Health and Human Services, 'The Healthy Marriage Initiative', (2007).

Valk, Pille, 'Religioooniõpetus Eestis' [Religious Education in Estonia], in Pille Valk (ed.), *Töid religiooonipedagoogikast I* (Tartu: Tartu Ülikooli Kirjastus, 2008).

Valverde, Mariana, 'Genealogies of European States: Foucauldian Reflections', *Economy and Society*, 36/1 (2007): 159–78.

Van Biema, David and Jeff Chu, 'Does God Want You to be Rich?', *Time Magazine*, 18 September (2006).

Van Gramberg, Bernadine and Penny Bassett, 'Neoliberalism and the Third Sector in Australia', Working Paper Series, Victoria University of Technology School of Management (2005).

Veidemann, Andra, 'Kirik ja riik on Eesti Vabariigis lahutatud' [The Separation of Church and State in the Estonian Republic], *Päevaleht*, 21 February (1991).

Veidemann, Andra, 'Toimetusse helistas.. ' [A Call to the Editors…], *Eesti Kirik*, 18 June (1992).

Venables B., Juan Pablo, *Diferentes e Integrados: Estudio acerca de la ética del trabajo en el Movimiento Pentecostal de la Región Metropolitana*. Thesis in Sociology submitted to the Faculty of Social Sciences (Santiago: Universidad de Chile, 2007), <www.cybertesis.cl/tesis/uchile/2007/venables_j/sources/ venables_j.pdf>, accessed 24 June 2011.

Wallace, Anthony F.C., 'Revitalization Movements: Some Theoretical Considerations for Their Comparative Study', *American Anthropologist*, 58/2 (1956): 264–81.

Wallace, Anthony F.C., *The Death and Rebirth of the Seneca* (New York: Vintage Books, 1972).

Wallerstein, Immanuel, *World-Systems Analysis: An Introduction* (Durham: Duke University Press, 2004).

Wallis, Jim, *The Great Awakening: Reviving Faith and Politics in a Post-religious Right America* (New York: Harper One, 2008).

Walzer, Michael, 'The Civil Society Argument', in Chantal Mouffe (ed.), *Dimensions of Radical Democracy: Pluralism, Citizenship, Community* (London: Verso, 1992).

Warner, R. Stephen, 'Work in Progress Toward a New Paradigm for the Sociological Study of Religion in the United States', *The American Journal of Sociology*, 98/5 (1993): 1044–93.

Warren, Mark R., *Dry Bones Rattling: Community Building to Revitalize American Democracy* (Princeton: Princeton University Press, 2001).

Warrington, Keith, *Pentecostal Theology: A Theology of Encounter* (London: T & T Clark, 2008).

Weber, Max, *The Protestant Ethic and the Spirit of Capitalism,* trans. Talcott Parsons (New York: Dover, 2003 [1905]).

Weber, Max, 'Introduction to the Economic Ethics of the World Religions', in Sam Whimster (ed.), *The Essential Weber* (London: Routledge, 2004).

West, Robin, 'Jurisprudence and Gender', *Chicago Law Review*, 55/1 (1988): 1–72.

Wiesenthal, Helmut, 'Markt, Organisation und Gemeinschaft als "zweitbeste" Verfahren sozialer Koordination', in Wieland Jäger and Uwe Schimank (eds), *Organisationsgesellschaft – Facetten und Perspektiven* (Wiesbaden: VS Verlag, 2005).

Wilcox, Clyde and Carin, Larson, *Onward Christian Soldiers: The Religious Right in American Politics* (Boulder: Westview Press, 2006).

Wilson, Bryan R., *Contemporary Transformations of Religion* (London: Oxford University Press, 1976).

Wimmer, Andreas and Nina Glick-Schiller, 'Methodological Nationalism and Beyond: Nation–state Building, Migration and the Social Sciences', *Global Networks*, 2/4 (2002): 301–34.

Wolfe, Joel, 'Populism and Developmentalism', in Thomas H. Holloway (ed.), *A Companion to Latin American History* (Malden: Blackwell, 2010).

Woodhead, Linda, 'Real Religion, Fuzzy Spirituality', in Dick Houtman and Stef Aupers (eds), *Religions of Modernity: Relocating the Sacred to the Self and the Digital* (Leiden: Brill, 2010).

Woodhead, Linda and Paul Heelas, *Religion in Modern Times: An Interpretive Anthology* (Oxford: Blackwell, 2002).

World Council of Churches, 'The Ecumenical Presence at the 4th World Social Forum', *World Council of Churches*, 21 January (2004), <www.oikoumene. org/en/resources/documents/wcc-programmes/public-witness-addressing-power-affirming-peace/poverty-wealth-and-ecology/neoliberal-paradigm/ the-ecumenical-presence-at-the-4th-world-social-forum.html>, accessed 25 November 2010.

Worsley, Peter, *The Trumpet Shall Sound: A Study of 'Cargo' Cults in Melanesia* (London: MacGibbon and Kee, 1957).

Wuthnow, Robert, *Saving America? Faith-Based Services and the Future of Civil Society* (Princeton, NJ: Princeton University Press, 2004).

Ziegler, Jennifer, 'Testimony to subcommittee on human resources of the House Committee on ways and means on February 10, 2005', U.S. House of Representatives Website, <waysandmeans.house.gov/hearings. asp?formmode=view&id=2969>, accessed October 2006.

Legal Sources

Laws

Canadian Charter of Rights and Freedoms, Department of Justice, Canada, <http://laws.justice.gc.ca/en/charter/>.

Constitution of the Republic of Estonia 1992, <http://www.president.ee/en/ republic-of-estonia/the-constitution/index.html>, accessed 20 February 2012.

Code criminel. 1892, 55–56 Victoria, Chap. 29 (1892) (Canada, Quebec).

Legal cases

Alberta v. Hutterian Brethren of Wilson Colony, 2009 SCC 37, [2009] 2 S.C.R. 567

Bedford c. Canada, 2010 ONSC 4264

Boucher v. the King, [1949] 96 C.C.C. 48

Bruker v. Marcovitz, [2007] 3 S.C.R. 607, 2007 SCC 54

C.C.C. 103 (C.A. Manitoba)

Dominion News & Gifts (1962) Ltd. c. The Queen, [1964] S.C.R. 251

Multani v. Commission Scolaire Marguerite–Bourgeoys, 2005 SCC 6, [2006] 1 S.C.R. 256

R. c. Butler, [1992] 1 R.C.S. 452

R. c. Caron, 2011 CSC 5, [2011] 1 R.C.S. 78

R. c. Labaye, [2005] 3 R.C.S. 728

R. v. Big M Drug Mart Ltd., [1985] 1 S.C.R. 295

R. v. N.S., [2009] O.J. 1766

R. v. Oakes [1986] 1 S.C.R. 103

Regina v. Dominion News & Gifts Ltd.[1963] M.J. No. 542; W.W.R. 65; [1963] 2

Renvoi relatif à l'art. 193 et à l'al. 195.1(1)c) du Code criminel (Man.), [1990] 1 R.C.S. 1123

Saumur v. City of Quebec, [1953] 2 S.C.R. 299

Syndicat Northcrest v. Amselem, [2004] 2 S.C.R. 551, 2004 SCC 47

Index

9/11 2, 140, 175, 207

activism 22, 28, 30–31, 36, 69, 81–82, 84,
    88, 102, 147
Acton, Harry Burrows 94
administration 13, 17, 60, 99, 101, 105–6,
    109–113, 115–7, 123, 126–7, 130,
    134, 137, 139, 141, 154, 156, 170
advertising 5, 28, 65–66, 186
advocacy 80, 84, 111, 161, 176
alienation 5, 16
Almeida, Ronaldo Rômulo M. de 29
Almond, Gabriel 121
alterglobalism 21–22, 31–36
Altnurme, Lea 147
Appleby, Scott 46
Ashcroft, John 99
atheism 25, 50, 145
audit culture 20, 70–71, 86, 90
auditing 77
austerity 59–61, 83, 90
authority 9, 11, 16–17, 49, 53, 66, 70–71,
    77, 81, 88, 106, 114, 120, 122,
    126–7, 132, 135, 150, 185, 196,
    199
autonomization 10

Bader, Veit 131–32
Barber, Benjamin 38, 43, 45–6
Beaumont, Justin 102
Bell, Daniel 5
Benedict XVI 49
Bentham, Jeremy 12, 180–81
Blair, Tony 14, 123
Bouchard-Taylor Commission 201
Bray, Michael 44
Brazil 29, 32, 34–35
Brenner, Neil 15
Brown, Gordon 123
Brown, Wendy 152, 195–8

Bruce, Steve 38–9, 146
Buckley, William F. 98
Buddhism 8, 40
bureaucracy 10, 15, 57, 112–3, 116, 118,
    121, 134
bureaucratization 6, 162, 176
Bush, George W. 99, 101, 105–6, 109–112,
    114, 117, 123, 126

Cameron, David 123
Canada 151, 178–9, 184–5, 187, 191,
    193–4, 197–8, 201–2, 208–9
capitalism 4–8, 22, 24, 27, 43–4, 72, 91,
    95, 116, 120, 124, 126–7
Carrette, Jeremy 6, 26
Carter, Jimmy 98
Casanova, José 2
Casas, Bartolomé de las 49
Catholicism 19–20, 28, 30–31, 34, 29, 49,
    51, 54, 55, 69–90, 101, 111, 137,
    144, 147, 154, 178
Chambers, Simone 114
Champion, Françoise 5
charismatic movement 7, 10, 28
Charitable Choice 99, 101, 109–10
charity 30, 81, 101, 104, 108, 111–2, 133,
    163–4, 166–8, 175–6
Chaves, Mark 112
Chile 29
choice 7, 25, 31, 38–9, 74, 78, 88, 131,
    143, 182, 185, 188–90, 196–7,
    202–5, 208
Christian Right 20, 26, 42, 51, 91–106
church-state relations 9, 41, 79, 88, 90,
    108, 130–3, 137, 139, 141, 144–5,
    149–50, 155, 198
citizenization 70
city churches 53–67

civil society 15, 20, 26, 32, 35–6, 43,
    69–90, 112, 114, 117, 127, 133,
    140, 157, 162, 164, 171, 177, 188
Clarke, Gerald 8
Cline, Austin 50
Clinton, Bill 14, 99, 109–11, 123, 126
Cole, Stewart 41
Coleman, John A. 82
commercialization 125
commoditization 15–16
communicative action 115–6, 118
competition 21, 24, 26, 30, 54, 56, 74,
    76–7, 87–9, 118, 131, 134, 163
Comte, Auguste 114
Connolly, William 23, 26, 96
conservative religion 37–45, 50
consumer society 7, 66, 143
consumerism 1–2, 5–6, 9–10, 15–7, 21, 26,
    31, 53, 163
consumerization 174
consumer-orientation 24, 67
consumption 4, 7–8, 15–16, 25, 28, 30, 59,
    66–7, 121
contractual 13, 17, 78, 83, 101, 112, 153,
    176, 180, 185, 190, 195
contractualization 155, 162
corporatism 81, 120–21, 123, 136
cost-benefit 78, 193–209
Coukos, Andrea 95
counterterrorism 140, 161–176
courts 154, 156–7, 165, 177–209
customer orientation 54–5, 61–62, 64, 67

Davie, Grace 8, 38, 147
de-Christianization 67
Deleuze, Gilles 23
democracy 25, 32, 43–4, 115–6, 119–22,
    125, 127, 141
democratization 15, 24–5, 35, 66, 183
Deng Xiaoping 13
depoliticization 95, 121, 190–91
deregulatation 1, 9, 13–4, 21, 24, 26, 47,
    94, 146–7, 152, 161
Dewey, John 12, 120
dialogue 35, 87, 129, 140
Dias, Candice 102
Dinham, Adam 9
downsizing 54–5, 59, 104, 106

Duchastel, Jules 16
Dumenil, Gerard 94
Durkheim, Émile 38
Dworkin, Ronald 12

economics 1–17, 143, 152, 161, 189
ecumenism 21–36, 148
efficiency 17, 21, 25, 58, 74, 77, 83, 113,
    155, 157
Eisenstadt, Shmuel 2
emotions 5, 7, 35, 111
Engels, Friedrich 3
entrepreneurialism 12, 21–36, 73, 76, 78,
    81, 86, 88–9, 91, 122, 188–90, 196
Estonia 143–60
ethics 4, 7, 29, 41, 51–52, 151, 181, 186
European Union 136, 154
Evangelicals 26, 31, 39, 41, 80, 84, 96–99,
    110–11, 114, 122, 124, 126

Faith-based Initiative 99–101, 106,
    109–128, 161
faith-based organizations (FBOs) 8, 20, 71,
    73–5, 78–9, 85, 87–9, 97, 91–129,
    133
faith-based welfare 91–129
Falwell, Jerry 91, 98
financing 123, 132, 145, 150, 162, 164–70,
    174
Finland 129–42
Fischer, Claude 38, 50
flexibility 5, 72, 135
Foucault, Michel 69–72, 75, 196
Freeden, Michael 14
Friedman, Milton 13, 93–5, 143, 152
Fukuyama, Francis 115
fundamentalism 37, 41–43, 45, 47, 50, 93,
    96, 106, 114, 122

Gaynor, Niamh 83
Germany 53–67, 95, 102
Gill, Anthony 157
Gill, Stephen 27
Giroux, Henry 114
globalization 1–3, 8, 15, 17, 21–24, 31–33,
    36, 43, 70, 72, 126, 130, 141, 155,
    162, 174, 196

governance 5, 8–10, 16–7, 28, 31, 70–71,
        74, 79, 83–4, 88, 90, 96, 129–142,
        145, 157, 159, 176
    at a distance 27
    global 22, 35
    meta- 135–6, 141
    multicentric 134–5
    multilevel 130, 135–6, 141
    neoliberal 32, 53, 78, 86, 88–9, 152–4
    networks 21, 130, 134–42
    pluricentric 130, 134, 136, 141
    technocratic 32
    unicentric 134–5
    welfare state 72
governmentality 21, 27, 69–78, 89
Greenberg, James B. 47
Guattari, Félix 23

Habermas, Jürgen 114–7, 120, 124–5, 127,
        177
Hackworth, Jason 9, 11
Hayek, Friedrich von 12–13, 93–5
Hays, R. Alan 103
health and wealth movement; *see*
        prosperity religion
hegemony 21–7, 35–6, 121, 123
Hervieu-Léger, Danièle 5
Hilton, Boyd 96
Hinduism 8, 37, 40, 43, 46
Hofstadter, Richard 41
homogenization 23, 44
Honohan, Iseult 80, 87
Hout, Michael 38, 50
Howard, John 161–62, 166
Hudson, Kenneth 95
Hume, David 12, 94
hypercommodification 36

individual choice; *see* choice
individualism 11, 16, 66, 75, 96, 108, 154,
        181, 186–8, 190
individualization 22, 57, 72, 75, 191
integration 3, 69–90, 132, 138, 194, 198
international law 9, 22, 132, 205
International Monetary Fund (IMF) 14,
        47, 94
Ireland 69–90

Islam 8–9, 37, 39–40, 43, 46, 80, 85, 87,
        129, 132, 136, 138–40, 161–177,
        207

Jehovah's Witnesses 149, 198
Jenkins, Philip 39
Jennings, Michael 8
judiciary 3, 116, 183–4, 191
Juergensmeyer, Mark 44–6, 50

Kahl, Sigrun 96
Kant, Immanuel 189
Keynes, John Maynard 12, 103
King, Richard 5, 26
Kintz, Linda 97
Kodacsy, Tamas 150
Kuo, David 110, 112

L'Estrange, Sean 81–82
Laar, Mart 143, 152
laïcité 89, 197
Latin America 24–35
legitimacy 2, 10, 14, 17, 20, 27, 43, 56,
        71, 76, 79, 81–83, 86, 90, 95, 103,
        116, 120–21, 123–8, 136, 140, 167,
        172–3, 175, 188
Lemke, Thomas 72
Leo XIII 49
Lévy, Chairman 34
Levy, Dominique 94
Ley, David 103
liberalism 10–14, 71, 74, 76, 94, 96, 114–5,
        119–23, 178, 180–81, 185–6,
        190–91
liberation theology 31, 33–43, 102, 105
libertarianism 27, 97–98
Lippmann, Walter 13
Locke, John 10–12, 94, 120, 184
low threshold offers 61–64
Lutheran 34, 101, 137–8, 144–8, 150–51,
        155, 158, 160

Madison, James 119
management 1, 5, 9–10, 15–7, 28, 53, 60,
        70, 76, 80, 85–6, 113, 129; *see also*
        New Public Management
managerialization 60
Mann, Simranjit Singh 44

market civilization 27
market economy 11, 72
market fundamentalism 47, 93, 114
market logic 194, 208
market society 11, 15, 17
marketing 5, 55
marketization 15–7, 31, 53, 59–60, 67, 79
marketplace 5–7, 16, 41
Marsden, George M. 41, 46
Martin, David 2, 206
Marty, Martin 42–3, 46
Marx, Karl 3–4, 38, 119–20
Marxism 5, 14–5, 145
Mauss, Marcel 56
Maussen, Marcel 132
McCain, John 127
McClain, Linda 78
McLoughlin, William 42
methodological nationalism 9, 133
Meyer, Birgit 8, 24
migration 1, 22, 69–90, 132, 137–8,
Mill, James 11, 94
Mill, John Stuart 12, 178, 180–81, 184–5,
    191
Miller, Peter 74–6
minoritization 23
minority 29, 80, 86, 140–41, 159, 199–200,
    206, 208
Mises, Ludwig von 12, 93–4
Mitterrand, François 14
mobility 5, 27, 29, 72, 122, 125
modernity 2, 10–12, 37, 41–43, 46, 57,
    114, 116, 119, 124
modernization 2, 4, 10, 16, 33, 41, 43
Mont Pelerin Society 13, 94
Mooney, Margarita 69
morality 5, 11–12, 30, 36, 40, 42–5, 49–53,
    64, 66–7, 71, 78–9, 108, 111,
    115–6, 120, 126, 149, 177–191
multiculturalism 3, 108, 178, 193–5, 201,
    208

Nagel, Thomas 12
Nasr, Seyyed Hossein 52
nationalism 4, 12, 37, 40, 46, 144, 184
nation-state 2, 4, 43–4, 70, 122, 125, 127,
    131, 137

neoliberal ideology 1–3, 9, 14–6, 21, 27–8,
    38, 72–3, 138, 141, 143, 152
neoliberal rationality 71, 73, 75, 82, 86,
    90, 196
neoliberalism 1–2, 9, 12–17
neoliberalization 14–5, 23–6, 189–91
network governance 21, 129–42
networks 5, 7, 9, 21–22, 27, 29, 31–33,
    35–6, 51, 75, 124, 127, 129–42
New Public Management (NPM) 9, 130,
    133, 137, 139; *see also* public
    sector reform
non-profit organizations (NGOs) 31–32,
    34, 73–4, 84–56, 88–9, 101, 105,
    113, 157, 162, 164, 166, 168, 171,
    173
Noreau, Pierre 177

Obama, Barack 123, 126–7
objectification 177
Olasky, Marvin 91, 105
opportunity structure 17, 132
Orthodox Christianity 80, 137, 144–5, 147,
    155–7
outsourcing 20, 59–60, 133, 137, 161–63,
    168, 171, 173

Parsons, Talcott 114–6
pastoral power 71–75, 86, 88–9
Pedersen, Anne Reff 136
Pentecostalism 3, 7–8, 22–31, 34–7, 39, 91
pluralism 7, 33, 35, 146, 195
pluralization 26, 142
Polanyi, Karl 11–12
polygamy 197
postmodern 125–7
privatization 21, 26, 47, 109–128, 131,
    137, 143, 152, 161
proceduralism 12, 121, 134, 184, 186, 191
projects 30–32, 62, 69–90, 135, 137–40,
    170–76
prosperity religion 7–8, 25, 28–9, 91–92
prostitution 177–191
Protestantism 4, 25, 28, 31, 39, 41–43, 49,
    65, 137, 148
public administration reform; *see* New
    Public Management, public sector
    reform

public sector reform 71, 83, 88; *see also*
    New Public Management
public sphere 2, 21, 23, 69, 116–8, 125,
    127–8
public/private 9, 72–3
Putnam, Robert 124

Quebec 89, 178, 184, 198, 201
Quesnay, François 10

Rand, Ayn 92
rational choice theory 6, 131, 196
Rawls, John 12, 108, 185, 191
Reagan, Ronald 13–4, 110, 152
recognition 3, 23, 29, 53, 76, 78, 83, 88,
    162, 201, 207
religion and economy 3–10, 31, 131, 146,
    151, 159
religious communication 60, 66
religious extremism 70, 79, 89
religious freedom 30, 132, 137, 144, 149,
    151, 154, 156, 159, 193–209
religious identities 21, 27, 35, 79
religious non-governmental organizations
    (RNGOs) 73–4, 88–9
Religious Right; *see* Christian Right
representation 17, 23, 87, 132, 139–40
restructuring 55, 70, 72, 108, 133, 161–62,
    164, 171, 173, 176
revitalization movement 37, 44–6
Richards, Jay 104
risk 21, 23–4, 29–30, 70, 76, 79, 162–6,
    168–9, 171, 175–6, 182, 190, 203,
    207
Robertson, Pat 110
Robertson, Roland 1
Roof, Wade Clark 6
Rose, Nikolas 74–6
Rougier, Nathalie 80, 87
Russia 95, 137, 144–5, 156

Sager, Ryan 97
Sakaranaho, Tuula 85
salvation goods 6
Scharbrodt, Oliver 85
Schulze, Emil 57
secularism 89

secularization 2–3, 9–10, 38, 40–41, 46,
    57, 61–62, 75, 84, 108, 131, 137,
    189, 191
securitization 2–3, 8, 193–5, 197, 202,
    207–8
security 9, 11, 17, 77, 87, 108, 132, 166,
    175, 186, 188, 190, 195–6, 203,
    204, 206–8
Sehested, Karina 136
self-governance 162, 165, 169–170, 172
Sen, Amartya 52
Sikhism 43–44, 194, 201, 207
Silva, Vágner Gonçalves da 28
Simmel, Georg 4
situative *Vergemeinschaftung* 65
Smith, Adam 10–1, 94
social capital 101, 112, 117, 124, 161, 176
social cohesion 70–71, 73, 79, 87, 141,
    163, 182
social contract 11–12
social Gestalt 55, 65
Social Gospel 102, 105
social justice 25, 33, 48, 81, 84, 86, 89
social policy 74, 76–8, 85, 141, 161
socialism 12–3, 24, 208
solidarity 22, 29, 32–3, 35, 53, 116
Sørensen, Eva 135–6
Soviet Union 137–8, 143, 145, 148–9, 156
spectacularization 125
Spencer, Herbert 114
spirituality 3, 5–6, 8, 10, 21–36, 65–6, 70,
    146–8, 158–9
Springer, Simon 27
Stiglitz, Joseph 47, 51
Stolz, Jörg 6
subjectification 177
subjectivation 75
subjectivization 26

Tadros, Mariz 79
Taylor, Charles 16
terrorism 50, 129, 132, 140, 161–76
Tham, Joo-Cheong 164
Thatcher, Margaret 13–4, 152, 190
think tanks 13–4, 94, 176
Tocqueville, Alexis de 125
Torfing, Jacob 135
total quality management 53

transnationalism 9, 14–5, 22, 31–2, 43, 132–3, 135
Trudeau, Pierre Elliott 184–5
Tsitsos, William 112
Turner, Bryan S. 2
Twombly, Eric 112–3

United States (USA) 29, 51, 91–106, 109–128, 151–2, 162, 168, 178, 195, 198, 201
utilitarianism 7, 12, 180, 189, 191, 196

values 5–7, 10–12, 16–7, 24, 26, 29–30, 32, 34, 41, 44, 72, 74, 77–8, 88, 114–116, 118–9, 122, 126, 128, 152, 163, 182, 184, 186–9, 193–6, 201, 205, 208
Venables, Juan Pablo 29
Verba, Sidney 121

Volcker, Paul 13

Wallace, Anthony 44–5
Warren, Rick 8, 92
Weber, Max 4–6, 16, 38, 66, 95–6
welfare provision 8, 82, 133, 138
welfare state 1, 12, 54, 73, 75, 77, 81, 88–9, 91, 95, 106, 139–40, 181, 193–4, 208–9
Williamson, Oliver E. 16
World Council of Churches 32–4
World Social Forum 32–5
World Trade Organization (WTO) 14, 32, 95
Wuthnow, Robert 112–3

Yu Hyongwon 49

zakat 163, 175–6

For Product Safety Concerns and Information please contact our
EU representative GPSR@taylorandfrancis.com | Taylor & Francis
Verlag GmbH, Kaufingerstraße 24, 80331 München, Germany